# Bandung Legacy and Global Future

## New Insights and Emerging Forces

# Bandung Legacy and Global Future

## New Insights and Emerging Forces

*Edited by*

Darwis Khudori

AAKAR

Bandung Legacy and Global Future: New Insights and Emerging Forces
*Edited by Darwis Khudori*



First Published 2018

ISBN 978-93-5002-548-2 (Hb)



Published by
**AAKAR BOOKS**
28 E Pocket IV, Mayur Vihar Phase I
Delhi 110 091
aakarbooks@gmail.com;
www.aakarbooks.com

Designed by
Limited Colors, Delhi 110 092

Printed at
Sapra Brother, Delhi 110 092

# Contents

# Preface

Bandung legacy poses a direct challenge to several hegemonic trends in the contemporary world. The growing political and militaristic domination in some parts of the world, directly or indirectly, has unleashed many streams of violence, civil wars, deprivation and distress migration. Capitalist globalisation has caused new forms of expropriation of local people's natural resources, generated more and more regional disparities and social inequalities and created a new global elite exploiting working people all over the world, especially in the developing countries. The effects of the development models propounded by the western countries and international agencies have led to severe damage to environment leading to climate change with serious consequences to the future of human life. The western domination in the cultural and communication fields, especially in information technology and satellite communications has undermined the dignity of local cultures, knowledge and value systems. The Bandung Conference of Asian-African countries in 1955 had a vision of defending sovereignty and countering hegemony of all kinds. That vision was reaffirmed and elaborated in 2005 in the New Asian African Strategic Partnership and further articulated in the Bandung Message of 2015 at the 60th Anniversary Conference attended by 91 States of Africa and Asia, 21 heads of state or of government, 15 observers, 10 international organisations. The essays in this volume address the historical as well as contemporary issues relating to old and new forms of hegemony.

This book incorporates the papers contained in the volume titled *Bandung at 60: New Insights and Emerging Forces* released on the occasion of the 60th anniversary at the conference of academics and social activists held in Jakarta and Bandung in October 27–31 2015. This edition also carries the important documents for ready reference namely, Bandung + 60 Declaration adopted at the October 2015 academic conference and Excerpts from Declarations adopted by the Bandung Conference of 1955, and also of 2005 and 2015 summit meetings.

The current world situation presents enormous responsibility upon independent academics and civil society activists to reflect on the contemporary crises facing humankind as the governments and international organisations operate under tremendous constraints arising out of the hegemonic environment. They can critique dominant political and economic strategies and recall the values upheld by the leaders of newly independent countries who had assembled in Bandung in 1955 to carry forward the visions of their liberation struggles to build a new world based on principles of sovereignty, equality, peace, disarmament and human rights. Three tasks that they had put before the world in 1955, namely strengthening the United Nations as the principal world body for peace, security and development, creating an equitable, just and democratic global economic order and reaffirming the value and dignity of all cultures, religions and knowledge systems—all three need to be reaffirmed today. The essays in this volume and the documents accompanying them show some directions to analyse and pursue these objectives.

The editor of this volume, the indomitable spirit behind this decade-old academic endeavour, Darwis Khudori must be congratulated for bringing together a great group of scholars and activists from different parts of the world to produce this valuable publication. I am sure this will give a fresh impetus to scholars and students of International Relations to re-examine their current theories and concepts and historical events and invite policy makers to rethink much of their assumptions and formulations.

Bandung Day
24 April 2017

**Manoranjan Mohanty**

# 1

# Bandung Conference and its Constellation

## An Introduction

*Darwis Khudori*

2015 is the year of the 60th anniversary of the 1955 Bandung Asian-African Conference. Several events were organised in diverse countries along the year 2014–2015 in order to commemorate this turning point of world history. In Europe, two of the most prestigious universities in the world organised special seminars open to public for this purpose: The University of Paris 1 Pantheon-Sorbonne, *Bandung 60 ans après: quel bilan?* (Bandung 60 Years on: What Assessment?), June 27, 2014, and Leiden-based academic institutions, *Bandung at 60: Towards a Genealogy of the Global Present,* June 18, 2015. In Africa, two events echoing the Bandung Conference are worth mentioning: *The World Social Forum,* Tunisia, March 25–28, 2015, and The Conference *Africa-Asia: A New Axis of Knowledge,* Accra, Ghana, September 24–26, 2015. In Latin America, the Journal *America Latina en movimiento* published an issue titled *60 años después Vigencia del espíritu de Bandung,* mayo 2015. In USA, a panel on *Bandung +60: Legacies and Contradictions* was organised by the International Studies Association in New Orleans, February 18, 2015. In Asia, China Academy of Arts, Inter-Asia School, and Center for Asia-Pacific/Cultural Studies, Chiao Tung University, Hangzhou, organised a conference on *Bandung – Third World 60 Years,* April 18–19, 2015. On the same dates, a conference on *Vision of Bandung after 60 years:*

Facing *New Challenges* was organised by AAPSO (Afro-Asian People's Solidarity Organisation) in Kathmandu, Nepal. In Indonesia, three conferences are worth mentioning: *Bandung Conference and Beyond: Rethinking International Order, Identity, Security, and Justice in a Post-Western World,* Gadjah Mada University, Yogyakarta, April 8–9, 2015; *Strengthening South-South Cooperation to Promote World Peace and Prosperity,*

Commemoration of the 60th Anniversary of the Asian-African Conference and the 10th Anniversary of the New Asian-African Strategic Partnership, organised by the Indonesian government in Jakarta and Bandung on April 19–24, 2015; *Rethinking Emerging Forces 60 years after the Bandung Conference: Building Sovereignty, Preventing Hegemony,* organised by academic institutions from Africa (CODESRIA) and Asia (LIPI Indonesian Institute of Sciences, Padjadjaran University and Trisakti University) in collaboration with ANRI (National Archives of the Republic of Indonesia) and MKAA (Museum of Asian African Conference), Jakarta-Bandung-Jakarta, October 27–31, 2015.

Why all these commemorations? What do they reveal? What are their outcomes? What can be taken as reference?

This book tries to answer these questions.

## Bandung in Global History

The Bandung Conference belongs to many histories: local history (of Bandung, for example), national history (of Indonesia, for example), Asian history, Cold War history, colonial and post-colonial history, etc. Among the scholars working on the Bandung Conference in a historical perspective, Samir Amin proposed to look at "Bandung" in "Global History"[1].

The term "Bandung" here has at least three meanings: 1) A conference that took place in Bandung, Indonesia, on April 18–24, 1955; 2) An international movement characterised by neutralism or non-alignment vis-à-vis two blocs of superpowers East and West; 3) A period of world history in which the non-aligned countries were able to lead a development based on their national, popular and sovereign interests by taking advantage of the antagonism of the two blocs of superpowers.

As for "Global History", it is the history of the world focused on capitalism that developed progressively to be a world system controlling all aspects of societal life. In his article "*La trajectoire du capitalisme historique: la vocation tricontinentale du marxisme*"[2], Samir Amin analyses the origin and the development of capitalism marked by three successive phases:

1. A long period of gestation that corresponds to the transition from a tributary system, which was the general form of pre-modern societal organisation (approximately 1000–1800 AD). This period was marked by successive waves of gradual inventions that constituted the elements of capitalist modernity. The oldest wave came from China at the 11th century, followed by the Arab-Persan World from the 13th to the 15th centuries and the Italian cities after the Crusades. The last wave was started with the European conquest of America and developed

during three centuries of mercantilism (approximately 1500–1800 AD). The historical capitalism that imposed itself to the whole world is the product of this last wave. Its mode of accumulation was based on dispossession, which created a polarisation between centres and peripheries, and which gave a destructive dimension to capitalism, marked by the genocide of the indigenous people of America and Australia, the importation of slaves from Africa to America and the colonisation of Africa and Asia.

2. A short period of maturity marked by the domination of "the West" to the whole world (19th century). It was initiated by two revolutions: British Industrial Revolution, which invented machines and urban working class; and French Revolution, which invented modern politic. Its mode of accumulation based on dispossession reached its final form and became a fundamental law of social order. But it is also in this period that capitalism created conditions allowing the emerging and development of 'alternatives' called utopianism, socialism and communism. Thinkers and activists like Owen, Fourier, Proudhon, Marx, Engels, … lived in this period. The concept *Communist Manifesto* (1848) and action *Commune de Paris* (1871) were the products of this period.
3. A long period of decline for two main reasons. On one hand, following the Commune of Paris, capitalism entered into crisis due to its development into monopoly capitalism, which Lenin qualified it as "the highest stage of capitalism", where its destructive dimension of accumulation started to dominate its progressive dimension. The most outstanding manifestations of the crisis were the two world wars, followed by the so called Cold War. On the other hand, towards the end of the 19th century, the dominated peoples in the peripheries of capitalism, especially Africa, Asia but also Eastern Europe and Latin America, started to take their right to control their own destiny. Among the first manifestations are Deobandi Muslim Movement in India (1867), Nahda Arab Renaissance in Egypt (around 1870), Indian National Congress (1885), Russian revolutions (1905 and 1917), Iranian revolution (1907), Indonesian National Awakening (1908), Mexican revolution (1910–1920), Chinese revolution (1911), Egyptian revolution (1919), etc. These movements developed into national liberation movements that succeeded to achieve their objective in the aftermath of the second world war.

Bandung (in the sense described at the beginning of this paper) is the crystallisation of these movements, *the first wave of the rise of the peripheries of capitalism,* now called the South. This victorious wave did however not last long. It started to go down in the 60s (with the overthrows and assassinations of its leaders such as Lumumba, Soekarno, Keita, Nkrumah, Guevara, Cabral, Nasser, …) and completely paralysed in the 90s (with the fall of Berlin Wall and the dissolution of Soviet Union). This happened for two reasons: internal weaknesses (lack of democracy, political instability, among others) and external attacks (recovery of capitalism).

With the fall of the East Block in the 90s, the West Block turned into a Single Superpower and ruled the world alone by strengthening its control over five basic needs of survival of every nation: *access to natural resources, technology, finance, media and armament.* However, this new domination did not last forever. In 2008, the most serious economic crisis in world history hit the heart of the centre of world capitalism and imperialism. On the other hand, in the same period, some countries in the peripheries of capitalism succeeded to consolidate their economic achievement and enter into G20, the group of the 20 largest economies in the world. Academics, analysts, activists, media, speak about the "rise of the South", the "Periphery", the "Emerging" economies, exemplified by Brazil, Russia, India, China and South Africa, known as BRICS, but also Argentina, Indonesia, Mexico, Turkey….

Thus, we witness since the beginning of the 21$^{st}$ century *the second wave of the rise of the peripheries of capitalism.* The word "emerging" is striking since it was put forward by Soekarno in the 60s in the historical context of Bandung Era. He invented the concept of NEFOS (New Emerging Forces, the peripheries of capitalism in Samir Amin's theory) as the antithesis of OLDEFOS (Old Established Forces, the centre of capitalism in Samir Amin's theory). What does it mean in the globalisation era? Does it mean that the "emerging" economies represented by BRICS have an affinity with the Bandung Era? Is it a coincidence or a continuity of the Bandung movement? What lesson to be learned for a better world order? What are the old and new challenges of the present globalised world to the Bandung Spirit-based international movements?

## Bandung Conference

The importance of the Bandung Conference in world history has been proven by the great number of works on or related to this Conference. Its history, its preparation, its organisation, its proceedings, its list of participants and their speeches, its final communiqué, its impacts, its follow-ups,... have been recorded in published documents (articles, books, audio-visual documents in divers languages) and unpublished documents (diplomatic and national archives in divers countries).

To summarise, the 1955 Bandung Asian-African Conference was a turning point in world history. For the first time representatives of the former colonised nations united their forces and proposed alternatives to the world order dominated by the superpowers. It is the birthday of the so-called Third World countries, a term that indicates the willingness of those nations to take position outside the two blocks of superpowers. The conference triggered solidarity movements among peoples, countries, states and nations of Africa and Asia. It made possible the representation of African and Asian countries in the UN and the recognition of the voice of colonised peoples in the world order. It accelerated the complete reconquest of independence of Africa and Asia. It led to the Non-Aligned Movement between the two blocks of superpowers. It allowed the newly independent countries to lead a development based on their national, popular and sovereign interests. It contributed enormously to the prevention of a possible third World War and to the evolution of humanity towards a more just and peaceful world.

## Bandung Spirit

The Bandung Conference gave birth to an idiom: Bandung Spirit. Yet, the exact meaning of the Bandung Spirit has not yet been defined. It is often associated with anti-colonialism, liberation, solidarity... Some claimed it as "non-alignment". During the Cold War, it was non-alignment to the two blocs of superpowers. After the fall of Soviet Union, it is now non-alignment to the "neoliberal globalisation" led by the single hegemony of the "Triad" (US, Western Europe and Japan). Based on the Final Communiqué of the 1955 Bandung Conference, the author of this introduction summarised the Bandung Spirit as a call 1) for a peaceful coexistence among the nations, 2) for liberation of the world from the hegemony of any superpower, from colonialism, from imperialism, from any kind of domination of one country by another, 3) for the equality of races and nations, 4) for building solidarity towards the poor, the colonised, the exploited, the weak and those being weakened by the world order of the day, and 5) for their development.

## Bandung Era

Following the Bandung Conference, the participating countries led their respective national development and at the same time struggled for securing their independence and sovereignty between the two blocs of superpowers. It was the period when Soekarno spoke at the UN "TO BUILD THE WORLD ANEW" and put forward the concept of NEFOS (New Emerging Forces) and TRISAKTI (political sovereignty, economic self-reliance, cultural self-assertion) as the antithesis of OLDEFOS (Old Established Forces),....

He proposed concrete actions through CONEFO (Conference of the New Emerging Forces) and GANEFO (Games of the New Emerging Forces). However, the period of development generated by the Bandung Conference started to end tragically sometime between 1965–1970 by the overthrow or assassination of the leaders inspired by the Bandung Spirit (Patrice Lumumba, Soekarno, Modibo Keita, Kwame Nkrumah, Ben Barka, Che Guevara, Amilcar Cabral…), the abortion of their development projects, the entry of their country into the Western Block circle. This period was called later the Bandung Era. The exact ending year of the Bandung Era has not yet been established unanimously. Some proposed 1970 as the ending year of the Bandung Era marked by the passing away of the two main leaders of the Bandung Conference: the African Gamal Abdel Nasser and the Asian Soekarno, and the following radical change of the political orientation of the two countries towards the Western Block (Indonesia under Soeharto's *Orde Baru* and Egypt under Anwar Sadat's *Infitah*). Certain suggested 1980 with the rise of Thatcher and Reagan in power leading the world under the neoliberalism and taking back the control over the Third World after their lost during the Bandung Era. Others put forward 1990 due to the fall of the Berlin wall and the end of Soviet Union, which means the end of bipolarism and non-alignment.

## Bandung Constellation

Like a big bang generating stars, planets, comets, meteors… the Bandung Conference generated conferences, cultural festivals, social and solidarity movements, associations/organisations/institutions, business fora, research institutes, study centres, academic periodicals, news magazines… forming a constellation based on, inspired or provoked by the Bandung Conference. In term of conferences, they are, for example, the Asian-African Student Conference, the Asian-African Writer Conference, the Asian-African Journalist Conference, the Conferences of Cairo, of Conakry, of Belgrade (Non-Alignment), of Moshi, of Havana (Tricontinentale), etc. In terms of organisation, they are, for example, AAPSO (Afro-Asian People's Solidarity Organisation), JAALA (Japan Asia Africa Latin America) Solidarity Committee, the Soviet Afro-Asian Solidarity Committee, Afro-Asian-Latin American Peoples' Solidarity, AFRASEC (Afro-Asian Organisation for Economic Cooperation), Association of Asian Studies in Africa (Zambia), AARDO (African-Asian Rural Development Organization), AALCO (Asian-African Legal Consultative Organization), AASGON (Africa Asia Scholars Global Network), etc. In academic world, the Bandung Conference gave birth to area studies dedicated to Africa and Asia, such as Graduate School of Asian and African Area Studies (Kyoto University, Japan), Research Institute for Languages and Cultures of Asia and Africa (Tokyo University, Japan), Ferguson Centre for African and Asian Studies (USA), Institute of Asian and African Studies (Moscow, Russia), Centre for African and Asian Studies (Great Zimbabwe University), Asian and African Cultural Studies Certificate (St. John University, USA), Institute of Asian and African Studies (The Hebrew University of Jerusalem), Department of Asian and North African Studies (Ca' Foscari University of Venice), Asien-Afrika-Institut (Universität Hamburg, Germany), Department of African and Asian Studies (Nnamdi Azikiwe University Awka, Nigeria), Department of African and Asian Studies (University of Khartoum, Sudan), Faculty of Asian and African Studies (Saint-Petersburg State University, Russia), etc. This is accompanied by publications of academic periodicals as well as news magazines, such as African and Asian Studies (Brill, the Netherlands), Asian and African Studies (Slovak Academy of Sciences in Bratislava, Slovakia). Journal of Asian and African Studies (SAGE, UK), Journal of Asian and African Studies (Tokyo University), Afro-Asian Journal of Finance and Accounting (UK), Asia and Africa today (Russian Academy of Sciences, Russia), Journal of Identity, Culture & Politics: An Afro-Asian Dialogue (CODESRIA, Senegal), Solidarity and Peace Journal of AAPSO Nepal (Nepal), news magazine Afrique Asie (France), etc.

## Bandung 60 Years On: What Assessment?

Now, 60 years after the Bandung Conference, colonisation has officially disappeared, the Cold War has ended, and the Non-Aligned Movement has almost lost its raison d'être. Yet, similar systems of domination by the powerful in the world order persist, wars continue to threaten humanity, mass hunger, diseases and poverty still characterise many parts of the world, and injustice has appeared in more sophisticated forms and larger dimensions. Why all these situtions? Is a better world still possible? Is there any alternative to the present course of globalisation?

The one-day seminar on "*Bandung 60 ans après: quel bilan?*" (Bandung 60 Years On: What Assessment?) at the University Paris 1 Pantheon-Sorbonne, June 27, 2014, gives some lights on the questions raised above. In addition to paper presentations, the discussions following every session of the seminar allowed the deepening and the extension of the theme of the day. Let us quote some of the most relevant points for our purpose3.

### *The essence of Bandung Spirit*

The essence of Bandung Spirit is non-alignment: non-alignment to the hegemony of the superpowers who unilaterally and for their own benefits imposed their rules on the whole world. Initiated in Bandung in 1955 and formalised in Beograd in 1961, it was the non-alignment to the two blocks of hegemonic superpowers of that day: West and East. Today, one hegemonic block remains: the Triad (USA, EU, Japan) that imposed unilaterally on the whole world "neo-liberal globalisation". The Bandung Spirit is to be interpreted today as non-alignment to neo-liberal globalisation.

### *The assessment of Bandung 60 years on*

Statements such as "Bandung has failed" or "Bandung did not keep its promises" or "Bandung did not give any alternative to the hegemony of superpowers it denounced" are not relevant. Bandung (in the sense of the Bandung Conference and the dynamic of development that followed it and that took place in the Third World, the Non-Aligned Countries, the South, the Periphery of the world capitalism, between 1955 and 1970, or even 1990, period known as Bandung Era) has demonstrated immense achievements. The proofs are numerous. However, Bandung has its limits that explain its erosion. It is these limits that should be studied.

### *The world without Bandung*

What would be the world if Bandung did not take place?

Bandung, or Bandung Era, between 1945 and 1990, is the first wave of the rise of the peoples of the South dominated by the North. Bandung has fulfilled great things. With Bandung, the North was forced to adjust itself to the request of the South. Before Bandung, the world was dominated completely by the capitalist-colonialist-imperialist North. After Bandung, the North has taken back its control over the world through neo-liberal globalisation. Today, there is a sign of affirmation of the rights of the peoples, the nations and the states of Africa, Asia and Latin America, which can be considered as the second wave of the rise of the South. At academic level, without Bandung, there will be no area studies linking Africa-Asia, and Africa-Asia-Latin America.

### *The enlargement of Bandung*

The alignment of Latin America to the Bandung movements started in the 1960s with the foundation of Non-Aligned Movement (Beograd 1961) and the Tricontinentale Conference (Havana 1966). However, the rise of the Non-Aligned Movement in Latin America really only started from 2000 (Brazil, Venezuela, Bolivia, Ecuador, Uruguay...). The time seems to have arrived for a larger alliance of peoples, nations and states of Africa, Asia and Latin America. In this perspective, the position of the peoples of the North is crucial: do they remain silent by supporting de facto the imperialist politic of their leaders; or are they willing to integrate themselves into the enlarged alliance of Bandung comprising the peoples of Tricontinentale and a number of citizens of the North?

Bandung is a world political success because it was led by the states. In order to make the second Bandung or the second wave of the rise of the South a success, it is necessary that the alliance of the peoples of the South and the North grows to be an alliance of the states.

### *The "emerging" countries*

The term BRICS to represent a group of "emerging" countries does not correspond to reality because it covers two contradictory phenomena: "lumpen development" and "emergence". The first is a development characterised by economic growth and at the same time pauperisation of the population. While emergence is characterised by a sovereign construction of a coherent, integrated and efficient national productive system capable of competition and exportation, accompanied by a rural development allowing an equal access to land for the rural population and a guarantee of national food sovereignty. According to these criteria, the only country really emerging is China. Some other countries have only certain elements of emergence like Brazil and India. While many countries do not have any element of emergence at all: they are more precisely "submerging" and suffering from "lumpen development", a development based on mainly natural resources and characterised by the growing middle class and the impoverishment of the popular class or the enlargement of the gap between the rich and the poor.

### *The China-Africa relationship*

In response to the call of the Bandung Final Communiqué, China is the only country participant of Bandung that has been developing economic and cultural cooperation with Africa in a methodical, systematic, consistent and continuous way since the end of the 1950s up to the present. Its approach is completely different from that of G7 (EU, USA, Japan). The latter takes a position of "donor" imposing severe conditions (especially liberalisation and privatisation), which put the national sovereignty of African countries into danger, for African countries wishing to receive their "aid". On the other side, the "win-win" pattern of Chinese approach does not impose any condition on Africa in its exchanges with China. Meanwhile, regarding

Chinese actions in Africa, many criticisms have been written, especially by representatives of the North, since China became the first trading partner of Africa in 2008, overtaking USA. This issue should be watched carefully by using scientific approaches rigorously.

*Other issues*

Some other issues have been evoked, without involving discussion, but may be developed in future meetings:

(a) The African problem. The relationship between Africa and the world (Europe, America, Asia) reveals the weakness of Africa: there is a risk that the destiny of Africa continues to be decided by others. Why? It is a vast theme of discussion to be treated in a meeting.

(b) China: sovereign or imperialist? China is sovereign, fine. But is not it also imperialist? Especially regarding its close neighbours: Myanmar, Cambodia, Laos, the Philippines, Vietnam… For example, the sovereignty claimed by China over almost all of the Eastern Sea (or the South China Sea) is "problematic"; it is the source of recurrent high tensions in these regions.

(c) The reunification of Korea

(d) The women question

(e) The question of religious diversity tearing up Africa and Asia

(f) The question of arms control

(g) The question of Palestine

It seems that the "emerging" countries are expected to accomplish the unfinished missions of the Bandung Spirit. Is it true? Is it possible?

## NEFOS or New Emerging Forces

The terms "New Emerging Forces" and their adversary "Old Established Forces" were invented by Soekarno during the hottest period of the Cold War.

In his annual speech celebrating Indonesian independence on August 17, 1963, under the title of *Genta Suara Revolusi Indonesia* (The Ringing of Indonesian Revolution), President Soekarno explained what he called NEFOS (New Emerging Forces):

> *New Emerging Forces are gigantic forces consisting of progressive nations and groups willing to build a New World full of justice and friendship among the nations, a New World full of peace and well-beings, a New World without imperialism, colonialism and exploitation de l'homme par l'homme et de nation par nation. New Emerging Forces consist of oppressed and progressive nations. New Emerging Forces consist of Asian, African and Latin American nations, socialist nations and progressive groups in capitalist states. New Emerging Forces*

> *consist of at least 2.000.000.000 human beings. Is not it a gigantic force, if it is well organised? I look forward to the second Asian-African Conference, I look forward to the first Asian-African-Latin American Conference, I look forward to the first Conference of New Emerging Forces in Indonesia! We will organise GANEFO, Games of the New Emerging Forces... CONEFO, Conference of the New Emerging Forces! In Indonesia, sisters and brothers! CONEFO in Indonesia, does not it show that Indonesia is in the forefront of New Emerging Forces? Let the forces of Progressive Nations be united! Let the Old Established Forces be trembling! Let the Old Established Order be collapsed!*[4]

The ideas of NEFOS and OLDEFOS became the doctrine of the Indonesian foreign policy during the Soekarno years of 1960–1965. They were a part of the "grand design" of Indonesian socialism, together with other doctrines such as BERDIKARI (*Berdiri di Atas Kaki Sendiri* or literally standing up on one's own feet, meaning self reliance), TRISAKTI (political sovereignty, economic self-reliance, cultural self-assertion), NASAKOM (the united force of the partisans of Nationalism, Religion and Communism), RESOPIM (Revolution, Socialism, Indonesia, National Leadership), etc.

Different from the Three World Theory of Mao Tse Tung (the First World consisting of superpowers, the Second World of lesser powers, and the Third World of exploited nations), Soekarno perceived the international order in a more radical way as an antagonism of two forces, not based on geographical boundaries or ideological stands (East-West or Capitalism-Communism), but more on the economic mode of production—which reminds us to Samir Amin's theory of "Centre-Periphery" in global capitalism. Soekarno considered an international conflict between the new and the old powers as determining feature of world society. This conflict would, in his view, lead to the ultimate and inevitable destruction of the old. In Soekarno's view, the root cause of international tensions lay in imperialism, colonialism and neo-colonialism, and not in the Cold War ideological enmity.[5]

The radical stand of Soekarno led Indonesia away from the West, especially the USA and closer to the East, especially China. It is in this context that Indonesia organised GANEFO (Games of the New Emerging Forces) in 1963 as alternative to Olympic Games perceived by Soekarno as dominated by OLDEFOS. It involved 2700 athletes from 51 countries of Africa, Asia, Europe and Latin America. The most radical measure taken by Soekarno was the withdrawal of Indonesia from its UN membership in 1965 as a protest against the OLDEFOS perceived by Soekarno as dominating the UN. In its place, Soekarno founded the conference of New Emerging Forces (CONEFOS). The building construction dedicated to this future UN alternative was started on the same date of the 10th anniversary of the Bandung Conference, April 19, 1965. However, before its completion, the famous tragedy of September 30, 1965, happened: seven generals were kidnapped and assassinated, the Communist Party was accused to be the author, the Army under General Soeharto took over the power, the Communist Party was dissolved, Communism, Marxism, Leninism were forbidden, hundreds of thousands of communists and their close relatives were massacred. The story of NEFOS ended together with the end of Soekarno's rule.

However, the CONEFO building survived, now being used as the Parliament Building of Indonesia. The same as the term "emerging", now being applied to economic performance of certain countries showing their resemblance with certain characteristics of the former West Bloc economy. So, the "emerging countries" of the 21th century, do they represent "emerging forces" of the Bandung Era? A study is needed to answer this question. On the long term goal, for example: do the "emerging countries" have a project of "changing" the international order like the ideal of NEFOS or a simple project of "catching-up" with the persistent West Bloc model? In the terms of Manoranjan Mohanty, do the emerging countries go towards "global restructuring" or "global rebalancing"[6]? Do the "emerging countries" have the objective of TRISAKTI (political sovereignty, economic self-reliance, cultural self-assertion) or accept to be sub-contractors of the former West Bloc master?

Meanwhile, the phenomenon of "emerging" does not appear only in macro-economic sector and at the level of nation-state, but also especially in socio-cultural sectors and at all levels of society (local, regional, national, transnational, international, global). Global and transnational social and solidarity movements emerged in the form of periodical World Social Forum and protests against capitalist establishments (IBRD, IMF, WTO, Wallstreet…). In addition to classical social movements claiming employment, salaries, subsidies… we have been attending a new phenomenon in social movements: the proliferation of demonstrations, not in the name of socio-economic well being as we found usually, but in the name of a collective identity, a collective reference to culture, religion, territory, environment, ethnicity, gender, sexual options,… Manuel Castell speaks about *The Power of Identity*[7]. They do not claim for the improvement of their socio-economic conditions, but for their right to exist, to be treated without discrimination, to decide on their own life, to control their environment, to maintain their cultural identity,…. In other words, they do not defend "what they do" but "what they are", their "self", their "meaning". Yet, not all of these movements are progressive. Some are regressive, even radicalised and acting with violence in the name of God, religion, belief, nation, ethnic group,... movements related to the fundamental categories of outdated mode of life, nowadays threatened by the contradictory and joint attacks of techno-economic forces and progressive social movements.

Among those "emerging" social movements, it seems that two of them will determine the future of humanity and its habitat: Feminist and Ecologist Movements. The first has a vocation not only to defend women's rights, but especially to change the whole structure of society at all levels of human existence (from familial, local, national, to global) based on patriarchy incarnated in male-capitalist-military domination of the present world. The second is expected to change the present model of development that threatens the survival of the planet. This model is based on economic and materialist interests, which puts on the top of priorities material productivity and profit, which transforms nature into commercial commodities, which pushes people to be greedy consumers. This model is enjoyed by a small number of economically rich countries, but which take the major part of natural resources of the planet for their own profit, comfort, pleasure and security. The application of this model to the whole world will lead to human-made ecological planetary catastrophes. That is why an alternative model of development is needed if human beings wish a sustainable world.

Where will this expected alternative model come from? Will it come from the North? Will it come from the South? Or, is this hypothetical division of North-South, Centre-Periphery, NEFOS-OLDEFOS, still relevant?

To answer these questions is beyond the aim of this introduction.

## Indonesia: Return to the Bandung Spirit?

The rise of Joko Widodo in Indonesia as an incarnation of people's sovereignty, his adoption of Soekarno's concept of TRISAKTI (political sovereignty, economic self-reliance, cultural self-assertion), his strong statements against global injustice and for solidarity towards the victims of global injustice, do they mean the return of Indonesia to the Bandung Spirit?

In Indonesia, the Commemorative Asian-African Conference organised by the Indonesian government in April 2015 gathered 91 States of Africa and Asia, 21 heads of state or of government, 15 observers, 10 international organisations. The two heads of state and government of the economically most powerful nations of the world were there: the Chinese President Xi Jinping and the Japanese Primary Minister Shinzo Abe, beside the Indonesian President Joko Widodo. The commemorative conference produced three documents: *the Bandung Message 2015*, *the Declaration on*

*Reinvigorating the New Asian-African Strategic Partnership* and *the Declaration on Palestine*.

Outside the official documents, Indonesian President Joko Widodo pronounced strong statements on divers world issues.

On global injustice in the sharing of world resources:

> *The world that we inherited today is still fraught with global injustice, inequality and violence. Our common dream of a new world civilization based on social justice, equality, harmony, and prosperity, has yet to become a reality. Global injustice and inequality are clearly on display before us.*
>
> *When the rich nations, which comprise a mere 20 per cent of the world's population, consume 70 per cent of the world resources, then global injustice becomes real. When hundreds of people in the northern hemisphere enjoy the lives of super rich, while more than 1.2 billion people in the southern hemisphere struggle with less than 2 dollars per day, then global injustice becomes more visible before eyes. When a group of rich countries think that they could change the world by the use of force, the global inequality clearly brings about misery, of which the United Nations looks helpless.*

On the unilateral force practiced by militarily powerful countries:

> *The use of unilateral force without a clear UN mandate, as we have witnessed, has undermined the existence of our common world body. Therefore, we, the nations of Asia and Africa, demands the UN reform, so that it could function better, as a world body that puts justice for all of us before anything else.*

On the obsolete international financial structure:

> *We also feel the global injustice when a group of established nations are reluctant to recognize that the world has changed. The view that the world economic problems can only be solved by the World Bank, the International Monetary Fund, and the Asian Development Bank, is an outdated view.*
>
> *I am of the view that the management of the global economy cannot be left only to the three international financial institutions. We must build a new global economic order, that is open to new emerging economic powers.*
>
> *We push for a reform of the global financial architecture, to eliminate the domination of one group of countries over other countries.*

On global leadership and the role of Indonesia:

> *The world needs a collective global leadership which is exercised in a just and responsible manner. Indonesia as a new emerging economic force, as a country with the largest moslem population on earth, and as the third largest democracy, stands ready to play a global role as a positive to fulfill noble goal.*

On the translation of Bandung Spirit into practice:

> *We can do all that by bringing the Bandung Spirit down to earth, by contextualizing the three core objectives that our predecessors had fought for sixty years ago.*
>
> *First, prosperity. We must cooperate closely to eradicate poverty, improve education and health services, promote science and technology, and provide jobs for our people.*
>
> *Second, solidarity. We must grow together, by increasing and expanding trade and investment between us. We must develop inter-regional economic cooperation between Asia and Africa, by helping each other in strengthening connectivity among us, by building infrastructures that connect our ports, our airports, and our roads. Indonesia will strive to be a maritime bridge that connects the two continents.*
>
> *Third, internal and external stability, and respect for human rights. We have to ask ourselves, what is wrong with us that many of our countries are plagued by internal and external conflicts that derail our economy.*

On Palestine:

> *For me, the global injustice feels more suffocating, when the Bandung Spirit, that demanded freedom for all nations of Asia and Africa, still left one outstanding debt for six decades. We, and the world, still owe it the Palestinians.*
>
> *The world is helpless before the suffering of the Palestinians, who live in fear and injustice, due to years of occupation.*
>
> *We cannot turn away from the misery of the Palestinians. We have to continue to fight with them, to support the birth of a free Palestine.*

It is the first time since the overthrow of President Soekarno in 1965 that an Indonesian president declared so clearly his attitudes expressing at the same time criticisms towards a group of states and institutions dominating the world, and solidarities regarding peoples and nations suffering from global injustice. Does it mean that Indonesia, under the presidency of Joko Widodo, is in return to the Bandung Spirit?

It is too early to answer to this question. What we can say at minimum and with certainty is that the Indonesian President Joko Widodo is a man of people, was born in a slum neighbourhood, hard worker for his success in life, studies, business, politics, simple in his behaviour, transparent in leading the government… During the presidential election, it was the popular mass who mobilised themselves and collected money for his success as presidential candidate. Fifty years after the end of the Bandung Era in Indonesia, he is the first president who does not belong to the political elite. It is the end of Indonesian oligarchy and the beginning of a new era. Now he is at the head of a vast country of 17500 islands, of a maritime territory of 5000 on 2000 kilometres, of 250 millions inhabitants, of 400 ethnic groups, of 5 world religions and hundreds of indigenous beliefs, and of 15$^{th}$ world economy. His first priority is to build and secure POLITICAL, ECONOMIC and CULTURAL SOUVERIGNITY as was conceptualised by Soekarno under the name of TRISAKTI. And for this purpose, he is aware that his country has to have a solid foundation: PEOPLE'S SOUVEREIGNTY of which he is an incarnation. He was elected one year ago. It is too early to judge his performance.

## This Book

This book is a fruit of the diverse commemorative manifestations mentioned at the beginning of this introduction. It is not based on a pre-conception. It comes out from a harvest of available articles. The structure comes later. Like a spontaneous building without architect, it is the materials that make the structure and not the structure that determines the materials. And the materials speak. Then the job of editor is to catch their voices and to put them in certain order to make them more useful, meaningful, beautiful and entertaining, if possible.

They speaks about issues presented in the previous lines. Some of them deal with the Bandung Conference and give new insights to this historical event; others reveal the signs of emerging forces inspired by the Bandung Spirit. They are ordered as a journey from the Past to the Present, from the Centre to the Periphery of the Bandung Constellation.

The order starts with HISTORY. The article of Darwis Khudori reminds readers that there are many books and articles on the Bandung Conference and not all of them are reliable. It is necessary to know which ones are "fundamental" when one is interested in this historical event—"fundamental" in the sense that they present the "fundamental" knowledge on the conference based on primary sources (official documents published by the organising committee during or following the conference, archives, interviews with people concerned directly by the conference, observations during the conference) and deserve therefore to be considered as a "must" to read. The article of Naoko Shimazu complements that of Darwis Khudori by telling the stories of the women in the Bandung Conference. It provides us with a new insight on the role of women in diplomacy: women generally were not as visible in what one might consider to be the formal diplomatic sphere at Bandung, whilst they were highly prominent in informal diplomatic settings.

The contributions of Manoranjan Mohanty and Noha Khalaf reveal the GLOBAL CHALLENGES that the Bandung Spirit-based movements have to face 60 years after the historical conference. For Manoranjan Mohanty, the realisation of the Bandung Spirit was frustrated during the Cold War and subsequently through the process of capitalist globalisation. But the struggles for those values of sovereignty of nations, equality and dignity of peoples and cultures and a development model that aimed at comprehensive fulfilment of material, cultural and political needs of all individuals, groups and regions went on. Thus has emerged the campaign through people's movements and regional multilateral organisations, for *'global swaraj'* or *'global movement for self-determination'* or *'self-realisation at every level from grassroots, regions and nations to the global level'*. While Noha Khalaf perceives the enduring and aggravated problems in Palestine are a part of global problems and that their solution does not concern merely practical politic but also and more fundamentally a theoretical framework elevated at global level in what she called *Thinking Global*.

Several articles concern INTERNATIONAL RELATIONS. Adams Bodomo speaks about the decisive role of the Bandung Conference in defining the international, areal and diaspora studies with Africa-Asia as a area of studies, which did not exist before the Bandung Conference. On his side, Lazare Ki-Zerbo reveals, from the archives, the importance of the ISGN (International South Group Network) founded at the Fort Hare University, South Africa, in June 1994. Its goal was to provide alternative content to the African Renaissance following the end of Apartheid in South Africa. It involved eminent scholars-activists from Africa and Asia. It produced documents referring to the Bandung Spirit as action plans for African Development. While István Tarrósy reviews how the Bandung Spirit, which was born in the "bipolar" context of international order, stays relevant in the "interpolar" globalism; how is possible that New Asian-African Strategic Partnership (NAASP) plays a role with the development of other frameworks of Asian-African co-operations such as TICAD, FOCAC, IAFS. Complementary to István Tarrósy, Mérick Freedy Alagbe compares the Final Communiqué of the 1955 Bandung Conference and the official document of the 2000 FOCAC (Forum on China-Africa Cooperation). He found a troubling similarities between the two documents. At the same time, he highlights the dynamisms at work in the international relations in this 21st century. Jason E. Strakes offers a less known case of the former Soviet Caucasus and Central Asia in their evolving relationship with Asia, Africa, Middle East and Latin America in the follow-up of the Bandung Conference. He poses the question of whether the principles embodied in the "Bandung Spirit" might offer a true alternative or "third way" that maximises both their political autonomy as newly sovereign nations, as well as their opportunities for sustainable and equitable development.

In EMERGING MOVEMENTS, two articles represent the "emerging forces" in global politic: gender and ecological issues. Seema Mehra Parihar reveals the gender injustice that still characterises the entire world in general and in Asia in particular. She offers theoretical frameworks and examples of governmental measures in India in promoting gender justice. On the other hand, Trikurnianti Kusumanto deals with the intricate relationship between food security and global environmental change. She underlines the importance of creating food systems that are resilient and equitable; allowing and supporting intensification of food production that is sustainable; making biodiversity and ecosystem services visible to informing decision and policymaking; viewing food and nutrition security as complex landscape covering different sectors, disciplines, institutions, and jurisdictions; governing interconnections between the diverse elements of food security.

Three articles concern what is called EMERGING COUNTRIES. Beatriz Bissio shows the continuity of the Bandung Spirit in the formation of Non-Alignment and BRICS. The Non-Alignment failed to fulfil most of its goals and BRICS seem to be determined to accomplish the Bandung missions. Tulus Tambunan and Ida Busnetty examine the Indonesian experience with two big economic crises in the past 12 years, namely the 1997/98 Asian financial crisis and the 2008/09 global economic crisis. One important finding from this study is that the Indonesian economy was much more resilience to the last crisis as compared to the 1997/98 crisis. Sit Tsui, Erebus Wong, Wen Tiejun and Lau Kin Chi present "Dilemmas of Development and Challenges for Emerging Countries" based on a comparative study of seven "emerging countries" that they call E7: Brazil, China, India, Indonesia, South Africa, Turkey and Venezuela. Within the historical framework of the progress of global capitalism, they examine and compare the development experiences of developing countries over the past century, particularly that of seven representative emerging countries. Each E7 country research team has provided a report of historical review on their development experiences. Based on their studies, the E7 academic team completes an overall cross-country analysis.

Meanwhile, the recent development of "emerging countries" has raised an EMERGING CONCERNS. Comparing China and India in agricultural question, especially land reform, Lin Chun found that the upsurge of a neoliberal, increasingly financialised global system intensified the question of land, threatening the livelihood of the world's remaining agrarian direct producers and the globe's environmental commons. In one way or another supported by state policies, big capital is further driving the "last peasantry" away from the land—land as a means of production and subsistence. For her, building a new moral economy through rural (re)organisation would be the only alternative to this relentless process of commodifying land and labour. In the same spirit, Lau Kin Chi examines the sustainability of China's economic development since the 1979 Reform by interrogating questions of socio-economic justice and ecological justice. She attempts to understand how the craze for Modernisation entraps China in socio-economic injustices and aggravating environmental crises.

A CLOSING REMARK ends the book. In his article, Aziz Salmone Fall underlines that most of the Non-Aligned Movement's agenda and its demands are still relevant today, notably: resisting the military control over the planet, advocating national and international policies for a more equitable management of resources for all people, safeguarding the rights of nations to choose their own independent development while ensuring peace and solidarity amongst nations.

The first edition of this book was launched during the Bandung+60 International and Interdisciplinary Conference that took place in Jakarta-Bandung-Jakarta on October 27–31, 2015, in Commemoration of the 1955 Bandung Asian-African Conference. Under the general theme of *RETHINKING EMERGING FORCES: Building Sovereignty, Preventing Hegemony*, the conference involved more than 80 speakers and chairs from 26 countries representing the Global South and progressive elements of the Global North. The main outcome of the conference is the BANDUNG+60 DECLARATION, which was submitted to the President of Republic of Indonesia, H.E. Joko Widodo, by the intermediary of the Chairperson of the Presidential Advisory Council, Prof. Dr. Sri Adiningsih. The BANDUNG+60 DECLARATION was not available before the conference. That is why it was not included in the first edition of this book. Now, the declaration is available and readers may find it as appendix of this second edition.

Last notice but not least: none of us, the authors of this book, is native English speaking person. It is a historical accident generated by imperialism and colonialism that led all of us to use English as a means of communication. Some of us use English as second, third or fourth language in our life. Our English is neither British, American or Australian, nor based on Cambridge or Oxford standard. All those formal categories are not relevant for us. What is important for us is that we understand each-other. For that respect, we are grateful to the team of English Department of Sanata Dharma University, Yogyakarta, Indonesia, who helped us harmonising our English in order to ensure that our English is understandable and that a chance of misunderstanding is avoided. This way is a part of our principle of self-reliance, including in language editing.

We have tried to do our best and we have an honour to wish you a nice reading.

## Endnotes

1. Samir Amin, *Histoire globale: une perspective afro-asiatique.* Paris: Les Indes Savantes, 2013, p. 276.
2. Samir Amin, 'La trajectoire du capitalisme historique: la vocation tricontinentale du marxisme' in *5 Samir-selection lectures.pmd – codesria,* http://www.codesria.org/IMG/pdf/4–Samir_Amin_Selections.pdf?3082 The English version of the article is available at http://monthlyreview.org/2011/02/01/the-trajectory-of-historical-capitalism-and-marxisms-tricontinental-vocation/
3. See the seminar report "Special report: the Bandung Confence sixty years on", *IIAS Newsletter* No. 69 Autumn 2014 available also online at http://www.bandungspirit.org/IMG/pdf/BANDUNG_60_YEARS_-_Seminar_Report_-IIAS-69–2014.pdf
4. Soekarno, *Di Bawah Bendera Revolusi* (Under the Banner of the Revolution), Vol. 2, collection of Soekarno's written work and speeches, Jakarta, Gunung Agung, 1964. The book is now available online for free on several websites, for example, http://thesoekarnofoundation.blogspot.co.id/2015/09/soekarnos-e-library_19.html
5. On the Indonesian Foreign Policy during Soekarno years of 1960–1965, see for example I Gede Wahyu Wicaksana, "Islam and Sukarno's Foreign Policy, with reference to Indonesia-Pakistan Relations 1960–1965" in International Journal.
6. Manonranjan Mohanty, 'Bandung spirit and the new Indian regime' in Latin America in movement, 03/06/2015, http://www.alainet.org/en/articulo/170099 of Indonesian Studies, Vol. 1 2013.
7. Manuel Castell, *The Power of Identity,* The Information Age: Economy, Society and Culture Vol. II. Cambridge, MA; Oxford, UK: Blackwell, 1997.

# 2

# Bandung Conference
## The Fundamental Books

*Darwis Khudori*

## Abstract

The 1955 Bandung Asian-African Conference took place around sixty years ago. Yet, people, states, civil society movements and academic world still speak about it and commemorate regularly its anniversary. Articles on or around the Bandung Conference are still written, sometimes marked by false information derived from quotations of quotations without verification of their original sources. The current mistakes such as the presence of Ho Chi Minh and Nkrumah in the conference continues to take place. This article is aimed at remedying this kind of ignorance by presenting the "fundamental" books on the Bandung Conference, "fundamental" in the sense that they present the "fundamental" knowledge on the conference based on primary sources of knowledge on the conference (official documents published by the organising committee during or following the conference, archives, interviews with people concerned directly by the conference, observations during the conference) and deserve therefore to be considered as a "must" to read for those interested in the Bandung Conference. They are nine books in this category, written between 1955 and 2007. This paper presents the nine books in three parts: 1) Annotated bibliography of the fundamental books, 2) Presentation of selected books and 3) Concluding remark.

*Keywords:* Bandung, Indonesia, Third World, Non-Alignment, Cold War.

Like a big bang, the Bandung Conference generated stars, planets, comets, meteors… forming a constellation of conferences, cultural festivals, social and solidarity movements, associations/organisations/institutions, business fora, research institutes, study centres, academic periodicals, news magazines… based on, inspired or provoked by the Bandung Conference. The contours and the content of the Bandung Constellation have not yet been known completely. They consist of at least four manifestations: Conferences, Organisations, Studies and Publications. The core of the Bandung Constellation is the Bandung Conference. Its history, its preparation, its organisation, its proceedings, its list of participants and their speeches, its final communiqué, its impacts, its follow-ups, its constellation,... have been recorded in three categories of documents: 1) Published documents on the Bandung Conference itself (the Bandung Conference as an autonomous subject); 2) Published documents that treat the Bandung Conference as a part of another subject (the Bandung Conference as an element of a subject); 3) Unpublished documents on the Bandung Conference and its constellation (the Bandung Conference in diverse national archives). This article concerns mainly the first category of documents, essentially the printed books published in diverse languages and countries following the conference until the present day.

## Annotated Bibliography of the Fundamental Books

1955: JACK Homer Alexander, *Bandung: On the Spot Description of the Asian-African Conference, Bandung, Indonesia, April 1955.* Chicago, Toward Freedom, May 1955.

This is the first publication on the Bandung Conference, printed for the first time in May 1955, earlier than the official publication on the conference by the Conference Organising Committee (the Indonesian Ministry of Foreign Affairs) in July 1955. According to my reading of the books on the Bandung Conference, this is the most complete, accurate, analytical and critical report on the conference, before the publication of Abdulgani's book in 1980. I will come back to this book in next chapter.

1955: APPADORAI A., *The Bandung Conference,* New Delhi, The Indian Council of World Affairs, June/October 1955.

This is the first publication of a synthetic and concise presentation of the Bandung Conference. The author was also a member of the joint secretariat of the conference. Different from the work of Jack presented previously, the work of Appadorai is focused on the decision of the Conference and his personal remarks. His work is limited to what was made public during the Conference because his position as a member of the Joint Secretariat of the Conference did not allow him to present all the contents of the Conference in an exhaustive way. Consequently, in term of quality and quantity of the information, the work of Appadorai is less important than that of Jack.

Nevertheless, his work has reached its target, which was the dissemination of the result of the Conference to a larger public, with Oxford University Press as distributor in the epoch where internet did not exist. Therefore,I will not come back to this book in the next chapter.

1955: MINISTRY OF FOREIGN AFFAIRS, Republic of Indonesia, Jakarta, *Asia-Africa speaks from Bandung,* July 1955.

This is the first official publication on the conference by the Indonesian Ministry of Foreign Affairs in Jakarta in July 1955. It is the conference proceedings comprising the documents and the transcriptions of the complete recording of the open sessions of the conference. In term of content, it completes the work of Jack. It can be seen as a kind of appendices of the Jack's work. In term of analysis, there is nothing significant. It presents the objective, the process and the spirit of the Conference. I will not come back to this book in the next chapter.

1955: WRIGHT Richard, *Bandoeng 1.500.000.000 d'hommes,* Paris, Calmann-Lévy, octobre 1955. The English version was published in 1956, *The Colour Curtain: A Report on The Bandung Conference.* Univ. Press of Mississippi.

It is a travel account on the Bandung Conference as the main event that provoked personal questionings and reflections to the African-American author. In term of facts and data of the Conference, Wright's work does not bring new elements compared to the previous books on the Conference. His strong points are to be found in his descriptions on the social conditions of the localities he visited at that time (Jakarta and Bandung) and his personal reflections on his experiences and on the phenomena he observed on site (colonial heritage, poverty, bureaucracy, racism, religion, communism, education, health, corruption, etc.). His main merit, in my view, is that he made known to the public the atmosphere of the Conference as well as its physical and societal environment through a fascinating and pleasing to read travel account. I will come back to his book in the next chapter.

1956: KAHIN George Mac Turnan, *The Asian-African Conference, Bandung, Indonesia, April 1955.* New York, Ithaca, Cornell UP.

This is the first document published by an academic institution. It contains a presentation of the Bandung Conference based on the official documents published during and after the Conference. The author added as appendices the supplementary speech of the Chinese Prime Minister Chou En-Lai in the Bandung Conference on April 19, his other speech in the political commission of the Conference on April 23, the report of the Bandung Conference presented by Chou En-Lai in front of the People's National Congress in Beijing on May 13, 1955, the speech of the Indian

Prime Minister Nehru in the political commission of the Conference on April 22. At the end, Kahin added his own remarks. The merit of Kahin is to be the first person who made known the Bandung Conference to the Western public, especially the English speaking academics. In term of contents, the work of Kahin is more descriptive than analytic. His remarks are very concise, very simple, and highly marked by the American preoccupation regarding the communist China. I will not come back to this book in next chapter.

1956: ROMULO General Carlos P., *The Meaning of Bandung.* Univ. of N. Carolina Press.

This is the first publication on the Bandung Conference written by an actor of the conference, who was the head of delegation of the Philippines and one of the eminent fighters of the conference representing the Pro-American position (with Thailand, Pakistan, Iraq, Turkey,...) against the neutralists (India, Indonesia, Egypt,...) and the communists (China, North Vietnam). The original elements of the book are to be found in the unpublished points of view and an attempt to appreciate the role of the Conference in the world context of 1955. I will come back to this book in the next chapter.

1965: CONTE Arthur (1965), *Bandoung, tournant de l'Histoire,* Paris, Robert Laffont.

This is the first most important book in French on the Bandung Conference as an autonomous subject, published ten years after the conference. Prior to this publication, there was already a book in French related to the Bandung Conference, written by Odette Guitard and published for the first time in 1961 under the title of *BANDOUNG et le réveil des peuples colonisés*. However, the Bandung Conference is just a part of the book dedicated more to the history of struggle for independence of the colonised countries of Africa and Asia.

The author did not bring new element in term of facts and data of the Conference (locality, country, organising countries, participating countries, delegates, speeches, sessions, result,...), which had been presented in previous books. The strong points of the book are to be found in the details of the Conference. Like in a novel, the details of gesture, cloth, physiognomy, expression,... are described as integral part of a character. The book forms a kind of "true novel" based on very accurate facts and data of the Conference, making the book easy, pleasing and instructive to read. I will come back to this book in next chapter.

1980: ABDULGANI Dr. H. Roeslan, *The Bandung Connection: Konperensi Asia-Afrika di Bandung tahun 1955.* Jakarta, Penerbit Gunung

Agung. Republished by the Indonesian Ministry of Foreign Affairs in 2011 and 2013. Its English version is *The Bandung connection: the Asia-Africa Conference in Bandung in 1955*. Singapore, Gunung Agung, 1981.

This is an essential book of the Bandung Conference for two reasons. On one hand, it was written by the Secretary General of the conference who was at the same time in charge of carrying-out the conference on the ground. On the other hand, he described the process of preparation and organisation of the conference, including details and anecdotes unknown by public before the publication. The added value of the book, compared to the previous ones, is in the personal account of the author as the main actor of the Conference on the ground, based on his personal notes and memories that cannot be found in any archive. I will come back to this book in the next chapter.

2007: AMPIAH Kweku, *The political and moral imperatives of the Bandung Conference of 1955: the reactions of the US, UK and Japan*. Folkestone (GB), Global Oriental Publishers.

This is the first true academic work on the Bandung Conference for two reasons. On one hand, the raw materials of the book were unpublished, taken from the American, British and Japanese archives. On the other hand, it brings new knowledge on the subject. I will comeback to this book in the next chapter.

Now, I will present the details of the books I consider fundamental.

## Presentation of Selected Books

1955: JACK Homer Alexander

The foreword of the book was signed by 23 well-known personalities at that time (including Roger N. Baldwin, Amiya Chakravarty, Norman Thomas, Quincy Wright,... please, check on Google how important these persons are). It says

> *Here is a comprehensive account of the Asian-African Conference in Bandung, Indonesia.*
>
> *It has been one of the most important international meetings in recent years. Dr. Homer A. Jack is a competent reporter and his description of the Conference and its results should receive widespread circulation in the United States.*
>
> *We hope you will read his report—and pass it on to your friends.*

"Homer Alexander Jack (May 19, 1916–August 5, 1993) was a Unitarian Universalist minister and early activist for peace, disarmament, racial equality and social justice. An accomplished writer and speaker, he organized and led a number of civil rights, disarmament, and peace organizations"[1]. The name JACK is a shortened version of JACOBOWITZ, a Jewish family who had immigrated from Central and Eastern Europe to avoid poverty and oppression. His visit to Europe at the period approaching the war determined his future life, as written in the CORE website: "As the clouds of war gathered over Europe in 1937, Homer A. Jack, a young Cornell graduate student, found himself teaching at a small college in Athens. He was completing his Ph.D. in biology and visited Europe to finish his thesis on the biological field stations of the world. On a tour of the continent at the end of the following school year, he visited Stalin's Russia, Hitler's Germany, and Mussolini's Italy. In Moscow, the authorities confiscated his camera, in Germany and Austria he witnessed overt anti-Semitism, and in Italy he observed ominous signs of spreading fascism. The lessons he learned about totalitarianism far outweighed the knowledge he acquired of the local flora and fauna. Returning home to upstate New York, Homer threw himself into peace activities to prevent America from being drawn into a second world war. He edited the Rochester No-War News and helped organize a rally that attracted 3000 people."

His engagement outside the USA started in the 1950s. "In 1952 Homer made the first of three trips to Africa, visiting South Africa and tracing the roots of Gandhian nonviolence and meeting African freedom fighters. His subsequent books, *The Wit and Wisdom of Gandhi* and *The Gandhi Reader*, helped introduce a generation of Americans to the father of nonviolence, including a young Alabama preacher, Martin Luther King. In then French Equatorial Africa, Homer visited Dr. Albert Schweitzer and was instrumental in helping to convince him to speak out against nuclear testing. Schweitzer's condemnation of atomic and hydrogen testing in his acceptance speech for the Nobel Peace Prize in Oslo electrified the world. In New Delhi, India, and Bandung, Indonesia, site of the nonaligned conference of 1955, Homer met Prime Minister Nehru who was also to become an ally in the campaign to end nuclear testing, along with Albert Einstein, Bertrand Russell, and other great humanitarians"[2].

### *Jack's Report*

His report on the Bandung Conference is less known and less quoted than the work of KAHIN published a year later. Nonetheless, his report is more analytical and more critical than that of KAHIN. There may be two reasons for that. On one hand, it was not an academic work nor published by an academic institution. It was a work of an activist for peace and humanity. It was published as a pamphlet of his movement. On the other hand, and that is probably the main reason, it was not in line with the US political orientation, in contrast to KAHIN's work.

## *Description of Bandung*

As a scientist-turned-journalist, Jack described in details the city of Bandung and the preparation made by the Indonesian government for the Conference. "In less than four months Bandung was transformed from a sleepy city, which was formerly a resort for the wives and children of Dutch colonials, into an efficient conference headquarters. Seventeen hotels and numerous small residences were requisitioned by the government and reconditioned. From Singapore were purchased 3,500 half woollen blankets (it can get chilly in Bandung despite its being only a few degrees south of the equator), 10,000 yards of lace curtain, 15,000 dinner sets, 600 plastic coat-hangers, 100,000 American and English cigarettes, and quantities of fruit juice, milk, and other foodstuffs normally in short supply. Special foods were imported, such as curries from Madras and nuts from Arabia. Hotels were given special instructions in preparing their menus and offered both European and Indonesian dishes, the latter including the famous *Rijstafel*." The major highways were also equipped with new mercury-arc lamps. More than 200 vehicles, some pastel-green Chevrolets and Plymouths, were taken over by the government. Each delegation was furnished a number of autos, with military and motorcycle escort. The supply of electricity was increased. The old Dutch Club, Concordia—renamed Gedung Merdeka—was entirely rebuilt to house the plenary sessions and press facilities. Generally the city was scrubbed and painted[3].

In term of communication, ample press facilities were arranged, with special cable and radio-telephone links to almost forty countries. The office of the Ministry of Information published a daily Conference Bulletin in English. The two Indonesian news agencies, ANTARA and PIA, published large mimeographed bulletins daily, also in English. More than 2,000 delegates, journalists, and observers descended on Indonesia beginning the middle of April. They were greeted by protocol officers and given almost immediate transportation to Bandung. No difficulties were experienced in Bandung and ample, often luxurious, facilities were provided for all. It was the consensus of delegates and journalists, many of whom were veterans at attending international conferences, that the facilities and hospitality at Bandung were superb[4]. Between six and seven hundred journalists came from perhaps fifty countries, representing a great variety of media: daily newspapers, weekly magazines, radio, television, and scholarly journals. There were large press delegations from China, Russia, India, and especially the USA, including several reporters from the American Negro press[5].

### *Delegates*

The book gives an overview of the conference participants and interesting details of the most important personalities of the conference: U Nu (Burma), Chou En-Lai (China), Sir John Kotelawala (Ceylon), Col. Gamal Abdel Nasser (Egypt), Kojo Botsio (Gold Coast), Jawaharlal Nehru (India), Ali Sastroamidjojo (Indonesia), Dr. Fadhil Jamali (Iraq), Tatsunosuke Takasaki (Japan), Mohammed Ali (Pakistan), Gen. Carlos Romulo (Philippines), Crown Pince Amer Faisal Al-Saud (Saudi Arabia), Prince Wan Haithayakon Krommun Naradhip Bongsprabandh (Thailand). The details include their age, their function, their personal character and their dress. On U Nu, for example, the book tells: *"48, Prime Minister since 1947. He is a poet and a student of Buddhism. He and the other Burmese delegates wore their mauve and yellow silken longyi with headdress of a matching color."* Kojo Botsio is described as following: *"39, Minister of State. A striking figure in his yellow woven toga, he studied at Oxford, edited a newspaper in Accra, and was imprisoned by the British in 1950."* On Mohammed Ali, the book says: *"45, Prime Minister. He was formerly ambassador to Washington. He came to Bandung with his new 28–year-old wife, the begum"*[6].

He also paid attention to observers representing different movements persecuted, ill-treated, stigmatised or opposing the political mainstream in their own countries: fighters for independence from Algeria, Morocco, Tunisia (against France), Malaya (against the UK), Jerusalem (against Israel), Cyprus (against the UK); fighters for equality from South Africa (against the Apartheid), for civil rights from Australia and the US. There were also fighters from West Irian for the integration of West Irian to Indonesia[7].

### *Conference*

The running of the conference was also described vividly, with the quotations of relevant and striking words of the speakers. Jack wrote about the "remarkable opening address", a "splendid speech", of the President Sukarno. He quoted also some key statements of Ali Sastroamidjojo, the Prime Minister of Indonesia who was elected as the permanent chairman of the conference. He mentioned a number of greetings sent from all over the world to the conference including those from Russia and the US. The chairman red some of the messages. K. Voroshilov, president of the Supreme Soviet of Russia wrote: *"I greet the participants of the Asian-African Conference which opens today; I express a sincere wish of fruitful work and success in accomplishing the lofty tasks facing the conference"*. From the US, the Prime Minister red a message from a group of fourteen Americans, including several Nobel Prize winners, who said that the *"way of Caesar is failing in Moscow and Washington as it has in Rome" and hoped the Conference would "develop independent solutions (and) enunciate the principle of a new society"*[8].

In Jack's account, the plenary sessions of the opening addresses were characterised by 1) a strong call for peace by Kotelawala of Ceylon, 2) a strong defence of military pacts by the Philippines, Turkey, Pakistan and Thailand, and 3) a basically conciliatory speech by China. Meanwhile, anti-communist speeches were pronounced by the chief delegates of the so called "committed" nations: Romulo from the Philippines, Mohammed Ali from Pakistan, Prince Wan from Thailand, Dr. Jamali from Iraq, and Zorlu from Turkey.

### *Chou En-lai*

The answer from Chou En-lai to the anti-communist discourses, especially in his mimeographed speech circulated to the public was, in Jack's words, a "clever document". He traced the history of colonialism in the two continents and said that *"the rule of colonialism in this region has not yet come to an end, and new colonialists are attempting to take the place of the old ones"*. He specifically mentioned the USA. He denounced that countries outside of Asia and Africa were establishing more and more military bases in the Asian and African countries. In his oral speech, Chou suggested that the Chinese delegation came to Bandung *"to seek unity and not to quarrel... to seek common ground, not to create divergence."* To the basically Muslim, Hindu, Buddhist audience, he admitted that *"we communists are atheists, but we respect all those who have religious belief."* Indeed, one member of the Chinese delegation was an Islamic leader. Then he talked about subversive activities and claimed that *"it is China that is suffering from the subversive activities which are openly carried on without any disguise by the United States of America."* He urged all delegates to come to China and see for themselves, since *"we have no bamboo curtain, but some people are spreading a smokescreen between us"*[9].

### *Closed Plenary Session*

It is in the closed plenary session that the delegates agreed upon

1. The Conference agenda of five separate headings: Economic cooperation, Cultural cooperation, Human rights and self-determination, Problems of dependent peoples, and World peace and cooperation;
2. The Conference way of decision making, which was based on unanimous agreement, rather than on a majority coming out from a

voting. However, the Conference was free to discuss any matter even if unanimity could not later be reached.

3. The formation of subcommittees on economic and cultural affairs, but no political committee. Instead there would be a series of informal meetings of the heads of delegations.

All the closed sessions took place in the *Gedung Dwi Warna* building toward the outskirts of Bandung. Only the brief communiqués were issued from these closed meetings, but some information was collected by *"enterprising journalists who buttonholed delegates as they left committee meetings"*[10].

Under the chapter "Behind Closed Doors", Jack wrote about four subjects: Formosa, colonialism, blocs and military pacts, Chinese openness.

On Formosa, although it was not in the conference agenda, it took a considerable place in the discussions. All the main actors of the conference were involved in the debates: Nehru, Krishna Menon, Chou En-Lai, Romulo, Prince Wan, Dr. Jamali, Prince Faisal, and other Colombo prime ministers. Independently, Sir John Kotelawala of Ceylon issued a statement to the press saying that *"Formosa should be neutralized for five years under the U.N. or Colombo powers trusteeship, that Quemoy and Matsu islands should be evacuated, and the U.S. should withdraw her fleet from the coastal waters"*[11].

On colonialism, it was Sir John Kotelawala who triggered the debate. *"If we are united in our opposition to colonialism, should it not be our duty to declare our opposition to Soviet colonialism as much as to Western imperialism?"* This brought forth a resolution endorsed by Turkey, Pakistan, Iraq, Iran, Lebanon, Libya, Liberia, Sudan and the Philippines. Mohammed Ali from Pakistan expressed fears of Soviet imperialism, but emphasized that China was not an imperialistic power. India and Burma stressed the need for finding common ground beyond the various political systems of different countries. China reiterated her intention of refraining from doctrinaire discussions in the interests of harmonious work in committee. In the end, all the parties agree to adopt a clause *"colonialism in all its manifestations"*[12].

On blocs and military pacts, Nehru opposed the existence of blocs and military pacts since this leads to armament race. This raised a debate with the bloc of Iraq, Turkey, Pakistan and Philippines. Chou En-Lai gave a conciliatory speech and expressed pleasure that China's name was not associated with expressions such as colonialism, imperialism, subversive action and infiltration. He gave assurances that he would take peaceful action regarding questions related to boundary differences and he extended the promise to Thailand, the Philippines, Cambodia, and Laos.

On Chinese openness, Chou En-Lai invited Prince Wan to go along with him and see for himself how things were along the Thai-Chinese border. Chou En-Lai repeated his invitation to Romulo to go along the Chinese coast to see if any warlike preparations were going on. He concluded by exhorting those present to make a start by bringing peace into the Conference hall.

## *Final Communiqué*

Jack's report includes the Final Communiqué of the Conference. Jack presented the entire text of the Final Communiqué, but also introduced his own view by adding subtitles such as TRADE FAIRS between paragraphs 5 and 6 of chapter A. ECONOMIC COOPERATION.

> *TRADE FAIRS*
>
> *6. The Asian-African Conference further recommended that: Asian-African countries should diversify their export trade by processing their raw material, wherever economically feasible, before export; intra-regional trade fairs should be promoted and encouragement given to the exchange of trade delegations and groups of businessmen; exchange of information and of samples should be encouraged with a view to promoting intra-regional trade; and normal facilities should be provided for transit trade of land-locked countries.*

And NUCLEAR ENERGY between paragraphs 9 and 10 of the same chapter.

> *NUCLEAR ENERGY*
>
> *10. The Asian-African Conference emphasized the particular significance of the development of nuclear energy for peaceful purposes, for the Asian-African countries. The Conference welcomed the initiative of the Powers principally concerned in offering to make available information regarding the use of atomic energy for peaceful purposes; urged the speedy establishment of the International Atomic Energy Agency which should provide for adequate representation of the Asian-African countries on the executive authority of the Agency; and recommended to the Asian and African Governments to take full advantage of the training and other facilities in the peaceful uses of atomic energy offered by the countries sponsoring such programmes.*

On chapter B. CULTURAL COOPERATION, he added NO SENSE OF RIVALRY between paragraphs 2 and 3.

> *NO SENSE OF RIVALRY*
>
> *3. It was not from any sense of exclusiveness or rivalry with other groups of nations and other civilisations and cultures that the Conference viewed the development of cultural co-operation among Asian and African countries. True to the age-old tradition of tolerance and universality, the Conference believed that Asian and*

> *African cultural co-operation should be developed in the larger context of world co-operation.*

And EFFECTIVE CONTROL inside the paragraph 2 dealing with armament of the chapter F. PROMOTION OF WORLD PEACE AND COOPERATION.

> *EFFECTIVE CONTROL*
>
> *The Conference considered that disarmament and the prohibition of the production, experimentation and use of nuclear and thermo-nuclear weapons of war are imperative to save mankind and civilisation from the fear and prospect of wholesale destruction. It considered that the nations of Asia and Africa assembled here have a duty towards humanity and civilisation to proclaim their support for disarmament and for the prohibition of these weapons and to appeal to nations principally concerned and to world opinion, to bring about such disarmament and prohibition.*

### *Analysis and Remarks*

At the end, the disguised journalist added his own analysis and remarks on the conference in three points: CONFERENCE BY PRODUCT, THE MEANING OF BANDUNG and WHAT WERE THE REAL GAINS OF BANDUNG?

In CONFERENCE BY PRODUCT, Jack put forward four items: 1) Formosa, 2) Dual Nationality, 3) Friendship, and 4) Indonesian Gains.

1. Formosa. After a number of informal meetings, on the last Saturday of he Conference, at the residence of Indonesian Prime Minister Ali Sastroamidjojo, "after lunch of chicken *sate* and *soto*", with the presence of Colombo prime ministers, Mr. Romulo and Prince Wan, Chou En-Lai issued the most significant statement of the entire Bandung Conference: *"The Chinese people are friendly to the American people. The Chinese Government is willing to sit down and enter into negotiations with the United States Government to discuss the question of relaxing tension in the Taiwan area".* This statement immediately caused repercussions in the capitals of the world, with the United States at first rejecting and later accepting the overture as a basis for further negotiations.
2. Dual Nationality. One of the controversial issues in Southeast Asia is the dual nationality of the millions of Chinese living in the Philippines, Thailand, Malaya, Indonesia and elsewhere. This issue was settled during the Bandung Conference, especially for the Chinese living in Indonesia. A treaty was signed by Chou En-Lai and Sunario

(Indonesian Minister of Foreign Affairs), calling for persons with dual citizenship to choose one of the two on the basis of free will any time before two years after the agreement comes into effect.

3. Friendship. Many of the delegates of the conference have never met each other. The Conference gave delegates an opportunity to live together, to work together, and to eat together. Many invitations were extended to delegates to visit other countries. Chou En-Lai issued a blanket invitation for all delegates to visit China. Several delegates, including Nasser and Chou En-Lai, spent additional days in Djakarta. Egyptian, Jordanian, and Lebanese delegates visited Japan after the Conference. President Sukarno promised to visit Egypt and Sir John Kotelawala publicly promised to visit China. During the Conference, a friendship treaty was signed between the kingdom of Afghanistan and the republic of Indonesia.
4. Indonesian Gains. The Conference did at least two things for Indonesia: firstly, it gave the people and the whole country an important psychological lift. Three centuries of Dutch colonialism had inculcated into the Indonesians the feeling of inferiority, of incompetence. The success of the Conference helped the Indonesians gain their self-confidence. Secondly, it strengthened the Nationalist party of Prime Minister Sastroamidjojo which was necessary to stabilise the political situation of the country.

In THE MEANING OF BANDUNG, Jack put forward his critical reflections on the Bandung Conference in five points

1. There was no organisation or permanent secretariat established following the Conference in order to implement the numerous decisions and proposals of the Conference.
2. The expectation on the development of the unity of Asia and the Middle East proved to be premature.
3. The delegates from Africa were far less experienced than those from Asia. There was no emerging leadership among the Africans in Bandung excepting Nasser who was more associated to the Middle East rather than to Africa.
4. Israel was unfairly treated by the Conference. Despite the hatred of the Arab Ligue, Israel should have been invited to the Conference for its geographical situation in Asia.
5. There was a good agreement for peace at the level of discussion and concern, but there was no orientation for actions.

In WHAT WERE THE REAL GAINS OF BANDUNG?, Jack enumerated the impacts of the Bandung Conference in ten points

1. Bandung has created a new bloc, the third one, which embraces two continents and almost two thirds of humanity. Despite its enormous diversity in all fields, a unity has been patiently built. This allowed the adoption of unanimous decisions on a number of controversial questions. This unity softened the extreme positions of the left and the right, of China facing the USA, of the Arab countries against Israel. The Conference was a successful "experiment of co-existence".
2. This unity produced the equivalent of a pact of non-aggression between China and all its neighbours.
3. Bandung forced the USA to re-examine their attitude and policy regarding Asia and Africa. The State secretary Dulles was obliged to revise several times his own attitude towards Bandung and President Eisenhower was called to reveal his new programme of aid for Asia during the Conference, including 200 millions USD for the Asian economic development.
4. Bandung will lead many of its members to economic improvement. It would take time and new capital resources. Japan will reinforce its trade relations with Asia and Africa.
5. Bandung will bring closer cultural relations between its nation members.
6. Bandung will help the dependent peoples in the world in general by the weakening of colonialism. The strong declarations made in Bandung against France on behalf of Algeria, Morocco and Tunisia; against the Netherlands on behalf of West Irian; against South Africa on behalf of the Africans, Pakistani and Indian descent; against the powers who hold Aden and the protectorates,… all this will give fruits.
7. Bandung witnessed the rise of China as an Asian great power and not only an isolated partner of Russia.
8. Bandung will mean the possible neutralisation of the "committed" countries like Thailand and the Philippines.
9. Bandung showed that the coloured people in the world do not need to be racist as their white fellows.
10. Bandung showed that communism in Asia and Africa is in any case unavoidable.

And Jack ended his report by the following words

*Bandung was at least five hundred years in the making. Not by arms, but by moral persuasion nourished by the world's great religions, will this third force help keep the peace the world so desperately desires. Bandung somehow caught the world's imagination and early its leaders were conscious that history was looking over their shoulder, but only time will tell if history will remember them. Bandung may just be the hinge of history.*

## 1955: WRIGHT Richard

African-American writer and journalist born in 1908, Richard Wright went in exile to France in 1946 in order to escape from the pursuit of American Federal Government against the communists. He lived in France until the end of his life in 1960.

Intrigued by an announcement of the Bandung Asian-African Conference in a journal, as he wrote in his book, he decided to go to Indonesia to participate in the Conference as journalist, with a minimum knowledge on Indonesia but with a personal sensitivity of a political exile and a descendant of slaves who suffered from racism in the USA.

There is nothing new in the book of Wright in term of content of the conference, compared to the book of Jack published in May 1955 and the official proceedings of the conference published in July 1955. The new elements for the readers at that time were his testimony, his view, his impression, his opinion, his thought around the conference. Let us quote some passages.

On the atmosphere around the Conference:

> *We drove past the conference building and saw the flags of the twenty-nine participating nations of Asia and Africa billowing lazily in a weak wind; already the streets were packed with crowds and their black and yellow and brown faces looked eagerly at each passing car, their sleek black hair gleaming in the bright sun, their slanted eyes peering intently, hopefully, to catch sight of some Prime Minister, a U Nu, a Chou En-lai, a Nehru... Then the air was periced by a screaming siren, heralding the approach of some august representative of some coloured Asian or African country. Day in and day out these crowds would stand in this tropic sun, staring, listening, applauding; it was the first time in their downtrodden lives that they'd seen so many men of their colour, race, and nationality arrayed in such aspects of power, their men keeping order, their Asia and their Africa in control of their destinies... They were getting a new sense of themselves, getting used to new roles and new identities. Imperialism was dead here; and, as long as they could maintain their unity, organize and conduct international conferences, there would be no return of imperialism...*[13]

On the physical living conditions of the poor people in Jakarta:

> *I passed those famous canals which the Dutch, for some inexplicable reason, has insisted upon digging here in this hot mudhole of a city. (...) I saw a young man squatting upon the bank of a canal, defecating in broad daylight into the canal's muddy, swirling water; I saw another, then another... Children used the canal for their water closet; then I saw a young woman washing clothes only a few yards from them...A young girl was bathing; she had a cloth around her middle and she was dipping water out of the canal and, holding the cloth out from her body,*

*she poured the water over her covered breasts... A tiny boy was washing his teeth, dipping his toothbrush into the canal...*[14]

For those who know well Jakarta, this kind of scenery is not a part of the past. It can still be found in Jakarta sixty years after the Bandung Conference.

## 1956: ROMULO General Carlos P.

Writer, journalist and diplomat, Romulo (1899–1985) joined the Allies during the WW II. Becoming American General, he was elected to be the president of General Assembly of the UN in 1949–1950. Invited to give lectures at the University of North Carolina, the USA, in 1956, he spoke about the Bandung Conference. His lectures were published afterward in a book form consisting of a foreword, two chapters and appendices.

The originality of his book consists of the unpublished points of view and an attempt to appreciate the role of the Conference in the events that took place in the world in 1955. The unpublished points of view were essentially the arguments that he and certain pro-Western, neutralist and communist delegates pronounced in the closed sessions of the Conference, in addition to his personal thoughts that were not pronounced during the Conference.

Representative of the US Allies, the author took a position as defender of the "free world" against the "neutralists" and the "communists". In his view, the neutralists were the "non-belligerent onlookers" in the struggle for mastery of the world between democracy and communism. That neutralism was often transformed to be "belligerent neutralism". The patent position of neutralism on the question of outlawing nuclear and thermo-nuclear arms, for example, was inconsistent. On one side, it was opposed to the West atomic experiments in the Pacific. On the other side, it stayed silent on the URSS atomic experiments. In this way, the neutralism gave advantages to communism[15].

His personal observations and opinions concerned especially the leaders of the three tendencies (pro-Western, neutralist and communist). The author appreciated the performances of the pro-Western leaders: John Kotelawala from Ceylon who attacked the communism as a new imperialism by citing the Soviet domination in East Europe; Nguyen Van Thoai from South Vietnam who blamed the dictatorial regime of North Vietnam who provoked the fleeing of one million Vietnamese to South Vietnam; Fadhel Jamali from Iraq who denounced the communism as a new form of colonialism worse than the old one and who defended its military alliances with the UK and Turkey in order to protect the "free world"; Prince Wan from Thailand who asked the communist nations to take out the spirit and the letter of what was called the "peaceful co-existence"[16].

On the other hand, the author criticised the neutralist and communist leaders, mainly Nehru and Chou En-lai. On Nehru, for example, he found that Nehru was anti-American but not anti-British despite his many years of imprisonment under the British rule in India. In fact, according to the author, due to his British education, Nehru had a secret admiration for everything British. He was not communist, he even fought the communism in India. However, he was predisposed, due to his anti-Americanism, to be pro-Russia. Moreover, the fact that he was Fabian socialist and confirmed agnostic kept him away from the US[17].

On Chou En-lai, the author was perplexed, astonished, surprised, of the fact that the behaviour of Chou En-lai did not correspond to the stereotypes known by the author on the communists impregnated by atheism, Marxism, materialism and, consequently, hostile to religions and spiritualities. Romulo wrote, for example, that Chou En-lai might be impressed by the fact that many speakers of the Conference invoked frequently the blessing of the Deity, so that in his policy statement during the open session he explained at length that communism was in general atheist but that his government allowed the freedom of worship. He pointed out that some of his delegates were followers of religions and he mentioned the numerous religious denominations, including Christianity, who were active in Red China. Then he asked the same tolerance for his "religious non belief" that his country observed towards believers. The author qualified Chou En-lai as "special pleader" when he repeated the prevailing Communist "tactical theme" where different political and economical systems could live together in peace and amity[18].

At the end, in the author's opinion, the neutralist and communist attempt to impose their ideas failed and the Final Communiqué represented the diplomatic victory of pro-West camp. The term "peaceful co-existence" (which was a Soviet political doctrine since 1952 and used in the China-India treaty of 1954), for example, was not accepted by the assembly for the Final Communiqué. The same as universal disarmament, including the prohibition of thermo-nuclear and other weapons of mass destruction, and further experiments of such weapons—pronouncement which would be difficult to oppose and constitute an obvious condemnation of the free-world coalition against communism. No such policy pronouncements issued from the Conference. Instead, the Final Communiqué exhorted nations to abide by a defined set of principles if they are "to live together in peace with one another"[19].

A faithful friend of the USA, the author pronounced with ease a series of severe criticisms towards the USA[20] but also at the same time gave them advices to answer those criticisms[21]. The Philippine delegation was the only one, he wrote, who attacked the USA in the Bandung Conference for supporting colonial policy of France, of Britain, of Belgium and of other colonial powers of Western Europe in the UN[22].

> *American continually talk of freedom and human rights. But they have supported the colonial policies of France, England, Belgium, and other colonial powers. They abstain in the UN whenever the questions of Cyprus, Tunisia, Algiers, and Morocco come up for decisions. In the UN Trusteeship Council they have adopted an amorphous attitude on fundamental questions affecting non-self-governing peoples. How can you believe in the sincerity of the Americans when their preachments and protestations do not jibe with their policy and actions?*
>
> *Why do American constantly boast of the superiority of the American way of life? It has its advantages and its blessings no doubt, but what is good for the Americans does not necessarily have to be good for us. Our way of life—which we have had for 2,000 years—may not offer the prosperity of the 200–year old United States, but there is something in maturity that cannot be bought with dollars or achieved with chewing gum, hot dogs, and comic strips.*
>
> *The latest expression of American materialism is not Hollywood; it is the nuclear weapon. Americans think that because they have superiority in this type of weapon of destruction they can stand alone and need not exert any effort to make friends or win allies. In fact, they are so ready for war they do not want to talk or enter into any negotiations. They are spoiling for a fight*[23].

One of his key answers to those criticisms was that *"The new Asia and Africa as shown in Bandung (…) is not taking the identical shape of a new Europe or a new America. Asia and Africa will go their own way, and the great hope of all mankind must be that they will share in a continuing partnership with what is best in America and Europe"*[24]. And he asked a fundamental question *"Whether the fabulous success of the American economy is something that can be imitated in… say Morocco, Egypt, India, and Indonesia or whether the American economy is something unique—the product of a unique geographical position and special history"*[25].

As for the Bandung Conference itself, Romulo gave full of praise appreciations. *"Bandung was, in a manner of speaking, a historical peageant, symbolizing the coming of age of Asia and Africa"*[26]. *"Democracy has its day in court at Bandung and emerged with flying colors"*[27]. *"Those who forcast that the Asian-African Conference would be a 'lynch party in reverse' look foolish indeed. Bandung was characterized by a rare degree of sanity and dignity"*[28].

*"The conference, though critical of certain Western powers, and rightly so, was far from hostile to the West as such. The conference went out of its way, in fact, to show understanding and charity toward wrongs and injustices, which, had the picture been reversed, would probably have not been overlooked at all"*[29]. And for this friend of the US, *"its meaning is even clearer now than before. And it is this: outside those lands where the Communists are now in control, there is an ever-growing devotion to the principles of democracy and freedom which are symbolized by England's immortal Magna Charta, by the French encyclopedists and the statement of the Rights of Man, and above all, by the American Declaration of Independence. We are achieving, in the free world, West and East, a common platform. And on this platform, we are bound to differ, to disagree, to make decisions at variance with one another"*[30]. *"In the over-all picture of man's quest for freedom and progress, Williamsburg, Philadephia and Bandung were related milestones"*[31]. *"Bandung did not provide the design for a perfect world; it did define, however, the basis for hope"*[32].

## 1965: CONTE Arthur

Arthur Conte (1920–2013) was presented on the book cover as a former minister, former President of the Assembly of Western European Union, several times extraordinary ambassador, French delegate for numerous international conferences. His book *Yalta ou le Partage du Monde* won the "Historia" and the "Le Plaisir de Lire" awards in 1964.

The book *Bandoung tournant de l'Histoire* was a part of collection "Ce jour là" (On that day) that proposed to make alive the great dramatic and historical days of the world. For that respect, the author consulted newspapers from all over the world and archives of numerous chancelleries. He had a chance also to meet face to face with ministers, heads of state, ambassadors who participated in the Bandung Conference.

It is from this book that we learn the process of the conference in details, the biography of the heads of delegation, the atmosphere of the conference, the confrontation of points of view among heads of delegation, and more. The authors succeeded to reveal, for example, the way the first closed session of the conference took place, which was not revealed in the previous books. The session was dedicated to fix the agenda and the procedure of the conference. The meeting was marked by disagreements and heated discussions, especially between Nehru, Sir John, Mohamed Ali and others. When Sastroamidjojo (the president of the Conference) proposed that the discussions be divided into five chapters following the Panchsheel Treaty (the five principles of peaceful co-existence treaty signed by China and India in 1954), Zorlu (Turkish head of delegation) reacted cynically:

"You are joking, your five principles are hollow like a bamboo". It was Nehru who intervened quickly and settled the question. Without referring to the Panchsheel Treaty, his proposal of five chapters were accepted easily: Economic Cooperation, Cultural Cooperation, Human Rights and Self-determination, Problems of Dependent Countries and World Cooperation for Peace.

However, Nehru was confronted with strong opposition when he proposed that there would be no public speech of the delegates for the reason that the twenty nine successive speeches would be wasting time. He proposed even not to hold public sessions as planned except for announcing the final communiqué. The delegates were to work discretely for preparing the final communiqué. The collective protestation against this proposal was immediate. "We have travelled a long way and we want to be heard," said the Ethiopian delegate.

Nehru: "Your twenty nine speeches would turn around the generality of condemning colonialism and you would risk also to make appear the profound gaps within the Asian-African block. I beg you to listen to my advice. I have experience".

Mohamed Ali: "I am Prime Minister of a sovereign and independent nation, and I am not accountable to the Indian Prime Minister".

Nehru insisted, stormed, grew irritated.

It was Chou En-lai who settled the problem. He intervened in the sense of the majority, persuading Nehru to renounce his proposal.

Thus, the discussion will be started by the public speeches of the heads of delegation[33].

## 1980: ABDULGANI Dr. H. Roeslan

ABDULGANI (1914–2005) was a fighter for Indonesian independence since his youth in the 1920s, which caused him expulsion from Dutch colonial school in the 1930s, close ally of Soekarno, then civil servant of the republic, minister of foreign affairs, minister of information, ambassador to the UN along the 1950s and 1960s. He was the secretary general of the Minister of Foreign Affairs when he was designated to be the Secretary General of the 1955 Bandung Conference.

The title of the book, "Bandung Connection" was inspired by a 1971 American film "French Connection" on a network of criminal organisation who imported from France the major part of the heroine consumed in the USA. The intrigues, tensions, surprises and climax revealing the relations between the criminal group and the French diplomatic world enlivened his memories of Secretary General of the 1955 Bandung Conference. For him, Bandung in 1955 played a role of "centre of connections" between countries and peoples of Africa and Asia in their struggle for independence from colonialism, imperialism and hegemony of super powers. Bandung was not only a centre of connections between governments, but also between activists of liberation movements of Africa and Asia: anti-apartheid activists from South Africa and Central Africa, liberation activists from Algeria, Morocco, Tunisia, Palestine,... civil rights activists from USA... all got together in Bandung.

There are interesting anecdotes revealed in the book. The most interesting one concerns the opening date of the Conference, which is April 18. The initial idea was to hold the conference on the last week of April 1955. Then it was realised that the last week of April 1955 was the beginning of Ramadhan, which is a sacred month for the Muslims where they observe their religious duty of fasting during the whole month starting from April 24 or 25. There was therefore an imperative to start the Conference around ten days in advance in order to allow the Conference to finish before Ramadhan. Otherwise all the Muslim participants from Pakistan, Iran and Arab countries would not come or would leave the Conference before its end. Meanwhile, April 15, 1955, was a sacred day for the Buddhists. The delegations from Burma, Thailand and Indochina would not be able to come to the Conference before April 17, 1955. Therefore, there was no choice: April 18 was the only possible date for the beginning of the Conference.

Toward the end of March, the author had to take care of two things: on one hand, to give ideas to president Soekarno for his opening speech and, on the other hand, to prepare strategic measures in order to anticipate the reactions of the USA which were hostile to the Bandung Conference project. Under this heavy pressure, he remembered vaguely that there was something happened on April 18 in the History of American Revolution. He then made a phone call to the US Ambassador Hugh Cumming with whom he had a good professional and personal relationship, asking him about the chronology of American Revolution. In the following day, he received some books of reference and found out that the 18th of April 1775 was a memorable day in the war of American independence. On the night of April 18, 1775, a young American patriot, Paul Revere, rode a horse in a gallop between Boston and Concord in order to wake up and inform people of the arrival of the British colonial army and called them for resistance. This event was immortalised by the American poet Henry Longfellow in his poem "Tales of Wayside Inn: Paul Revere's Ride". Hence, April 18 was a historical date in the struggle for American independence. Why not integrate this element in the opening speech of the Conference?

Soekarno agreed. That is why Soekarno recited the poem of Longfellow in his opening speech:

> *The battle against colonialism has been a long one, and do you know that today is a famous anniversary in that battle? On the eighteenth day of April, one thousand seven hundred and seventy five, just one hundred and eighty years ago, Paul Revere rode at midnight through the New England countryside, warning of the approach of British troops and of the opening of the American War of Independence, the first successful anti-colonial war in history. About this midnight ride the poet Longfellow wrote:*
>
> *A cry of defiance and not of fear,*
>
> *A voice in the darkness, a knock at the door,*
>
> *And a word that shall echo for evermore…*
>
> *Yes, it shall echo for evermore, just as the other anti-colonial words which gave us comfort and reassurance during the darkest days of our struggle shall echo for evermore. But remember, that battle which began 180 years ago is not yet completely won, and it will not have been completely won until we can survey this our own world, and can say that colonialism is dead.*

The impact was extraordinary, especially on the American journalists and activists of civil rights. Their sympathy to the Conference was immediate. Ambassador Hugh Cumming himself came to the author after the opening speech to give him his hand. They shook their hands without words but with wide smile and brilliant eyes full of mutual appreciation[34].

## 2007: AMPIAH Kweku

Lecturer-researcher specialised on Japanese studies at the University of Leeds, the UK, the author started to be interested in the subject in 1991 when he did his first research on the Japanese participation in the Bandung Conference. He discovered with astonishment that most of the Japanese academics ignored the subject despite the Japanese participation in the event and its extensive implication in the post-colonial economic development in Southeast Asia. His initial intention then was focusing his research on the participation of Japan in the Bandung Conference. After some reflection, he found that a comparative study on the responses of the US, the UK and Japan to the Conference might give justice to the event. Moreover, studies on the American and British responses to the event were far from being exhaustive.

What were the reasons of worries and the major preoccupations of the US regarding the Conference? How did the US try to settle the problems? To what extent did the British share its worrying preoccupations with the US, and how did it respond? What did the US expect from Japan in their efforts to minimise the threat from the expected union of the Neutralists and the Communist China, and how far did Japan cooperate in this exercise? Those are among the questions on which the author tried to work.

His accurate, analytic and synthetic presentation of the American, British and Japanese reactions to the Conference constitute his major contribution to the knowledge of the subject and its global repercussion at that time.

### *The USA*

For the USA, the Bandung Conference was a headache. It amplified the US' worries for the Cold War in Asia, especially for the possible loss of allies and friends in the region. The Department of State believed that the cohabitation of Pan-Asianism and Neutralism was a step towards Communism. This made the Secretary of State nervous. As Dulles confessed, he was stressed by the question of how the affair would turn out in the region. At the beginning, the USA did not wish its friends to attend the Conference. When it became clear that Washington would not be able to prevent its friends from participating in the Conference, and after considering the risk of not being represented at all in the Conference, Washington changed completely its strategy. It let its friends to participate in the Conference while suggesting that they were to be represented by the best possible delegation and with the approval of Washington. This implicated the Department of State to find a strong leader able to represent the pro-American countries in the Conference. The global objective of the strategy was to find someone who could contain Chou En Lai and Nehru. For Washington, Chou En-lai was the incarnation of communist threat to the Conference. That is why Washington was determined to find somebody who could held him and break his charisma. This created anxieties in the Department of State and produced many comments on the Prime Ministers of Pakistan and Ceylon considered not to have the required qualities. At the end, the performance of Chou in the Conference, his intelligence and moderation, became object of many comments in the Department of State. It was clear that Chou turned the diplomacy towards his advantage and that his offer to settle the question of Formosa in amicable way provoked a trouble in the Department. The answer of the Department was cold. In spite of all, the US global assessment to the Conference was positive. The Department of State saw the moderate tone of the Final Communiqué as a victory for the West, victory attributed to friends defenders of the cause of the West (especially Turkey, Lebanon, Iraq, Pakistan, Thailand, Ceylon and the Philippines). Meanwhile, this did not waive the US impression on the lyrical and powerful performance of Chou in the Conference. His offer to facilitate a political settlement of the Formosa question troubled Dulles and the Department of State because it made China acceptable to the Asian countries, which remained a threat in the mind of the USA political decision makers.

*Great Brittain*

Whitehall and the British Government were very concerned by the Bandung Conference, mainly for its impacts on the British colonies in Africa. The perception was strong, especially in the Colonial Office (CO), that the Asian countries were trying to lead the African countries against the Empire. The invitation addressed to the Gold Coast, the Federation of Central Africa and Sudan for the Bandung Conference was perceived as an encroachment on the British interests. Consequently, Whitehall did all the possible to soften the risks for the UK of their participation in the Conference. As a result, the Central African Federation declined the invitation, the Gold Coast went to Bandung as observer. On the other hand, Sudan participated as a full member.

The recommendations of the Conference on the economic development of African and Asian countries were considered by Whitehall to be more serious than the supposed threat of Communism. They were perceived as an attempt of African and Asian countries to form an economic bloc excluding other countries, especially of the West. The recommendation on the countries producing raw materials was perceived particularly threatening.

As the main US ally, the UK shared naturally the US concerns on the communist expansion. However, Whitehall was not obsessed by the threat of China as did the Department of State.

As for its national interest, the UK was more concerned by the colonial issue put forward by India and also coincidently by the USA. The latter considered the UK's colonial possession as a reason for Communist expansion and wished its disappearance.

In a memorandum following the Conference, the Colonial Office identified the problems posed by the Conference in three themes: Anti-colonialism; Asian commitment to African affairs; Emergence of African-Asian bloc in the UN. On Anti-colonialism, the sentence "colonialism as an evil in all its manifestations" in the Final Communiqué of the Conference, which was formulated thanks to countries friends of the West, was considered better than a declaration addressed directly to Western colonialism. However, this sentence was considered at the same time harming because it put in equation Colonialism and Communism.

On the second and third themes, they were a reality to anticipate.

At the end, like the US, the UK found the result of the Conference moderate and satisfying.

*Japan*

Ostracised by its Asian neighbours for its aggressions in Asia from the end of the 19th century to 1945, Japan found the Conference an opportunity to reintegrate itself into Asian community. That is why Japan had decided to participate in the Conference before the US did it for Japan. Yet, the Japan's position was very delicate, between maintaining its good relation with the US and developing its independent policy based on its own interests. This is in addition to the trauma suffered by Asian countries participating in the Conference due to the Japanese imperialist behaviour before its defeat. In a metaphor quoted by the author, Japan came to participate in the Conference like "a cat at a mice's convention with a bell around its neck" but had to behave carefully in such a way that it appeared like "a mouse at a cat's convention". The Japanese delegation was prepared to avoid questions related to Japanese national interests, which might raise controversies among the Asian countries participating in the Conference or criticisms on Japanese actions before and during the war.

After the war, Japan was determined to make a distance with military tensions. Consequently, in the framework of "peaceful co-existence", Japan decided to develop amicable relations with all countries, including the USSR and the PRC. In the Bandung Conference, Japan did not want to serve as messenger of the US grand strategy in Asia, contrary to what the US expected. For example, Japan did not say about supporting SEATO. Despite its cooperation with the US before the Conference, Japan did not show sufficiently its pro-American qualification during the Conference, in the contrary to the Philippines, Turkey and Pakistan. In other words, Japan refused to defend directly the US interests in the Conference, leaving others to do the job. This was a test of the determination of the Hatoyama's administration in Japanese independent foreign policy vis-à-vis the USA. In this way, while remaining subordinated to the hegemonic power of the US, Japan was able to manage well its position in order to reach its objectives within the dominant discourse of the Conference.

Japan's main interest in the Conference was the economic imperative of the event. That is why Japan did not involve in the political meetings of the Conference but in the economic meetings. This was not without consequence, especially in the interior affairs of Japan. The critics accused the government of hiding behind a camouflage of "Diplomacy of Peace" in order to concretise better its primary intention to dominate the economies of Southeast Asia. The Socialist Party, which was in opposition, expressed its dissatisfaction regarding the Government that put in priority national economic interests on the top of international policy.

## Concluding Remark

It seems clear that the Bandung Conference, its actors, its process and its products have been revealed by the fundamental books presented previously. The work of Ampiah, however, gives a new perspective, which is the Bandung Conference seen from outside, mainly from the points of view of the states concerned by the conference, in this case the US, the UK and Japan. Meanwhile, there are other states that were also concerned in diverse degrees by the conference, such as France, the Netherlands, but also Russia, Portugal, Australia, South Africa, Israel,... Yet, we do not know how did those countries perceive, anticipate or react to the Conference. Thus, it seems that there is still something to be written on the Bandung Conference seen from outside. Researches on diverse national archives of the countries concerned by the Bandung Conférence may bring probably new elements or new perceptions on this historical event.

## Endnotes

1. *Dictionary of Unitarian & Universalist Biography*. See http://uudb.org/articles/homeralexanderjack.html (consulted on July 7, 2015).
2. Core Congress of Racial Equality. See http://www.congressofracialequality.org/homer-jack.html (consulted on July 7, 2015).
3. Jack Homer Alexander, *Bandung: On the Spot Description of the Asian-African Conference*, Bandung, Indonesia, April 1955. Chicago, Toward Freedom, May 1955, pp. 4–5.
4. Ibid., pp. 5–6.
5. Ibid., p. 9.
6. Ibid., pp. 7–9.
7. Ibid., p. 9.
8. Ibid., pp. 11–12.
9. Ibid., pp. 13–14.
10. Ibid., p. 15.
11. Ibid., pp. 15–16.
12. Ibid., p. 16.
13. Wright Richard, *The Colour Curtain: A Report on The Bandung Conference*. University Press of Mississippi, 1956, pp. 114–115.
14. Ibid., p. 82.
15. Romulo General Carlos P., *The Meaning of Bandung*. University of North Carolina Press, 1956, pp. 8–9.
16. Ibid., pp. 21–27.
17. Ibid., p. 12.

18. Ibid., pp. 16–17.
19. Ibid., p. 7.
20. Ibid., pp. 42–47.
21. Ibid., pp. 49–53.
22. Ibid., p. 49.
23. Ibid., pp. 43–44.
24. Ibid., p. 53.
25. Ibid., p. 41.
26. Ibid., p. 35.
27. Ibid., p. 36.
28. Ibid., p. 48.
29. Ibid., p. 48.
30. Ibid., p. 56.
31. Ibid., p. 48.
32. Ibid., p. 36.
33. Conte Arthur, *Bandoung, tournant de l'Histoire*. Paris, Robert Laffont, 1965, pp. 252–253
34. Abdulgani Dr. H. Roeslan, *The Bandung Connection: Konperensi Asia-Afrika di Bandung tahun 1955*. Jakarta, Indonesian Ministry of Foreign Affairs, 2013, p. 56.

# 3

# Women "Performing" Diplomacy at the Bandung Conference of 1955[1]

*Naoko Shimazu*

## Abstract

How can we attempt to better understand the role played by women in international diplomacy? How did women perform as diplomatic actors at the Bandung Conference of 1955? Diplomacy is often regarded as a highly male-dominated sphere, even more so than national politics. Was the Bandung experience any different from other international diplomatic events? What this paper argues is that women generally were not as visible in what one might consider to be the formal diplomatic sphere at Bandung, whilst they were highly prominent in informal diplomatic settings. In order to illustrate this duality, I start by offering a critical re-reading of 'the Freedom Walk'—the iconic walk made by all delegations along Jalan Asia Afrika, mostly from Hotel Savoy Homann or Hotel Preanger, to attend the opening plenary session on 18 April in Gedung Merdeka or the Freedom Building—which I introduced in my previous work. Then, I examine situations of informal diplomacy where women had high public visibility, notably in scenes of 'sociability in diplomacy'. What becomes evident is that the visibility or invisibility of women as diplomatic performers depends much on the definition of 'who' constitutes diplomatic performers. Moreover, when we refer to visual sources as significant primary sources, women suddenly feature very prominently at Bandung. I conclude that we need to expand the scope of enquiry to include non-traditional sources, especially visual sources, in order to gauge more inclusively performative roles of women in the study of international diplomacy. This work constitutes one part of my current monograph project on Diplomacy as Theatre: The Bandung Conference and the Making of the Third World.

*Keywords:* women, formal diplomacy, informal diplomacy, sociability, visual sources, performance

How did women perform in diplomacy at the Bandung Conference? Diplomacy is a notoriously male-dominated sphere. Arguably, the Bandung Conference was no different than most other international diplomatic events in that women's roles as diplomatic performers appeared marginal, and limited, in scope. This paper argues that we need to expand generally the scope of intellectual enquiry pertaining to the study of diplomacy if we are serious about wanting to understand more fully how women were integrated into the iconography of diplomacy at Bandung. To this end, diplomacy will be examined in general terms of two complementary dimensions: formal diplomacy, and informal diplomacy. Under formal diplomacy, we question why women remained, on the whole, invisible in formal enactments of diplomacy, most notably in, what I have previously termed, 'the Freedom Walk'. In informal diplomacy, however, we observe the diametrically opposite phenomenon, which is the constant visibility of women, particularly when we privilege visual over textual sources. By including the people of Bandung as local audience, with a performative function in the theatre of diplomacy, women again become prominent. In all, this paper argues for widening the scope of scholarly enquiry in the study of diplomacy, and attempts to situate international diplomacy in the realm of the everyday.

## I. Gendering the Freedom Walk

I have argued elsewhere that one of the most powerful performative moments at the Bandung Conference was the 'Freedom Walk'[2]. On the opening day of the conference, delegates walked along Asia Africa Road to the principal conference venue, Gedung Merdeka or Freedom Building, from either Hotel Savoy Homann or Grand Hotel Preanger about fifty metres and hundred metres respectively down the road. Even the chiefs of delegations who had been put up on hillside bungalows arriving in their sedan cars were asked to get out of the car and walk the last stretch to the venue, in order to avoid congestion around the Freedom Building. This walk turned into a 'parade of nations' as each delegation walked along Asia Africa Road, clapped and cheered by the local crowd who had gathered from early morning to catch the glimpse of famous world statesmen. According to an Indonesian weekly magazine, *Lukisan Dunia*: 'it's not clear whether the public was happy because they can see one by one members of the delegations arrive at such a short distance or whether they were attracted by the variety of national clothes worn by the delegations of the Gold Coast,

Ethiopia, Ceylon, Burma, and India which looked very attractive'[3]. What made this walk symbolic was that it created an 'interactive space' between these statesmen, some of them iconic figures, such as Nehru, Zhou Enlai, Nasser, and the local people, both sides performing their respective roles as statesmen and audience, lending to the iconography of the Bandung Conference. I argued that this mutually reinforcing interaction resulted in the forging of a bond, often emotive, between leaders and the people, based on shared revolutionary experiences for struggles of independence.

An alternative reading of the Freedom Walk through the lens of gender gives rise to an entirely different, and highly critical, picture from what the celebratory reading of the Freedom Walk elaborated above would suggest. The Freedom Walk, which is so powerfully evocative because of its ability to project three-dimensionally the pro-independence dream of 'the road to freedom' through the very act of walking towards the Freedom Building, was equally striking for the conspicuous absence of women. Apart from a handful of women who paraded alongside the men, Freedom Walk for women ended up being about performing their invisibility in international diplomacy—hence, what one may call, a non-performance as performance.

Who were the women taking part in the Freedom Walk? *Ceylon Daily News* was disparaging about the abysmal state of female representation at the conference, namely that not a single woman delegate was present in the conference that represented the 1.4 billion people worldwide[4]. Indira Gandhi accompanied her father to the conference, where she was given a privileged limelight due to the stature of her father, Nehru, as she began to act as his official consort in all diplomatic duties from the time he became prime minister in 1947. Insofar as her conference participation was concerned, she sat in on committee meetings, attending many functions, though always in an unofficial capacity. More significantly, President Sukarno and Vice-President Mohammad Hatta were both accompanied by their wives, as was Prime Minister Ali Sastroamidjoyo who was accompanied by his wife, Ibu Sri, on their Freedom Walk. In the photographs of the Walk, we can see Sukarno's wife, Fatmawati, walking to the left side of her husband; and Madam Hatta, nearly invisible, behind Fatmawati. What this arrangement reveals is that it mattered greatly to Sukarno and Hatta as well as the Joint Secretariat that their wives formed part of the Indonesian presidential party at the world historic conference: as an important political statement to make of their revolutionary credentials in the eyes of the Indonesian public; and a diplomatic statement to make for Indonesia as a leading new modern state in the eyes of the global audience.

Paradoxically, it was the paucity of women in the Freedom Walk that had the effect of highlighting contemporary feminist politics in some Asian societies—the burning issue of polygamy, which had been practiced by two leaders amongst the Colombo Powers, the sponsoring states of the Bandung Conference. Polygamy was one of the two pressing, and longest standing, issues in women's movement in Indonesia dating back to the colonial period, the other being women's education. Ironically, the very visibility of Sukarno's parading with Fatmawati in her role as the First Lady, had opened up a public debate on Sukarno's ongoing scandal over a parallel relationship he was having with Hartini whom he met in 1953. Sukarno's relationship with Hartini at the time of Bandung was an open secret—in fact, he marries Hartini in 1955. Sukarno would go on to have another wife after Hartini in Naoko Nemoto (a Japanese national). Sukarno's espousal of polygamy, had antagonised Indonesian women's groups during the conference, but was also symptomatic of the post-colonial predicament of women's movement, with its unfulfilled revolutionary promises, more generally across the newly decolonised states.

Small wonder then that the Pakistani Prime Minister, Mohammed Ali, who paraded along with Madam Ali, to whom he had only gotten married some two weeks before the conference, got under fire from women's movements in Pakistan and Indonesia. Madam Ali was the prime minister's second wife, and her presence at Bandung caused quite a stir, and consternation, for a number of reasons. A news headline screamed out: 'Mrs Ali No. 2 is now in Bandung'[5]. *The Pakistan Times* published an article, 'Protest Against Ali's Second Marriage', in which it reported a meeting of Pakistani women demanding of the boycott of second wives, stating that polygamy was only allowable 'if a wife is incapable of bearing children, or has been suffering from some disease'. It voiced 'regret' over the attendance at the conference by Ali's second wife, demanding that status and the title of the First Lady should belong to Begum Hamida Mohammed Ali, and not to the second wife, a Canadian-Lebanese, who had been the social secretary of the prime minister's before the marriage. In fact, this issue resulted in a protest march of Pakistani women to the Pakistani Prime Minister's residence, and an 'anti-polygamy letter' was delivered by the group, the Protection of Rights of Women, which had been formed in Karachi, the day before[6]. The editorial took an uncompromising position, supporting the women's group, that the second marriage of the prime minister had 'cause[d] considerable damage to Pakistan's prestige abroad' and that he had behaved 'most improper[ly]' by celebrating his second marriage with a huge ceremony, mobilising even the Governor-General of Pakistan to give a banquet on return from honeymoon, and displaying wealth by obtaining a special permission to import large quantities of gold and precious stones[7]. Because of his official role as prime minister, Mohammed Ali's personal life choice had become a symbolic public matter, causing national embarrassment to Pakistan and the Pakistani people in the eyes of the international audience. This issue had been noted also in other international newspapers, such as in the *Daily News* of Colombo:

> Pakistan's Premier Mohammed Ali has stirred up quite a lot of hot air among women of Indonesia, as a result of bringing with him his second wife—his former social secretary mistakenly described as Canadian but actually Lebanese. She sat this morning clad in a white saree, usually she wears frock, next to India's Indira Gandhi, who hardly spoke a word to her. The Perwari—equivalent to the Womens' Progressive group with the difference that it is a live force here and taken seriously—had not invited her to a reception to the wives of the delegates. The boycott by the group follow the pattern of their protests against Dr Soekarno, the Indonesian President taking with himself a second wife. Their protests succeeded in that she was not allowed to take precedence over the first[8].

Not to be outdone, the Indonesian women's magazine, *Wanita*, also made its views known:

> Within this celebratory situation in Bandung, there's a dark cloud in the minds of Indonesian women. The arrival of PM Mohammed Ali of Pakistan who brought his second wife with whom he has just married on 2 April, depressed the happy situation. Indonesian women, who are still fighting for their rights, were taken aback because Ali brought his second wife. Once again we are forced to swallow a bitter pill. It appears that women's struggle is still 'full of sharp tongues'. So be it. We will continue fighting. And, at the time, we are the host, madam, so all odd feelings have to be put aside, and the state guests must be greeted properly. Indonesian women have to have big heart for the honour of the country[9].

In any case, Mohammed Ali's case had even reached the Home News Service bulletin of the BBC:

> In Karachi, a group of women delivered a letter at the home of the Prime Minster, Mr. Mohammed Ali, today, in protest against the Prime Minister's second marriage early this month, during the lifetime of his first wife. The group, representing a number of women's organisations in Pakistan, arrived shortly before Mr. Mohammed Ali left on his way to the African-Asian Conference at Bandoeng, in Indonesia. In their letter, they asked that both the Prime Minster's wives should be given an equal place at State and Social functions. They also called on the Prime Minister to give his first wife the status of first lady of Pakistan, in the absence of the wife of the Governor-General.[10]

The Indonesian public dissatisfaction in some quarters over demonstrations of polygamy by two of the five Colombo Powers' leaders can be traced to the beginnings of feminism in Indonesia during the Dutch colonial times. Kartini—the first widely acknowledged feminist of the Indonesian people, was a Javanese aristocrat, and polygamy ranked as one of the two objectives for activism in her short but influential life. Since then, polygamy remained as the most important feminist platform, leading into the post-independence era.[11] Polygamy was a fight for equality for women as the Indonesian women's movement fought alongside the Indonesian nationalist movement to overthrow the Dutch. Ali Sastroamidjoyo was involved in the first Indonesian Women's Congress, held in Jakarta in December 1928, co-organised by Ali Sastroamidjoyo's sister, Sukonto, where he addressed the issue of Islam and the customary law on the position of women. Polygamy as a national feminist issue that united various women's movements belonging to Christians (both Catholics and Protestants) and Muslims, also became the bone of contention as there existed a fundamental disagreement on the degree to which each side had wanted to push for either the complete ban of polygamy on the part of Christians, or to better women's lot without abolishing the institution altogether on the part of Muslims[12]. Mohammed Sjafei wrote in *El Fadjar* (The Light) of the Young Muslim Association: 'Polygamy is not prohibited by Islam, but it is distressing that many abuse their rights…They practice a "polygamy de luxe"…and I mean by this that such polygamy is inspired entirely by man's passion.' In fact, there was a tendency to denigrate polygamy because it was practiced mainly by the well-to-do class of men. Polygamy continued to be a key issue as in the second meeting of the Indonesian Women's Congress in 1929, a larger umbrella organisation was formed in the Federation of Indonesian Women's Associations (PPII). From henceforth, Indonesian representatives would be sent to annual Congress on Asian Women, the first of which took place in Lahore in January 1932, when polygamy was condemned. In 1929, Putri Indonesia was formed under the Yong Java movement, taking a much hardliner stance on polygamy. Sukarno had even addressed a meeting held in Bandung by Putri Indonesia. In 1930, this group had a splinter group in Isteri Sedar (The Alert Woman) in Bandung, with its own organ *Sedar*. Sukarno supported Isteri Sedar which soon turned into a political movement. The leader of Isteri Sedar, Suwarni Pringgodigdo wrote an article 'The Question of Polygamy' in 1934 in which she argued that 'The Indonesian woman has a right to justice and independence and polygamy is the very denial of justice and independence'.[13]

Undoubtedly, Sukarno amongst the three key Indonesian leaders at the conference—others being Mohammad Hatta and Ali Sastroamidjoyo—was the most traditional in his outlook on women and marriage. What exacerbated Sukarno's position was that he had been an ardent supporter of women's movement in the period of nationalist struggle, encouraging all women to be part of the revolutionary struggle, only to be exposed that it was a lip-service he had paid to have women join the struggle in attaining equality of Indonesians both men and women. Hence, Sukarno was hypocritical in his stance, mainly because his revolutionary rhetoric and daily practice diverged considerably. To make matters doubly worse, the social class most affected by problems of polygamy was the well-to-do class, only the top few percentage of the Indonesian population.[14] These were the women that participated in the revolutionary struggle most visibly, and paradoxically, it was their class that was most affected by polygamy.

Let us return to the Freedom Walk and consider the particular significance of Fatmawati and Madam Hatta being part of the iconography of the Bandung Conference in the eyes of the Indonesian public. In the now familiar photographs taken on 17 August 1945 when Sukarno and Mohammad Hatta read out the Proclamation of Independence from the balcony of 11 Jalan Diponegoro in Jakarta, Fatmawati and Madam Hatta stood with their husbands in their Javanese dress on the balcony to be part of the historic occasion. During this ceremony, the new Indonesian flag was raised. As the popular revolutionary lore goes, it was Fatmawati who had made the Indonesian flag of *merah-putih* (the red and white) by sewing together two pieces of cloths—one red and one white—which became the very first official flag of the newly proclaimed Republic of Indonesia.[15] Mostly because of this, Fatmawati had been portrayed as the 'Mother of the Country' or 'Ibu Negara', symbolically representing Indonesian women, at the moment of independence. Hence, both Fatmawati and Madam Hatta were, in the eyes of the public, part of the iconography of the birth of the nation. Therefore, it made much political sense for these women to be parading (though in a subservient position of being behind their husbands) with their husbands as heirs to the revolution, representing the female population of Indonesia; the fact of the presence of these few women can be interpreted as a symbolically significant gesture in the revolutionary narrative which had been a gender-inclusive, pan-Indonesian narrative of the attainment of sovereign independence for the republic.

Relative to the contributions made by Indonesian women in the revolutionary struggle, the fact of their invisibility from the official Freedom Walk in the post-colonial celebration at Bandung, belied the reality of women's position in the post-colonial Indonesia. Moreover, the symbolic invisibility of women in formal diplomacy as epitomised in the Walk, had wider implications for the role of women in newly post-colonial countries generally, such as in Pakistan, and indeed, further afield. Women's movements shared their collective disillusionment with the onset of the status quo in their respective societies after the initial euphoria of independence had been died down, as women's issues became marginalised in public debates on post-colonial state-building.[16]

Nonetheless, Bandung did have an immediate influence in terms of establishing a new international association known as the Asian-African Conference on Women, the first meeting held in Colombo in 1958, where the twenty-nine Bandung nations were represented. This was the result of an Indonesian initiative taken in the Cultural Committee of the Bandung Conference, in order to 'implement the aims and principles of the Universal Declaration of Human Rights as related to women and to discuss the cooperation between Asian-African women in regard to matters of common interest'[17]. Bier argues that the 'Bandung Spirit' had its effect beyond diplomacy and foreign relations, as it had an impact on global feminism, which 'challenges conventional historical narratives of international feminism' because Bandung 'provided an alternative political and organisational space to the prewar, Western-dominated, imperial international women's feminist movement' that situates primary agency in British and American initiatives.[18]

## II. Women in Informal Diplomacy

As I have already stated above, women were generally speaking invisible from formal documentation of diplomatic activities. This is mainly reflective of the dearth of women in high politics generally, in the lack of female statesmen and female diplomats. Yet, how do we account for the overwhelming visual evidence of women during the Bandung Conference? Women are highly visible in a variety of conference activities such as manning the Information Desks in conference buildings, journalists, social events, entertainments, and most prominently as members of the local audience. A number of Indonesian journalists noted this fact in an article entitled, "Women's Activities Behind the Scenes at the Asian-African Conference". In fact, the prominence of women who were actively participating in the conference preparations (including manning the press office) and cultural activities in Bandung was so striking that Nehru notes it in his 'recollections of the conference'. He was convinced that it must have left an impression on Arab delegates[19]. Hence, it becomes critical to expand the range of intellectual enquiry to incorporate non-official sources, especially visual sources, in the study of diplomacy in order to make women visible in the diplomatic sphere[20]. In this section, I argue that women performed as agents of informal diplomacy during the conference.

Let us turn our attention for a moment to the official photograph album compiled of the Thai delegation, where we see a relatively high number of photographs of Phibubenjang Kitiyakorn who was the wife of Prince Wan Waithayakorn, the chief of the delegation to the Bandung Conference[21]. She is portrayed arriving with her husband at the Bandung Airport, two photos of her sitting next to her husband in front of Zhou Enlai, two of her at a reception organised by the Women's Association of Indonesia in Bandung attended also by Fatmawati, Madam Hatta, Mrs Mohammad Ali of Pakistan, two of her in a reception for the Thai press hosted by Prince Wan Waithayakorn in the Pasar Baru Restaurant after the conference, four of her arrival back at Bangkok's Don Mueang Airport after the conference. All in all, she appears in eleven photographs out of eighty-three photographs of delegates, whereas her husband scored a surprisingly modest twenty-four as the head of delegation. The frequency of her photographic appearances in the official album suggests that there was a recognition of her role as a diplomatic consort in Thai diplomacy, and that this had the effect of projecting the image of Thailand as a modern Asian state where women were visible in the diplomatic sphere. Moreover, the fact that in most photographs she is not wearing the ethnic dress is another projection of modernity, as there is no sartorially-based gender contrast created between Prince Wan and his wife, as it was the case with the Indonesian leaders like Sukarno, Hatta, Ali Satroamidjoyo whose wives wore the Javanese dress, or Mrs Mohammed Ali who likewise wore the sari at official representations at Bandung. It may be worth pointing out that though Zhou Enlai's wife, Deng Yingchao, did not attend the Bandung Conference, Zhou soon recognises the importance of the performative role of the diplomatic consort, and recommends that wives of officials play a role in Chinese diplomacy from 1960 onwards[22].

Arguably, the role of the diplomatic consort[23], particularly when occupied by women as wives, can be made into a highly visible performative role for a number of reasons. As in the Indonesian and Pakistani cases, diplomatic consorts can project visibly the national/ethnic identity of their countries through the manipulation of the dress. Hence, the dress plays part in the non-verbal communication in international diplomacy. Because of the paucity of women actors in diplomacy, female diplomatic consorts stand out visibly by default. Moreover, diplomatic consorts are dispatched to perform in informal diplomacy, such as participating in social events, cultural activities, and social welfare visits. What is noteworthy about the underlying agenda of these 'soft power' activities is that it is primarily about the politics of inclusion—in other words, it is not about staking out national differences through diplomatic consorts (though they would often be wearing their respective national dress) but about demonstrating the togetherness of these women representing different countries. Hence, it plays a complementary, and augmenting, role to formal diplomacy, even when national delegates may be at odds with each other in committee meetings, yet in the informal diplomatic sphere, consorts' primary performative objective would be to emphasise amity, show interest in other cultures, and express concern for the socially disadvantaged. And, the most important aspect of this performance is the photographic evidence portraying female sociability in inclusiveness, one could say almost a type of female solidarity, as they jointly play their 'supportive' role to their male spouses. Hence, we see a clear demarcation between formal and informal diplomacy when we attempt to understand women's role in it.

Within the range of entertainment activities involved, women played principal roles as guests and entertainers[24]. Most notably, the attitude of the Joint Secretariat revealed through its official bulletin is self-revelatory, when it comes to the social events during the conference. The official reception held at the end of the opening day at the Governor of West Java's residence hosted by President Sukarno, Fatmawati, Vice-President Hatta, and Madam Hatta, was written up as 'the formal opening of the Conference "season"'[25]. The suggestion that the week-long conference was the equivalent of a 'season' of entertainments—in some sense, was not too far from the truth as many post-colonial 'debutants' in the form of newly independent states, were introduced by the five sponsoring powers into 'society'—being an international society of states. In this week-long season of entertainments, women performed a prominent role as informal agents of diplomacy. In depicting scenes of sociability, women are on an equal playing field with men, mainly because women now feature centrally as the objective of discursive and visual materials.

Women's Committee of the Asian-African Conference played a central role in organising various activities for women visitors. A 'Club House' had been set up at Pintu Terbuka on 3 Jalan Braga, which doubled as the committee's conference headquarters, where women participants can refresh themselves, take a rest, and meet other women. As one of the events, the Panitia Hari Kartini (Kartini Day Committee) sent an open invitation to conference participants to celebrate the anniversary of the birth of Raden Adjeng Kartini (1879–1904), who was 'one of the pioneers in the women's struggle for emancipation in Indonesia'. Kartini had attained a cult stature of a nationalist heroine after her premature death at the age of twenty-five from childbirth, the year she had established a school for daughters of Javanese officials as an ardent advocate of female education. The Kartini Foundation was set up, alongside other schools in Jakarta, Semarang and other cities in Java[26]. This was to be held in the Erlangga Building on Jalan Riau on 21 April[27]. Quite markedly, this notice of the open invitation for the Kartini Day was placed next to a large photograph of Mrs. Ali Sastroamidjoyo speaking to Nehru by the podium of the main conference hall in the Freedom Building (Gedung Merdeka). After the Kartini Day celebrations, the ladies then moved to the next venue which was the Governor's Residence:

> A fashion show of many Indonesian national costumes aroused much interest. Dresses from East Sumatra, with the rich cloth interwoven with gold and silver thread, the Balinese temple dress with its elaborate headdress of real flowers, the different costumes of Jogjakarta including the dress of a Princess with its richly embroidered jacket and the bare-shouldered style worn in the Sultan's court, and the colourful costumes of Makassar, Minahassa and the Moluccas, were all widely admired.
>
> An unusual feature was the women's gamelan orchestra which accompanied a fine performance of the Tari Topeng or Mask Dance. Later a choir of girls from the training school for kindergarten teachers in Bandung sang the song of Kartini, leader of women's emancipation, and played the angklung. This is an orchestra of bamboo instruments, each of which plays only certain notes. Since 1943 angklungs have also been made with western tone scales[28].

The Women's Committee had managed to co-opt the sultan's families from the royal courts of Yogyakarta and Surakarta, as their princesses had modelled in the above mentioned fashion show, alongside professional models[29]. The fashion show of indigenous dresses from various parts of the Indonesian archipelago, to this extent, contained within it a highly political significance. Arguably, the different dresses exemplified Sukarno's motto of Bhinekka Tunggal Ika (Unity in Diversity), as he spoke in his opening speech of the diversity of the Indonesian archipelago in ethnic and religious terms. These descriptions of entertainment are almost always supplied with photographs of the occasion. The above featured piece in the official bulletin had contained two photographs with only women in them, one with a female dancer, and a half-page photograph of female guests at the tea party hosted by the Governor of West Java on 20 April, with the young Indian girl dancer[30]. Even batik became an object of cultural diplomacy, as two batik shows were organised, one a benefit show for charities on 20 April at the Naga Mas Restaurant, and another for the benefit of the blind children to be held at the Savoy Homann Hotel on 25 April at 8pm[31]. Apparently at the fashion show, 'The most original dress of the show was a pale pink strapless, embroidered with "Afro-Asian" conference April 1955'[32]. Judging from the frequency of photographs featuring social occasions featuring women in the official conference bulletin, the Joint Secretariat of the conference must have considered informal diplomacy which consisted in large part of various activities promoting sociability amongst delegates, as integral to the overall success of the conference.

## Conclusion

What becomes clear in this attempt to understand the role of women in the study of international diplomacy at the Bandung Conference is that traditional diplomatic sources based on textual materials, mostly official archival materials, have a dearth of material on women's participation in diplomacy, mainly because of the perceived lack of women's involvement in policy-related issues. However, if one investigates a larger pool of sources, which privilege visual materials, one begins to gain a different perspective on the role of women in diplomacy. Truth be told, women are prominent in visual representations at Bandung, making up a significant part of the iconography of the Bandung Conference. Hence, the range of sources consulted can have a direct bearing on the understanding of the role of women at Bandung. If one only consults official archival materials, women remain nearly invisible as it was in the case of the Freedom Walk; whereas if one consults visual materials, one is struck by the 'visibility' of women. Therefore, the move to expand the range of sources to include the visual would be the first step in the direction towards a democratisation of diplomacy that includes women and, as I have already argued elsewhere, the people. In this sense, the role of women in diplomacy seems to occupy a more prominent position when recast under the notional framework of 'diplomacy as theatre'—and yet remains largely a silent one.

## Endnotes

1. This is a work-in-progress paper, which will form part of my monograph, D*iplomacy as Theatre: The Bandung Conference and the Making of the Third World*. I am grateful to Darwis Khudori for encouragement in including this paper into the conference volume.
2. Confer Naoko Shimazu, 'Diplomacy as Theatre: Staging the Bandung Conference of 1955', *Modern Asian Studies* 48:1 (January 2014): 225–252.
3. 28 April 1955, No. 17, year 3, *Lukisan Dunia* (Jakarta).
4. *Ceylon Daily News*, 18 April 1955.
5. *Ceylon Daily News*, 19 April 1955.

6. *Pakistan Times* (Lahore), 18 April 1955.
7. *Pakistan Times* (Lahore), 18 April 1955. Intriguingly, this statement was recanted by the paper in a small piece on 20 April 1955.
8. *Ceylon Daily News* (Colombo), 20 April 1955.
9. 'Bandung that lovely city' (title in English), *Wanita*, No. 9, year 7, 5 May 1955.
10. Home News Bulletin, 6 p.m., 16 April 1955, BBC Written Archives, Caversham Park.
11. Jayawardena, Kumari. *Feminism and Nationalism in the Third World* (London: Zed Books, 1986), p. 146.
12. Ibid., p. 149.
13. Cora Vreede-de Stuers, *The Indonesian Woman: Struggles and Achievement* (The Hague: Mouton & Co., Publishers, 1960), pp. 100–106.
14. Elsbeth Locher-Scholten, *Women and the Colonial State: Essays on Gender and Modernity in the Netherlands Indies* 1900–1942 (Amsterdam: Amsterdam University Press, 2000), p. 189.
15. J.D. Legge, *Sukarno: A Political Biography* (Harmondsworth: Penguin, 1972), pp. 219–220.
16. The aforementioned Jayawardena's work demonstrates that there was a common thread running through many of the dilemmas faced by women's movements in newly post-colonial states.
17. Asian African Conference: Meeting of the Committee on Cultural Co-operation, 19, 20 and 22nd April 1955 (Verbatim Reports – uncorrected), issued by the Conference Secretariat, Ajia-Afurika kaigi kankei no ikken, giji yōroku, B'-0050, B6.1.0.24–4, Diplomatic Archives of the Ministry of Foreign Affairs of Japan, Tokyo.
18. Laura Bier, 'Feminism, Solidarity, and Identity in the Age of Bandung: Third World Women in the Egyptian Women's Press', in Lee, Christopher J. ed. *Making a World After Empire: The Bandung Moment and its Political Afterlives* (Athens, Ohio: Ohio University Press, 2010), p. 150.
19. Letter from Nehru to Edwina Mountbatten, 30 April 1955, Gopal S. (general editor), *Selected Works of Jawaharlal Nehru* (New Delhi: Jawaharlal Nehru Memorial Fund, 1981), p. n/a.
20. I agree with Jean Gelman Taylor that it matters whether or not women are in the photograph. See Jean Gelman Taylor, 'Official Photography, Costume and the Indonesian Revolution', in Jean Gelman Taylor, ed. *Women Creating Indonesia: The First Fifty Years* (Clayton: Monash Asia Institute, 1997), p. 91.
21. 'Kanprachum aechia-aefrika na mueang bandong prathet indonisia 18–29 mesayon 1955' (Asian-African Conference at Bandung, Indonesia, 18–29 April 1955), Chulachomklao Royal Military Academy (CRMA), Nakhon Nayok, Thailand.
22. '"Wife diplomacy": Women behind Chinese diplomacy', *Global Times*, 24 May 2014, http://mobile.globaltimes.cn/content/862502.html, accessed 16 June 2015.
23. Generally speaking, there is a dearth of studies on diplomatic consorts in modern and contemporary history. What is available tends to be mostly anecdotal in nature, which focus on personal experiences as wives of diplomats. For example, Sally James, *Diplomatic Moves: A Wife in the Overseas Service* (London: Radcliffe Press, 1995); Brigid Keenan, *Diplomatic Baggage: The Adventures of a Trailing Spouse* (London: John Murray, 2006); Cherry Denman, *Diplomatic Incidents: Memoirs of (Un)diplomatic Wife* (London: Hodder Paperbacks, 2011).
24. 'Kanprachum aechia-aefrika na mueang bandong prathet indonisia 18–29 mesayon 1955' (Asian-African Conference at Bandung, Indonesia, 18–29 April 1955), Chulachomklao Royal Military Academy (CRMA), Nakhon Nayok, Thailand.
25. *Asian-African Conference Bulletin*, No. 9 (24 April 1955), p. 17.
26. Jayawardena, p. 145.

27. *Asian-African Conference Bulletin*, No. 5 (20 April 1955), p. 12. The photograph of Mrs Ali Sastroamidjoyo is on page 13 of the same issue.
28. ‘World Opinion: Statements by Visitors to the Conference’, *Asian-African Conference Bulletin* No. 7 (22 April 1955), p. 15.
29. *Asian-African Conference Bulletin* No. 8 (23 April 1955), p. 6.
30. ‘World Opinion: Statements by Visitors to the Conference’, *Asian-African Conference Bulletin* No. 7 (22 April 1955), pp. 15–16.
31. *Asian-African Conference Bulletin* No. 8 (23 April 1955), p. 6.
32. ‘A-A dress most original at Bandung batik show’, *Indonesian Observer*, 22 April 1955.

# 4

# Bandung, Panchsheel and Global Swaraj

*Manoranjan Mohanty*

## Abstract

The legacies of the anti-colonial struggles and aspirations of newly independent countries were embodied in the Bandung Conference Declarations in 1955 and in the Panchasheel Principles the preceding year. But their realisation was frustrated during the Cold War and subsequently through the process of capitalist globalisation. But the struggles for those values of sovereignty of nations, equality and dignity of peoples and cultures and a development model that aimed at comprehensive fulfilment of material, cultural and political needs of all individuals, groups and regions went on. Thus has emerged the campaign through people's movements and regional multilateral organisations, for 'global swaraj' or 'global movement for self-determination' or 'self-realisation at every level from grassroots, regions and nations to the global level'.

*Key words:* Bandung Spirit, Panchasheel, anti-colonial movements, BRICS, Multilaterism, Swaraj

## Bandung Spirit, Panchasheel Vision and the Age of Self

On 27 September 2015 the UN General Assembly adopted the post-2015 Sustainable Development Goals (SDGs) in a Summit of world leaders. It showed the possibilities and limits that existed in the prevailing world system. The possibilities accrued from the fact that the crucial demands of people everywhere for livelihood with dignity, equality among individuals, groups and regions and harmony with nature cannot be put aside in the contemporary world under any pretext. But were these only concessions to the restive people around the world or did they acknowledge the need to reconsider the dominant economic, political, military and cultural outlook of the global elites? The Millennium Development Goals (MDGs) reflected the same ambivalence. Their much needed objectives were often used for legitimising the neo-liberal growth drives of global capital. The SDGs however face even stronger challenges for dominant forces. The global elite's preoccupation with achieving economic growth, military domination and coping with crisis after crisis emanating from outbreak of violence of one kind or the other has been so intense that the humankind's common aspirations for peace, equity, happiness and harmony with nature have in effect, receded to the background. But history presented many moments when such cherished goals were affirmed and renewed with new vigour. The Bandung conference of Afro-Asian Nations in April 1955 and the preceding year's Declaration of Panchasheel (Five Principles of Peaceful Coexistence) by India and China in April 1954 were among such historical moments. Adoption of the UN Charter in 1945 and Universal Declaration of Human Rights in 1948 were some of the other examples. Unfortunately, the pursuit of power and dominance in local, regional and global levels has been so intoxicating among the elites of the various countries that the agenda of transformation to achieve freedom and equality for individuals, groups and regions has been subsumed under the power objective. Sophisticated theories of balance of power and realism and neo-realism have dominated the discourses on policy and strategy. Panchasheel and Bandung, UN Charter and UDHR are dismissed as "idealistic" at best and "utopian" as the worst championed. The media, think tanks and research bodies are filled with securely fastened tank tops guarding the thick stopper so that the elite's pipeline of refined fuel flowed without interruption.

But the stopper seemed to crack and tanks burst periodically frightfully upsetting the elite order. Uprisings within countries from time to time and military and economic shocks internationally and natural disasters now and then remind the rulers to re-examine their fond beliefs and listen to people's movements whose voice they detested and whom they had treated as disrupting their 'national' or 'good-for-the-globe' agenda.

## Bandung Legacy

Bandung Spirit, Panchasheel Vision and the UN Charter affirmed the principle of equality, freedom and dignity of all individuals, countries and cultures and resolved to enable them to find their ways to achieving their aspirations. Thus the central vision of all liberation struggles was *'swaraj'* or *'self-rule'* or *'self-determination'* or *'self- realisation'*. Today this *'self'* has emerged as the centre of all political activities which seeks fulfilment of its material, cultural and political needs. This is not the concept of self as in liberal political theory that defines it as the atomistic individual. It is the self that treats others as self and engages constantly in transforming their relations into one of mutual self-realisation. Hence, swaraj inherently involves *'ubuntu'* (*I am because you are-* in Zulu language which was revived as the post-Aparteid framework by Mandela and Desmond Tutu in South Africa).

The global political, economic and cultural order that Bandung and Panchasheel had envisaged were founded in the values of swaraj and ubuntu and such other civilisational legacies of entire humankind from all parts of the world as would contribute to achieving their common aspirations.

The year 2015 happens to mark the centenary of the return of Mohandas Gandhi from South Africa to India and along with the Bandung celebrations many in India were celebrating the beginning of the new phase of India's freedom struggle. Therefore, it was a fitting moment to affirm the significance of swaraj as the goal of all individuals, groups and regions across the world. Swaraj according to Gandhi did not mean only achievement of political independence from the British, but all round liberation of humans from all kinds of bondage. People's struggles, especially women's movements, environment movements, indigenous people's movements and human right movements during the second half of the twentieth century and the early decades of the twenty first had evolved many new dimensions of liberation which were already ingrained in swaraj. Defending sovereignty of nations was central to swaraj, but to make it real it meant many other things that guaranteed autonomy and self-governance of groups and regions. Thus 'global swaraj' had emerged as a common goal of humanity founded on the pillars of Panchasheel and Bandung.

The sixtieth anniversary celebration at Bandung in April 2015 rekindled hopes of the possibility of regaining the momentum of democratic transformation of the global order. As Indonesia's President JokoWidodo said in his address: "this revival of Afro-Asian Voice cannot be replaced by anyone". Extending the Bandung framework to South America and thus making it a movement of the South or ASAFLA (Asia, Africa and Latin America) assuming the role of the driving force for global future is a major development in the contemporary time. The Bandung Message 2015 adopted at the Conference gave a comprehensive perspective on global transformation by putting climate change, energy security, human rights, women's empowerment, food security, poverty eradication and disaster management as the core of the development program[1]. Focusing on civilisational dialogue involving all cultures and regions of the world in a framework of peace-building, mutual respect was a timely response to the alienating consequences of the current wave of globalisation and power politics by forces of hegemony.

Setting up a Banding Centre as a permanent secretariat and coordination of these programs, putting in place mechanisms of coordination with various multilateral organisations, building an Afro-Asian University Network and above all declaring April 24 as the Bandung Day to be celebrated every year in all the Afro-Asian countries are bound to have long-term significance. The fact that the Bandung Conference had a special program to protect the interest of the small island countries of Pacific and other regions sent out a distinct message. In 1955 many politicians from the US and other western countries shared this perspective and took part in Bandung even though US Secretary of State John Foster Dulles introduced the antagonistic frame, setting the terms of the Cold War. Today many in the US wish to support the Bandung perspective that can help the US to reorient its hegemonic perspective and be a partner in a global democratisation process while its dominant elites still affirm its dominant leadership role in the world. That produces similar hegemonic policies in all regions to balance each other. Against this international politics based on neo-realist theory, Bandung represents the global politics of creative theory that locates itself in the dynamics of democratic transformation promoting the fulfilment of creative potential of all individuals, groups and regions in a framework of mutuality and interdependence.

## Global Rebalancing and Global Restructuring

In the contemporary discourse on global transformation there are two contending perspectives. One is the path of 'global rebalancing' that maintains the essential features of the post-World War II international political and economic order inviting the newly rising economies such as the BRICS (Brazil, Russia, India, China and South Africa ) to join the high table of the industrialising countries of G-8. The other is the path of what can be called 'global restructuring' which aims at transforming the prevailing, unequal global political and economic order including the Breton Woods system into an equitable, just and fair world order. It is an irony of our times that the ruling elites of the rising economies such as those of India, China and Brazil send out contradictory messages as to whether they are engaged in rebalancing or restructuring of the present world economic order. Their bilateral relations, and their global role in multilateral forums including in UN reflect this situation. On the one hand, they wish to be known as 'responsible powers' respecting international norms as demanded by the West. At the same time, they realise the consequences of working within the prevailing order together with its neo-liberal economic agenda and a security system based on balance of power which produced greater inequality between and within nations and give rise to manifold alienation of disadvantaged groups, cultures and regions. They know full well that the prevailing order is a source of much instability, insecurity and violence in the contemporary world.

## Global Initiatives for Transformation

The evolving process of civilisational movement has been the result of three trends in the world all of which are likely to gather further momentum in the near future. They are: social movements in various countries, the world people's movement and regional organisations of states. Let us briefly deal with the way they are affecting the global process of change.

First is the rise of social movements in the various countries such as the women's movement, indigenous people's movements, anti-caste movements, environment movements besides the peasants and workers movements. The upsurge of these movements has brought about a creative society in many countries of the world in which each oppressed group is more conscious of its creative potentiality than before and is determined to carry on the struggle to reduce the constraints on the realisation of their potentiality. It is the coming of the creative society that has redefined the parameters of development as social development and civilisational movement. In India, for example, the autonomy movements, the tribal and peasants movement and the dalit movement have acquired unprecedented momentum and are likely to be more and more assertive in the coming years. The autonomy movements and the land rights movement and the civil liberties movement are likely to grow stronger in China as well[2]. In Brazil, the indigenous people's movement, the unorganised workers movement and the peasant movement for land rights will continue to influence the course of politics[3]. This is true in many other parts of ASAFLA where self-determination movements of one kind or the other are going on.

In case of the movements who challenge the state in their own countries often there is state repression that sometimes incapacitates the movements. The Indian experience presents a typical case in which even though the functioning liberal democracy allows movements to emerge and flourish pursuing non-violent as well as violent methods, both kinds of movements face severe repression from time to time. The movements also face the challenge of fragmentation into splinter groups and manipulation by ruling parties. However, their cumulative impact on the agenda-forming of the polity is clearly noticeable. Some of the laws such as NREGA (National Rural Employment Guarantee Act, 2005) and Forest Rights Act, 2006 and the right to Education Act, 2009 may actually be the responses to the social movements. India has been a typical example of both responsiveness to and repression on people's movements. The autonomy movements in Kashmir and Northeast have been subjected to severe repression as has been the Maoist movement in central Indian tribal region. But occasional initiatives for dialogue and development measures are also visible. The movements opposing displacement caused by mega mining projects in Odisha, Chhatishgarh and elsewhere have raised serious issues of the nature and pattern of development, especially during the neo-liberal phase. Over all it is clear that the people's movements have a major impact on the shaping of the development discourse in India[4].

The second major current that has influenced the global transformation process is the world people's movement through the solidarity groups across countries. Since 2000 the World Social Forum (WSF) has been the key example of this trend articulating the alternative to the World Economic Forum, the latter representing the forces of globalisation of capitalist market forces. Social movements from various countries come together in this forum that generally holds its annual meetings in Porto Allegre in Brazil and demands restructuring of the current world order[5]. WSF upholds the rights of the oppressed groups of the world and focuses on the interests of the countries and regions of the South. The groups in the WSF also take up issues relating to environment in a major way. With the slogan "Another World is Possible", the WSF has become a crystallised platform of many of the ideas represented in the concept of civilisational movement. All continents of the world are represented in the forum which is basically a powerful voice of the South supported by sympathetic activists and intellectuals of the North[6].

Even before the WSF came into being the UN summits played an important role in bringing the NGOs together in a parallel summit. The Rio de Janeiro Earth Summit in 1992, the Vienna Summit on Human Rights in 1993, the Copenhagen Summit on Social Development in March 1995 and the Beijing World Congress on Women in September 1995 were land mark events which brought the world thinking on fundamental issues of human progress into the common consciousness of humankind. Thereafter, the agenda of each country on such issues was scrutinised to assess the record of achievements and failures. Later the UN Summit on Racial Discrimination in Durban in 2001 and the Environment Summit in Johannesburg in 2002 were also milestones which charted courses of action for the transformation of global agenda. Some of the subsequent summits to review the UN processes and country performances on the same issues created major platforms of global opinion on matters relating to people's rights and environmental concerns. Some of the new structures in the UN system are clearly the outcomes of this process. The formation of the Human Rights Council in 2006 and the UN Women in 2011 are example of this process. Some of UN's existing agencies get more and more energised despite the political constraints of the big power pressures. For example, the ECOSOC whose Committee on NGOs coordinated much of the interaction among the NGOs has become more important in the recent years. In a world dominated by nation-states the global people's movement has many limits in its functioning. Only those NGOs who are permitted by the national governments to go abroad are represented in such forums. As distinct from NGOs there are social movements who may not have funds to travel abroad. Some who manage to do so are supported mostly by foreign agencies who may have their own motivations for supporting such movements. Despite all such limitations, one can see the emergence of a multi-stranded global civil society contributing to the evolving civilisational movement.

The third agency is the rising trend of regional organisations of countries which originally came together for economic cooperation, but in the process influenced the course of history impacting on the structure of the global political economy. They range from regional initiatives of informal kind or organisations still in the making, to steadily consolidating regional institutions. The IBSA forum consisting of India, Brazil and South Africa started in 2003 as an informal grouping of three major developing countries belonging to three continents. As three large multi-ethnic societies with liberal democratic systems the IBSA Dialogue Forum has emerged as an important initiative for alternative thinking from the perspective of the South. With China included in this grouping in course of the environmental negotiations at the Copenhagen Summit in 2009, a new grouping was born called BASIC. This now acquired added clout in global discourse. Brazil, Russia, India and China (BRIC) came together in their first summit in 2009. The prediction made by Goldman Sachs in 2003 that these four countries will be the leading markets in the coming decades and China and India would be the two leading economies by 2050 began to be seen in concrete terms. With the inclusion of South Africa this formation became BRICS. Now they hold annual summits and their ministers and joint task forces plan to meet frequently on the burning issues affecting global economy. In the recent years they have coordinated their views on environmental issues and have taken collective positions on trade and finance issues in world forums. The coming of what is called 'emerging markets' of China, India and Brazil has vastly influenced the prevailing structure of power in the world[7]. Even though US Dollar remains the most powerful world currency, the Chinese economic growth, especially its exports to the world market, especially to US has established China's special status in the world economy. The high rate of growth of India and Brazil in addition to China's also has had a similar effect as their markets are also growing.

This new situation has brought about a new grouping called G-20 – the group of twenty largest economies of the world which has replaced the G-8 of the industrialised countries which until recently were deciding the rules of world trade and finance. The developing countries known as G-77 or the Group of 77 whose number later rose to 112 countries at one point used to make appeals and present proposals to the G-8. The latter started inviting leaders of China, India and a few other countries to attend its extended meetings during the recent years. The emergence of the phenomenon of G-20 may have heralded the coming of a new period of world history with the western industrialised countries losing pre-eminence over world economy. China surpassed Japan's US$ 5 trillion GDP in July 2010 and became the second largest economy of the world after US. This development has been in the making for some years now. Combined with the US military interventions in Iraq and Afghanistan this process has been described as the decline of US empire[8]. That the Orient had a higher GDP than Europe until early eighteenth century and now had regained its economic preeminence has been pointed out by many scholars[9]. *Adam Smith in Beijing* is a title of the Chinese success story of regulated market economy that has brought a new global status to China[10]. 'Peaceful Rise of China'has been a theme of much Chinese discourse in the past two decades[11].

Would G-20 carry forward the banner of G-8 and promote the path of global capitalism or is it likely to put the world on a new course of equitable development? It is clear that the path advocated by G-8 generates uneven development worldwide and inside countries and ecological destruction as well as alienation, social inequality and consumerism. To what extent is it likely that the developing countries among G-20 would represent the liberation urges of the post-colonial societies and pursue a path of equitable and sustainable development and thus become a part of civilisational movement? That is still an open question.

We have two contrasting models of regional organisations, one consolidating the existing world order dominated by capitalist market economy and another seeking to alter it. During the Cold War period, transformation of the world political economy into an equitable and just order was the principal goal of the Panchasheel Agreement (Five principles of peaceful coexistence) signed by India and China in 1954, the Bandung Conference of newly independent Afro-Asian countries in 1955, and the Non-Aligned Movement which started in 1961 and continued to meet even today. The developing countries took the initiative in the UN to launch a drive for NIEO (New International Economic Order) – an initiative which got swept away with the coming of the neo-liberal wave of globalisation promoting free trade through WTO. But regional initiatives of various kinds continued to be pursued.

The relatively well institutionalised EU (European Union) is very clearly wedded to promoting market economy and liberal democracy at the global level. Having shared the military line of NATO under US leadership it is the epitome of the industrial revolution models of development. The other institutionalised grouping, ASEAN (Association of South East Asian Nations) started as a Cold War security grouping against communist party-ruled states like China. But it has evolved into a free market economic block which has also initiated many regional trade and security measures. The ASEAN plus three (China, Japan and South Korea) has emerged as a formidable economic zone. The East Asia Summit which includes India, Australia and New Zealand in addition to ASEAN plus three has emerged as an important annual forum to take stock of the world economy. Another important grouping is SCO (Shanghai Cooperation Organization) which started as a neighborly cooperation forum of China, Russia, Kazakhstan, Kyrgyzstan, Tajikistan and Uzbekistan in 2001. But over the years it has grown into a comprehensive economic and security organisation in East and Central Asia with India, Pakistan, Afghanistan and Mongolia as observers in it. It is also a grouping of market economies seeking a regional role in tackling regional problems. Unlike ASEAN, the SCO with China and Russia as the major players in it clearly has the objective of making their presence felt in the region in competing with the US and EU. However, EU, ASEAN and SCO are all pursuing the paths of industrial revolution and market economy while also pursuing a security policy of balance of power.

As distinct from the EU, ASEAN and SCO, an alternative trend in global political economy is symbolized by the ALBA (Bolivarian Alliance of Latin America) which has a transformative vision not only for Latin America, but for the whole world. It aims at restructuring the world political economy so that it is more equitable and just. Starting as a joint initiative of Venezuela and Cuba in 2004 it was joined by Bolivia, Nicaragua, Ecuador and several other smaller states by 2010. Opposing the free trade system which is promoted by the US-led effort to form the FTAA (Free Trade Area of the Americas) or the already functioning NAFTA (North American Trade

Agreement) ALBA promotes equitable exchange and solidarity among states and peoples to struggle for freedom, equality and justice both globally and in their own countries. It is interesting to note that the BASIC countries share the same general perspective but are not as explicit as ALBA in their action program[12].

In Africa, the decade-old African Union has also been actively pursuing a transformative perspective through regional cooperation. Established in 2002 as a successor to OAU (Organization for African Unity) AU has 53 member states with the objective of achieving greater unity and solidarity among the African countries, defend sovereignty, promote political and socio-economic integration of the continent and African common positions on issues of interest to the continent. During the decade of its existence it has undertaken a number of economic and social measures in support of human rights and democracy. Despite being a large continental organisation with diverse tendencies, its historical legacies make it a transformative body rather than a regional front of Western capitalist countries[13].

There are many other organisations in different parts of the world aiming at achieving regional cooperation, but not all of them are geared towards altering the dominant patterns of global development. But as the world politics gets more pluralised such organisations acquire greater autonomy. For example, the objective of SAARC (South Asian Association for Regional Cooperation) was mainly to facilitate regional trade and cooperation in social development matters. But gradually it took collective positions in climate change negotiations vis-à-vis the Western powers. But SAARC has been unable to make substantial progress in regional cooperation due to bilateral problems of member countries, mainly India and Pakistan. There are initiatives such as the RIC (Russia-India-China), the BCIM (Bangladesh-China-India-Myanmar), BIMSTEC (Bay of Bengal Scientific, Technological and Economic cooperation), the ECO (Economic Cooperation Organisation ), MERCOSUR (launched by Argentina, Brazil, Paraguay and Uruguay in 1991 joined by Venezuela in 2006) and many others in different continents which seek to promote regional cooperation. All of them strive to secure regional autonomy in their respective spheres and hence have the potential of reducing the influence of big powers. The cumulative effect of all these inter-state initiatives on the restructuration of global political, economic and cultural relations may not appear dramatic at a point of time, but over a long period they definitely alter the pre-existing global structure. Such effects are clearly visible in the functioning of the UN agencies, World Trade Organisation, climate change negotiations and other spheres.

The three catalytic trends of the contemporary world, namely, social movements in various countries, the world people's movements and the regional organisations, together constitute a massive historical force propelling civilisational movement of the human race. Besides these, the new global initiative represented by the BRICS shows the nature of the trends which are complex but has the potentiality of contributing to the process of global restructuring along the lines of the Bandung and Panchasheel principles.

## Emergence of BRICS

BRICS is a unique formation of five big countries spanning four continents i.e. all the major ones except North America, covering 43 per cent of the world's population. In 2012 in PPP terms BRICS accounted for about 30 per cent of the global GDP poised to be 45 per cent by 2030. The international financial agency Goldman Sachs takes the credit for conceptualising this acronym for putting together the five 'emerging markets' in 2003 to prepare the western economies to cope with this phenomenon in not too distant a future. This was a classic statement of 'global rebalancing'. But the reality is that the coordination among these big developing countries had started much earlier in the forum of Group of 77 in course of WTO negotiations. Already much common ground was visible in the policies of India and China in the Doha round negotiations and climate change talks. Russia joined the process as a part of its economic reconstruction and linked up its fast developing relations with China and India with that process. The Shanghai Cooperation Organisation (SCO) facilitated the new thrust in the trilateral relations of Russia, India and China which was already in the making since 2001. Thus the first summit of four BRIC countries in Yekaterinburg in Russia in 2009 was an initiative clearly aimed at restructuring the global financial system. The second summit in Brazil in 2010 decided to invite South Africa to the grouping. At the third summit in Sanya in April 2011 South Africa joined the group and the five member BRICS was in place. In this process it had become clear that the new initiative was treading cautiously.

For example, it is noteworthy that the Fourth BRICS Summit held in New Delhi in March 2012 as well as the Fifth Summit held in March 2013 in Durban did not explicitly challenge the structure of the prevailing economic order, thus playing safe with the Western powers which were yet to take serious note of the formation of BRICS. The Indian Prime Minister made a cautious statement pledging to "work closely for the reform of global institutions of political and economic governance like the UN Security Council and the International Monetary Fund that reflects the contemporary realities[14]. At the same time the leaders of the five countries called for reforms of the quota and governance system in the World Bank and IMF, initiated measures such as to form a new Development Bank for the BRICS and other emerging and developing countries. The Durban Declaration put it thus: "As the global economy is being reshaped, we are committed to exploring new models and approaches toward more equitable development and inclusive global growth by emphasising complementarities and building on our respective economic strength"[15]. In fact they took steps on many fronts which have the potential for restructuring the power relations in world scale.

When the Fourth Summit was held in New Delhi, BRICS had moved into a new stage of development. It enacted two important agreements indicating the transition from the present world economic arrangements into a more dispersed one. First, the Agreement on Extending Credit Facility in Local Currencies reduces dependence on the dollar as the main medium of international trade. This phenomenon is already growing in other cases of bilateral trade involving BRICS countries. Second, the BRICS Multilateral Letter of Credit Confirmation Facility Agreement signed by Development Banks is another significant step facilitating intra-BRICS trade. In the Fifth Summit in Durban the decision to form the BRICS Development Bank was taken and a US $ 100 billion BRICS Contingency Fund was launched. The process of trading among BRICS countries using local currencies was further streamlined. A BRICS Business Council met to plan out steps to promote intra-BRICS trade.

The Fifth Summit of BRICS not only took a number of economic and financial initiatives, it addressed a number of major global issues. On Syria it supported dialogue among the parties as advocated by the UN-Arab League representative. On Palestine it reaffirmed the two state solution with 1967 border. The BRICS stressed the need to handle the Iranian nuclear issue through dialogue respecting Iran's right to use nuclear energy for peaceful purposes. Afghanistan according to them needed support to build itself as a peaceful, stable country, free of terrorism. On issues of climate change, Millennium Development Goals and human rights too they spelt out common positions in the Durban Declaration. The Sixth Summit in Brazil's Fortelaza in 2014 was a landmark event that brought the New Development Bank into existence with its location in Shanghai having an Indian CEO and Russian Chairperson of the Board of Management and with a branch in South Africa. The Seventh Summit in Ufa, Russia in July 2015 consolidated this process with many new structures laid down in economic, communication and educational spheres. India's commitment to the new multilateral organisation despite a change of regime from the Congress-led UPA to the BJP-led NDA continued as an active participant in the evolving networks[16]. Thus at the end of the first seven years cycle of the summits BRICS had emerged as a new global force not only representing the interests of these five countries but developing countries as a whole. That itself was a democratising trend in the world order. Was it a trend of rebalancing or restructuring?

Ever since the world took note of the economic successes of China and India the new concept of global rebalancing had been in frequent use. But it gathered even greater salience after the global economic crisis of 2007–2009. Pushed by the IMF, the G-20 forum was formed in 2008 to propagate this line of thinking mainly to persuade China to accept the balancing role in the world economy by promoting domestic demands and revaluing its currency and so on. China, India and other rising economies are also called upon to play the role of the major stake-holders in environment, information, peace-keeping and other spheres, besides getting integrated with the prevailing financial and trade system of world economy. Thus global rebalancing process seeks to incorporate the emerging powers in the big power club to run the existing global political and economic order.

Global restructuring, on the other hand, refers to fundamental restructuring of the world political economy to fulfil the demands for equity, justice and autonomy at every level in all regions of the world from local to global realms in all spheres, economic, political, cultural, science and technology, information and knowledge spheres. The need for fundamental restructuring of the power relations and reordering of values was felt because of the intensified crisis that we encounter in the contemporary world. The crises manifest in many spheres including economy, environment, cultural alienation, terrorist violence and wars. But under the pressure of the existing rules of the game the inter-state organisations cannot frankly talk about them. Still we can discern the historical trend that places BRICS in the process of global restructuring.

The BRICS vision of global future has to be placed in the emerging process of global democratic transformation. This vision brings together two sets of trilateral efforts which had started independently a few years before BRICS was formed. They were the RIC (Russia-India-China) and the IBSA (India-Brazil-South Africa). It is important to observe that even after the formation of BRICS the two trilaterals continue to exist because they had a distinct value of long-term significance in the process of global transformation. IBSA Forum represented not only legacies of liberation movements in three continents, but also experiences of democracy in three developing countries. The RIC embodied traditions of three large, populous countries which were contiguous and had legacies of revolution and freedom struggle have a specific significance of its own. The RIC vision to build an equitable and democratic world order which was proclaimed in RIC Foreign Ministers Communiqué in Wuhan in November 2010 is clearly linked to the process of global restructuring rather than merely global rebalancing. Even if a transition from a "unipolar" world to a "multipolar" world is often mentioned as a goal of many countries and multilateral organisations and it was also in the Wuhan Communiqué, that may be conceived only as a part of the further democratisation of the world order where the affairs of the world are not left to be managed by an oligopoly of a few countries. One of the main trends in the contemporary world is persistent challenge to any exercise of hegemony by any power in any part of the world. Hence the world order should be based upon "principles of international law, mutual respect, cooperation, coordinated action and collective decision-making by all states" – a vision that was stated in the Wuhan Communiqué and which embodied the Panchasheel (Five Principles) legacy of 1954 and consistent with the Bandung Spirit.

The role played by India and China in the evolving global order is the product of their modern history of struggling against colonialism and domination. If we miss the linkage with that history we cannot understand the debates taking place in their countries over their development strategy and their foreign policy. The legacies of civilisational interaction between India and China, the values which guided their freedom struggles and the post-colonial transformation remain central to the contemporary assessment of their growth performance and global role.

## Global Swaraj

The contemporary moment in world history is witnessing interesting debates on human future as people in every part of the world review the achievements, failures, mixed outcomes and indeterminate experiences of the past one or two centuries. In every part of the world there is a realisation of the interconnection of the experiences of people across the globe while at the same time they are more conscious of the nature of their relationships with one another. People assess the extent of freedom they enjoy and the magnitude of domination they feel in different realms. Technology of information, communication and transport on the one hand and the new consciousness of self-determination of individuals, groups and regions on the other, have created a new democratic environment in the history of human civilisation. Hence reflecting upon and articulating global futures from one's spatial, temporal, social, cultural and political vantage points is becoming more and more possible in course of debates and discussions today. During the colonial era and the Cold War years visions of human progress were articulated by the dominant forces in certain ways which are challenged today in course of the contemporary struggles against hegemonic globalisation. The new visions of human future which emerge from the discourses in the developing world now encompass not only political freedom and economic growth, but comprehensive social development and environmental preservation. They have acquired deeper civilisational dimensions entailing newer relationships between humans and between humans and nature.

Many of the new issues echoed stirrings of the liberation struggle in Asia, Africa and Latin America. Gandhi had said in *Hind Swaraj* that long after political swaraj or independence was achieved there would still be a continuing struggle for achieving swaraj. Literally swaraj meant self-rule but in effect this means self determination or self-realisation. Gandhi's concept of swaraj referred to swaraj for the village, for women and by implication swaraj for each oppressed person and region. Struggle for the realisation of the creative potentiality of each individual, group and region by removing structural and practical constraints to that process is a continuing process. Besides, Swaraj for Gandhi was grounded in the concept of harmony between humans and nature. Thus human progress has to be visualised in terms of freedom of one and all accomplished in harmony with nature. This vision is recalled to challenge the drive of capitalist globalisation which increases disparities, destroys natural resources and generates cultural alienation[17].

This is where the debate in the development discourse is re-enacted today and the struggle over contending lines of thought is likely to continue in the near future. Proponents of economic growth argue that growth will percolate down to alleviate poverty while social movements assert that issues of justice, equity and environmental sustainability as well as autonony, cultural and religious dignity and sovereignty are more important than growth.

The greatest legacy of the twentieth century is the rise of self-realisation urges of human beings. This was embodied in the anti-colonial struggles, the socialist and democratic revolutions and the multiple social movements of peasants and workers, women, indigenous people, the anti-race, anti-caste and human rights movements especially of the last few decades of the century. This trend is fast acquiring civilisational dimensions and in the near future the assertion of self-realisation as being the central goal of global history of civilisations is likely to gather greater and greater salience.

One of the recent moments of articulation of this phenomenon was the centenary of M K Gandhi's work *Hind Swaraj* (Indian Home rule) in 2009 when the concept of swaraj took centre place in deliberations in India and abroad. Swa-raj (literally self-rule) did not mean, according to Gandhi only political freedom from colonial rule, but fuller realisation of the self. The self was conceived as individual, group or region. Writing in 1909 he had presented a critique of the Western civilisation for its preoccupation with materialism. Though many commentators might disagree with such a monolithic characterisation of a civilisation, Gandhi was focusing on the dominant theme of the industrial revolution that colonialism had spread. Self-realisation had to be accomplished in moral, material and political terms as had become clear in course of Gandhi's practice of Satyagraha[18]. His critique of industrialism was based on similar premises. Gandhi had pointed out that the Western path of industrialisation had destroyed traditional skills of people and had ultimately produced an acquisitive society of mass production and mass consumption that also increasingly depleted natural resources. This critique of industrialism was recalled by many social movements in course of their campaigns against globalisation when its high tide was unleashed during the 1990s and later. Gandhi had also denounced parliamentary democracy as it had centralised political power and promoted corruption. These assertions will continue to be debated from various vantage points. But the centrality of swaraj as a civilisational goal is the essential message of Gandhi's life and works. What is important to note is that he stood by the text of this short book written in form of a dialogue till his death because swaraj was considered as an endless pursuit of freedom for individuals, groups and regions. Swaraj for the oppressed peasant and worker, swaraj for the oppressed races and castes and for adivasis or indigenous people, and for women and religious minorities meant continuous struggle for achieving their aspirations. Village self-government or Gram Swaraj in a system of decentralised, participative institutions of politics and government was Gandhi's political order of swaraj. For realising the self-determination urges of a village or a region a host of policies had to be pursued. Thus I would argue that swaraj has emerged as a civilisation goal in the twenty first century as this is the common feature of all the democratic upsurges of the contemporary times and this is likely to be an even more powerful trend in the coming years.

This civilisation discourse on development and social transformation is based on the premise that all people everywhere in the world have their own civilisations embodying creative potentiality of their beings[19]. The colonial construction of world history that graded societies with degrees of civilisation stands fundamentally challenged today. The claim that Europe represented the most advanced stage of human civilisation in the eighteenth and the nineteenth centuries and currently the US represents the same kind of superior civilisation does not carry much weight at present. Now it is clear that the so-called civilising mission of colonialism was more of a military aggression for world market and political domination than its professed goals. Theory of civilising mission stands firmly discredited today. The so-called dark continent that Africa was described as, now we know, did have a high civilisation of its own having strong influence on both Europe and Asia[20]. The indigenous people in every part of the world represented important aspects of human civilisation as well. Therefore, we are already witnessing a recasting of cultural discourse in the twenty first century.

In the new civilisational discourse, all civilisations are regarded as deserving of respect and equal status. No civilisation in any part of the world has only positive glorious traditions. Each has both positive and negative traditions and legacies with many diverse trends in their histories. This includes the European, American, Indian, Chinese and Arabic-Persian civilisations. In other words, no civilization is monolithic as assumed by the clash of civilisation theorists[21]. Paradoxically, even the proponents of 'dialogue among civilisations'[22] have monolithic notions of civilisations focusing on harmonious aspects. Besides, all civilisations experience civilisational movements or a dynamic process of change in which basic orientations of life, culture and art and attitudes towards nature as well as cosmic outlook in addition to patterns of politics and economy undergo changes. Such changes may not be immediately discernible, but become prominent features of human existence over time.

The presently ongoing civilisational movement has addressed the human aspiration for swaraj or self-realisation in several concrete ways. Whenever the preoccupation with material needs has been prominent either under capitalism or under socialism the demand for political freedom and social justice has become prominent.When both these aspirations have occupied full attention in a society the cultural aspirations have appeared as more significant and identity demands have surfaced. The perspective on equity and justice has steadily acquired ecological dimensions. Thus freedom, in fact, swaraj has acquired a comprehensive meaning with material, political, cultural and ecological dimensions. The contemporary debates are likely to take these issues into new heights in the near future. The debate on consumerism is bound to grow and make humankind more and more aware of the limits of the availability of natural resources. The crisis of environment is likely to generate more responsibility for appropriate plans for production and consumption. Whether the distribution process is expanding the realm of social justice for workers, peasants, women, dalits, adivasis and minorities will be a major task of politics.

The concept of swa or self in swaraj or self-realisation has three elements built into it which present an alternative cosmology to the one that is embedded in the capitalist epoch of industrialisation. Firstly, it is a concept of self that treats everyone else also as self. The dichotomous notion of "self and the other" that has been a central idea of the era of colonialism, capitalism and caste ideology is conceptualized differently in the swaraj notion. The contradictions among individuals, groups and regions represent relationsips which may be relationship of domination and exploitation at a point of history, but they had to be handled through struggle and transformed into relationships of mutual reinforcement. This concept of the self is also represented in the South African concept of Ubuntu which in Zulu language means "I am because you are". It implies that "I can develop only when you develop". The existence of all beings is seen as coexistence with mutual respect for one another and all development can only mean mutual development according to the Ubuntu framework[23].

Secondly, the concept of self is a concept of the human as a creative being. Civilisation is also conceived as a long and unending process of the unfolding of human creativity.The individual or a group has enormous creative potentiality which is yet to be fully realised because of many structural constraints such as class, ethnic, race, caste, gender domination. Social struggles and public policy aim at resolving these contradictions so that an individual or a group is free from the bondage or the obstacles to achieving their creative potential[24].

Thirdly, the notion of self conceived in terms of human beings is integrally connected with nature and other species who are also treated as 'self'. Thus the relationship between humans and nature is to be understood as one of coexistence, mutual support and exploration. This understanding challenges the proposition on 'man's expanding conquest over nature which has been strongly pushed by the votaries of technological development and industrial revolution during the past two hundred years. The swaraj concept of nature explores nature to know its laws with humility admitting that humans know about only a small part of nature and they ought to utilise that knowledge for the creative good of humans as well as of other species and of nature as a whole. This view has a significant message to preserve natural resources and follow a development path that has minimum depletion of natural resources and energy. Above all it promotes a lifestyle that is committed to the swaraj concept of nature.

## Endnotes

1. file:///C:/Users/Dr.%20Mohanty/Downloads/Bandung%20Message%202015%20(1).pdf
2. Manoranjan Mohanty et al (eds), *Grassroots Democracy in India and China* (New Delhi, Sage, 2008). See also Monoranjan Mohanty et al (eds), *Building a Just World: Essays in Honour of Muchkund Dubey* (New Delhi, Orient BlackSwan, 2015).
3. Monica Bruckmann, "Alternative Visions of the Indigenous People's Movement in Latin America: Reflections on Civilisation and Modernity", *Social Change* Vol. 40, No. 4 (December 2010) pp. 601–608.
4. Medha Patkar and Amit Bhaduri, "Industrialization for the people, of the people and by the people", *Economic and Political Weekly*, Vol. 44, No. 1 (January 3, 2009) pp. 10–14.
5. Walden Bellow, *Deglobalization: Ideas for a New world Economy* (London, Verso, 2009).
6. Jai Sen and Peter Waterman (eds), *World Social Forum: Challenging Empires* (New York, Black Rose Books, 2007), see also Samir Amin and James Membrez, *The World We wish to See: Revolutionary Objectives in the Twenty-first Century* (New York, Monthly Review Press, 2008).
7. Abdul Nafe, *IBSA, Trinity of the South: Potential of India-Brazil-South Africa Partnership* (New Delhi, Research and Information System, 2008), see also Alan S. Alexandrof and Andrew Fenton (eds), *Rising States and Rising Institutions: Challenges for Global Governance* (Washington DC, The Brookings Institution, 2010).
8. Chalmers Johnson, *Dismantling the Empire: America's last best hope* (New York, Metropolitan Books, 2011), Immanuel M Wallerstein, *Decline of American Power: The US in a Chaotic World* (New York, The New Press, 2003).
9. Andre Gunder Frank, *ReOrient: Global Economy in the Asian Age* (New York, Sage, 1998).
10. Giovanni Arrighi, *Adam Smith in Beijing: Lineages of the 21st Century* (New York, Verso, 2009).
11. Zheng Bijian, *China's Peaceful Rise: Speeches of Zheng Bijian 1997–2005* (Washington DC, The Brookings Institution Press, 2005).
12. ALBA and LA, see Olivier Dabene, *The Politics of Regional Integration in Latin America* (New York, Pallgrave Macmillan, 2009).
13. John Akokpari et al (eds), *African Union and its Institutions* (Johannesburg, Jacana Media, 2009).
14. Manmohan Singh, Closing Speech at the fifth BRICS Summit at Durban on 28 March 2013.
15. *Durban Declaration and Action Plan,* 27 March 2013 (www.brics5.co.za), *The Ufa Declaration of Seventh BRICS Summit,* 9 July 2015 (http://www.brics.utoronto.ca/docs/150709–ufa-declaration_en.html).
16. Prime Minister Modi reaffirmed the commitment in his speech at Ufa, http://www.privatejobshub.in/2015/07/narendra-modi-7th-brics-summit.html. However, the Modi government's attitude towards Bandung conference and Panchasheel showed marked change. See Manoranjan *Mohanty, Bandung Legacy and the New India Regime*, Mainstream, Vol. LIII No. 26 (20 June 2015).
17. See the text with commentary in Anthony J Parel (ed), *Gandhi, Hind Swaraj* (Cambridge, Cambridge University Press, 1997), see also Bhikhu C Parekh, *Colonialism, Tradition and Reform: An Analysis of Gandhi's Political Discourse* (New Delhi, Sage, 2003).
18. Parel, op. cit.
19. Manoranjan Mohanty, "Recasting Cultural Questions for a Harmonious World", *Social Science Probings*, Vol. 20, No. 2 (June 2008).

20. John J Jackson, *Introduction to African Civilizations* (New York, Citadel Press, 1970, 2001).
21. Samuel Huntington, *The Clash of Civilizations and Remaking of the World Order* (New York, Simon and Schuster, 1998).
22. UN initiative declaring the year 2001 as the year of Dialogue among Civilizations and the subsequent activities under the auspices of UNESCO had a similar notion. See for example the International Congress of Cultures and Civilizations in Yemen in June 2004.
23. *South Africa: Vision 2020 Towards Ubuntu* (Johannesburg, 2005).
24. Manoranjan Mohanty, "Social Movements in Creative Society" in Manoranjan Mohanty et al (eds) *People's Rights* (New Delhi, Sage, 1998).

# 5

# Thinking Global
## Challenge for Palestine

*Noha Khalaf*

## Abstract

On the occasion of the commemoration of the sixtieth anniversary of the Bandung Conference, it seems necessary and vital to undertake the elaboration of a new theoretical framework which would allow us to state the right questions about the failure of the Twentieth Century to provide a brighter future for the Arab world and to solve its central complex problem of Palestine. Ironically, while Western capitalist thinkers are constantly elaborating new concepts to explain and transform the world to their advantage, the Arab Nation which had sought unity in 1955, has become divided, and fragmented while falling into the lethal trap of the 'clash of civilizations'. From 1955 onwards, various concepts have been omitted and others have been introduced into Arab nationalist thought and instead of uniting in the face of the Zionist occupation of Palestine and solving the Palestinian refugees problem through the effective exercise of their right of return, new conflicts have emerged leading to a new outpour of refugees from other surrounding Arab countries, thus relegating the Question of Palestine to the backstage. This article attempts to analyse some of ideological changes that have occurred at all levels on the world stage in the era of globalisation, making it necessary to elaborate new concepts and engage in 'global thinking' and 'action' to solve the Palestinian problem.

*Keywords:* Arab World, Bandung Spirit, Middle East, Palestine

## Introduction: 'Thinking Global'[1]

In view of the escalation of violence and the evolution of the actual dangerous situation in Palestine with the most recent attacks against Al Aqsa Mosque in Jerusalem by the forces of Zionist occupation in September 2015 (67 years after the occupation of Palestine in 1948, and almost fifty years after the fading away of the aura of Arab Nationalism, following the 1967 June war), it seems more than ever vital to look into the internal and external reasons that have aborted one of the most engaged attempts at the regional and global levels to unite the new emerging nations of the South in the face of the great powers and neocolonial policies, through the holding of the important Bandung Conference in 1955[2]. One of the most important examples of this failure, being the continued occupation of Palestine.

Therefore, in commemoration of the sixtieth anniversary of the Bandung Conference, it seems necessary to attempt to elaborate a new theoretical framework which would allow us to state the right questions about the failure of the Twentieth Century. This is meant to provide a brighter future for the Arab World and to solve its central complex problem of Palestine, which is one of the main causes of the present catastrophic situation in the Middle East.

In order to proceed in elaborating that framework, we shall start by comparing briefly between two historical moments. The first one is the seemingly optimistic general trend of the times in the mid Twentieth Century, when the Arab nations were emerging from their colonial past and witnessing the rise of 'Nasserism' and 'Ba'thism', as unifying Arab ideologies and part of the anti-colonialist movement, in conjunction with the struggle of Algeria which was still fighting for its independence. The second one is the present pessimistic mood in the Arab World, due to its exposure to a long and deep crisis of fragmentation, disunity, chaos and strife with a resurgence of 'neocolonialist' forces and the persistence of Zionist colonial policies, which are fomenting and benefiting from the general disarray.

It is also worth noting that the sixtieth anniversary of the Bandung Conference coincides with the centennial of the Sykes-Picot agreements of 1916 which were followed by the Balfour declaration of 1917, both of which represent the main historical documents that spelt the death toll for Palestine.

It is also necessary to recall that the Bandung Conference took place only three years after the Young Officers took over power in Egypt in 1952, and only seven years after the 1948 catastrophe that befell Palestine due to the establishment of the Zionist colonial entity in the heart of the Arab world, in application of both the Sykes-Picot agreements and the Balfour Declaration[3].

So paradoxically, while the mood of some Arab nations seemed optimistic in 1955, the question of Palestine which had just gone through the 1948

'Nakba' with its refugees scattered around the Arab World lingering in refugee camps, was not seriously addressed.

It is also ironical that Nasser, the hero of the Arab World and of Arab Nationalism had stressed on two occasions in his 1955 pamphlet entitled "The philosophy of revolution" that Palestine was not one of the priorities of the Egyptian revolution[4].

Today, the vital questions that have to be addressed are more complex, since they have to analyse the past while attempting to elaborate frameworks of thinking for the future. New concepts have to be envisaged, other than those used in the mid of the Twentieth Century.

Old concepts and new concepts often combine together to form what some theoreticians have referred to as 'webs of concepts'[5].

As we proceed we shall attempt to pinpoint the dilemmas which led to transformations of 'webs of concepts' due to changing political contexts. Such dilemmas emerged in the life span of 'Arab Nationalism' as well as in the life span of 'the spirit of Bandung'. Although dilemmas have also risen within capitalist, liberal and even imperialist movements, they have always invented new concepts to face such dilemmas and to integrate them in their world views.

It is, therefore, vital for African and Asian Nations to be equally aware of the need for new concepts to explain changing contexts.

## 1. The Coincidence between 'The Climax of Arab Nationalism' and 'The Bandung Spirit'

Albert Hourani, one of the most reputed historians of the Arab World, refers to the years 1950–1960 as those of 'the Climax of Arabism'[6]. According to Hourani:

> This was the period when the idea of the 'Third World' became important: the idea that is, of a common front of countries in process of development, mainly belonging to the former colonial empires, keeping themselves uncommitted to either of the two blocs, that of the 'West' and that of the communist 'East', and exercising a certain collective power through acting together, and in particular through their command of a majority in the General Assembly of the United Nations. A second element was the idea of Arab unity: that the newly independent Arab states had enough in common, in shared culture and historical experience as well as shared interests to make it possible for them to come in close union with each other, and such a union would not only give them greater collective power but would bring about that moral unity between people and government which would make government legitimate and stable. To these elements another one was now added—that of socialism—that is to say the idea of control of resources by government in

> the interests of society, of state-ownership and direction of production, and equitable distribution of income through taxation and the provision of social services[7].

This last idea was a reflection of the strength of socialist and communist movements all over the world. Consecutively communist and socialist groups and parties were emerging in the Arab World in opposition to both imperial rule, but later against their new governments, especially that independence had been reached in several countries by manipulations, both internal and external[8].

Communist parties were fragmented but attempts were undertaken to create movements which could combine all the three concepts. The centre of this activity was in Egypt where historians began to interpret Egyptian history in Marxist terms: Mahmud Amin al-'Alim and Abd al 'Azim Anis offered a socialist critique of Egyptian culture[9]. However, due to the fragmentation of the left, other important attempts to amalgamate the main concepts of Arab nationalism were elaborated. The most important one was the ideology elaborated by the ideologue of the Ba'th party in Syria, Michel 'Aflaq. For him there was a single Arab Nation with the right to live in a single united state.

In the mid fifties the Ba'th party became more overtly 'socialist'[10]. The appeal of its ideas spread in Lebanon, Jordan and Iraq and in some countries of the Arabian peninsula. The Ba'th played an important role both in the attempt to create the United Arab Republic in 1958 and in its dissolution three years later[11].

The other important trend of Arab Nationalism was developed by the army officers which took power in Egypt in 1952, with Abdel Nasser as the uncontested leader calling for social reform, justified by an idea of 'Arab socialism', different from Marxism, where the whole society was supposed to unite around a government representing the interests of all[12].

According to Hourani, while these were the two main trends which solidified the idea of Arab nationalism in the fifties, these started to disintegrate after 1967, leading to what he called 'a disturbance of spirits'[13] where ethnic and religious divisions emerged to the forefront in countries such as Lebanon, Iraq, Kuwait, Bahrain, Saudi Arabia, Syria due to the presence of large Shi'i populations. However, according to Hourani "A certain Islamic element would always remain important in that combination of ideas which made up the popular nationalism of the age.... Whether it was the Islam of the modernists or that of the 'Brothers', but it remained on the whole a subordinate element in the system"[14].

If one adapts the methodology based on 'Webs of concepts' to Hourani's analysis of Arab Nationalism, we would find that the central concepts are the 'Third World', 'Arab Unity' and 'Socialism' with the question of religion being marginal in the central web.

## 2. Nasserism And The Third World: From "Anti Colonialism" to "Anti Communism"—the Gradual Eviction of the 'Socialism' Concept

Since the most important figure representing the Arab World at the 1955 Bandung Conference was Gamal Abdel Nasser, the main hypothesis in this following section is that while Egypt played a major role in this movement at the start, its internal political and social contradictions constituted later as the main reason for the fading away of the 'Bandung' momentum a few years later.

According to Anwar Abdel-Malek, the late famous Egyptian thinker and sociologist, there was no mention in 1954 of 'positive neutralism' or even of 'neutrality' in Nasser's "Philosophy of the Revolution". Further, "no definition of principle regarding the relationship with the forces who are competing for the world", yet according to the author, from 1955–1956, 'positive neutralism' took root in the land of Egypt for the first time as one of the three main elements that made up the ideology of the military regime, which Anwar Abdel-Malek refered to as 'nationalitarism', as distinct from 'nationalism[15].

"The orientation towards neutralism was influenced therefore both by negative and positive elements". 'Negative' as a result of Western policy towards the military regime; and 'positive', as a result of the ideological and political influence of foreign countries, mainly Asian. The negative elements compelled Nasser to abandon the traditional orientation of Egypt towards Europe. In the middle of Anglo-Egyptian negotiations, he said that "it is not useful to talk about neutrality since the term has no meaning, especially in times of war, unless the countries adhering to it are strong enough to maintain their neutrality"[16].

Salah Salem, Minister of 'national orientation' in Nasser's regime, explained what was meant by neutrality, "you can call our new political orientation 'neutrality' or any other name as you please. Some might have a different notion of neutrality. What we mean is that we take a hostile posture towards anyone who stands against our dignity and freedom, while we support and collaborate with anyone who helps and supports us"[17].

At the same time that socialist ideas were being debated in Egypt, paradoxically, Anwar Sadat, one of Nasser's closest allies was presiding in the foundation of the Islamic Congress, which was at first led by him, and then by Hussein Kamel al-Din after January 1961[18].

The Islamic Congress aimed at creating a permanent link between Egypt and the entire Muslim World in Asia, Africa and other continents. Its intention was to work for the spread of Islam, through economic rapprochement and the organisation of programmes of cooperation between the different Muslim countries.

It is, however, thanks to the initiative of Nehru that 'positive neutralism' became a mainstay of Nasserist policy starting in 1955. Nehru visited Egypt twice—in 1952 and 1953—seeking to elaborate a common front against the great powers. After the second visit, an Egyptian spokesman said that "it is possible that Egypt aligns with the neutralist bloc of Asian countries to try to put an end to the imperialist occupation of the Suez Canal by the Great Britain". The five principles adopted by Nehru and Chu En Lai became known in Egypt in 1954. On April 6, 1955, a treaty of friendship was signed between Egypt and India in Cairo. From the 18th to the 24th of April, the conference of twenty nine countries of Asia and Africa, met in Bandung, on the initiative of the 'Group of Five'of Colombo. Later 'the other Europe' joined the movement through the implication of the president of Yugoslavia Tito. On February 5th, 1955, the first meeting between Tito and Nasser took place. The Yugoslav head of state then made his first official visit to Cairo between the 28th December 1955 and January 6, 1956, but the Egyptian-Yugoslav agreement was consolidated during the Brioni meeting in July 1956, when joined by Nehru, the Heads of State formulated the main thesis of positive neutralism: "the current division of the world into powerful blocs tends to kindle our fears. (...) We must try to achieve peace, not by division but by global collective security, hence, by extending the area of freedom and ending domination of one country over another. It is essential to move towards disarmament to reduce the fear of conflict. (...) Continued efforts to accelerate the development of newly independent countries is one of the main tasks leading to the establishment of a permanent and stable peace between nations... "[19].

It was, therefore, obvious that the first major negotiations with the socialist countries were intended to send a message to the 'West' which was at the time consolidating its military presence in the region through the signing of the Baghdad Pact on February 24, 1955 between Turkey, Iraq, Pakistan and Britain. Nasser responded to it by establishing a tripartite Arab command between Egypt, Syria and Yemen. Following the unfruitful negotiations in view of purchasing weapons from the West, Nasser announced on September 2, 1955 the conclusion of an arms deal with Czechoslovakia. Nasser made it clear that if the Americans refused to finance the construction of the High Dam, (except under their conditions), Nasser was out to seek substitutes.

In Africa, Nasser's policy provided political, military and financial support to nationalist movements. In 1955, Egypt set up the 'African Liaison Office', and since 1959 offices for representatives of African liberation movements were opened: the freedom fighters from Rwanda and Burundi from 1959 to 1961, the National Democratic Party in Southern Rhodesia from 1960, the Congress of the African League (ALC) and the ANC of South Africa, MPLA and UNITA of Angola from 1961 to 1972, of the PAIGC Guinea-Bissau from 1961 to 1974, FRELIMO of Mozambique in 1963–1975, ZANU and ZAPU in 1964, Zimbabwe in 1965. During the summer of 1957 the 'Voice of the Free Africa', which broadcasted programmes in seven African languages, had been launched from Cairo. In fact, 'Egyptian neutralism' from1955 to 1958 was supported by three fractions of Egyptian society according to Abdel-Malek. First, the large industrial and banking bourgeoisie, traditionally anti-communist, was forced to defend itself against the West, by participating in 'bargaining tactics'; second, the left wing movement represented by the group of 'al Misa' who believed in the anti-imperialist struggle based on the perspective of ex-colonised or colonised nations in view of establishing peace and coexistence. And third, in the centre, stood the military who tried to balance these centrifugal tendencies.

While in Bandung Nasser became the arbiter of a coalition composed of the centre and the left, back in Egypt an intensification of Islamic propaganda was disseminated by the Islamic Congress of Anwar Sadat.

In the solidarity conference of Afro-Asian peoples, held between December 26, 1957 and the first of January 1958, the focus was on the fight against underdevelopment and all forms of neo-imperialism. This conference was initiated by Asian left parties, including the Indian PC and participated by delegations from 46 Asian and African countries. At this conference, the Egyptian left was playing a prominent role, powerfully aided by revolutionary groups in different countries. Despite the censorship in the previous composition of the Egyptian delegation, the Egyptian government was alarmed. Sadat, then, reacted by electing a rightist, Youssef al Seba'i, to the key post of permanent secretary general, in order to neutralise the growing Communist influence, including that of Popular China, and prevent the success and overflow of the Egyptian Marxist left.

Other factors had interplayed to produce the offensive against the left in Egypt between January and March 1959. The unification of the communist movement, the arising differences with the Syrian Communist party and the left turn of the Iraqi revolution were established. From April 29 to May 16, 1958, Nasser went to the Soviet Union, where he declared diplomatically his friendship and gratitude, but later, expressed in closer circles his intimate apprehensions and the need to distance himself from an "immeasurably powerful" ally. Upon his return to Cairo, he declared to the crowd coming to greet him that he had been informed that the United States had adopted a new policy with regard to the United Arab Republic (UAR) and that they would respect its neutrality and independence. In early summer, the censorship of the press was instructed to forbid any attack against Foster Dulles and against US policy in general. This readjustment in policy continued and Nasser's anti-communist speech on December 23 at Port Said was a prelude to the offensive against the left. This led to a change in perspective from 'neutrality' to 'non-alignment'. This is why 1958 could be considered as the 'the transition year' of change from 'positive neutralism' to 'non-alignment'[20].

In 1959 the UAR declared itself non-aligned and Khrushchev publicly criticised the new anti-communist orientation of the UAR. Between September and December 1959, relations had also deteriorated with Beijing, which declared that Egyptian anti-communism was incompatible with the Afro-Asian movement. In the eyes of the Egyptian leaders, Bandung no longer existed.

Mohamed Hassanein Haykal, one of Nasser's closest advisers and spokesman declared: "Bandung was a step (...), loved moments we have experienced (...). But the page is turned". He explained the evolution of the neutralist ideology in three stages: 'non-engagement', prior to 1955, when the Third World countries felt too weak and helpless to act; 'positive neutralism' after Bandung and Suez, when the imperialist offensive forced the young independent states to ally with the 'devil'; and finally 'non-alignment' at the time of the 'nuclear balance' between the two main blocks[21].

These same themes were expressed by Nasser in his speech at the Belgrade Conference on September 1, 1961, and were included in the 25 resolutions of the Conference. According to Abdel-Malek, in Belgrade, a clear differentiation occurs in the Afro-Asian World. "Neutralism, an Asian initiative after the Second World War, had found its way to Africa and moved towards Latin America". For Abdel-Malek "nothing illustrates better the new face of non-aligned Egyptian neutralism than its African policy between 1960 and 1962". Finally, according to Georges Corm, "the Third World countries subsumed under the name 'non-aligned' reorganised themselves in the 'Group of 77', as a middle road between East and West"[22]. According to this author, this group still exists today, but has become insignificant in the course of international events, while concurrently, the Organisation of the Islamic Conference (OIC) led by Pakistan and Saudi Arabia, the 'two tenors of anti-Sovietism, customers of American power', have been competing with the non-aligned trend[23].

## 3. The Middle Eastern Rift: the Gradual Eviction of the Concepts of 'Arab Unity' and 'Third World' and the Introduction of the Concept of 'Clash of Civilizations'

It is my contention in this essay that revisiting Samuel Huntington's theory "The Clash of Civilizations", published in 1993 in Foreign Affairs, which has greatly influenced US policy makers, might be of great significance in shedding light on the overwhelming Middle Eastern rift, which has pervaded all aspects of the Middle East today. This theory had influenced the Middle Eastern political elite, especially its traditional variant, who adopted blindly some of its precepts, in a lopsided manner. This is what can be deduced today, given the great dilemma and tight straits through which the Middle East is passing and which has submerged Arab societies in a murderous impasse.

When coining his theory, the US Hawk, Huntington, was in fact searching for a formula which would preserve Western hegemony over the globe at the end of the Cold War. He reached the conclusion that the best way would be through transferring armed and violent conflicts away from the Western ivory tower towards the non-Western World and the Eastern hemisphere. He explained his basic precepts in the following terms: "It is my hypothesis that the fundamental source of conflict in this new world will not be primarily ideological or primarily economic. The great divisions among humankind and the dominating source of conflict will be cultural. Nation states will remain the most powerful actors in world affairs, but the principal conflicts of global politics will occur between nations and groups of different civilizations. The clash of civilizations will dominate global politics. The fault lines between civilizations will be the battle lines of the future. Conflict between civilizations will be the latest phase in the evolution of conflict in the modern world" and he added further "In the politics of civilizations, the peoples and governments of non-Western civilizations no longer remain the objects of history as targets of Western colonialism but join the West as movers and shapers of history".

One of the obvious flaws in his theory at first hand is his classification of civilisations. According to him "Civilization identity will be increasingly important in the future, and the world will be shaped in large measure by the interactions among seven or eight major civilizations. These include

Western, Confucian, Japanese, Islamic, Hindu, Slavic-Orthodox, Latin American and possibly African civilization. The most important conflicts of the future will occur along the cultural fault lines separating these civilizations from one another".

Huntington also distinguished between what he referred to as variants and subdivisions within civilisations. "Civilizations obviously blend and overlap, and may include sub-civilizations. Western civilization has two major variants, European and North American, and Islam has its Arab, Turkic and Malay subdivisions. Civilizations are nonetheless meaningful entities, and although the lines between them are seldom sharp, they are real. Civilizations are dynamic. They rise and fall. They divide and merge. And, as any student of history knows, civilizations disappear and are buried in the sands of time".

My main hypothesis, which I shall try to develop briefly in this article, is that the Huntington's theory was simplistically understood by Arab intellectuals as one calling only for a 'civilisational' and cultural war between Western and Islamic civilisations. Despite various criticisms addressed at this theory, many intellectuals fell in its ideological trap and believed in the relevance of a 'civilisational' clash in contradistinction to an ideological or economic one. This led them to magnify the importance of the concept and consecutively their own importance by concentrating their efforts in attempting to prove and demonstrate the superiority of their own civilisation while engaging in a show of force in competition with Western culture and values. By so doing they inflated their narcissistic tendencies as thinkers and intellectuals, over blowing their own egos, with the encouragement of some Western institutions which promoted an intellectual trend which could be referred to as 'Islamo-philia' in contradistinction to an increase in Western 'Islamo-phobia', to the extent that several of these intellectuals ignored the real dangers that were threatening to erupt within their own societies and which had been implicit within the theory of the 'Clash of Civilizations', namely: 1) The question of transferring future armed conflicts from the West to the East, since the West had already experienced armed conflict within its boundaries through the first and second World Wars and was not ready to experience once again such conflicts, and that therefore the 'democratic West' which is composed mainly of the US and Western Europe and their allies, will resort to a peaceful resolution of its own conflicts which are mainly based on economic rivalry and competition, while the 'despotic East' including Eastern Europe and southern countries shall resolve their inner conflicts by armed and violent means. 2) The propagation of the theory concerning the end of ideologies, was sustained by other

American post cold-war theoreticians like Fukuyama with his theory 'The end of History'. The aim of such theories was the relegation of socialist ideas into the dustbins of history, leaving scope for the mushrooming of neo-liberalism as the ideological counterpart of Western hegemony and neo-colonialism as the dominant form of relationships on the international level, while camouflaging the inner economic and class distinctions within the boundaries of Western societies themselves. 3) The propagation of an anti 'Third World' ideology, aiming at abstracting Third World conflicts from their economic dimension and reducing them to 'cultural' and 'civilisational' ones, in view of eliminating the possibility of the reemergence and empowerment of international trends like those of non-alignment and preventing the resurgence of political moods similar to those emanating from the Bandung Conference and the emergence of Third World leaders such as Tito, Nehru and Abdel Nasser.

The superficial and subjective response of Arab intellectuals to Huntington's theory led to the appearance of an ideological fashionable 'vogue' based on misconceptions in the thought of political elites. It included both the liberal minded and the conservative classical religious factions who were unable to think outside the religious paradigm. They called for a linkage between Islam and socialism, Islam and nationalism, and finally between Islam and neo-liberalism. On the other hand, secular and left-oriented thinkers were marginalised since they did not conform with the trend, and their intellectual production remained stalled while living in the nostalgia of the golden and glorious age of Socialism, Marxism and Communism.

The political elite, with its Arab pseudo intelligentsia, also started to neglect the growing economic tentacles of the Zionist state in the Third World and its increasing impunity in dealing with the Palestinian people and Arab lands. A neglect which was encouraged by the dwindling peace process and the Oslo accords. At the same time Western capitalist concepts were fabricated by institutions such as the World Bank and the International Monetary Fund in the name of 'restructuring' and 'sustainable development', with a new political jargon of 'responsibility', 'liability', 'transparency', 'good governance', 'accountability' and 'liberal democracy' versus 'tyranny and despotism' replacing the old socialist and Marxist jargon. The neoliberal Arab elites blindly gulped and propagated these concepts, without adding any local input and thus failing to give them any positive practical resonance. At the same time such elites had fallen prey to the strict conditions of foreign aid and funding.

Thus three years ago, with the Arab popular revolt gaining momentum, one faction of the Arab elite was busily engaged in its mythical civilisational and religious war with the West. It unleashed the emergence of a panoply of religiously dominated factions, some of which were more fundamentalist and extremist than others. While the more liberal factions were busy reaping the fruits of foreign funding through various non-governmental as well as governmental institutions, the global economic condition was looking dim. The rich were getting richer through speculation while the poor were getting poorer due to their total abandonment by the state apparatuses which had fallen in the hands of corrupt speculators referred to as 'the new businessmen'. US strategists had, by then, added other 'bright' concepts to the theory of the Clash of Civilizations, such as the theory of 'creative chaos' conceived by Condolezza Rice and her neoconservative bedfellows with all its catastrophic consequences in Iraq, Lebanon and presently in Syria.

In the face of such 'chaos', the centrality of the Palestine problem was being drowned and the question of Palestinian refugees was relegated to the background due to the growing numbers of refugees from the surrounding Arab countries.

Due to the magnifying effect of the religious factor within the mindset of the Islamic movements which had gained confidence in their self-acclaimed capacity as the new heroes and dynamic agents of social change in the Arab World, while encouraged by various Western institutions, their leaders were lured into believing that the time had come to revive the grandeur of their Civilisation. They jumped on the long sought bandwagon of political supremacy in order to establish Islamic rule and went as far as the claim of *the restoration of the Caliphate.* In reality a neoliberal pro-Western faction of businessmen had mushroomed within their ranks, consuming all kinds of modern goods, utilising modern technologies but paradoxically calling for a return to a pure past free of all such technologies.

Due to the absence and marginalisation of any coherent political elite, Western and Arab media exploited the political and cultural void by 'instrumentalising' religious extremism. They did so by stirring up traditional and latent inherited differences between the two main trends within 'Islamic Civilisation' until they evolved into violent and destructive armed conflict. They left the Israeli state, a so called offshoot of Western civilisation, immune and protected by its military arsenal. They expanded and engulfed Arab territory while appearing in the eyes of Arab populations as an equal to Arab regimes, in their capacity for destruction and killing, and as a democratic and peaceful island in a sea of Arab barbarians, in the eyes of the whole world. Therefore, the main question which remains unanswered is whether the Arab political elites will be capable of putting an end to this rift and of extracting the Arab region from the vicious cycle of violence and destruction, while starting at last to face the real dangers that threaten their societies, such as poverty, hunger and foreign control of their economies, by forming alliances with other third world and southern countries to challenge an unjust world order, instead of indulging in the game of "civilisations" which has overturned the tables against the Arab populations and transformed Arab states into 'failed states'.

## 4. From the 'Clash of Civilizations' to the 'Clash of Ideas': Reinventing New Concepts?

A special issue of Foreign Affairs, published in January and February 2012, on the occasion of the 90th anniversary of this influential political periodical had as its major theme "The Clash of Ideas: The Ideological Battles That Made the Modern World and Will Shape the Future"[24].

In the era of globalisation, it seems necessary to review the ongoing ideological debates in the West and worldwide in order to see whether these debates and clashes affect the ongoing ideological clashes in the Arab region and whether one can detect their repercussions on the Arab revolutions.

The first impression from the adoption of the term 'clash of ideas' is that it was meant to be a reminder or an answer to the famous theory of the 'Clash of Civilizations', elaborated by Samuel Huntington in 1992[25].

Several other writers had adopted the same framework through various other less hawkish forms such as the book entitled "Jihad versus Macworld" published by Barber in 1995.

By the end of 2001 and especially after 9/11, Huntington's theory seemed like a bad dream come true, with all its nightmarish consequences, ending with Islamo-phobia becoming the name of the game and replacing totally the old Communist phobia.

Interestingly, however, a careful revision of the ideological debates of the time (end of eighties and beginning of nineties after the dismantlement of the Soviet Union) reveal that Huntington's 1993 article on 'The Clash of Civilizations' had emerged as part of a raging ideological debate of the time in counter trend to Francis Fukuyama's famous theory entitled 'The End of History'.

The philosophical debate that had been raging at the time was in fact between these two schools of Western Thought: that is between Fukuyama's liberal ideology and Huntington's conservative and hawkish rightwing philosophy.

Fukuyama, as a liberal philosopher, was also staunchly anti Marxist but a faithful adept of Hegelian idealism. He therefore saw history as evolving through a 'clash of ideas' instead of through a 'struggle between classes', and thus concluded that its 'end' would come when one ideology would become dominant on a global scale, instead of the hegemony of one class, the proletariat, according to Marxist materialism.

Put in a nutshell, Fukuyama's philosophy could be summarised in the following terms according to his own words: "What we may be witnessing is not just the end of the Cold War, or the passing of a particular period of post-war history, but the end of history as such: that is, the end point of mankind's ideological evolution and the universalisation of Western Liberal Democracy as the final form of human government"[26].

The famous French Philosopher Derrida in his book Specters of Marx[27] published in 1993, declared that the quick celebrity achieved by Fukuyama's ideas was nothing but 'a symptom of the anxiety' on the part of the intellectual branch of current 'Western Hegemony' to ensure the 'death of Marx' while spreading its 'New Gospel'. Derrida added "instead of celebrating the end of ideologies and the end of the great emancipating discourses, let us never neglect this obvious macroscopic fact, made up of innumerable singular sites of suffering: no degree of progress allows one to ignore that never before, in absolute figures, have so many men, women and children been subjugated, starved or exterminated on the earth"[28].

Two decades later, it seems that the old debate is still ongoing with a tilt by Foreign Affairs, in favour of the framework based on the 'clash of ideas' rather than 'the clash of civilisations'. What seems to add to the significance of this 2012 special issue of Foreign Affairs is its publication of a more recent article by Fukuyama, the philosopher of the late eighties, which surprises us by celebrating the return of 'history' on the intellectual scene, since it is entitled 'The Future of History: Can Liberal Democracy Survive the decline of the Middle Class?"[29] contrary to his previous views about the 'end' of history.

In this new article Fukuyama seems to revise his past optimism about the success of liberal democracy as the dominant global ideology. His points are worthy of consideration, not so as to celebrate the good of liberal democracy, but in order to reach a better understanding of the main ideological trends in the era of globalisation, especially that such trends have permeated the international arena reaching the Arab World, despite the denial of intellectuals who still believe in national and cultural specificities.

Fukuyama, starts his article by saying "something strange is going in the world today", and this thing appears to be "the lack of left wing mobilisation" adds: "that the chief reason for this lack is 'a failure in the realm of ideas' leading 'the ideological high ground on economic issues to be held by a libertarian right. The left has not been able to make a plausible case for an agenda other than a return to an unaffordable form of old-fashioned social democracy. This absence of a plausible progressive counter-narrative is unhealthy, because competition is good for intellectual debate just as it is for economic activity. And serious intellectual debate is seriously needed, since the current form of globalised capitalism is eroding the middle class social base on which liberal democracy rests".

Finally one can say that Fukuyama's main hypothesis is that the erosion of the middle class, which is becoming apparent in Western societies, will threaten the supremacy of the liberal democratic model of governance, and that one of the main reasons for this development is 'globalisation' where "the benefits of the new order accrued disproportionately to a very small number of people in finance and technology". Fukuyama considers that one of the "most puzzling features of the world in the aftermath of the financial crisis is that so far, populism has taken primarily a right wing tone, not a left wing one" and he explains the failure of the left as being an 'intellectual one' given that 'it has been several decades since anyone on the left has been able to articulate, first a coherent analysis of what happens to the structure of advanced societies as they undergo economic change and second a realistic agenda that has any hope of protecting a middle class society'. Further dissecting the left with sarcasm, he adds: "the main trends in left wing thought in the last two generations have been frankly disastrous, as either conceptual frameworks or tools for mobilisation. Marxism died many years ago and the few old believers still around are ready for nursing homes. The academic left replaced it with post modernism, multiculturalism, feminism, critical theory and a host of other fragmented intellectual trends that are more cultural than economic in focus'.

In his attempt to visualise a future ideology for the West, Fukuyama states that most of the ideas have been around in bits and pieces. For some time the scribbler would have to put them in a coherent package and "the critique of globalisation, that is, would have to be tied to nationalism as a strategy for mobilisation in a way that defined national interest in a more sophisticated way..." and "the product would be a synthesis from both the left and the right, detached from the agenda of the marginalised groups that constitute the existing progressive movement", concluding that "the ideology would be populist; the message would begin with a critique of the elites that allowed the benefit of the many to be sacrificed to that of the few and a critique of money politics, especially in Washington, that overwhelmingly benefits the wealthy".

Another article published in that same issue, entitled "the Democratic Malaise: Globalisation and the threat to the West", by Charles A Kupchan[30], professor of international affairs at Georgetown University and Senior Fellow at the Council of Foreign Affairs, speaks of 'the crisis of governability' that has engulfed the world's most advanced democracies" adding: "It is no accident that the United States, Europe and Japan are simultaneously experiencing political breakdown; globalisation is producing a widening gap between what electorates are asking of their governments and what those governments are able to deliver, the mismatch between the growing demand for good governance and its shrinking supply is one of the gravest challenges facing the world today".

While Fukuyama's analysis concerns mainly the West and particularly the United States, it seems so flagrantly appropriate for an understanding of the dynamics of the social movements that have engulfed the Arab World and that constitute what is referred to as the 'Arab spring'.

The similarities are striking on a number of levels. First: financial interests in the Arab World have been so unjustly distributed, with only a few incurring all profits at the expense of the many who are increasingly impoverished. Second: the middle class is ailing and starting to disappear as a result of this unjust distribution of wealth. Third: Left wing movements are almost invisible from the political scene and have failed to engage with the Arab revolts constituting the 'Arab Spring', making leeway for the more religious Islamic parties, which have a more populist ideology. Fourth: The main 'clash of ideas' in the 'Arab Spring' was often referred to as the 'clash' between 'Liberal' parties and 'Religious Islamic' parties as was the case in Egypt, without any clear explanation of what 'Liberalism' means in the Arab World.

Following these observations, several issues need to be debated seriously in the Arab World, especially those concerning the relationship between global ideological trends and regional ones on the one hand, and that between regional trends and national ones on the other hand.

Several questions have to be clearly stated concerning the 'clash of ideas' in the Arab World and attempts to find convincing answers will definitely enrich the highly required and necessary ideological debate.

## 5. Thinking Global: Towards the 'Global Intellectual'

In an article entitled "Mainstreaming Utopia: a global challenge"[31], Marc Fleurbaey, professor at Princeton, presents a 'few thoughts' about 'how ideological evolutions as well as the globalisation trend in society and science require reviving the interest in social transformation but also shaping the new efforts in a quite different way from the previous intellectual endeavors and social movements that made the twentieth century eventful, and sadly, terribly lethal'. In summary the points he makes are the following:

- Utopian thinking, understood not a delusionary dreaming but as the rational study of social transformation, is needed especially nowadays.
- Research in social transformation can no longer be left to the 'solitary intellectual' who was the typical utopian thinker of the previous centuries.
- A simple, concrete way of making progress might be to congregate the available knowledge about principles and possibilities for social change into a report produced by a panel of experts, in interaction with the relevant social actors[32].

The author adds that "the need for reviving the studies of social transformation and more specifically the interest in social 'progress' (a word that has fallen into disrepute) is as strong as ever nowadays, in a time of deep economic, social and moral crisis".

The globalisation trend itself which promised to erase boundaries and shorten distances has been exploited by the wealthy and the powerful to increase their supremacy. The new utopian research that is needed has to do with a rational study of the perspectives for social change, with a special focus for the most disadvantaged populations. Such a study has to combine a normative component since "social change without social ethics is like a ship without a compass". In as far as social transformation can be led by conscious and organised efforts of social actors, these actors need to know, discuss and coordinate on the direction they wish to pursue[33].

Fleurbaey adds: "Today social scientists look back with some melancholy to the glorious time of intellectuals and the aura that surrounded their domain in the second half of the 20$^{th}$ century. Perhaps we should instead welcome the fact that the charisma of the intellectual has vanished, if this protects us and our descendants from new waves of simplistic and totalitarian doctrines"[34].

The author concludes that what is required today is a new kind of scholar who works in a more cooperative way and adopts a more modest attitude: The 'global intellectual' that is now needed is a group, a network, a cooperative endeavour. Social sciences, paradoxically, have remained the most individualistic of the academic disciplines, but we do observe an increase in collective projects involving teams, as well as the growing importance of articles as opposed to books, reflecting the larger proportion of contributions which are highly specialised. This fragmentation can be viewed in a positive light because it provides the building blocks for new better forms of syntheses.

Edgar Morin the French philosopher in an article *"Au delà du réductionnisme et du holisme : la complexité du global"*[35] states that one has to avoid what he calls 'réductionism' since we cannot understand the 'whole' by starting with the 'parts' given that the 'whole' is more than the sum of the parts according to Aristotelian logic.

According to Morin 'global thinking' contains within it, and shall always contain an element of uncertainty, the 'unexpected'. It is therefore a thinking that is in permanent movement has to be 'correlated' with different places on earth, since from every area around the globe emerges different points of view which are in fact complementary. Global thinking is an adventure, a 'dangerous' adventure but also a 'marvellous one' and it is the only adventure that we can undertake. Morin adds "it is the only adventure that concerns our lives, individually and collectively. It is the only adventure that links us to others, to our co-citizens, and to humanity"[36].

## 6. Thinking Global for Palestine

Finally, since the original aim of this paper was to put back the Question of Palestine within a global context, several questions have to be addressed concerning the past while trying to elaborate a blueprint for the future.

Ironically, the Palestinian problem still persists despite the rise and fall of several ideologies, whether Arab Nationalist, Marxist or 'Third World' ideologies such as those embodied in the Bandung spirit.

In my opinion, the question involving the persistence of an illegitimate military occupation for over sixty years, and the subjugation of an innocent population which identifies itself as part of the world liberation movement, is proof of the failure of the intellectual elites of the Twentieth Century on the Arab, Palestinian, the Third World and international levels to state the right questions and look for the right answers.

The Palestine problem lies at the crossroads of a central web of issue that need to be addressed to reach a more just world order. In Palestine a local population is being subdued and subjugated by a fierce military occupation. In Palestine the original population is assassinated, and massacred: starting with the Deir Yassin Massacre of 1948, passing through the Sabra and Shatila Massacres of 1982 to the more recent ones in the besieged city of Gaza in 2014, and in Al Aqsa Mosque in September 2015. While arrested, besieged, and became more and more impoverished everyday, with its environment polluted, its waters diverted, its cities, homes, Mosques and Churches destroyed and violated, the Palestinian people still resist in all possible ways: the prisoners with hunger strikes, the children with stones and the women and mothers of martyrs with incredible patience, will, and courage. Palestinian refugees are denied the inalienable right of return to their cities of origin, while that right is being usurped to allow other foreigners to the area to immigrate on a religious basis, making of the Palestinian refugee problem an exceptional one in history.

It is impossible at this point to go over all the details of Zionist ideology and its use of religion to oppress other people. So much has been written and said to that effect, but any person with honest and clear insight can see that the disintegration of the Arab World today benefits the Zionist expansionist dream.

Unfortunately, all the ills produced by capitalist globalisation have also found roots in that small area. A small but influential part of its elites have been co-opted just like others in the Arab World by the global order, while 'Israel' which is recognised by the Western world as a 'democratic state' and which has the fourth most powerful army in the world and is engaged in arms sales and training of mercenaries throughout Africa and Asia, bastions of the 'Third World'.

The Palestine problem is proof of a 'failed' Twentieth Century, in terms of its capacity to restore justice and establish peace in a more human world. I think Palestine needs new 'global intellectuals' who think of the future, not simply through the existing international agencies which often function as shields to the real problems of humanity. Only a new 'global intellectual' collective enterprise can restate the right questions in order to elaborate a functional strategy to restore peace and justice in Palestine. Such an endeavour must at first question all the false attempts that have claimed to be adequate solutions to the Palestine problem, such as the Oslo accords of 1993. Such a critique can only be launched within forums such as those that had emerged in Bandung 60 years ago. However, they should be undertaken by wiser independent intellectuals and not necessarily by governments who might still be under indirect colonial hegemony and of the 'liberal capitalist world order' which encourages all kinds of inhuman practices and ideologies such as Zionism and racism, while making tremendous profits from a flourishing arms industry.

This is why we shall attempt through this distinguished forum to debate how all emerging and peace loving forces in the world can support Palestine in view of liberating it from one of the most lethal and brutal occupations in history.

## Endnotes

1. Penser global: Internationalisation et globalisation des sciences sociales et humaines, sous la direction de Laurent Levi-Strauss et Gwenaelle Lieppe, Maison des sciences de l'homme,

Paris 2015. This book is a collective work with about thirty contributions from various social scientists and philosophers in the search of new approaches in social sciences.

2. "Bandung Sixty years later: The Arab World from Sunrise to Sunset", published in Arabic, Rai al Youm, April, 2015, by Noha Khalaf, reconstitutes the spirit and context of the time and the political personalities who were the spiritual mentors of such a project as well as the followers who attended the Bandung Conference.
3. For a detailed analysis of the Balfour Declaration, see, Noha khalaf, Balfour's Legacy: Between Past and Present, a paper presented to the Conference held in Haddington, Scotland, November 13–14, 2005.
4. Gamal Abdel Nasser, *The Philosophy of Revolution*, (Falsafat al Thawra), 1955.
5. The term 'web of concepts ' has been elaborated by various authors to study changes in ideology, such as Reinhart Kosellek, author of *Futures Past: On the Semantics of Historical Time*, 2004. His studies direct themselves to the semantics of central concepts in which historical experience of time is implicated. Webs of concepts is a constellation of concepts evoked by members of a movement. Within a web of concepts, concepts are evoked, omitted, contested and modified by various members of a movement. They are not fixed. Bevin in the "Logic of the history of ideas", 1999, suggests that dilemmas are points at which webs of beliefs change in order to adapt to new contexts, whereas deliberately or unintentionally new concepts are added and previous concepts expelled to make room for new beliefs.
6. Albert Hourani, *A History of the Arab People*, Warner Books, 1991, p. 401.
7. Ibid.
8. Ibid.
9. Ibid., p. 402
10. Ibid., p. 404
11. Ibid.
12. Ibid., p. 405.
13. Ibid., p. 435.
14. Ibid., p. 436.
15. 'Nationalitarisme' was a term used by Abdel-Malek in distinction to 'nationalisme', he explains this difference: "we could say that 'nationalisme' is the period of national edification—whereas 'nationalitarisme' refers to a period engaged in 'positiveness' and the creation of progressive values and institutions", Anouar Abdel-Malek, La Pensée Politique Arabe Contemporaine, Seuil, 1979, p. 19.
16. Anouar Abdel-Malek, *Egypte Société Militaire*, Editions du Seuil, 1962.
17. Ibid., pp. 220–225.
18. Ibid.
19. Ibid.
20. Ibid., p. 130.
21. Ibid., pp. 231–232.
22. Georges Corm, *Orient-Occident, la fracture imaginaire*, Editions La Decouverte, 2002, p. 26.
23. Ibid.
24. *Foreign Affairs*, January-February 2012.
25. Samuel Huntington, *The Clash of Civilizations*, Foreign Affairs, 1993.
26. Ibid.
27. Derrida, *les Spectres de Marx*, 1993.
28. Ibid.

29. Francis Fukuyama, "The Future of History: Can Liberal Democracy Survive the decline of the Middle Class?", *Foreign Affairs*, January-February, 2012.
30. Charles A Kupchan, "The Democratic Malaise: Globalization and the Threat to the West", *Foreign Affairs*, op. cit.
31. Marc Fleurbaey, "Mainstreaming Utopia: A global Challenge" in *Penser Global*, op. cit. pp. 93–102.
32. Ibid.
33. Ibid.
34. Ibid.
35. Edgar Morin, "Au-delà du réductionnisme et du holisme : la complexité du global. Le débat", in *Penser Global*, op. cit. pp. 449–457.
36. Ibid.

# 6

# Africa-Asia Relations

## Bandung's Role in Redefining Area and International Studies

*Adams Bodomo*


## Abstract

The first major Afro-Asian Conference in April 1955 in the Indonesian town of Bandung constitutes a watershed for Africa-Asia relations. I argue in this paper that it not only constitutes a watershed, a point of departure for international relations, especially involving African and Asian governments, but it also redefined the way scholars practice international studies, especially involving the areas of Africa and Asia. As empirical basis for this argumentation, I present, based on quantitative and qualitative studies, a complex sociocultural profile of an Afro-Chinese diaspora community in China, showing that this community is neither exclusively an inquiry for African Studies nor for Chinese/Asian studies but an inquiry that has to come from comparative areal, international, diaspora, and global studies perspectives. To the extent that the Bandung Conference was a watershed for Africa-Asia relations, it helped define the way we do areal, international, diaspora, and global studies involving Africa and Asia.


*Keywords:* Bandung, Africa-Asia, Area Studies, International Studies, Diaspora Studies

## 1. Introduction

In April 1955 government delegations of 29 mostly independent African and Asian countries met in the Indonesian town of Bandung to, among others, promote Afro-Asian economic and cultural cooperation and to oppose colonialism or neocolonialism by the United States, the Soviet Union, or any other imperialistic nation.

The Bandung Conference has become a major point of reference in discussing official relations between Africa and Asia and these relations have developed into more specialised country to country relations. However, scholars also need to look at how we studied Africa and Asia before Bandung and how Africa and Asia have been studied or should be studied after Bandung. Talking about studying Africa and Asia is essentially talking about studying them as geopolitical areas of inquiry. I argue in this paper that before Bandung it would have been possible to study Africa and Asia as separate and separated entities but that after Bandung Africa and Asia were intrinsically linked at the government-to-government level, and Africa-Asia studies have to move from just mere area studies to international studies since we can now study government-to-government relations between the two entities. I discuss some basic definitions in this introduction and then give a background of Bandung before using the formation of African diasporas in Asia, particularly China, to illustrate the changing nature of area and international studies in a world of globalisation, claiming that Bandung was a watershed to all these changes. This leads to a development of a theory illustrating how we might approach international studies from an areal, global and diaspora perspective within academia.

I conceive of *area studies* broadly as an interdisciplinary field of research that focuses on studying the peoples, cultures, and institutions of a particular geopolitical region and migrants from that region in other parts of the world. I also conceptualise *global studies* as a field of research that focuses on analysing globalisation, a process which involves an increasing interaction of people of different cultures, languages, and identities as more and more efficient transportation and communication technologies facilitate the movement of peoples, goods, and services across vast expanses of the world. Global studies must be distinguished from *international studies* which observe and analyse international relations, i.e. dealing mostly with government-to-government relations.

I advance the argument, based on the experience of doing research on Africans in China, that doing area studies in an era of globalisation actually involves doing international, global, and interdisciplinary studies, and in the case of relations between Africa and Asia Bandung made this possible. Theoretically, I expand my bridge theory of migrant indigene-relations (Bodomo 2010, 2012) for the study of Africans in China into a bridge theory for global, areal, and diaspora studies (the GADS theory).

## 2. Background of Africa-Asia relations: Bandung and Beyond

Even though not all African and Asian nations participated in the Bandung Conference, most aspects of contemporary Africa-Asia relations, that is, government-to-government relations are predicated on the experiences and influences gathered at the Bandung Conference of April 1955.

This conference was organised at the initiative of five Asian nations including Burma, Ceylon (Sri Lanka), India, Indonesia, and Pakistan, with the leadership spear-headed by Indonesia's first President, Sukarno, who saw himself leading a new, emerging power in the world which he called NEFOS (Newly Emerging Forces), somewhat a very prophetic name for what is happening now in the name of BRICS that five groups of emerging economic powers (including Brazil, Russia, India, China and South Africa) call themselves, which I have renamed elsewhere as the Group of Emerging Economic Powers (GEEP) as contained in Bodomo (2011).

Some of the leading academic works that document the Bandung conference include Ampiah 2007, Choucri 1969, Kahin 1956, Khudori 2006, Lee 2010 and Roberts 2013. Most of these woks cite the ten core principles of the Bandung conference, which were unanimously adopted as follows:

1. Respect for fundamental human rights and for the purposes and principles of the Charter of the United Nations
2. Respect for the sovereignty and territorial integrity of all nations
3. Recognition of the equality of all races and of the equality of all nations, large and small
4. Abstention from intervention or interference in the internal affairs of another country
5. Respect for the right of each nation to defend itself, singly or collectively, in conformity with the charter of the United Nations
6. (a) Abstention from the use of arrangements of collective defence to serve any particular interests of the big powers (b) Abstention by any country from exerting pressures on other countries
7. Refraining from acts or threats of aggression or the use of force against the territorial integrity or political independence of any country
8. Settlement of all international disputes by peaceful means, such as negotiation, conciliation, arbitration or judicial settlement as well as other peaceful means of the parties own choice, in conformity with the charter of the United Nations
9. Promotion of mutual interests and cooperation
10. Respect for justice and international obligations

These 10 principles are often seen as precursors to core values of the Non-Aligned Movement, and even extend to the core principles of the United Nations.

The influence of the Bandung Conference is seen in the speed with which many African and Asian countries quickly established diplomatic relations. Right after Bandung many African countries beginning with Egypt in 1956 and followed in quick succession by 10 African countries by 1960 established diplomatic relations with China.

The African presence in China, especially the formation of relatively large communities in 21st Century could not have easily happened without the events of Bandung and the establishment of diplomatic relations with China. This African presence in China and other parts of Asia is not new, as there are accounts of very early interactions between Africans and Chinese (Wyatt 2009, Rashidi and van Sertima 1995), especially the voyages of a Ming era Chinese Admiral, Zheng He, to the east coast of Africa in the early part of the 15th Century. However, the formation of Diaspora African communities, especially by African traders, is a very new, 21st Century phenomenon. This was triggered by the Asian financial crises of 1997 and China's entry into the WTO in 2001. African traders who were in neighbouring Southeast Asian regions adversely affected by the crisis began to move into the markets of Guangzhou and other southern Chinese cities to escape the financial crises and to take advantage of market opportunities as China's economy became more and more open. Now there are about half a million Africans in China with Guangzhou hosting the largest community.

The African presence in China is only one aspect of burgeoning relations between Africa and China. As China's economy steadily developed into one of the most important economies in the world, it needed raw materials to fuel an economy growing at neck-break speed. It turned to Africa in a most intensified way since the turn of the millennium, and this resulted in very close government-to-government relations between China and the various governments of Africa. These government-to-government links led to growing people-to-people relations, with Chinese visiting and settling in Africa and Africans visiting and settling in China in substantial numbers. There are now more than two million Chinese in Africa compared to half a million Africans in China. Africa-China relations as sketched here have been the subject of many studies including Brautigan (2003, 2011); Brautigam and Tang (2011); He Wenping (20009, 2010); Holslag (2011); Li Anshan (2005); Li Pengtao (2010); Li Weijian, Zhang Zhongxiang, Zhang Chun, and Zhu Ming (2010); Liu Hongwu (2008); Meng Deli and Nie Dianzhong (2011); Michel and Beuret (2009); Mitton (2002); Park

(2009); Rotberg (2008); Sautman and Yan (2007); Song (2011); Strauss and Saavedra (2010); I. Taylor (2006, 2008); M. Taylor (2011); Zhang Zhongxiang (2011); and Zhao Minghao (2010).

In this section, we provide a general background of this African Diaspora in China in the form of socio-cultural facts and statistics describing the community in broad terms, derived from fieldwork lasting over five years in six main cities in China. This then leads to a discussion of specific issues of linguistic repertoire (language use and language choices in specific contexts). Issues of language and cross-cultural communication comprise some of the best ways to illustrate the blurring of territorial boundaries with regards to issues of identity as people constantly migrate from one area of the world to the other. It shows that area studies can no longer be bounded geographically and that we have to redefine them to fit into an international, globalised study paradigm. We will first look at some methodological issues before returning to the core arguments of the paper.

## 1. Methodology

The research results reported in this talk are part of results derived from a study lasting over five years by the author and his team of African and Chinese research assistants. To address the main theme about the everyday lives of Africans in China, i.e., what it is like to be African in this country, we have had to pose and try to answer questions about this community such as who these Africans are, where they come from, why they come to Guangzhou, how communication takes place, how the communities are organised and how they contribute to the economy of their adopted country of residence—we decided to do an empirically-based socio-linguistic and urban anthropological survey of six main cities in China: Hong Kong, Macau, Guangzhou, Yiwu, Shanghai, and Beijing. In terms of analyses, the focus is more on Guangzhou in this paper.

## 2. General Statistical profiles

Collating the statistical profiles of the various cities together, we have 736 returned and valid responses, though our research team interacted with between 800 and 1000 Africans during this research project over five years.

In terms of gender distribution, majority of the Africans in China are male. At the beginning of the African influx into China between 1997 and the turn of the Millennium, African women were hardly seen among the trader populations. A salient socio-cultural feature of the African family system is that, in the average family business structure, it is usually the husband who travels to look for new sources of supply for the business but with time the women begin to travel out as well. As African men got to know China well, more and more women began to arrive and now, including some rather young women who are yet to marry and establish a family business. This number is destined to rise as more and more females come to do business and to study.

With regards to levels of education, most of these immigrants have at least completed secondary education followed by those who have completed university/college, and a few who have completed postgraduate study.

There are more traders or businessmen in China among the African migrants than any other profession. The second largest group comprises of students.

Age-wise, most Africans in China are between the ages of 25 and 34. This indicates that this is a relatively young population that is in one of the most economically productive age brackets, which may vary from place to place but which can be said to be between the ages of 20 and 55, especially with regard to work involving physical strength.

One of the most crucial questions we had to frequently address early on in our research of the African presence in China was which countries these Africans come from. The top 10 countries of origins of the Africans in our survey group are Nigeria, Ghana, Mali, Guinea, Senegal, Tanzania, Congo, Kenya, Cameroon, and Niger. The order of listing is from the country with the highest number of immigrants (Nigeria) to the one with the least number of immigrants (Niger). The list also suggests that there are more West Africans in China overall.

## 3. Linguistic Repertoire

With the above broad characterisation of the community, let us analyse the linguistic repertoire of Africans in China, especially that of African traders. The term linguistic repertoire, for us, refers to the gamut of languages that a community (such as the African community in China) speaks, reads, and writes and the choices members of this community make in the use of these languages in various communication situations. The term has been defined more broadly as "…a fluid set of linguistic resources that members of an ethnic group may use variably as they index their ethnic identities" (Benor 2011: 142). As we do more and more linguistic analysis of Diaspora communities in what may be termed "Diaspora Linguistics", terms such as linguistic repertoire will become more and more salient, and indeed feature prominently in sociolinguistic interactional studies (e.g. Gumperz 1962, Hillery 1955, Hymes 1972, Labov 1972, Ochs 1993, and Patrick 2002).

Beginning with the number of African languages represented in China, there are totally 98 native languages spoken by the respondents.

In addition to their native languages, most of the respondents can speak English while a few others can speak French.

We investigated how long the respondents have been staying in China, for this might influence the make up of their linguistic repertoire, as it might be the case, for instance, that longer term Africans would speak Chinese more fluently. It is found that many of them only stay in China for a short period of time spanning from one month to 1 to 3 years. This is a result of rather restrictive immigration rules.

A question investigates the respondents' proficiency in Chinese. Many respondents do not speak any Chinese at all. Those who can, also, do so poorly. However, there are a very few who claim they have excellent proficiency in Chinese.

Another question investigates their proficiency in English. Whereas some respondents claimed that their proficiency in English is excellent, majority think their proficiency is good. It is a common feature among Africans in China that they tend to embellish their proficiency in the former colonial languages, English and French.

We also wanted to seek the respondents' opinion on whether English is a common language in China around their business district. Some respondents think that English is a common language, and indeed often insist on the Chinese learning "their" language, i.e. English in the case of Africans from Anglophone countries and French for Africans from Francophone country.

Although some respondents claim they have never encountered communication problem, majority claim they have come across such situation. This issue is related to the phenomenon of "calculator communication" extensively discussed in Bodomo (2012). Most Africans think that even in the absence of an effective lingua franca, they can still communicate with their Chinese customers in the markets of Guangzhou by the use of their calculators.

One of the questions aims at investigating how the respondents perceive their identity, whether and to what extent they would identify themselves as Chinese. Some said categorically that they would not identify themselves as Chinese.

Still on the issue of identity one question investigates whether and to what extent the respondents think they are different from Chinese people. Some respondents think that they are different from Chinese people to a very large extent.

We also sought to know to what extent the respondents think they are connected to the local Chinese community. Many people think they have no social connection to the local Chinese community. Some respondents think that they are only connected to the local Chinese community to a small extent.

In terms of analysis, this last set of questions is seeking a broad answer to the issue whether Africans in China would like to integrate into Chinese communities in China or they just want to be on their own. The answers here indicate that, at this point in their China sojourn, Africans in China do not try or even strive to fit or "integrate" into Chinese communities; this is not happening now in any appreciably large scale, except maybe for those Africans married to Chinese, but even they hardly do this. Africans from my research are just happy to *interact* businesswise and cross-culturally, but not to *integrate* into Chinese culture and family settings. Given that Africans cannot even get Chinese citizenship straight-forwardly, among many other issues, Africans in China do not seem to want to integrate into Chinese culture and society; they want to live by themselves and interact happily with Chinese at public places such as in markets and work places.

## 3. Everyday Life in Guangzhou

Having provided a background of Africans in China, and looked specifically at their linguistic repertoire, we supplement these quantitative studies with some in-depth interviews with three people, an African man from Zambia, an African woman from Zimbabwe, and a Chinese woman from Jiangxi Province.

### In-depth interview III:

Questionnaire no. 59

Mr. J, a Zambian of about 28 years old at the time of our research, had been doing business for two years after he graduated from university. He ran a business retailing phones and clothes. His business involves importing manufactured goods from Dubai and China to countries like Zambia, Tanzania, and South Africa. He explained that as his business was still in the developing phase, he did not own a shop himself. Instead, he sold his goods in his friends' shops in Lusaka, the capital of Zambia. Guangzhou was Mr. J's first and only point of contact with China because of business. He planned to stay in Guangzhou for only a week on the trip during which we interviewed him. Asked how he got around, he said he got to know a lot about the city from his countrymen who had been there earlier; now he knows a lot about TianXiu and was indeed now staying at the TianXiu

Hotel. In fact he chose to live at TainXiu Hotel because it is close to shopping centers like TianXiu Building and it is at a good location and therefore highly accessible to other places. During his first trip to China and Guangzhou, he encountered some communication problems due to language barriers. As he does not speak any Chinese himself, he does not understand Guangzhou people who, according to him, do not speak good English. He said he sees himself as a smart businessman and would thus not let the language problem hinder his business. On the other hand, he also finds that Chinese, who are keen at business, have a special way to communicate with their customers by using calculators. Therefore, though they do not speak the same language, they still do business successfully with each other. Although China is very new to Mr. J, he already finds a lot of difference between doing business in Guangzhou and other places like Dubai. To him, Guangzhou is not a very safe place and you have to take good care of your belongings whereas in Dubai, you can leave your goods along the corridor and no one will steal them. However, goods are cheaper in Guangzhou than in Dubai and this is why he wants to do business with China.

In-depth Interview VI:

Questionnaire no. 53
Mrs. A., from Zimbabwe, told us that she was an English teacher at Sun Yat-sen University in Guangzhou; and she had been living in Guangzhou for more than 3 years with her family at the time of our interview. She no longer teaches English at Sun Yat-sen University now as she only had a one year contract to come and teach. She is now running a small import and export business in Guangzhou. As a foreigner she found that it is difficult to get a job in Guangzhou. And that is why she is running her own business now. Mrs. A perceived that there are a lot of cultural differences between Africa and China which make intercultural interaction difficult. She thinks that people would not employ her if they do not even understand her, explaining why it is difficult for her to land a job. Mrs. A added that she does not understand Chinese either. For example, she does not understand why Chinese people spit on the floor. And she believes that this is because they are not educated. So she thinks that is not their fault if they do that since it is because of lack of education. For the same reason she believes that Chinese people discriminate against Africans mainly because they are not educated in matters of interracial sensitivities. Finally, Mrs. A believes that someday there will be better intercultural understanding given enough education.

## In-depth interview VII (Chinese interviewee)

Ms R came to Guangzhou from Pingxiang in Jiangxi Province two years ago at the time of our interview and had been working in the TianXiu Building since then. She attended High School so she thinks she can speak fluent English. Therefore, she did not come across any communication problems with her African customers. It is clear that the ability to speak English is an advantage in the TianXiu Building and any other African business places in Guangzhou. Nearly every shop in the TianXiu Building wants an English translator and sometimes a French translator because many African businessmen in Guangzhou speak French. According to Ms R, Africans in the TianXiu building mainly came from West Africa, for example, Guinea, Ivory Coast, Mali, and Niger. Ms R main job is to take orders and pre-orders, and sustain regular contact with the customers. However, Ms R had not been receiving many orders in the days before our interview. She mentioned that when she first came to the TianXiu Building, there were many African businessmen and hence more orders. Many African businessmen owned shops in the building. The shop opposite to Ms R's shop is owned by an African businessman. Ms R mentioned that some African businessmen even owned factories in Guangzhou. Now, however, many African people have left Guangzhou and sold their shops to Guangzhou people. Although Ms R could observe all these changes involving African business activities in Guangzhou, she does not know much why there are such changes. She does not have a strong connection with the African people with Guangzhou. They are her customers only.

Besides these three in-depth interviews I also participant-observed Africans in an African restaurants and was able to get the following important complaint about the everyday harassment Africans feel they are being subjected to at the hands of the Guangzhou immigration authorities.

"You want to know what it is like for me to live in China?… Every day before I leave my house… to go to the markets… factories… or even to go eat… to come here for dinner… for African food in this restaurant, I spend about, what… ten minutes gathering all the documents that prove that I am legally resident in China; I cannot walk out of my house… my hotel without my passport, my room key, and anything that shows that I am legally resident in China. And I have done this for the past 3 years that I have been in and out of China."

## 4. Making Sense of It all: A New Territory for Area Studies, International Studies, Global Studies, and beyond?

From these quantitative and qualitative studies depicting the background of the African presence, especially the everyday life of the Africans in Guangzhou, and the general condition of what it is like to be African in China, what can we make of this in terms of area studies and related fields? This African presence has been dubbed Africa's newest Diaspora because it is a 21st Century phenomenon, only barely 15 years old. It is a relatively complex Diaspora community and we need insights from many areas of study, including African Studies, Chinese/Asian studies and various fields such as sociology, anthropology, linguistics, and history to understand the community. It is hard, for instance, to understand Africans in China without understanding the sociocultural context in which they grew up in Africa, and it is hard to understand Africans in China without understanding the sociopolitical context in which they are operating in China. As a specific illustration, to fully account for the relative complex linguistic repertoire and cross-cultural communication intricacies in the markets of Guangzhou one needs insights from African culture of buying and Chinese savvy business transaction skills, among many other issues. This kind of approach involves an interaction of different area studies to the point that it might be best to just talk of global, areal/international, and Diaspora interdisciplinary studies. There are already studies, such as Looser (2102) that point to area studies being geared "towards the study of larger scale society" (Looser 2012: 97).

I propose in this paper that the best way to approach this relative complexity that involves a blurring of geographical as well as academic boundaries is to evolve a theory that bridges boundaries: what I call the bridge theory of global, areal and Diaspora studies (the GADS theory). This GADS theory is clearly stated as follows: *in an era of globalisation characterised by constant movement of people, goods, and services, Diaspora communities serve as bridges between geographical areas of the world, linking their areas of origin to their areas of domicile, a study of which then requires interdisciplinary insights from different areas of study*. The GADS theory is an extension of my earlier bridge theory of migrant-indigene relations (Bodomo 2010, 2012) that was developed to account for the interaction between Africans and Chinese. It is not all scholars who see migrant communities as serving as bridges. Lyons, Brown and Li (2012), for instance, contest my bridge theory and attempt to provide evidence to show that African communities in Guangzhou constitute an enclave, disconnected from their host communities because of tensions between these communities. While there are often tensions between migrant and host communities, these tensions cannot always constitute counter-evidence for a bridge theory if we look beyond migrant-host relations. Whereas migration has often been looked at two-dimensionally, in terms of the migrant community and its relations with the host community (i.e. situated in a particular geopolitical area), the bridge theory proposes that migration is, at least, a three-dimensional phenomenon involving the target migrant community, its source community, as well as its host community. When looked at this way we can see that socioculturally, socioeconomically, and sociopolitically, a migrant community most often serves as a bridge that mediates relations, interactions, and perceptions of its host cultures to its source cultures. For instance, on the one hand, Africans visiting Guangzhou often get their initial insights about the Chinese society through the eyes of Africans already living in China, including insights about the good relations as well as the tensions between Africans and Chinese. On the other hand, Guangzhou people, whether or not they like or dislike Africans, get to experience certain African cultural mannerisms from Africans living among them even before they get to know where Africa is.

This bridge theory of migrant-indigene relations is essentially a theory that attempts to make sense of the confusing, blurring boundaries between global, areal, international, and Diaspora Studies. The theory allows one to study Africans in China from the perspectives of African studies, from the angle of Asian studies, from the insights of Diaspora studies, and generally from the emerging preoccupations of global and international studies as these market places that we see in Guangzhou and other parts of China have become global market places involving a mix of people from all parts of the world, including Africans, Asians, and Westerners. Bandung and its successor platforms that established stronger African and Chinese/Asian relations made this reinterpretation of area studies as global and international studies possible

## 5. Conclusion

I argue in this paper that the Bandung conference of 1955 has redefined the way we do area and international studies in a world of globalisation, especially in regards to the relations between Africa and Asia. In other words, Bandung not only constitutes a watershed, a point of departure for international relations, especially involving African and Asian governments but it also redefined the way scholars practice international studies, especially involving the areas of Africa and Asia. I have used my study of the African diaspora in China to illustrate this thesis throughout the paper.

To fully account for what it is like to be African in China, to understand the everyday experiences of Africans in the markets of Guangzhou, one needs insights from many disciplinary and interdisciplinary areas of study such as African Studies, Asian Studies, Diaspora Studies and, ultimately, global interdisciplinary studies. Africa's newest Diaspora constitutes an exciting new territory for Area Studies in the era of globalisation. Indeed, the study of Africa in an Asian context is more meaningful when we draw in comparative angles between Africa and Asia from various perspectives including the historical, the cultural, and the political.

In this paper I have presented evidence based on empirical, quantitative, and qualitative surveys of more than 700 Africans in China, located mostly in Guangzhou, to produce a profile of this community and to depict the everyday lives of these migrants from Africa. This profile indicates a complex sociocultural Diaspora community, and thus necessitates a careful study of African and Chinese political, economic, cultural, and especially linguistic systems—giving rise to what might be called "diaspora linguistics"— in order to make sense of this complexity. I have thus proposed a bridge theory of global, areal, and Diaspora studies (GADS) as a theoretical, methodological, and interdisciplinary platform to analyse Africans in China. The African Diaspora in China comprises a new, exciting research territory for a range of disciplines, including African Studies, Asian studies, and global studies. Once of the most enduring legacies of the Bandung conference of 1955 is that it helped redefine area and diaspora studies involving Africa and Asia as international and global studies.

## References

Ampiah, Kweku (2007). *The Political and Moral Imperatives of the Bandung Conference of 1955: the Reactions of the US, UK and Japan*. Folkestone, UK : Global Oriental.

Bertoncello, Brigitte, & Bredeloup, Sylvie (2007). The emergence of new African "trading posts" in Hong Kong and Guangzhou. *China Perspectives*, 1, 94–105.

Bodomo, A. B. (2005). Some cultural and linguistic parallels between Africa and China: The case of some West African and some southern Chinese. Unpublished paper, University of Hong Kong.

Bodomo, A. B. (2007). An emerging African-Chinese community in Hong Kong: The case of Tsim Sha Tsui's Chungking Mansions. In Kwesi Kwaa Prah (Ed.), *Afro-Chinese Relations: Past, Present and Future* (pp. 367–389). Cape Town, South Africa: The Centre for Advanced Studies in African Societies.

Bodomo, A. B. (2009). Africa-China relations in an era of globalisation: The role of African trading communities in China [全球化时代中的中非关系：非洲在华贸易团体的角色]. *West Aisa and Africa* [《西亚非洲》], 8, 62–67.

Bodomo, A. B. (2010). The African trading community in Guangzhou: An emerging bridge for Africa-China relations. *China Quarterly*, 203, 693–707.

Bodomo, A. B. (2011). South Africa joins the Group of Emerging Economic Powers (GEEP): Rise of African economy to international prominence. *Pambazuka*, Issue 511. http://www.pambazuka.org/en/category/features/69855.

Bodomo, A., & Silva, R. (2012). Language matters: The role of linguistic identity in the growth of the Lusophone African community in Macau. *African Studies* 71, No. 1, pp. 71–90.

Brautigam, D. (2003). Close encounters: Chinese business networks as industrial catalysts in sub-Saharan Africa. *African Affairs*, 102(408), 447–467.

Brautigam, D. (2011). Aid "with Chinese characteristics": Chinese foreign aid and development finance meet the OECD-DAC aid regime. *Journal of International Development*, 23(5), 752–764.

Brautigam, D., & Tang, X. Y. (2011). African Shenzhen: China's special economic zones in Africa. *Journal of Modern African Studies*, 49(1), 27–54.

Gillespie, Sandra (2001). *South-South transfer: A study of Sino-African exchanges.* New York: Routledge.

Gumperz, John J. (1962). "Types of Linguistic Communities." *Anthropological Linguistics*, 4(1), 28–40.

He Wenping [贺文萍]. (2009). Sino-African relation: Facts and distortions [中非合作互利共赢的实证分析]. *Asia & Africa Review [亚非纵横]*, 6, 48–55, 63.

He Wenping [贺文萍]. (2010). How far can China go in Africa [中国在非洲还能走多远]. *People's Tribune [人民论坛]*, 22, 38–40.

Hevi, Emmanuel (1964). *An African student in China*. London: Pall Mall Press.

Hillery, George A. (1955). Definitions of community: Areas of agreement. *Rural Sociology*, 20(4), 111.

Holslag, J. (2011). China and the coups: Coping with political instability in Africa. *African Affairs*, 110(440), 367–386.

Hymes, Dell (1972). Models of the interaction of language and social life. In J. Gumperz & D. Hymes (Eds.), *Directions in sociolinguistics: The ethnography of communication* (pp. 35–71). Oxford: Blackwell (Revised from 1967 paper).

Kahin, George McTurnan (1956). *The Asian-African Conference: Bandung, Indonesia, April 1955.* Ithaca: Cornell University Press, 1956.

Khudori, D. (2006). Towards a Bandung spirit-based civil society movement: reflections from Yogyakarta commemoration of Bandung Asian-African conference. *Inter-Asia Cultural Studies* 7: 1, 121–138. http://www.tandfonline.com/doi/pdf/10.1080/14649370500463240.

Labov, William (1972). *Sociolinguistic patterns*. Philadelphia: University of Pennsylvania Press.

Le Bail, H. (2009). Foreign migrations to China's city-markets: The case of African merchants. *Asie Visions*, 19, pp. 1–22

Lee, Christopher J., ed, (2010). *Making a World After Empire: The Bandung Moment and Its Political Afterlives.* Athens, OH: Ohio University Press.

Li Anshan (2005). African studies in China in the twentieth Century: A historiographical survey. *African Studies Review*, 48(1), 59–87.

Li Pengtao [李鹏涛]. (2010). The development of Sino-African relations and new Chinese migrants in Africa [中非关系的发展与非洲中国新移民]. *Overseas Chinese History Studies [华侨华人历史研究]*, 4, 26–32.

Li Weijian, Zhang Zhongxiang, Zhang Chun, & Zhu Ming [朱伟建; 张忠祥; 张春; 祝鸣;]. (2010). Towards a new decade: A study on the sustainability of FOCAC [迈向新的十年：中非合作论坛可持续发展研究]. *West Asia and Africa[西亚非洲]*, 9, 7–12, 81.

Li, Zhigang, Laurence Ma, & Desheng Xue (2009). An African enclave in China: The making of a new transnational urban space. *Eurasian Geography and Economics*, 50(6), 699–719.

Lyons, Michal, Alison Brown and Li Zhigang (2012). In the Dragon's Den: African Traders in Guangzhou. *Journal of Ethnic and Migration Studies*, Vol. 38, Issue 5, pp. 869–888.

Liu Hongwu [刘鸿武]. (2008). On the experience of accumulation and theoretical response of the thirty years China-African relations [论中非关系三十年的经验积累与理论回应]. *West Asia and Africa [西亚非洲]*, 11, 15–20, 81.

Looser, Tom (2012). The Global university, area studies and the world citizen: neo-liberal geography's redistribution of the "world". *Cultural Anthropology*, Vol. 27, Issue 1, pp. 97–117.

Meng Deli, & Nie Dianzhong [蒙德利; 聂佃忠]. (2011). Sino-Africa relations and the challenges under the new situation [新形势下的中非关系及其挑战]. *Special Zone Economy [特区经济]*, 5, 94–95.

Michel, Serge, & Beuret, Michel (2009). *China safari: On the trail of Beijing's expansion in Africa*. New York: Nation Books.

Mitton, Todd (2002). A cross-firm analysis of the impact of corporate governance on the Asian financial crisis. *Journal of Financial Economics*, 64(2), 215–241.

Monson, A.B. (2009). *Africa's Freedom Railway: How a Chinese Project Changed Lives and Livelihoods in Tanzania*. Bloomington: Indiana University Press.

Nazli Choucri, "The Nonalignment of Afro-Asian States: Policy, Perception, and Behaviour", *Canadian Journal of Political Science / Revue canadienne de science politique,* Vol. 2, No. 1, (March, 1969), pp. 1–17.

Park, Yoon (2009). *A matter of honour: Being Chinese in South Africa*. Lanham, MD: Lexington Books.

Patrick, L. Peter (1999). The speech community. Retrieved July 13, 2010, from http:courses.essex.ac.uk/lg/lg232/SpeechComDefs.html.

Prasad, Kiran Kamal, & Angenot, Jean-Pierre (Eds.) (2008). *TADIA: The African Diaspora in Asia, explorations on a less known fact.* Bangalore: Jana Jagrati Prakashana.

Rashidi, Runoko, & van Sertima, Ivan (Eds.) (1995). *The African presence in early Asia* (Rev. ed.). New Brunswick: Transaction Press.

Roberts, Brian Russell (2013). Artistic Ambassadors: Literary and International Representation of the New Negro Era. Charlottesville: University of Virginia Press. pp. 146–172.

Rotberg, Robert (Ed.). (2008). *China into Africa: Trade, aid, and influence*. Washington, DC: Brookings Institution.

Sautman, B., & Yan, H. R. (2007). Friends and interests: China's distinctive links with Africa. *African Studies Review*, 50(3), 75–113.

Song, H. (2011). Chinese private direct investment and overseas Chinese network in Africa. *China and World Economy*, 19(4), 109–126.

Strauss, Julia, & Martha Saavedra (Eds.) (2010). *China and Africa: Vol. 9: Emerging patterns in globalisation and development*. Cambridge: Cambridge University Press.

Sullivan, M. (1994). The 1988–89 Nanjing anti-African protests: Racial nationalism or national racism? *The China Quarterly*, 138, 438–457.

Taylor, I. (2006). China's oil diplomacy in Africa. *International Affairs*, 82(5), 937–959.

Taylor, I. (2008). China in Africa. *Journal of Modern African Studies*, 46(2), 325–326.

Taylor, M. (2011). China and Africa: Emerging patterns in globalisation and development. *Political Studies Review*, 9(2), 287–295.

Vertovec, Steve (1999). Three meanings of "Diaspora", exemplified among South Asian religions. *Diaspora*, 7(2), 277–299.

Wyatt, D. (2009). *The Blacks of premodern China*. Philadelphia: University of Pennsylvania Press.

Zhang Zhongxiang [张忠祥]. (2011). China-Africa relationship [中非关系研究综述]. *West Asia and Africa [西亚非洲]*, 5, 65–70.

Zhao Minghao [赵明昊]. (2010). China's perspectives on current people-to-people links between China and Africa [中非民间交往进展及面临的挑战]. *Global Review [国际展望]*, 6, 7, 57–60.

# 7

# International South Group Network (ISGN)

## Experience, Lessons and Perspectives for Human Rights in Global Africa

*Lazare Ki-Zerbo*

## Abstract

This article aims to reference the participation of the Centre for Studies on African Development (CEDA/CSAD) at the International South Group Network founded at the Fort Hare University in June 1994. The goal of the network was to provide alternative content to the African Renaissance advocated by New South Africa. Materials were collected in order to retrace the birth and evolution of ISGN and highlight the multifaceted heritage of Bandung, of the South Commission headed by J. Nyerere and Pan-Africanism. Methodologically speaking, the research allows checking the challenges of electronic records and archives of contemporary social movements. It also constitutes a witness experience in order to understand the critical theories on international relations among authors such as Rajagopal Balakrishnan or Vijay Prashad. In particular, it offers a background to foresee and impulse the actions planned by the Bandung Spirit Network and within the United Nations, including the initiative from the South, for a binding international treaty concerning multinational companies.

*Keywords:* Bandung, Human Rights, International Relations, Multinational Companies, South

## From Bandung to post-apartheid South Africa

In June 2014, the African Union Summit on Agriculture and Food Security was being held in Malabo (Equatorial Guinea). A petition had already attracted nearly two million signatures, entitled "From rhetoric to action" whose aim was to transform agriculture and food security in Africa. Besides food security, the issues of conflicts affecting in particular the Sahel, from the Horn of Africa to the north of Mali, through the Central African Republic, were also included. This holistic approach to security is legitimate and based on a comprehensive analysis of the social challenges that affect African people's lives.

It is obvious that the wealth's non-redistribution in Africa, added to the interventions of foreign actors (as in Libya[1]), is the root cause of these conflicts. Bernard Founou Tchuigoua is right in writing: *"The radical critical approach promotes a comprehensive idea to human security that incorporates socio-economic, political, internal and external dimensions, therefore a holistic and truly global human security. It offers the humanistic goal of eliminating the factors of inequality of economic developments and growing inequalities in the distribution of income and wealth, and of course the democratisation of societies and the international system. This approach is based on facts like popular majority peripheries, differences between the new phase of human insecurity and the Cold War that are less important than the similarities"*[2].

In fact, this debate was already the order of the day when the official end of apartheid was supposed to take place in South Africa, with the elections of April 27, 1994, followed by the historic speech of Nelson Mandela on June 13, 1994 about African renaissance[3]. We must keep in mind the historic experience of South Africa even if this country is not what we expected: a very powerful nation able to contribute to the rapid transformation of the entire Continent. Mandela and the ANC were conscious that social change was crucial and launched the Reconstruction and Development Program (RDP) whereas the conservative forces inside and outside drove the country to the brink of civil war with the deadly attacks of the Inkatha.

We have to remember South African experience in order to avoid an eternal resumption. Bandung, the Pan-African ideal[4] must not be invoked by an abstract ideal, as a nostalgia and without an affective will to transform the present situation marked by the persistence and strengthening of imperial domination in the South, especially in Africa, for instance in Mali. Issa Shijvi writes about this in his lecture on *The Silence in the NGO discourse: the role and future of NGOs in Africa: "History is not about assigning or sharing blames nor is it about narrating the 'past', which must be forgotten and forgiven or only remembered once a year on remembrance of heroes or independence days. History is about the present. We must understand the present as history so as to change it for the better"*[5].

It is this historical perspective that explains my decision to share the experience of the *International South Group Network (ISGN)* with the Bandung Spirit Network of activists and researchers. The archives of the Third World resistance and construction of a better world are also guidelines for the present and the future.

In this article, I started this work for the ISGN. We managed to retrieve some archives but there is a lot to be done, especially in South Africa itself[6]. Such an enterprise goes through certain methodological difficulties; ISGN archives are largely electronic, whereas the network is not operational any longer. In the first part, I will show the evolution of the ISGN activities since the inaugural conference of June 1994 until the tribute to Joseph Ki-Zerbo organised in Nairobi in 2008; then the assessment on the network and finally I will propose a few conclusive and prospective remarks based on a creative interpretation of Third World resistance by critical thinkers such as Rajagopal Balakrishnan.

## Fort Hare, June 12–16, 1994

*Bandung, South Commission and African Renaissance*

On April 27, 1994, the African National Congress (ANC), the oldest movement of African liberation born on January 8, 1912, allied with the Congress of South African Trade Unions (COSATU) and the South-African communist party, wins the first democratic elections of South Africa with 62,65% and Nelson Mandela took an oath at the National Assembly on May 10, 1994: it is the culmination of a transition process which started since his release from prison on February 11, 1990. On June 13, 1994, Nelson Mandela gave a historical speech[7] while attending, for the first time as president, African Unity Organisation Summit in Tunis. He spoke about the African Renaissance, one of the themes highlighted by Thabo Mbeki.

In fact, many Africans of the continent and the Diaspora, including the author of the present article, saw the New South Africa with hope, as if it was the beginning of an automatic transformation of the global geo-political order in the Continent, especially the fight against neocolonialism. In the press release published for the Fort Hare Conference, we can read about it: *"the primary concern of the University of Fort hare (...) is to avoid the neocolonial trap that has prevented other Third World countries from achieving genuine independence from its past colonial masters*"[8].

In the first national unity government, two ministers are remarkable because of their political affiliation with the Inkatha Freedom Party (IFP): Ben Ngubane, Minister of Arts and Culture, Sibusiso Bengu, Minister of Education. The latter was a Lutheran World Federation collaborator who was close to Oliver Tambo, ANC president from 1958 to 1991. But he also became distant from the controversial leader of the IFP Mangosuthu Buthelezi. His participation in the first government of Mandela testifies in any case the confidence he enjoyed, despite its affiliation with the IFP, at the direction of the ANC and his accession to the progressive agenda of the Tripartite Alliance ANC-COSATU-SACP[9].

Anyway, it was as Vice-Rector of the oldest Black South African University, in Fort Hare[10], created in 1916, that Sibusiso Bengu organised from December 17, 1993, Congress of NGO representatives of Africa, Asia and Latin America. He was assisted by Tamara Kunanayakam[11], who was at the time a Sri-Lankan diplomat based in Geneva. Participation went beyond the Asian-African area of Bandung and included Latin America. To understand this extension, it should be noted that an 'Interim Committee of the Southern Group' was associated with the organisation of the meeting. Nelson Mandela and Julius Nyerere, President of the South Commission, were also mentioned in the provisional program but did not attend.

The South Commission[12] was composed of development experts such as Widjojo Nitisastro from Indonesia, Michael Manley of Jamaica, Marie-Angeline Savane of Senegal, as well as representatives from Brazil, Venezuela, Zimbabwe ... It was created with the financial support from the South, the largest donors being Venezuela, India, Kuwait, Malaysia, Nigeria, Botswana, Zimbabwe, Korea, China, Cuba, Brunei. By establishing an interim group of the South, the South Commission, which had a limited mandate in time, certainly considered the sustainability of its action, beyond the intergovernmental treaty creating the South Centre[13].

We can therefore say that the vision of the African 'Renaissance', and the ideal of the self-centred development in the Third World promoted by the South Commission development, is the main sources of inspiration for ISGN. For example, the very name of the conference, "International consultation for people-centred development alternatives for the south", refers to the plea made in the above report, published few years earlier.

Invited as the Director of the Centre for the Study of African Development (CEDA), Joseph Ki-Zerbo was linked with this current as a theorist of progressive endogenous development on African continent[14]. Ten years earlier, he had participated—in Arusha—at a meeting of the Socialist International movements of liberation[15]. He was also related with structures such as the Geneva University Institute of Development Studies (IUED) and the World Council of Churches, which had contributed to the launch of CEDA activities[16].

After his exile in Senegal during the revolution period in Burkina Faso (1983–1987), the Fort Hare Conference was therefore part of a new beginning for the Pan-Africanist historian. He had created the National Convention of Progressive Patriots / Social Democratic Party (CNPP / PSD)[17], a member of the Socialist International. Its parliamentary group was the largest party of the opposition with its twelve members.

## Conference: philosophy and synthesis

An ISGN illustrative file[18] found in the documents of the Centre of Studies on African Development in Ouagadougou and the invitation card received by Professor Fernando Leiva in order to attend the Fort Hare Conference, allows a complete vision on the meeting's reference terms and proceedings.

The aim of the network is the following: *"The broad objectives of the meeting would be to initiate a process of inter-regional collaboration and consultation with a view to explore areas of common interests, defining alternatives that are relevant and responsive to the needs of people, developing common strategies and a broad based organisational framework, for South-South solidarity and cooperation. It is hoped that the outcome of this Conference will include a declaration and program of activities as well as a plan for the establishment of a network*"[19]. The concept of 'network' is launched. It was certainly at the centre of the approaches of Geneva NGOs. Southern Group had, however, specific objectives coming from Bandung ideas:

(i) Promote values putting people above profit;
(ii) Promote peoples' right to self-determination in all its dimensions;
(iii) Promote an approach of human development and democratic rights concerning environment, peace and their link;
(iv) Promote direct access and equal participation to the process of decision at the international level and democratisation of international institutions[20].

This file describes the international context and underlines the Bandung collapse, whereas it points out how the new world risks the implosion of nation-states and the liquidation of social gains.

The consultation is therefore against this post-Berlin neoliberalism (1989) and tries to suggest an alternative based on popular aspirations. It echoes to the African Charter for Popular Participation in Development and Transformation adopted in Arusha in February 1990.

Professor Bengu, Minister of education, declared in his opening speech: *"The people of South Africa fully recognise that the recent achievement of political democracy is but a phase in the longer struggle for the attainment of genuine socio-economic democracy*"[21], referring to the reconstruction and development programme, abandoned after Mandela, and now claimed by many South Africans. The ambition of the South Group was to develop a self-reliant development in new South Africa and in Africa. It was during this meeting that one had to resist the neoliberal trend of post-1989 period.

Much closer to ANC than IFP, Bengu carried on: *"the main item on the agenda of the progressive force of the South [is] a careful reassessment of their structures of resistance and their activities, which up until the recent past had been largely shaped and conditioned by the politics of the Cold War. (...) the issue reduces itself to the fundamental question of how we can impact upon and restructure the non-democratic, people-sensitive system. (...) The quest to evolve a popular democratic system on a world scale must simultaneously become a process of building and strengthening democratic South organisations at home and internationally. (...) We also need a revitalised international alliance of democratic and other people*'s *organisations and structures*"[22].

He also comes back to the question of the ideological content of political commitment of the South: according to him (and this confirms his distance from Inkhata), popular and socialist class must be addressed to.

After his opening speech, the participants had to study the comparative analysis of the situation in the Southern countries, from the political and economic point of view (June 13–14). Headings were especially dedicated to the global governance: United Nations institutions' role, Bretton woods, neoliberal policies disruptive social impact. June 15 concerned the analysis of the situation in South Africa and June 16 the proposal of alternative programmes[23].

The file contents list out conference's resolutions, among which was in Africa.

The topic of women's situation was scheduled for the following year (violence against women, linked with exploitation, poverty, hunger etc.).

Another resolution condemned NATO and American intervention such as calls for a nuclear free world.

In the final declaration, the wars against Vietnam, Philippines, India and Indonesia (the 'peoples of the rainforest') are quoted as examples[24].

The meeting underlines its preference for a decentralised strategy, instead of Cold War marked by world's centrality ('one centre or some Grand Design') in each of the blocks.

This option leads to the final decision—on June 16, 1994—to implement an 'International coordinating committee' at the University of Fort Hare. The conference elected an International Coordinating Committee (ICC) composed of representatives from each region: Joseph Ki-Zerbo for Africa, Fernando Leiva for Latin America, Francisco Pascual for Asia/Pacific, and

Viola Plummer for North America. It was the task of the ICC to guide and direct the work of the network. Professor Ki-Zerbo attended ICC sessions in South Africa, September 14, 1998.

Concerning the way of financing, the principles of the Asian/Pacific group was retained: diversity of financing sources, transparency, responsibility and subsidies without conditionality.

It should be noted that Norwegian Agency for Development Cooperation (NORAD) and Karibu Foundation were strong partners.

## Cape Town (1997)

The President of ISGN, S. Bengu invited the Office of the ISGN in Cape Town in a local church in December 1997. This meeting led to the entry of new members in the governing structure. This is Dr. Molefe Tsele from NGO ESSET (Ecumenical Service for Social and Economic Transformation)[25], Dr. Alejandro Bendana from the Centre for International Studies, Nicaragua (he was a Sandinista who studied at Harvard University). Sonia Soto (Philippines) also made her entry as a representative of a Filipino Women organisation, Kaisa Ka, committed against militarism and for genuine security[26].

During 1999 session, Professor of Economics in Fort Hare, Pricilla Munyai, made her entry in the ICC (International Committee of Coordination). The ICC of Cape Town is in accordance with the decentralisation philosophy of South Centre. Other organisations following this idea are: CEDA (Burkina Faso), ESSET (South Africa), IEC (Nicaragua), the Development Economics Department of Fort Hare University, Resource Centre for the Development of People (Philippines), Kaisa Ka (Philippines), Direction and SEATINI (Zimbabwe). CEDA specialises in land issues and food security.

## Harare-Ouagadougou (1997–2001): the issue of land issues and biodiversity in the heart of the action of ISGN

As a result of this meeting, ISGN was founded, led by the International Coordinating Committee, ICC / CIC with Professor Joseph Ki-Zerbo as president, Professor Yash Tandon, Ugandan economist based in Harare (Zimbabwe), the South African pastor Molefe Tsele.

The ISGN was conceived as a network organisation of civil society for an equitable economic order and against neoliberal globalisation, like the international African forces for development founded twenty years before at Dakar in April 1975. According to Roland Colin, "International African forces for the development" presented itself as an international movement to bring together forces of civil society committed to development in Africa[27].

At that time Joseph Ki-Zerbo defended an alliance between intellectuals, workers and peasants that echoes several revolutionary theories, especially that of Cabral. This is certainly due to the participation of Professor Ki-Zerbo to the Constitutive Conference of Fort Hare.

## Progressivism

We can understand the connection between Joseph Ki-Zerbo and Bengu. As an intellectual committed to supporting the liberation movements, and following the experience of Thomas Sankara, followed by a political shift of the country towards the wild liberalisation, CEDA director certainly saw in the ISGN a consistent approach of the Pan-African ideal as formulated by Bengu: "some sort of socialist and people centred ethos"[28].

Their progressive vision is based primarily on the appropriation of what was called the Scandinavian model. For example, during the round table on Sustainable Consumption and Production held in Oslo on December 8, 1995, Bengu, invited as Minister of Education, states: "*The Nordic people are endowed with an admirable sense of responsibility for the welfare of others and a belief in the virtues of fairness and equality. It is no wonder, therefore, that this Roundtable is taking place in Oslo. I hope that this will imbue our discussions with the Nordic spirit of civic responsibility*"[29]. *Ki-Zerbo was a political partner of the Swedish Social Democratic Party and close collaborator of Dag Hammarskjöld Foundation as editor of its journal Development and dialogue.*

## The Rio conference, ecology and land issues

In his speech, Bengu says: "*We are gathered here as government representatives, academics, environment and development practitioners and activists, to consider the subject of environment and development as being critical for the survival of human kind.(…) All possible solutions to overcome the environment and development crisis must, therefore, concentrate on the enhancement of human beings so that they may become the agents of development*"[30].

Twenty years later, in the context of the World Climate Conference held in Paris in December 2015, this position is still the same. It raises the question of the link between ecology and social justice, as source of conflict between the Northern and Southern countries, on the priorities set in the context of the fight against global warming.

As for Joseph Ki-Zerbo, the environment has an important place in his vision of endogenous development, including the role of habitat or Mother Earth as a template for the construction of identity in Africa[31]. With French economist Michel Beaud[32], Calliope Beaud, Larbi Bouguerra, Pierre Calame, Maurice Cosandey, Venant Cauchy, he was a member of the Vezelay Group established in 1986, to think about global challenges, world responsibility and solidarity, as part of the Charles Leopold Mayer Foundation after the World Conference on environment in Rio[33]. With this foundation under Swiss law, he published *Companions of the Sun: anthology of great texts of humanity on the relationship between man and nature*[34].

Twenty years after Rio, Pierre Calame, previously Director of Charles Léopold Mayer Foundation for the Progress of Man, offered a living testimony at the conference in honour of Joseph Ki-Zerbo, held at UNESCO in May 2012: *"It is especially thanks to him that the Vezelay group understood very quickly that the European and American thinking on what was beginning to be called 'sustainable development' won't have a way out if it didn't induct right from the beginning the question of poverty and instability in many countries of the South, especially African ones"*[35].

This context will be decisive in the ISGN's action under the leadership of Yash Tandon, Ugandan progressive economist who lived the great era of universities of Makerere and Dar el Salaam[36].

The Charter of Southern Africa on the Earth, Work and Food Safety[37], of the conference on the same topic held in Harare in April 1997 and to which the author of this article participated on behalf of CEDA, reflects the aspirations of democratic organisations at this critical period.

Indeed fifteen years after the independence of Zimbabwe and with the arrival of the ANC to power, the issue of land reform and enhancement of endogenous knowledge was more than ever at the order of the day. The situation was explosive. It was not a UN intellectual agenda but an acute social contradiction. The Government and UNDP was preparing an International Conference on Land Reform. For example, as Horace Campbell shows in his study on Zimbabwe, quoting the exemplary work of Yash Tandon[38], the traditional seed conservation techniques were threatened by the intensive mode of capitalist agricultural production force in the settlements of southern Africa.

It is for this reason that the Charter adopts the following advanced positions:

1. Advance lobbying and pressure tactics, and develop networks and joint action within SADC countries to curtail, regulate or stop practices of MNCs against workers and people;
2. Acknowledge that equal access to and ownership of land is a basic human right;
3. Call for a revolutionary, holistic land and agricultural reform based on the principle of "land to the tiller";

4. Demand recognition of farmer's rights to indigenous seeds and their in situ conservation, and that developed countries meet their commitments to provide funds for such conservation.

Taking into account the differences between the social situation in Southern Africa and West Africa, CEDA contributed to ISGN's programme on land (Land project), organising a consultation on the same challenges, given the liberalisation policy implemented by the Government with the support of international institutions[39].

The reflections of J. Ki-Zerbo at the symposium of the Research Centre for Endogenous Development (CRC) held in Bamako in 1989[40] were also oriented towards the promotion of endogenous knowledge, including local seeds[41]. From one end to the other of the continent convergence was real.

Moreover, between Harare (1997) and Ouagadougou (2001), there was the memorable protest at the WTO conference in Seattle in 1999, Burkina Faso and the powerful popular movement "Enough is enough"[42]. Following the murder of journalist Norbert Zongo, on December 13, 1998, radicalisation of struggles emerged. Popular protest era of late twentieth century is based on decentralisation and coordination of groups in struggle[43].

During its meeting in Johannesburg on November 21–22, 1999, the CIC of ISGN noted that the financial crisis which shook Southeast Asia was a serious questioning of the orthodoxy advocated by international financial institutions. That orthodoxy does not structurally bind the trade negotiations to development issues. *"In the South the issues of trade and WTO, financial architecture and debt are linked to development"*[44]. The progress report also notes the partnerships developed with Via Campesina, Jubilee, Third World Network.

## SEATINI, heritage of ISGN

SEATINI (Southern and East African Trade, Information and Negotiations Institute) is an institute of ISGN, specialising in negotiations and trade-related information, established in 1996 as the ISGN programme directed by Yash Tandon. The institute was created after the First Conference of the WTO of Singapore in December 1996, but also as part of a programme called "Consumption and Production systems changes" (Capscan).

SEATINI organised his first workshop in Harare in April 1998 for the international negotiation with specialised senior executives from 17 countries. The theme was the impact of the WTO on African states. The second workshop was held from March 4 to 9, 1999, in Kampala with the participation of Uganda's trade minister Manzi Tumubweine, and resident representatives of UNDP and UNCTAD.

The good news is that SEATINI Institute is still active in Uganda. The local office is managed by the historian Mrs. Jane Seruwagi[45].

## Perspectives in the context of the post-2015 agenda

The pioneering work of ISGN is at the confluence of historical struggles and discourse: the anti-apartheid movement organised within the ANC, the South African black youth and the University of Fort Hare. Heir to the Pan-African movement in Twentieth Century, it had to be vocal in 1994 in order to prevent South Africa from falling into neocolonialism prevailing on the Continent. In Burkina Faso, in the Centre for Study on African Development, intellectuals coming from the Pan-Africanist Movement of National Liberation (Joseph Ki-Zerbo, Aly Lankoandé, Pierre Bandré, Rose-Marie Sandwidi, Jacqueline Ki-Zerbo, Aimé Damiba ...), brought their contribution to this adventure[46], thus perpetuating the ideal of the African international forces for development (IAFD) launched with Mamadou Dia[47].

This modest version of a "grassroots resistance" as Rajagopal Balakrishnan once put it[48] is an inspiration to resume the fight for an effective exercise for the right of development in the world, particularly in the context of the resolution of the board of Human Rights on June 26, 2014, calling for a binding treaty pertaining to multinationals[49]. It was sponsored by Bolivia, Cuba, Ecuador, Venezuela and South Africa. Asian and African countries have supported against the West. The appeal of Bangkok made by NGO coalition, during the first People and Business Forum (November 5–7, 2013) supports this initiative. In July 2015 Ecuador began the complex procedure to progress toward this objective[50]. The review, published by the working group on the Right to Development in 2013[51] also states useful milestones.

However, this fight must be based on a more substantial participation of Southern countries themselves, as was the case for the South Commission. If that commitment is effective, then the people of the South will reinforce their popular sovereignty. Before illustrating this continuing process, it must be recalled what lies under the idea of "international law from below" as coined by Balakrishnan.

## From resistance to effective reconstruction

The idea of an epistemological rupture with the dominant Eurocentric history of human rights and history that gave birth to the Third World Approach to International Law (TWAIL) is not new. It is consubstantial with the evolution of the nationalist movements. What is important is that peoples and leaders from the South knew from living experience the link between human rights and everyday life, particularly in economics and trade. Slavery, forced labour, occupation of fertile land, all the injustices committed during slave trade and colonial eras made them understand that exclusion and domination was practiced and organised legally. According to Balakrishnan, the themes developed by the 29 nations attending the Indonesian conference in Bandung in April 1955, (the "spirit of Bandung") form the cornerstone of the New International Economic Order (NIEO) dreamt by former "subject people"[52]. "*It came to symbolise the new spirit of solidarity in the Third World*"[53]. Two events illustrate the post-Bandung later, even if they happened much later: the OPEC mobilisation in 1973 and the 6th special session of the United Nations General Assembly (UNGA) in April 1974 in Alger. The Declaration on the Establishment of a NIEO "*called for an order based on equity, sovereign equality, interdependence, common interest, and cooperation among all states irrespective of their economic and social systems*"[54]. The principle of permanent sovereignty over national resources was already included in the article 2 of the two UN Covenants on civil and political rights, so as economic, social and cultural rights (1966), but was now proclaimed in order to transform political and economy world. As for UNCTAD[55], "*the momentum created at Bandung was resulting in the concrete political contestation*"[56].

However, as Vijay Prashad[57], Balakrishnan is not totally apologetic. He underlines the limit of the state-centric and inherited flaws of a modernist vision of Third World nationalism.

## Decolonising human rights curricula and policies

Today, the struggle for national, Pan-African, popular sovereignty in the Global South is going on with different versions. In October 2014 and September 2015, the people of Burkina Faso have shown that the resistance to corrupted regimes wanting to change the constitution is an important challenge. But after the departure of African "strong men" what will replace the oligarchy and the structural dependence on the so called "aid"?

Two examples can be made: the first is about the history of human rights in Africa and the Diaspora; the second would be about human rights approach to the debate about the currency of West African economics and monetary union (WAEMU) and the Economic Community of the States of Central Africa (ECSCA), the African Financial Community franc (CFA in French).

Keba Mbaye, one of the greatest African lawyers, points out that the remarks of the French historian of law Frédéric Joüon des Longrais on Asian judicial culture can be applied to Africa: relations with parents and community are more important than equality guaranteed by the right of the individual. This is an old debate. What is important is that Keba Mbaye thinks African and Asian laws belong to the same paradigm or tradition where collective rights are important[58]. The idea of a relational foundation of the bearer of rights can also be applied to the idea that links, connections: this sharing is more important than goods, property ("*les liens sont plus importants que les biens*"). To meet this need, more study on the history of African law system is still to be done. It is not an old-fashioned approach when one considers the issue of land property: is land a good or a common social good?

The same critical approach is relevant for the prevention of torture and cruel, inhuman and degrading treatment in the 1984 Convention Against Torture. Knowing the codification of torture in the European laws at the time of slavery and the rejection of them by African, a counter-hegemonic genealogy of international human rights is necessary to introduce torture prevention in societies that still bear the stigmata of these practices. For instance, the *Declaration of the Rights of the Negro Peoples of the World,* adopted by the United Negro Improvement Association had already mentioned "*inhuman, unchristian and uncivilised treatment*" (art.12) and protested against "*the lynching, by burning, hanging or any other means, of human beings as a barbarous practice and a shame and disgrace to civilisation*" (art.17)[59]. Thus without falling in the trap consisting in attributing all the violations of human rights to colonialism and slave trade, one cannot eradicate the social and cultural impact of the enormous violence perpetrated during these periods. After Yash Tandon, Rajagopal Balakrishnan[60], let us quote writer V.S. Naipaul whose book *The loss of Eldorado: A colonial history*[61] illustrates with vivid details the intimate relation between production of law and oppression in the colonial world.

Angela Davis is also relevant[62] and helps us understand the contribution of struggles for freedom in the South concerning minorities and oppressed peoples in the North.

To conclude, let us mention the mobilisation of engaged scholars such as Kako Nubukpo and Nicolas Agbohou on the issue of the CFA currency[63]. This campaign is gaining in popularity: beyond economics, human rights-based approach to development should play a role. How?

According to the third article of the WAEMU treatise,—which stipulates that "*The Union respects in its activities the fundamental rights expressed in the Universal Declaration of Human Rights of 1948 and the African Charter of Human Rights and Peoples of 1981*"[64]—awareness of the citizens of WAEMU about the constitutionality of the monetary policy of the central bank of the states of West Africa is raised. One should underline that this bank is for people and citizens' rights of the Union and not for the states only. Democratic states must serve their people. It is odd to know that 600 billion CFA are kept abusively by West African central bank because of its monetary policy, while, at the same time, chiefs of government feel compelled to lobby for funds outside of the Union. At the same time, important infrastructures such as the regional inter-states railway are privatised for the benefit of French private companies such as Bolloré.

Says Professor James Heintz: "*The official mandates of most central banks are excessively narrow, leading to conservative monetary policies and an inability to address to extreme economic crises. These mandates could be changed in a way that includes a consideration of human rights*"[65]. International and regional human rights law is full of resources for such an advocacy. For instance the UN special 'rapporteur' on extreme poverty[66] is a legal instrument of the Office of High Commission for Human Rights that can be targeted, in coordination with the efforts concerning a legally binding treatise related to the TNCs. The data produced by this special rapporteur on banking and austerity measures (once in Africa, now in Greece, Portugal…) are useful contributions to national and popular efforts for a better world.

## Conclusion

Twenty years ago the International South Group Network anticipated the international resistance that is now associated to Seattle, Porto Alegre or anti-Davos riots. It gave an impulse to African renaissance project and created a space where activists from Burkina Faso and Zimbabwe, South Africa and Philippines could interact for a people's centred development platform. This endeavour, a modest version of a "united democratic front", was linked to the Bandung heritage through the South Commission. It was looking for social alternatives that the democratic spring of the 1990's in Africa did not realise. Today, the African youth is looking for power shift in Burkina Faso, Congo and many countries, which is legitimate. But alternative is the best solution.

Thirty years after the declaration on the right to development (1986), the Bandung Spirit Network and its members can contribute to the analysis and spreading of critical perspectives on human rights coming from the South. It must link with international and non-governmental actors for whom the "*We the people*" of the UN Charter means power of the people and not power on the people.

# Endnotes

1. See H. Campbell, *Global NATO and the catastrophic failure in Libya*, Monthly Review Press, New York, 2013.
2. B.F. Tchigoua, « La sécurité humaine dans la perspective d'une Renaissance de la solidarité afro-asiatique » XIe Assemblée générale du CODESRIA : 06–10 décembre 2005, Maputo (Mozambique), p. 7, http://www.codesria.org/spip.php?article711&lang=fr
3. http://www.anc.org.za/show.php?id=4888
4. Cf. L. Ki-Zerbo, J.-J Ngorsene, The Pan-African Ideal, CODESRIA, Dakar.
5. http://www.pambazuka.org/en/publications/pz_sr_14.pdf
6. I wish to thank MM Hubert Tapsoba previously librarian for the archives of the Centre for the Study of African Development (CEDA), Oystein Tveter (Norway), the Chilean professor Fernando Ignacio Leiva (USA). I wish to express my special gratitude to Professor Yash Tandon for his important e mail dated February 7, 2015. Many thanks also to Dr. Ama Biney for her first proof reading.
7. Cf. http://www.anc.org.za/show.php?id=4888
8. Conference documents, mimeo, Fort Hare, June 1994, p. 3.
9. South African Communist Party.
10. Robert Sobukwe, one of the historic leaders of the Pan-Africanist Congress (PAC) of South Africa, Nelson Mandela, Oliver Tambo, Robert Mugabe, studied at Fort Hare.
11. Until this year Ms Kunanayakam was the Chairman and Rapporteur of the UN Working Group on the Right to Development. UNCTAD was one of the last bastions where the South could express its vision of human rights in connection with the development centred on people. The letter of December 17, 1993, was signed only by Mr. Bengu.
12. As a reminder, the South Commission was launched in 1990, after the summit of the Non-Aligned Harare in 1986, on the initiative of the Malaysian Prime Minister Mahathir Mohamad. After publishing the report *The challenge of the South,* the South Centre in Geneva was established.
13. Refer to the Treaty on the South Centre website : http://www.southcentre.int/wp-content/uploads/2013/02/Intergovernmental-Agreement_EN.pdf
14. Cf. my article "Joseph Ki-Zerbo (1922–2006): an evangelical pan-Africanism perspective?", *In Black & Asian Studies Association Newsletter*, No. 61, November 2011, p. 11–13, http://www.blackandasianstudies.org/newsletter/diamond.pdf
15. See J. Nyerere, J. Oop den Uyl, T*he Arusha Conference. Conference on Southern Africa of the Socialist International and the Socialist Group of the European Parliament with the Front Line States, ANC and SWAPO*. Arusha, Tanzania, September 4–5, 1984; London, Socialist International, 1985, p. 135.
16. See the Joseph Ki-Zerbo Foundation's website of: http://www.fondationki-zerbo.org/; unfortunately, under the National Council of Revolution (1983–1987), the CEDA library was sacked.
17. Later became the Party for Democracy and Progress / Socialist Party (PDP / PS) following a split within the CNPP / PSD. The PDP became the advocate of endogenous development.
18. *International South group network-Mission statement*, 1994.
19. Letter dated May 21,1994, of Mme Kunanayakam to M. Leiva.
20. *Mission statement*, pp. 5–6.
21. Conference documents, unpublished, Fort Hare, june 1994
22. *Mission statement*, pp. 17–18.
23. On June 16, 1976, took place the revolt of the youth of Soweto against the introduction of

Afrikaans in schools attended by black Southern Africans. This is the Youth Day in South Africa and the African Union.

24. Resolutions, Conference documents, Fort Hare, June 1994
25. http://www.esset.org.za/
26. http://www.genuinesecurity.org/partners/kaisaka.htm
27. Annick Gouba, *Introduction à l'histoire du MLN, mémoire de maîtrise*, Université d'Aix en Provence, September 2004, p. 156.
28. Conference documents, Fort Hare, June 1994, op. cit., p. 19.
29. Roundtable on sustainable consumption and production, conference documents, Oslo, 8th December 1995.
30. Conference documents, Fort Hare, June 1994, op. cit.
31. Read "The development in mind", Introduction to *La natte des autres*. For endogenous development in Africa, Ed. Karthala / CRC, 1992, Paris, Dakar, p. 51; also the preface to Kélétigui Mariko, *La mort de la brousse, Ed.Karthala*, Paris, 1996, on the environmental degradation in Sahel.
32. M. Beaud with Calliope Beaud and Larbi Bouguerra (dir.), *L'état de l'environnement dans le monde* (The state of the environment in the world), Ed. La Découverte, Paris, 1993.
33. Cf. following site of references: : http://www.alliance21.org/2003/rubrique231.html; http://www.world-governance.org/IMG/pdf_Plateforme_web.pdf
34. Ed. La Découverte, Paris, 1992.
35. *Joseph Ki-zerbo: humanist, historian committed intellectual*, Proceedings of the International Conference held at UNESCO Headquarters, Paris, May 24, 2012. Version 25 June 2012, p. 25.
36. Cf. the right synthesis by H. Campbell, *Reclaiming Zimbabwe. The exhaustion of the patriarchal model of liberation*, David Philips, 2003, especially Chapter 7: "Executive lawlessness and the land issue in Zimbabwe". Campbell participated in the work of the Southern Africa Regional institute for policy studies (SARIPS) whose director was Sam Moyo, read "Agrarian Question and reconciliation in Zimbabwe", in Contemporary Zimbabwe, Ed Karthala, 1995, p. 211–274. It is symptomatic that Y. Tandon has prefaced the collection of recently published texts by the Centre Europe Tiers Monde (CETIM): *Julius Nyerere, Collected texts* introduced by Yash Tandon, Editions CETIM 96 pages, 2014.
37. The Charter published in the *African journal of political science* is available on line http://sanweb.lib.msu.edu/DMC/African%20Journals/pdfs/political%20science/volume2n2/ajps002002008.pdf
38. Op. Cit. (note 36), pp. 4–5.
39. Cf. *Land issues, food security and biodiversity*, CEDA, Ouagadougou, 2001.
40. The work *La Natte des autres* constitutes the Proceedings of the symposium.
41. Cf. *La Natte des autres* (The other's mat), p. 50: references to the work of Kenyan researcher Thomas Odhiambo. Of the latter, one can read a free access in 1975 conference on the website of the University of Nairobi: http://www.uonbi.ac.ke/sites/default/files/odhiambo%20T.pdf.
42. Cf. Augustin Kounkine SOME, *The collective struggle against impunity in Burkina Faso*. Civil society is mobilising against the killings orchestrated by the state apparatus, February 2001, consulted on February 6, 2015 on the link http://www.irenees.net/bdf_fiche-dph-5378_fr.html ; C. T. Miniwo, Burkina Faso, emergence of a 'social governance', in *Etat des résistances dans le Sud. Afrique*, Ed. Centre Tricontinental, Syllepse, 2010, pp. 87–92.
43. Cf. *ISGN Triennum program (2000–2002)*, "the international context", pp. 1–2.
44. ISGN Triennum program, p. 2.
45. See the site http://www.seatiniuganda.org/ consulted on January 12, 2015.

46. One of the latest activities of ISGN paid full tribute to Joseph Ki-Zerbo in the presence of former Zambia President Kenneth Kaunda; this was during the World Social Forum of Nairobi (2007).
47. Cf. R. Colin, *Sénégal notre pirogue, au soleil de la liberté*, Ed. Présence africaine, Paris, 2007.
48. See R. Balakrishnan, *International law from below. Development, social movements and third world resistance*, Cambridge University Press, 2003, 2004, pp. 146–161.
49. Cf. http://ap.ohchr.org/documents/dpage_f.aspx?s=58, about the 14/07/2014 A / HRC / RES / 26/9 resolution. Council of Human Rights on the elaboration of a legally binding instrument on transnational corporations and other business enterprises and rights. See the synthesis carried on (in French) this link: http://openews.eu/le-conseil-des-droits-de-lhomme-de-lonu-favorable-a-la-fin-de-limpunite-des-multinationales-la-france-et-lue-votent-non/
50. See http://www.cetim.ch/tncs-and-human-rights-succes-of-the-first-meeting-of-the-united-nations-working-group/
51. *Realising the Right to Development. Essays in Commemoration of 25 Years of the United Nations Declaration on the Right to Development*, OHCHR publication, consulted on January 9, 2015 on http://www.ohchr.org/EN/Issues/Development/Pages/RTDBook.aspx
52. R. Balakrishnan, op. cit. (note 48) , pp. 74–78.
53. Op. cit (note 48), p.74.
54. Op. cit. (note 48), p. 79.
55. Op. cit. (note 48), pp. 82–88.
56. Ibid.
57. See *The Darker Nations: A People's History of the Third World* (New Press People's History, 2008). The French translation of this title by *Les nations obscures* (The obscure nations) is not satisfying at all. We must not forget the struggle over the beauty of darkness as W.E.B du Bois envisioned it his fiction *Dark princess (1928)*, a romance between an African-American worker and an Indian princess.
58. See *Les droits de l'Homme en Afrique*, Ed. Pedone, Paris, 2002, p. 72.
59. See also art. 18 and 19: "*We protest against the atrocious crime of whipping, flogging and overworking of the native tribes of Africa and Negroes everywhere. These are methods that should be abolished and all means should be taken to prevent a continuance of such brutal practices*" and "*We protest against the atrocious practice of shaving the heads of Africans, especially of African women or individuals of Negro blood, when placed in prison as a punishment for crime by an alien race*". On Pan-Africanism and human rights see also D. Nault "A voice of tremendous power: Africa, the UN, and the emergence of third generation rights", paper presented at the 10th international conference of the Asia Association for Global Studies (AAGS), Tokyo, Japan, July 18–19, 2015; https://www.academia.edu/13490565/A_Voice_of_Tremendous_Power_Africa_the_UN_and_Third_Generation_Rights
60. See R. Balakrishnan, "The prohibition of torture and the normalisation of pain", op. cit., pp. 182–185.
61. *The loss of Eldorado: A colonial history*, Pan Macmillan, London, 2001.
62. *Are prisons obsolete?*, Seven Stories Press, New York, 2003.
63. K. Nubukpo, *L'improvisation économique en Afrique de l'Ouest, Ed. Karthala*, Paris, 2011; N. Agbohou, *Le franc CFA et l'Euro contre l'Afrique*, Ed. Solidarité mondiale, Paris, 2000.
64. Article 3, http://www.uemoa.int/Documents/TraitReviseUEMOA.pdf
65. "Central banks: do they have human rights obligations?" Issue No. 2, available online on the website www.rightingfinance.org
66. See Aisha Maniar, "Show me the money: can human rights offer an alternative discourse of resistance to austerity?" available on the website www.opendemocracy.net

# 8

# Bandung in an Interpolar Context
## What 'Common Denominators' Can the New Asian-African Strategic Partnership Offer?

*István Tarrósy*


## Abstract

The essay intends to point at the importance of the unique discourse that goes back 60 years to the conference of Bandung, and the non-aligned, the framework of a 'third way' of politics and solidarity during the bipolar world, but also with potentially lasting impact and implications for the interpolar globalism of the twenty-first century. It will critically look into the chances of a new intercontinental setting—maybe the New Asian-African Strategic Partnership (NAASP)—while acknowledge strongly developing processes, which overarch and interconnect co-operations of different kind in the form of summit diplomacy (such as TICAD, FOCAC, IAFS) driven by and organised on the basis of competing national interests of major Asian actors. How much can the 'Spirit of Bandung' stay relevant in our interpolar setting, and how the NAASP can mean a distinct framework of reference will be visited from a number of angles.


*Keywords:* interpolar, multipolar, Spirit of Bandung, Bandung conference, New Asian-African Strategic Partnership

## The Interpolar Context[1]

After the collapse of the Soviet Union and the dissolution of the Eastern Bloc, first, the international community had the feeling to experience a 'unipolar moment'[2], but gradually had started witnessing the 'emergence of a more multipolar world' (Smith 2012:52), with the United States of America as undoubtedly still 'by far the most powerful state on the face of the earth' (Mearsheimer 2006:113), and with an increasing number of emerging powers exerting a growing influence in the global arena. This is especially important as human communities have been facing a number of challenges of global nature—the hardest one to cope with being the events of 9/11 and what followed with the rise of transnational terrorism —, all of which need collaborative efforts to tackle. Some other views are also heard about the system of inter-and-transnational affairs: according to Richard N. Haass, for instance: "the principal characteristic of twenty-first-century international relations is turning out to be nonpolarity: a world dominated not by one or two or even several states but rather by dozens of actors possessing and exercising various kinds of power"[3]. Although his view on acknowledging the presence of 'numerous centers with meaningful power' is relevant, today's international context is best described as 'interpolar' with the moment when 'major global and regional powers cooperate to manage deepening interdependence, and build a viable and effective multilateral order' (Grevi 2009:7). Is there a chance for a newly defined (or rather re-confirmed) framework of solidarity and collaboration among Asian and African states to get more attention and voice in this interpolar globalism? How much can the 'Spirit of Bandung' contribute to the rise of Asian entities in Africa, and how much African agency can get strengthened via the special Afro-Asian relationship and its New Asian-African Strategic Partnership (NAASP)?

## Bandung and its revitalised Spirit?[4]

It is beyond doubt that sixty years ago, in April 1955, the Indonesian city of Bandung, in the words of Jawaharlal Nehru, 'became the capital of Asia and Africa' for a week. The conference of Bandung offered an opportunity in diplomatic terms for almost thirty countries to meet and lead talks over certain heavy issues affecting continents in a polarised world in a way that had not been possible earlier. The event itself had contributed to attaching greater value to the diplomatic significance of Asian and African countries and to allowing them to step into world politics as key factor with their 'third-way' proposals. Ampiah clearly argues, that the ambitions of conference participants 'were to be further channelled into an articulate and coherent 'third force' in a world supposedly frozen into two camps by the Cold War' (1999:39).

At the Bandung conference, as Kahin rightly underlined, "the delegates [...] were able to establish, or at least delineate much more clearly than before, several important common denominators of their international orientation" (Kahin 1956:1). We can agree with Lumumba-Kasongo, that most of the scholarly works published on the Bandung conference, to mention only a few such as: Kahin, McTurnan (1956); Nazli (1969); Mackie 2005; Seng and Amitav (2008); McDougall and Finnane (2010); Lee (2010), "underlined positive energy that derived from the conference toward the development of new way of thinking in terms of Africa-Asia relation and their collective relations with the European-American powers" (Lumumba-Kasongo 2015:6). His stance is also relevant especially in terms of critically examining the potential of the conference "to challenging the dominant system" (ibid). Can the 'Bandung Spirit' mean something extra/unique to countries of the Global South to position themselves with a substantial voice in a setting desired to be more equal and fair than in the past?

Although there have been promising macro indicators of a 'rising Africa' for the last ten years or so, it is better to stay cautious with the new mantra. "The ongoing dynamics deepen Africa's dependent position in the global economy", argues Taylor (2014:3). Problems are worsened as a result of the deepening inequalities among different parts of the world, which according to others, can be characterised by a neo-colonial global disorder, which is in favour of maintaining disparity as such. It seems that most of the countries of Africa get bogged in poverty and corruption, while Asian states are on the rise. "Where is the Afro-Asiatic solidarity today?", asked Claude Arpi in an article published in April 2005, at the fiftieth anniversary of the original conference. Did the philosophy of non-alignment ever really exist? According to Matthew Quest when giving a review of Richard Wright's *The Color Curtain* forty years later, "non-alignment was clearly a tactic, not a philosophy"[5], especially when during the Cold War skilful diplomacy was needed in manoeuvring among opposing bloc interests.

In 2003 South-African President Thabo Mbeki, the Non-Aligned Movement chair at the time "warned that the movement's future depended on its response to global challenges. He called on the NAM to take stronger resolutions on issues of concern"[6]. Almost the same was underlined by Josef Purnama Widyatmadja in his article entitled 'The Spirit of Bandung' appeared in The Jakarta Post on April 6, 2005: "Fifty years after the Bandung conference [...] Asian and African leaders seem to have lost their enthusiasm to fight for their aspirations. [...] it is important for Asia-Africa to engage in extensive dialogue to identify the challenges and opportunities the movement has to address [...] The role of Asia-Africa in promoting a just international order will depend largely on its inner strength, unity and cohesion". But is this cohesion a reality or a myth? How can this spirit be revitalised for the benefit of Afro-Asian linkages and more opportunities for the developing world?

## Multipolarity and the 'southern way'

What came out of Bandung 1955 has, no doubt, become fundamental for the international system, think about the Non-Aligned Movement (1961), the G77 (1964), the 'largest intergovernmental organisation of developing countries in the United Nations'[7], promoting South–South cooperation, or the Association of Southeast Asian Nations, ASEAN (1967).

Already during the Cold War a third point of reference and framework of political thoughts helped the participants of the Bandung conference, directing them towards a platform of expectations and intentions of the South. After the end of the bipolar world the new dichotomy of North and South and the newly defined aspirations of the now 'Global South' remained well articulated enough to let us think even more of a transforming system with not only one, but several centres of gravity, forming (slowly and gradually) a more multipolar setting. We are required to stay cautious enough, however, with 'today's multipolar mania', as William Wohlforth (2007:44) warns us in his clear power analysis. What we can easily do is to profoundly relate the position of the 'new actors' to that of the U.S. and foresee the potential redistribution of power in the international system in a gradually more multipolar environment. There are scholars who argue that in such an arena 'many nations will possess military and economic might sufficient to be recognised as greatpower states' (Yeisley 2011:75). Yet 'multipolarity's rapid return' (Wohlforth 2007:44) after the collapse of the Soviet Union, in the post-Cold War era, is not a realistic scenario in the short term, and time is needed before great power status is achieved by some of the emerging entities.

The majority of the critics of the non-aligned movement say that in the post-Cold War era NAM remained a kind of sleeping beauty. Poulose draws our attention to the role it may play in the new global climate; this includes "involvement in global environmental issues, contribution to the emerging global water crisis, ushering in a new world trade order, [...] [together with] campaign for the abolition of nuclear weapons and other weapons of mass destruction" (Poulose 2003:3), all helping set the international agenda focused on issues such as poverty, democracy and fair trade, all of them highly important for countries of the Global South. "At a time when no country, whatever its development status, can afford to go it alone", as Singapore's Minister of State for Foreign Affairs Zainul Abiden Rasheed noted at the conference entitled 'Globalisation and Economic Success: Policy Options for Africa' in November 2005, organised by the Brenthurst Foundation, South Africa, "it was appropriate [...] [to] reaffirm the ancient links of global commerce between Asia and Africa" (Mills et al. 2005:87). This statement also confirms the re-increased expectation about South-South co-operation, which should be enhanced by the more powerful member-states within NAM and the Group of 77 '(India, Brazil, South Africa, Nigeria, as well as Arab oil-producing countries) which have reached a higher degree of development and technological advancement' (Jazić 2005:66).

As I wrote in an article in the year of the 50th anniversary of the Bandung conference[8], third-way politics, or politics of the former Third World successfully influenced the thematic setting of the global agenda in the first years of the new Millennium. Today, North-South relations and the issues connected with the development of countries of the South have become one of the main inertia systems of our global world, and in formulating potential answers to global challenges, it is unimaginable that Southern views and demands, for example, the opinions and suggestions put forward by the non-aligned in the UN, are not taken into account per se. This leads us to the obvious conclusion that there is a need, ever increasing, for such southern dialogue and co-operation, along the traditional network of non-alignment, in the sense of alliance formation and concerted efforts, and coupled with what Jazić proposes, "a fight for multilateralism, the central role of the UN and its Millennium programs [...] make the existence of the NAM no less necessary than before" (ibid). I still think that to allow this 'third way', or better to say, 'southern way' to stay as a real alternative to global solutions, unanimous, clear and strict reforms must be carried out by the respective countries.

## New Asian-African Strategic Partnership (NAASP) Reaffirmed?

The 60th anniversary conference in April 2015 has produced some further re-encouraging rhetoric. Indonesian president Joko 'Jokowi' Widodo 'boldly declared before closing the conference: "This is [the] revival voice of Asian-African nations that cannot be replaced by anyone"[9]. Under the motto 'Strengthening South-South Cooperation to Promote World Peace and Prosperity' one main objective was to make a commitment to the 'Declaration on Reinvigorating the New Asian-African Strategic Partnership', which basically reaffirmed support for the New Asian-African Strategic Partnership accepted at the 50th anniversary event. The commitment to foster a 'stronger, more inclusive and sustainable' partnership was again stated. But what has the NAASP added to partnerships existing and working among countries of the Global South—on a bilateral basis, in a triangular framework or within a multiplayer setting? Triangular collaboration has been on the rise, for instance, since the early 2000s—without such a declaration and 'new' framework anyway. Twenty-first-century international relations show a different scenario compared with the bipolar setting, as there is a "shift from post-cold-war US-led unipolar to a multipolar global order in which the emerging powers of the global South will be key players [...] particularly in the face of the retreat of the Washington Consensus and its rather poor record in Africa" (Cheru and Obi 2010:1). The signatories of the Declaration on the New Asian-African Strategic Partnership underline exactly this aspect of their continued efforts to cooperate when they say: "[...] we have not yet attained commensurate progress in the social and economic spheres. We recognise the need to continuously strengthen the process of nation and state-building, as well as social integration" (NAASP 2005:1). We may agree with Cheru and Obi, therefore, when they also point out that what such a partnership—together with all other emerging schemes of involvement—seems to strive for in the case of Africa, for instance, is 'providing support and an enabling international environment for the [African] continent to chart its own alternative developmental course' (ibid).

When hearing such optimistic tones, also presented in the Declaration, it is better to stay critical, as does Ian Taylor in his book *Africa Rising? BRICS – Diversifying Dependency*[10], which rather raises attention about the extended group of entities that—as external forces—create more dependent linkages for African actors. Taking trade as a major connecting thread, Taylor points out that the structures of emerging countries with Africa "do not exhibit any exceptionalism and are comparable to the relationships established by the capitalist core since the colonial period" (2014:147). Taylor also emphasises that there are obvious opportunities for African states in diversifying their relations with all those 'hungry for' natural resources and new markets if the African agency can take control of its own resources. He also quotes Cabral[11] underscoring the 'starting point for any true rise of Africa': "national liberation takes place when, and only when, national productive forces are completely free of all kinds of foreign domination" (ibid:160).

To be able to produce a new political vision and all the necessary capacities for something 'different' though, signatories of Declaration want to stick to the Spirit of Bandung and African-Asian solidarity. They are also "committed to develop an institutionalised process of the NAASP" (2005:5), which at the same time is not an easy aspiration as far as the intergovernmental level is concerned. The text of the Declaration goes on saying that the already existing initiatives, such as the Tokyo International Conference on African Development (TICAD), the Forum on China-Africa Cooperation (FOCAC), or the India-Africa Summit Forum (IASF) will be complemented the NAASP, it is hard to see in concrete terms how such an idea can really turn into a functioning operation for the benefit of all parties involved.

## Concluding Remarks

Lumumba-Kasongo is right in emphasising that the essential political issue is "to develop first the state's welfarism as the foundation of African-Asian solidarity" (2015:16). This is what may then contribute to a new type of 'appreciation' of the new type of African-Asian solidarity and partnership initiative. As opposed to the international environment and momentum of 1955, today, representatives of African and Asian nations have a harder job to "clearly delineate common denominators of their international orientation", quoting again Kahin from 1956. Although in rhetoric there are still opportunities to make firm political distinctions from others (of the Global North), it remains very difficult to offer true alternatives not only as opposed to the U.S.-dominated neoliberal Washington Consensus, but also amongst themselves, compared with one another, for instance, to the African continent. Still, there may seem to be hope in terms of the tones and connotations, which are ever so important for close cooperation: all the entities of the system of Afro-Asian partnership want a change envisaging a "caring Asian-African society where the people live in stability, prosperity, dignity and free from the fear of violence, oppression and injustice" (NAASP 2005:3). This looks to stay a true driving force for the coming years.

## Endnotes

1. This part uses Tarrósy 2013.
2. As proclaimed by Charles Krauthammer in 1990. See Krauthammer, C., 1991, 'The Unipolar Moment', *Foreign Affairs*, Vol. 70, No. 1, pp. 23–33. and also Krauthammer, C., 2002, 'The Unipolar Moment Revisited', *The National Interest*, No. 70, pp. 5–17.
3. See Haass 2008 on the Internet: http://www.foreignaffairs.com/articles/63397/richard-n-haass/the-age-of-nonpolarity
4. The majority of the information on this section and the following one of the paper is drawn from Tarrósy 2005.
5. The article was downloaded from http://www.spunk.org/library/pubs/lr/sp001716/bandung.html
6. Mbeki's thoughts and the profile of NAM is summarised in an article published by BBC on http://news.bbc.co.uk/go/pr/fr/-/2/hi/in_depth/2798187.stm
7. As stated on the official website: http://www.g77.org/doc/ , having over 130 members today.
8. See Tarrósy 2005.
9. As reported by Prashanth Parameswaran in The Diplomat: http://thediplomat.com/2015/04/did-indonesia-revive-the-asia-africa-strategic-partnership/
10. See the full review of the book: Tarrósy 2015.

11. Cabral, A., 1979, *Unity and Struggle: Speeches and Writings of Amilcar Cabral,* New York: Monthly Review Press, p. 143.

## Bibliography

'Conversations in International Relations: Interview with John J. Mearsheimer (Part I),' *International Relations,* Vol. 20, No. 1, pp. 105–123.

'Declaration on the New Asian-African Partnership', Bandung, Indonesia, April 24, 2005.

Ampiah, K., 1997, *The dynamics of Japan's relations with Africa: South Africa, Tanzania, and Nigeria.* London, New York: Routledge.

Arpi, C., 2005, 'Was Bandung in vain?', rediff.com. 22 April 2005. Accessible on the Internet at: http://www.rediff.com/news/2005/apr/22claude.htm

Cheru, F. and Obi, C. (eds), 2010, *The rise of China and India in Africa. Challenges, opportunities and critical interventions,* London, New York: Zed Books – NAI.

Grevi, G., 2009, 'The interpolar world: a new scenario,' Occasional Papers No. 79, European Union Institute for Security Studies, pp. 1–44.

Haass, R. N., 2008, 'The Age of Nonpolarity', *Foreign Affairs,* May/June, Vol. 87, No. 3, pp. 44–56.

Jazić, Ž., 2005, 'The Non-Aligned Movement Yesterday and Today – in the Process of Globalisation: Critical View', Croatian International Relations Review. Vol. 11, No. 38–39, pp. 59–66.

Kahin, G. M., 1956, *The Asian-African Conference. Bandung, Indonesia, April 1955,* Ithaca, NY: Cornell University Press.

Lumumba-Kasongo, T., 2015, "Rethinking the Bandung conference in an Era of 'unipolar liberal globalisation' and movements toward a 'multipolar politics'", *Bandung: Journal of the Global South,* Vol. 2, No. 9, pp. 1–17.

Martin, A. S., 2012, *Power in the Changing Global Order. The US, Russia and China,* Cambridge-Malden: Polity Press.

Poulose, T. T., 2004, '13th NAM Conference. Rising Against Unilateralism', *Asian Affairs.* April 2003. Downloaded from the Internet at: www.asianaffairs.com/april2003/non_aligned_13.htm, accessed on May 5, 2005.

Smith, M. A., 2012, *Power in the Changing Global Order. The US, Russia and China,* Cambridge – Malden, MA: Polity Press.

Tarrósy, I. 2013, "'Chimerican' Interests, Africa Policies and Changing US-China Relations", *BiztPol Affairs,* Vol. 1, No. 1, pp. 11–28.

Tarrósy, I., 2005, 'Need for non-alignment in our global world? The Non-Aligned Movement Today and Tomorrow', *Croatian International Relations Review,* Vol. 11, No. 40–41, pp. 157–163.

Tarrósy, I., 2015, 'Africa Rising? BRICS – Diversifying Dependency by Ian Taylor', *Journal of Modern African Studies,* Vol. 52, No. 2, pp. 244–246.

Taylor, I., 2014, *Africa Rising? BRICS – Diversifying Dependency,* Woodbridge – Rochester, NY: James Currey.

Wohlforth, W., 2007, 'Unipolar Stability. The Rules of Power Analysis', *Harvard International Review. Spring,* Vol. 29, No. 1, pp. 44–48.

Yeisley, M. O., 2011, 'Bipolarity, Proxy Wars, and the Rise of China', *Strategic Studies Quarterly,* Vol. 5, No. 4, pp. 75–91.

# 9

# In Search of International Order

## From Bandung to Beijing, the Contribution of Afro-Asian Nations

*Mérick Freedy Alagbe*

## Abstract

For decades, aid-dependency and recurring calamities have earned the South a compassionate attention from the rest of the world. Political disorder, uprising, disease, ill governance, ethnic conflicts, drought, dire poverty etc. have been the striking features of that part of the world. Consequently, international donors, NGOs, UN peacekeeping missions streamed into the South to heal the traumas of its hapless people. This rousing generosity though highly desirable, has unfortunately overshadowed every inch of progress made by the developing world and downplayed the significance of its contribution to the world order. Yet, on different occasions, the developing world has taken a clear stance on international affairs and set a good example to the rest of the world. The Asian-African cooperation has particularly played a leading role in that field by repeatedly calling on the international community to abide by rules that promote peace and stability.

Two major events—when carefully considered with regard to their ultimate outcomes-add weight to this suggestion. These events refer to the Bandung Conference of April 1955 and the FOCAC meeting in Beijing in October 2000.

The article below scrutinizes the documents released at the closing of these two meetings and highlights the startling similarities they featured. It shows the great faith the Southern nations place in international institutions and rules that govern them. The South's ideal of a peaceful and stable world has remained unflinching from the launch of the Bandung initiative throughout the 20$^{th}$ Century. Another interesting point is the analysis of some new dynamics at work in the 21st Century's international relations, which challenge the long-standing North South division-based theory. Increasingly allusive challenges facing the world are progressively eroding the wall between the North and the South, forcing the international community to think globally and value principles and institutions that promote peace. Of course, there is still a long way to go before peace becomes reality. However, one must acknowledge that the resounding call made by the Asian-African cooperation in 1955 has definitely shed light on some of the crucial issues harming world stability.

*Keywords:* Africa-Asia, Bandung, China-Africa, International Order, North South cooperation

The definition of order hinges on two elements: First, a set of shared values and binding rules; next, a legitimate authority to enforce them. To the latter, H. Kissinger prefers "*a balance of power that enforces restraint where rules break down, preventing one political unit from subjugating all others*".[1] Yet, since the emergence of the Westphalia system, the world has been lurching from one crisis to another, failing miserably to set up these two intertwined pillars. So far, the dream of building a genuine international order has remained unreachable. On occasions, international order has embodied what a small cluster of powerful nations driven by national interests deemed convenient. As consequence, in default of an effective and fair international order, the world has resorted to systems of balance made of alliances and temporary coalitions. When facing major humanitarian disasters, as witnessed during the two World Wars, winners and losers will grieve together a fleeting moment, and then pick up the pieces and resume hostilities. These have been the unshakable rules governing the international relations since the inception of the modern world. The creation of international organizations and other decision-making bodies, and the adoption of a huge number of conventions and treaties have failed to change these firmly entrenched practices.

Among other factors hampering the establishment of an effective international order, is countries' sovereignty. The latitude tacitly granted to all sovereign States to join, dismiss or revoke any international agreement; to abide by or challenge any established authority or supranational leadership seems to be at the heart of the woes facing the world. The situation turned even more complex with the rise of new actors on the international scene following the demise of the State-based world after World War II. It is widely acknowledged today, more than ever before, that besides the mainstream Nation-States—the key players on the international scene—there is a growing number of new stakeholders viz. international organizations; multinational firms; NGOs; media; influential circles (religious organizations, professional consortia, lobbies etc.). Some analysts add to this endless list, with good reasons, lawless groups such as terrorist organizations, drug cartels, and irregular armed groups.[2] In such a complex environment, building up an international order is rather a tough job.

Yet, there have been some landmark political events in contemporary history of international affairs, which brought about relevant concepts of international order and suggested ways forward to a greater global stability. One of them was undoubtedly the Bandung Conference of April 1955. This first heartfelt appeal to the world in the post-World War II period, came from the Southern nations, most of them newly independent, entering the world stage and discovering a limping international system governed by rules, practices, foreign ideologies that are at odds with their internal reality, history and aspirations. These new States then started a long struggle through collective action for international recognition, by first creating the non-aligned movement in Belgrade in 1961. A long stream of achievements followed throughout the second half of the 20th Century.

Unfortunately, what the world recalls today of the historic meeting in Bandung is a vast gathering of disgruntled nations seeking to have a say in the international arena. Nevertheless, Bandung was far beyond this flimsy assessment and therefore needs to be rehabilitated in the current international context.

So, what is the legacy of that initiative? To what extent has, the Bandung Conference reshaped the international order? What have been the transformations observed in the Bandung *spirit* since the beginning of the 21st Century? Is the Bandung spirit still prevailing in the South?

## 1. The Contribution of the Bandung Conference

The final communiqué of the Bandung Conference[3] provided relevant ingredients for the building of an international order. Ingredients that can effectively preserve peace and the well-being of everyone. In the post-war ideologically divided world, where the search for allies and arm races have become the driving forces of cooperation between States, Bandung came opportunely to refocus attention on top priorities.

Two key elements emerged from the final communiqué: Firstly, the reminder of the common rules and secondly, the designation of the legitimate leadership. These two points spark interest as they heavily influence the international environment. Indeed, in the first half of the 1950s, the Bandung Conference revived the principles and values that represent the cornerstones of the governing of the world and hailed the universal role of the United Nations as an organization safeguarding these values. The 10 principles enshrined in the communiqué summarized the essential rules for guiding the world to more stability.[4] Some of them carried considerable weight in the context of the time. Among them are, *self-determination*; *non-interference in the internal affairs of States* and *respect for basic human rights*. The Bandung Conference also called on the international community to consider some key aspects impeding global stability. For this, the communiqué raised on one hand, the question of representation of developing countries within the UN agencies: "*The Conference considered that the representation of the countries of the Asian-African region on the Security Council, in relation to the principle of equitable geographical distribution, was inadequate*"[5]. On the other hand, the question related to the risk of nuclear proliferation: "*The Conference considered that disarmament and the prohibition of the production, experimentation and use of nuclear and thermo-nuclear weapons of war are imperative to save mankind and civilization from the fear and prospect of wholesale destruction*"[6]. These guidelines are essential in a world where only rivalries prevail.

The conference also put emphasis on the key role of the UN and recognized the institution as central to the organization of international relations. The UN Charter has remained the primary reference throughout the final communiqué regarding issues of great concern. More than just a reference to the UN, the Bandung Conference also known as Asian-African Conference, has attributed specific tasks to the UN, corroborating by this means its role as leader and judge on the international stage. On the chapter of international cooperation, the final communiqué mentioned that "*The Asian-African Conference, taking note of the fact that several States have still not been admitted to the United Nations [...] called on the Security Council to support the admission of all those States which are qualified for membership in terms of the Charter*".[7] In addition, in its call on nuclear arms, the Conference urges the United Nations to intensify their efforts towards disarmament. On the economic front, the Conference called on the United Nations to establish a fund for economic development to support developing countries. These recurring appeals position the United Nations as regulator of the international system. After all, the quest of the Bandung Conference can be defined in two ways: first, it was an attempt to draw attention on the existence of these new countries on the international stage and a bid to share their vision of what could be referred to as order within the international community. The South that is usually regarded as weak and poverty-stricken, pooled their strength together and mooted these guidelines at the Bandung Conference, for the building of a stable international society.

The legacy of Bandung has gone through generations and its spirit remained intact until the 21st Century. The new chapter in the Chinese-

African cooperation, which began with the first summit of the FOCAC (Forum of Cooperation on China-Africa) in October 2000 in Beijing, is an irrefutable testimony. Principles and Declarations of the FOCAC are part not only of the foundations laid by the Bandung Conference, but a resounding reminder of this historic event.

## 2. The Beijing Declaration as reminiscence of Bandung

The 21st Century opened with the advent of a new China-Africa cooperation. The first edition of the Forum on China-Africa Cooperation was launched in Beijing in October 2000. Since then, the forum brings together African and Chinese leaders at a pace of a summit every three years, alternately in Beijing and in an African city.

Few events have aroused as much passion, curiosity, questions, speculations and conceptualization as the Chinese-African cooperation. The presence of China on the African continent is breeding concerns in some capitals around the world. What are the socio-economic, security, cultural and political implications of this new partnership, as it portends a profound shift in the sharing of power in the international relations? These questions are particularly baffling for traditional global powers and cannot be neglected by them, given the weight in terms of financial resources and demography the China-Africa cooperation encompasses. According to figures from the PRB,[8] the Chinese population in 2015 is about 1,371,900,000 and that of Africa 1,171,000,000 representing more than one-third of the world population and making the FOCAC one of the most important multilateral negotiation frameworks in the world.[9] As for the resources, besides the demographic dynamism,[10] they relate firstly to China's colossal financial resources, fueled by an annual economic growth rate of 7.4% (despite the global gloom)[11], and secondly, to the vast reserve of natural resources in Africa (minerals, water resources, forestry, etc.). According to recent studies, China's trade with Sub-Saharan Africa has maintained its upward trend, reaching a total amount of US$170 billion in 2013.[12] Chinese FDI to Sub-Saharan Africa soared during the same period as well, representing 7% of global FDI flowing into the continent.

The Chinese-African cooperation is based on a set of texts, agreements and treaties that guide the FOCAC and inspire its action. Out of these documents, the Beijing Declaration of 12 October 2000 is the most important as it provides a synopsis of the principles of the Chinese-African cooperation, which actually take roots in previous similar initiatives.[13] The Beijing Declaration also expressed the way the two parties perceive the world in the 21st Century and their common conception of a stable and fair international order, thereby revealing its first great similarity to the final communiqué of the Bandung Conference. From an analytical point of view, readers may find startlingly similar the content of the two declarations despite the forty-five years gap between the two events. How could the Bandung *spirit* resist so tenaciously the erosive effect of time?

In the South a series of concerns and a certain perception of the world remained unchanged. Like a copycat of the Bandung outcomes, the China-Africa meeting in Beijing clearly reaffirmed the central role of the UN in maintaining international order. Much more than a framework for multilateral discussions, the United Nations is perceived as a key driver and supervisory body for global stability, hence the need to consolidate its authority. The Beijing Declaration refers to this stating that:" The *purposes and principles of the UN Charter [...] must be respected [...] The primary role of the UN Security Council in safeguarding world peace and security should be respected and enhanced and vigorous efforts should be made to push forward the reform of the United Nations and international financial institutions*"[14].

The Sino-African meeting emphasized the importance of this regulatory institution in a world where unilateralist impulses and abuses of sovereignty seriously threaten peace.

Similarly, some issues raised by the Bandung Conference were present on the agenda. People's self-determination and non-interference in the internal affairs remained a constant concern. In Beijing, the China-Africa Summit pointed out: *"No country or group of countries has the right to impose its will on others, to interfere, under whatever pretext, in other countries' internal affairs, or to impose unilateral coercive economic measures on others"*[15]. These principles while particularly protecting weaker countries, guarantee the stability and security of the world. Similarly, the question of the representation of developing nations in the UN agencies re-emerged. From the Beijing Declaration it is said that: *"The developing countries should be more adequately represented in the UN Security Council and international economic and financial institutions so as to fully reflect the democratic principle governing international relations".*[16] Both summits focused clearly on the Security Council, attaching therefore a specific requirement to their claim. This issue has also mobilized African leaders for decades, and many efforts have been made to reach a common ground.[17] Finally, on security issues, both documents also chime with each other in expressing serious concerns about the presence of nuclear weapons in the world and proliferation risks it breeds. The Beijing Declaration extends the final communiqué of Bandung when it stated that: *"All the parties concerned should strive to advance the process of disarmament and nuclear non-proliferation, with a view to realizing the ultimate goal of complete prohibition and thorough destruction of nuclear weapons and other weapons of mass destruction, so as to ensure security to all countries".*[18]

In short, from Bandung to Beijing, the South has made a concrete bid for a better regulation of the international relations. The relentless quest of the nations for order has found a relevant answer with these two historic summits. These initiatives of the South reflect a lucid awareness of their common exposure to abuses and bullying in the international system. The marginalization in major international decisions; the subjection to unfair rules and exposure to challenges facing the developing world, are among other reasons why these countries stuck together and managed successfully to build a common understanding of what an equitable world means. However, the 21st Century brings many changes in the international arena that modify the parameters for analysis and accelerate global convergences, necessary for the formation of a genuine international order. These developments impel us to rethink the Bandung *spirit* in its posterity.

## 3. Towards the Fulfilment of the Bandung Dream?

Bandung is an initiative from States that share the common identity of belonging to the South. This is a fundamental fact to consider because most of the issues raised by the Conference constituted a greater concern among those States, given their situation. The search for an alternative international order in the fragile and arbitrary system represents a vital need for these countries. Nevertheless, the 21st century ushered in a new era where course of events has been changing rapidly, with positive signals pointing ahead. The international environment has changed dramatically since the Bandung Conference. Traditional North-South fractures are somewhat blurred with the emergence of new challenges. Some key actors have seen their status deeply changed and their claims taken different emphases. New actors have appeared with powers sometimes underestimated. Even within the developing world, new positions have emerged and mark the entry into an era that could definitely be described as post-Bandung. What are the new ingredients of the current international configuration? What hope do they carry in leading the world to a more equitable order?

First, the traditional distinction between the North and the South essentially based on economic disparities has turned out to be meaningless in the globalized era. A. Kloke-Lesch and C. Gleichmann pointed that *"In the G20, industrialized countries and emerging economies do not meet as blocs representing the North and South. In the search for solutions to global problems, interests and alliances cut across traditional groupings".*[19] The same applies to the concept of Third World, which is blurred by the emergence of a multitude of subcategories and many outliers escaping any classification. Consequently, the world is no longer as clearly compartmentalized as it was in the mid-1950s. Therefore, the October 2000 Sino-African summit in Beijing, notwithstanding its coalition-like move of developing nations, cannot conceal the profound changes occurred in recent decades. While China continues to portray itself in official rhetoric as being a developing country[20], macroeconomic data and progress made in many areas over the last 40 years sharply belie this claim. Its role in the international aid system now earns it the name of "emerging donor".[21] At the same time, China appears to have designed its own aid principles.[22] Along the same lines of changes, a noteworthy emergence of a new category of developing countries occurred in early 2000, which dismissed the traditional binary reading of North and South. This new category is called BRICS.[23] The economic and diplomatic weight of this group reshuffles the cards and increases the pressure for some readjustments in the international system; at least the one of development cooperation.[24]

Beyond perceptible changes in the traditional categories, there is a beginning of convergence regarding some main concerns throughout the world. Political rallying slogans usually wielded by the South in collective actions are now echoing in the North and are not likely to lose resonance in the coming decades. Issues that were of great concern in the South have become global and many countries in the North are grappling with them. For example, *self-determination*, which was long a hobbyhorse in the South, has now insidiously taken root in the nationalism voiced by many peoples in developed countries. Sometimes it takes the form of separatist aspirations like in Belgium, Spain, and the UK, or it takes shape in the exaltation of some of the mundane far-right political bids from politicians as seen in France, Sweden, the Netherlands and the UK. The issues of poverty, wealth redistribution, public debt, blurring of cultural references are no longer the preserve of developing nations. It is noticeable that, doubt has grabbed peoples' long-standing and deep conviction of the superiority of their cultural model, and they are now rushing to search for recipes in the heart of the South. Jacques Attali, a distinguished French economist summarized the drift in these raw words:

*"We also should declare openly that Western civilization has something to learn from others. An efficient society should be able to organize both the expression of differences and the creation of an enduring collective view. Civilizations that draw on other philosophical and ethical beliefs—whether Confucianism or Buddhism—seem to be succeeding where we are failing in efforts to maintain human dignity, foster solidarity, and give long-term*

*meaning to our decisions by fostering a vision of what sort of world we hope to have in the 21st Century.*[25] *[...] Asian societies suggest possible answers to the contradictory tenets of the market and democracy; by allowing a stronger role for the state in protecting citizens against some of the risks of competition, these societies balance the contradictory forces".*[26]

Across the world, civil societies are pulling together actively, mobilizing somehow the same means against the same evils. The devastation inflicted to local economies by capitalism or the perpetuation of domination system are denounced with the same vigor in all parts of the world; and are giving rise to the same coalitions within civil societies. The birth of the anti-globalization movement in the late 1990s brought a dazzling demonstration.[27] The anti-globalization movement rallied people of all political hue, from all parts of the world against the prevailing international system. World public opinion had appeared so homogeneous and powerful on major international issues in the early 2000s that some analysts described it as a counter-power to the US hyper power.[28] In recent years, popular uprisings claiming more or less openly ties with alter-globalism grew and flourished everywhere and represented a fierce reaction against the international system. These include the *Occupy Wall Street* movement in the US; *Indignados* in Spain; the "*Y-en-a-marre*" movement in Senegal; even the so-called *Arab spring* revolts etc.

Also, the acceleration of globalization even though it has opened up new opportunities (markets, borders, labour mobility...), also brought its share of torment. Terrorism has become a global security issue, which is exported as easily as market goods and services. It threatens the interests of both poor and rich countries. Therefore, fighting against violence proponents requires global solidarity. Moreover, the very fast and tight interconnection between different parts of the world, strengthened by the development of transport and telecommunications is not without consequences for the tranquility of peoples. Epidemics can spread with great speed today as we witnessed with the EBOLA outbreak in West Africa, tricking containment systems in place even in the most developed countries. On the other hand, constant flow of information in this interconnected digital world, however useful it may be, also carries considerable disadvantages. Finally, global warming and its aftermaths is affecting mankind as a whole without distinction between rich and poor, nor developed and underdeveloped countries. Thus there's a growing clamor for reducing the gap between the North and the South in terms of environmental knowledge.[29] This common fate in the hardships of our existence brings together rich and poor and annihilates the cleaving Third World theories of previous decades. Therefore, the movement initiated in Bandung, which involved exclusively developing nations and those newly freed from colonial rule around common concerns, is doomed to wane in the 21st Century where challenges and anxieties are universally shared. It is not excessive to forecast that in the coming decades, the issues that will serve as a rallying point to only developing nations might become increasingly rare. Does this suggest that the world has become more homogeneous and more equitable? Such conclusions would certainly be clumsy or reckless because common exposure to the same challenges does not necessarily imply identical status or conditions. Development gaps between countries are still considerably wide. Moreover, the challenges outlined above do not arise to the same extent in all countries. However, as economic globalization inseparably goes along with "globalization" of threats, this might ultimately dam selfish national interests that have long undermined attempts to build an international order. The 21st Century revives hopes of a worldwide awareness and the possibility of establishing a balanced international order. The progress made in the negotiations at Paris climate conference in December 2015, the so-called COP 21, where all the 196 attendees agreed to limit greenhouse gas emissions between 1.5°C and 2°C by 2100, is perhaps the first chapter of this new era.[30]

## Endnotes

1. Henry Kissinger, *World Order*, London, Penguin Books, 2014, P.9
2. Fareed Zakaria, *Le Monde post-américain*, Paris, éd. Perrin, 2009, p. 42.
3. The Ministry of Foreign Affairs, Republic of Indonesia (Ed.). Final Communiqué of the AsianAfrican conference of Bandung. Djakarta 24 April 1955, pp. 161–169. Follow link http://www.ena.lu/final_communique_asian_african_conference_bandung_24_april_1955-2-1192 (For a French version, see Communiqué final de la Conférence Afro-Asiatique de Bandoeng, 24 Avril 1955, Annuaire Français de Droit International, 1955, Vol. 1, No. 1 pp. 723–728).
4. Ibid, p. 7.
5. Ibid, p. 6.
6. Ibid, p. 6.
7. Ibid, p. 5.
8. Population Reference Bureau, 2015 World Population Data Sheet, Washington DC, August 2015, pp. 11–14 http://www.prb.org/wpds/2015/
9. FOCAC today gathers 50 African countries (having diplomatic ties with China), the People's Republic of China and the Commission of the African Union.
10. Studies forecast 2.4 billion inhabitants for Africa by 2050. Population Reference Bureau, op. cit, p. 11. For other sources, see United Nations/Department of Economic & Social Affairs, World Population Prospect/The 2012 revision, New-York, Vol.1, réf: ST/ESA/SER.A/336, 2013 , p. 2.
11. IMF, World *Economic Outlook: Legacies, Clouds, Uncertainties*. Washington DC, October 2014 , p. 54.
12. Miria Pigato and Wenxia TANG "China and Africa: Expanding Economic Ties in an Evolving Global Context" World Bank/Investing in Africa Forum, March 2015, p. 2.
13. These principles were issued for the first time in April 1954 jointly by Zhou-en-lai and Nerhu in a bilateral treaty on Tibet. See "Agreement between the Republic of India and the People's Republic of China on Trade and Intercourse between Tibet Region of China

and India" Government of Republic of India, Ministry of External Affairs / Indian Treaty Series, Peking 29 April 1954.

14. The People's Republic of China, Ministry of Foreign Affairs, Beijing Declaration of the Forum on China-Africa Cooperation, Beijing 12 October 2000.
15. Ibid.
16. Ibid.
17. For further insight into the question, read Déclaration d'Harare (OUA, AHG/decl.3 (XXXIII), Déclaration sur la réforme du conseil de sécurité, 33e session ordinaire de la conférence des chefs d'Etat et de gouvernement, Harare, Zimbabwe, 4 juin 1997, p. 2) ; le Consensus d'Elzuwini issu des travaux du comité des « Quinze » (UA Ext./EX.CL./2(VII), Position commune africaine sur la réforme des Nations unies, 7e session extraordinaire du conseil exécutif, Addis-Abeba, 7–8 mars 2005, p. 10) or read MANOKOU Lucien, «L'Afrique et le Conseil de sécurité de l'ONU (1946–1990) », *Guerres Mondiales et Conflits Contemporains*, Paris, No. 196, décembre 1999, p. 10.
18. The People's Republic of China / Ministry of Foreign Affairs, Beijing Declaration of the Forum on China-Africa Cooperation, op. cit.
19. Adolf Kloke-Lesch and Colin Gleichmann, "Global development beyond the North- South paradigm", in Thomas Fues / Peter Wolff (Ed), *How can the new summit architecture promote pro-poor growth and sustainability?*, German Development Institute, Bonn 2010, p. 13.
20. Tull Denis M., "The Political Consequences of China's Return to Africa" in Alden Christopher, Large Daniel and de Oliveira Ricardo Soares (dir.), *China Returns to Africa: a rising power and a continent embrace*, London, C. Hurt & Co Publishers, 2008, pp. 111–128, p. 111.
21. The term was popularised by Jean Raphael Chaponnière to mean countries that are considered aid recipients but are allocating aid to poorer ones. See Chaponniere Jean Raphael «°L'aide chinoise à l'Afrique: origines, modalités et enjeux°», *L'Economie Politique*, No. 38, avril 2008, pp. 7–28, p. 9.
22. Kenneth King, in a remarkable analysis found that principles China apply to its aid program are not similar to the ones used by mainstream western donors. See Kenneth King, "China and Africa: new approaches to aid, trade and international cooperation", Comparative Education Research Centre, March 2006. p. 3.
23. The presence of Russia in this group does not allow it to be considered as belonging to the Third World.
24. "The Role of BRICS in the Developing World", European Parliament/ Policy Department, April 2012, p. 4. The study started with its executive summary mentioning this: "BRICS are at the forefront of using their economic weight to induce change, which is challenging traditional western donors in general and the EU in particular".
25. Jacques Attali, "The Crash of Western Civilisation: The Limits of the Market and Democracy", *Foreign Policy*, No. 107, summer 1997, pp. 54–64.
26. Ibid.
27. According to some analysts the alter-globalism movement owes its origin to the widespread resentment over the international system in both the South and the North.
28. Patrick E. Tyler, "Threats and Responses: News Analysis. A New Power in the Streets", *New York Times*, February 17, 2003. See article on : http://www.nytimes.com/2003/02/17/world/threats-and-responses-news-analysis-a-new-power-in-the-streets.html
29. Sylvia Karlsson, "The North-South knowledge divide: Consequences for Global Environmental Governance", Global Environmental Governance, p. 20.
30. See Center for Climate and Energy Solutions "Outcomes of the UN climate change conference in Paris" http://www.c2es.org/international/negotiations/cop21-paris/summary , consulted on January 31st, 2016. NB: The new US administration has withdrawn from the Paris agreement.

# 10

# The Former Soviet South in the Global South

## Reinvigorating "Bandung Spirit" as a Path Between Hegemonies?

*Jason E. Strakes*


## Abstract

While the recently independent nations of the former Soviet Caucasus and Central Asia exhibit many of the characteristics associated with post-colonial or developing states, the study of these countries in the U.S. and Western European academies has traditionally been relegated to a generic "post-communist" or "Russian and Eastern European" subfield. At the same time, much academic and policy discussion continues to frame their international relations according to narratives of an enduring geopolitical dichotomy between power centres representing "East" (Russia) and "West" (US/NATO/EU). This dominant perspective and discourse has caused many to overlook their evolving relationships with Asian, African, Middle Eastern and Latin American countries and institutions in the past two decades. Most recently, the major global powers have presented these states with a choice between two possible hegemonies: the neoliberal development model as represented by incorporation into Euro-Atlantic institutions and trade and investment regimes, and its alleged alternative advocated by Russia, Brazil, South Africa, India and China, as represented by the newly established structures of BRICS and post-Soviet regional integration projects such as the Russian-sponsored Eurasian Economic Union (EAEU). The present article poses the question of whether the principles embodied in the "Bandung Spirit" might offer a true alternative or "third way" that maximises both their political autonomy as newly sovereign nations, as well as their opportunities for sustainable and equitable development.

*Keywords:* Bandung Spirit, bipolarity, Caucasus, Central Asia, development, hegemony, post-Soviet

## Introduction

While the recently independent nations of the former Soviet Caucasus (Armenia, Georgia and Azerbaijan) and Central Asia (Kazakhstan, Kyrgyzstan, Tajikistan, Turkmenistan, and Uzbekistan) may exhibit many of the conditions and characteristics associated with "post-colonial", "developing" or "Global South" states—including struggles with hegemonic influences, economic inequality, political incapacity and unresolved conflicts—during the past two decades the study of these countries in the U.S. and Western European academies has typically been relegated to a generic "post-communist", "Russian and Eastern European" or "Eurasian" subfield. Although the comparability of the former Second and Third Worlds has been the subject of some debate in international relations and political economy since the 1990s (Skak 1996; Ma 1998; Snyder 1998; Sakwa 1999; Gammer 2000; Beissinger and Young 2002), much of this discussion has taken place within post-colonial studies, which originated in the field of literary criticism rather than the social sciences (Chioni-Moore 2001, 2006). Another justification for isolating the cluster of cases traditionally known by Sovietologists as the "Southern Tier" is their present self-delineation between "European" and "Asiatic" regions of the post-socialist space. Yet paradoxically, with limited exceptions (Vatanabadi 1996; Kandiyoti 2002; Adams 2008; Heathershaw 2010; Tlostanova 2010) it is the Baltic and Central Eastern European states rather than Muslim-majority Azerbaijan or the Central Asian republics that have been prominently identified as an appropriate domain for analysis and interrogation of post-colonialism (Kelertas 2006; Korek 2007; Annus 2011). The conventional classifications above have also been partly attributed to the significantly different condition of these countries from the traditionally defined Third World, as well as from one another (Tarkhan-Mouravi 2014, 98–100).

## Post-Soviet Development and Post-Colonialism: Distant Cousins?

Yet, a review of changes in economic and human development indicators within these sub-regions across time challenges this standard of separation. One prominent European research foundation suggests that in the early years of independence, the Caucasus and Central Asian states were included by international financial institutions (IFIs) and specialised agencies of the UN system in the category of "South countries", in which foreign assistance programmes were directed at the promotion of "development" rather than "transition" as in Central Eastern Europe (French National Research Agency 2011: 5). Other scholars have suggested the inclusion of those former Second World countries distinguished by a relative lack of advanced economic development—such as the five Central Asian republics—into a revamped or expanded category of "underdeveloped" nations (Maksoud, 1993; Randall, 2004: 43). While previous studies reveal that by the late 1990s, Eastern Europe and Central Asia exhibited rates of poverty comparable in both relative and absolute terms to Latin America and to a lesser extent Africa, in more recent years the majority of these states (save for impoverished Kyrgyzstan and Tajikistan) have become concentrated in the "middle-income" category defined by the World Bank, thus potentially facing the limited growth "trap" experienced by many developing countries (Bangura 2002: 5; Slay 2012). This perspective accepts the premise that during the late Soviet era, these societies experienced a level of modernisation comparable with that of the advanced Western industrialised nations, along with the international status and prestige associated with belonging to a superpower. At the same time, the socialist mode of development and its accompanying ideological doctrine of "national liberation" was advertised as a model for emulation by Asian and African nations, buttressed by the Russian academic tradition of Oriental Studies, or specialised training in the history, languages and literatures of "Eastern" countries. Yet with the collapse of centralised planning and state-directed production systems and sudden entry into the global economy, accompanied by drastic reduction in per capita gross domestic product (GDP) and a sharp increase in poverty rates, the former republics began a rapid decline to the status of a new "South", this time juxtaposed with the "North" located in the former Moscow metropole (Ohayon et al 2014: 3–5). It is this condition that introduces the question of domination and hegemony familiar to post-colonialism into the post-Soviet context. As the Caucasus and Central Asia have become highly susceptible to the influences projected by regional and global powers, along with the dramatic effects of the rapid introduction of neoliberal reform policies during the past two decades, the eventual recovery of economic growth has been linked to a transformation in the composition of GDP from major manufacturing and processing industries to the export of raw materials, agricultural goods and migrant labour combined with expansion of the service sector. According to this perspective, in contrast with the ideal of universal prosperity envisioned by multinational corporate globalism since the 1990s (Gurtov 2007: 8), this transition has instead solidified their position on the periphery of the "world-economy", or the advanced capitalist social system characterised by transnational trade and production processes as traditionally defined by scholars of the *dependencia* and world systems schools. However, the manner in which this process has transpired exhibits wide divergences and variations across post-Soviet countries (Ohayon et al 2014: 5).

At the same time, much academic and policy discussion continues to frame the international relations and external orientations of these countries according to narratives of an enduring geopolitical dichotomy between competing power centres representing a retrograde "East" (Russia and its allies) that seeks to preserve the previous order based upon authoritarianism, corruption and clientelistic economies, and a unified "West" (US/NATO/EU), in which liberal democracy, social progress and economic prosperity prevail. This popular ideological construction serves to reinforce and perpetuate their perceived status as once-and-future imperial subjects versus achieving "sovereignty" and "independence" (i.e., the freedom to integrate with Western institutions), rather than identifying those factors that might allow them to attain real social, political or economic transcendence according to their own interests and needs. In turn, this prevailing perspective and its associated discourse has caused many to overlook their evolving relationships with Asian, African, Middle Eastern and Latin American countries as well as institutions representing the interests of developing nations in the past two decades.

For instance: based upon their productive diplomacy with states in South and Southeast Asia and longstanding membership in forums such as Organisation for Islamic Cooperation (OIC), representatives of Azerbaijan and all five Central Asian republics attended the April 2005 Asian-African Summit held in Jakarta, Indonesia on the 50th anniversary of the 1955 Bandung Conference, while Azerbaijan, Kazakhstan and Tajikistan were signatories to the first Declaration on The New Asian-African Strategic Partnership (NAASP), which sought to revitalise its principles and objectives for the 21st Century (Republic of Indonesia MFA, 2005, 2009). The document also laid the foundations for the NAASP Capacity Building for Palestine Coordinating Unit co-chaired by Indonesia and South Africa and implemented by the Palestinian National Authority (PNA), through which Jakarta has served as programme funding coordinator for Azerbaijan along with twenty other developing nations. Azerbaijan, Kazakhstan and Kyrgyzstan were participants in the follow-up and evaluation mechanism NAASP Ministerial Conference on Capacity Building for Palestine in July 2008, while the NAASP Coordinating Unit meeting in Amman, Jordan in June 2009 reported that Kazakhstan had contributed humanitarian assistance to the PNA in the equivalent of $150,000, while Kyrgyzstan was among the countries that pledged to implement seven related projects in the near future (Kingdom of Thailand MFA, 2009; *Tabloid Diplomasi* 2010: 11). Azerbaijan and all five Central Asian states further sent delegates to the Asia-Africa Youth Forum of NAASP member countries on achievement of the UN Millennium Development Goals (MDGs) at Bandung in August 2010 (Asia-Africa Youth Forum 2010: 3). Other recent examples of such common identification are provided by the case of Tajikistan, which in September 2010 became the second former Soviet republic (following Turkmenistan) to enter the Group of 77 & China after a decade of activism in international organisations related to sustainable development issues; and Azerbaijan, which in May 2011 became the fourth (following Uzbekistan, Turkmenistan and Belarus) to enter full membership in the Non-Aligned Movement (NAM) after seventeen years of observer status. Most recently, representatives of Azerbaijan and Kyrgyzstan also delivered addresses pertaining to major national and international issues—the Armenia-Azerbaijan Nagorno-Karabakh conflict in the first instance, and the global development-security nexus in the latter—at the Summit of the 60th Asian-African Conference Commemoration (AACC) and 10th Anniversary of the NAASP in April 2015, while Azerbaijan, Kazakhstan and Kyrgyzstan sent delegates to the New Asia-Africa Youth Conference Plus 2015 held in Bandung during the same month (Kabar 2015; News.Az 2015).

## Hegemony and Counterhegemony: A New Bipolarity?

Yet, most recently the major global powers have presented the governments of these states with a framed "choice" between two possible developmental futures: one signified by continued incorporation into the global neoliberal architecture through integration into Euro-Atlantic institutions and trade and investment regimes via mechanisms such as the Eastern Partnership (EaP) Association Agreement/Deep and Comprehensive Free Trade Area (AA/DCFTA), and its ostensible "multipolar" or "counterhegemonic" alternative advocated by mid-level or emerging powers such as Russia, Brazil, South Africa, India and China. These are represented by the newly established structures of BRICS, in particular the New Development Bank (NDB) founded in July 2015, as well as post-Soviet regional integration projects such as the Russian-sponsored Eurasian Economic Union (EAEU), which was formally inaugurated together with Belarus and Kazakhstan in January 2015. Despite promotion of the expected "benefits" to their societies of either option in public diplomacy and popular commentary, both arrangements are essentially asymmetric in character. Whereas the first imposes requirements on recipient states to implement costly domestic legal and institutional reforms to harmonise their political and economic systems with Brussels without guarantees of either short-term improvements in standards of living or eventual accession, the second involves submission to potentially restrictive and suboptimal common external tariff and non-tariff barriers and customs regulations, as well as acceptance of obvious power differentials represented by Russia's regional dominance and pursuit of global power status. While crisis-ridden Ukraine, Moldova and Georgia became signatories to the former in June 2014, Armenia and Kyrgyzstan have both acceded to the latter in January and May 2015 respectively, with EAEU membership under consideration by the government of Tajikistan.

However, in reality all three Caucasus states had already established preferential trade relations with the European Union under the United Nations Conference on Trade and Development (UNCTAD) Generalised System of Preferences Plus (GSP+) programme introduced by the European Commission in December 2008, which granted tariff-free market access to thirteen other developing countries including Bolivia, Colombia, Costa Rica, Ecuador, Guatemala, Honduras, Sri Lanka, Mongolia, Nicaragua, Peru, Paraguay, El Salvador, and Venezuela (UNCTAD 2008: 15). At the same time, over 30 African, Middle Eastern, South, and South/East Asian states including Zimbabwe, Egypt, Iran, Syria, Jordan, India, Mongolia, China, Vietnam and Japan have expressed interest in concluding free trade agreements with or membership in EAEU, as its emphasis on non-interference in domestic affairs in favour of pragmatic economic cooperation has made it compatible with previous efforts at Asian regionalism and South-South cooperation (Satubaldina 2015).

These ambiguities identify an important qualification lurking within the professed challenge to the international political and economic status quo presented by BRICS/EAEU: the distinction between "emergence", or the genuine generation of wealth across sectors of the national economy through mobilisation of productivity at all levels of society, and "submergence" or "lumpen development", as characterised by the rapid expansion of the middle classes through natural resource-export driven growth alongside drastic increases in income inequality (Bandung Spirit 2015: 3). This interpretation is underscored by the fact that while Russia may exhibit the strongest economic performance relative to the Caucasus and Central Asia, it is major local energy (oil and natural gas) producers such as Azerbaijan and Kazakhstan that have achieved the highest levels of annual per capita GDP (Asian Development Bank 2009: 131; International Business Publications 2015: 34). Such distinctions thus demonstrate the potential for the emergence of intraregional hegemonies that complicate the simple assignment of a "North-South" or "core-periphery" division to the post-Soviet domain (Thorez 2014: 222).

## Conclusion

Two main questions therefore result from the discussion above: First, how might the principles embodied in the "Bandung Spirit" offer a viable alternate strategy or "third way" that maximises both the self-determination of post-Soviet countries as recently sovereign nations, as well as their opportunities for sustainable and equitable development? Secondly, how might these conceptual and practical issues be addressed using the analytical tools and approaches familiar to the study of international relations? A significant obstacle to this effort is presented by the tendency for observers to analyse the foreign policies of these countries within a narrow East-West framework, rather than recognising their increasing interest in and pursuit of cross-regional diplomacy during the past decade. A concise explanation for this trend is provided in the context of economic development, as Azerbaijan and the Central Asian republics in particular are "more focused on building relationships with South Asia, Sub-Saharan Africa and Latin America rather than...[the] traditional Euro-Atlantic construct. These aforementioned regions represent reciprocating markets and resources, while the EU limits their trade horizons with its trade quotas"[1].

Thus, in order to surmount this definitional dilemma, a necessary task for analysts and policymakers alike is to question or even challenge the paradigm of enduring bipolar competition that has become institutionalised in academic and public discourse on post-Soviet and Eurasian affairs. One such method would be to develop a comparative framework for analysing the participation of the eight states of the Caucasus and Central Asia in Asian-African institutions and South-South cooperation since independence in 1991. This would identify and examine the causal links between their domestic developmental characteristics, their appraisals of hegemonic and counter-hegemonic arrangements in the international order, and the compatibility of their foreign policy approaches with the ten Bandung principles as reaffirmed in the documents of Global South conventions such as NAM, NAASP, and AACC. For instance: Since full inclusion into the NAM, Azerbaijan has expressed strong identification with the Bandung principles in its public diplomacy, although its participation in its deliberative mechanisms has yet to develop more fully beyond seeking support among member states for its campaign for the non-permanent UN Security Council seat from 2012–2013 and its position in the Nagorno-Karabakh conflict (Strakes 2015a: 16). In recent years Armenia, Azerbaijan, and Kazakhstan have become active in the UN Alliance of Civilizations (UNAOC) and the Malaysia-sponsored Global Movement of Moderates (GMM) as referenced in paragraph 8 of the Bandung Message 2015, while Azerbaijan, Kazakhstan and Turkmenistan voted in favour of the UN General Assembly "Culture of Peace" draft resolution in June 2015 (Bandung Message 2015: 2; UNGA 2015: 1). Armenia and Kazakhstan (to be followed by Kyrgyzstan) signed and ratified the Multilateral Agreement on Establishing an International Think Tank on Landlocked Developing Countries (LLDCs) based in Ulaanbaatar, Mongolia in October 2010 (referenced in paragraph 26 of the Bandung Message 2015), which implements research programs to promote regional trade and development (Bandung Message 2015: 6; UN 2010). Representatives of the financial sector from Armenia, Azerbaijan, Kyrgyzstan and Tajikistan attended the Asia-Pacific High-Level Consultation on Financing for Development sponsored by the United Nations Economic and Social Commission for the Asia-Pacific (UNESCAP) and the Indonesian Ministry of Foreign Affairs in preparation for the Third International Conference on Financing for Development (FfD) in Addis Ababa, Ethiopia in July 2015 (Bandung Message paragraph 26), in which the first major post-Soviet donor institution, the Azerbaijan International Development Agency (AIDA) played a prominent role (Bandung Message 2015: 6–7). In contrast, as the smallest and poorest nation in Central Asia, Tajikistan has assumed a foremost position in development diplomacy and global governance concerns (MDGs/SDGs) due to its intimate relationship with the UN specialised agencies, aligning itself with the Group of 77 & China in multiple issue areas, and participating in various Asian regional organisations in order to secure foreign assistance and investment, as well as attaining observer status in NAM in 2009 (Strakes 2015b). In sum, a more systematic consideration of the variables that influence these policies could provide a template for interpreting the motivations of post-Soviet states in seeking to move beyond the residual (or reconstructed) power structures of the Cold War, towards the attainment of true political and developmental autonomy within the contemporary international system.

## Endnote

1. Correspondence with Zhyldyz Oskonbaeva, Senior Advisor and Eurasian Liaison at Research Institute for European and American Studies, and co-founder of Black Sea Caspian Sea International Fund (BSCSIF), 13 July 2015.

## Bibliography

Adams, Laura L. (2008), "Can We Apply Postcolonial Theory to Central Eurasia?" in *Central Eurasian Studies Review*, Volume 7, Number 1, Spring, pp. 2–7. http://centraleurasia.org/wp-content/uploads/2013/01/CESR-VII-1.pdf

Asia-Africa Youth Forum (2010), *Reviving Asia-Africa Spirit to Accelerate the Achievement of MDGs. Administrative Arrangements*, Bandung, 23–27 August. http://sman28jkt.sch.id/userfiles/file/Aministrative%20arrangement%20AAYF%20final.rtf

Asian Development Bank (2009), "Azerbaijan", in *Asian Development Outlook 2009: Rebalancing Asia's Growth*. March http://www.adb.org/Documents/Books/ADO/2009/AZE.pdf

Annus, Epp (2011), "The Problem of Soviet Colonialism in the Baltics" in *Journal of Baltic Studies*, Vol. 43, No. 1, pp. 21–45.

Bandung Message (2015), *Strengthening South-South Cooperation to Promote World Peace and Prosperity*. http://www.bandungspirit.org/IMG/pdf/bandung_message_2015.pdf

Bandung Spirit (2015), *Building Sovereignty, Preventing Hegemony: The Challenges for Emerging Forces in the Globalised World*, http://www.bandungspirit.org/IMG/pdf/bandung_60–tor-main_text.pdf

Bangura, Abdul K. (2002), *Mario Fenyo on the Third World: A Reader*, Writer's Club Press.

Chioni-Moore, David (2006), Is the Post- in Postcolonial the Post- in Post-Soviet? Toward a Global Post-colonial Critique, in Violeta Kelertas (ed.), *Baltic Postcolonialism*.

____ (2001), Is the Post- in Postcolonial the Post- in Post-Soviet? Toward a Global Post-colonial Critique, *PMLA*, Vol. 116, No. 1, pp. 111–128.

Beissinger, Mark and Crawford Young (eds.) (2002), *Beyond State Crisis?: Postcolonial Africa and Post-Soviet Eurasia in Comparative Perspective* (Washington, DC and Baltimore, MD: Woodrow Wilson International Center for Scholars Press and Johns Hopkins University Press).

French National Research Agency (2011). "Conference Concept Paper" in *The Caucasus and Central Asia, twenty years after independences: Questioning the notion of South countries*, 25–27 August, Almaty, Kazakhstan, pp. 5–6. http://www.cercec.fr/materiaux/doc/publications/2011%20–%20The%20Caucasus%20and%20Central%20Asia,%20twenty%20years%20after%20.pdf

Gammer, Moshe (2000), "Post-Soviet Central Asia and Post-Colonial Francophone Africa: Some Associations" in *Middle Eastern Studies*, Vol. 36, No. 2 (April).

Gurtov, Mel (2007), *Global Politics in the Human Interest*. 5th Edition, Lynne Rienner Publishers.

International Business Publications (2015), *Kazakhstan: Energy Policy Laws and Regulations Handbook*, IBP Inc, USA.

Kabar Agency (2015), "Deputy Foreign Minister of KR participated in Ministerial Council and Asia-Africa Summit", 24 April. http://kabar.kg/eng/politics/full/12816.

Kandiyoti, Deniz (2002), "Post-Colonialism Compared: Potentials and Limitations in the Middle East and Central Asia" in *International Journal of Middle East Studies* 34, pp. 279–297.

Kelertas, Violeta (ed.) (2006), *Baltic Postcolonialism* (On the Boundary of Two Worlds: Identity, Freedom, and Moral Imagination in the Baltics, Vol. 6), Amsterdam and New York: Rodopi.

Korek, Janusz (2007), *From Sovietology to post-coloniality: Poland and Ukraine from a postcolonial perspective*. Stockholm: Södertörn Academic Studies 32.

Ma, Shu-Yun (1998), "Third World studies, development studies and post-communist studies: definitions, distance and dynamism" in *Third World Quarterly*, Vol. 19, No. 3, pp. 339–348.

Maksoud, Clovis (1993), "Redefining Non-Alignment: The Global South in the New Global Equation" in Phyllis Bennis, Michel Moushabeck (eds.), *Altered States: A Reader in the New World Order*, New York: Olive Branch Press, pp. 28–37.

News.Az (2015), "Azerbaijani Delegation Attends Asian-African Conference in Jakarta", 24 April. http://www.news.az/articles/politics/97389

Ohayon, Isabelle, Silvia Serrano and Amandine Regamey (2014), "Introduction: The Post-Soviet Caucasus and Central Asia: Another South?", in Sophie Hohmann, Claire Mouradian, Silvia Serrano, Julien Thorez (eds.), *Development in Central Asia and the Caucasus: Migration, Democratisation and Inequality in the Post-Soviet Era*. Paris: I.B. Tauris, pp. 1–16.

Randall, Vicky (2004), "Using and Abusing the Concept of the Third World: Geopolitics and the Comparative Political Study of Development and Underdevelopment" in *Third World Quarterly*, Vol. 25, No. 1, pp. 41–53.

Republic of Indonesia, Ministry of Foreign Affairs (2010), "Bandung Spirit: Dukungan Negara Asia-Afrika untuk Kemerdekaan Palestina" in *Tabloid Diplomasi*, No. 33 Tahun III, Tgl. 15 Juli-14 Augustus.

____ (2009), "Declaration on the New Asian-African Strategic Partnership" in *The New Asian-African Strategic Partnership (NAASP) Senior Officials' Meeting (SOM)*, Jakarta, 12–13 October 2009. http://kemlu.go.id/Documents/NAASP/Hyperlink%201.pdf

____ (2005), "List of NAASP Participating Countries: Asian Countries". http://kemlu.go.id/Documents/NAASP/Hyperlink%204.pdf

Sakwa, Richard (1999), "Postcommunist Studies: Once Again through the Looking Glass (Darkly)?" in *Review of International Studies*, Vol. 25, No. 4, October, pp. 709–719.

Satubaldina, Assel (2015) "Over 30 countries interested in signing free trade agreement with EEU" in *Tengri News*, 21 July. http://en.tengrinews.kz/politics_sub/Over-30–countries-interested-in-signing-free-trade-agreement-261289/

Skak, Mette (1996), *From Empire to Anarchy: Postcommunist Foreign Policy and International Relations*. London: Hurst & Company.

Slay, Ben (2012), "The 'Rise of the South' and post-communist Europe and Central Asia" in UNDP in Europe and Central Asia, 14 November. http://europeandcis.undp.org/news/show/87D85445–F203–1EE9–BBF1704483E89CCC

Snyder, Jack (1998), "Introduction: Reconstructing Politics amidst the Wreckage of Empire" in Barnett Rubin and Jack Snyder (eds.), *Post-Soviet Political Order: Conflict and State-Building*. NY: Routledge.

Strakes, Jason E. (2015), "Azerbaijan and the Non-Aligned Movement: Institutionalizing the 'Balanced Foreign Policy' Doctrine" in *Istituto Affari Internazionali (IAI) Working Paper Series 15/11*. http://www.iai.it/sites/default/files/iaiwp1511.pdf

____ (2015), "Tajikistan in the Global South: Development Diplomacy, Non-Traditional Security and International Prestige" in *Norwegian Institute for International Affairs (NUPI) and OSCE Academy Central Asia Policy Briefs No. 27*, Bishkek, July 2015. http://www.osce-academy.net/upload/file/Policy_Brief_27.pdf

Tarkhan-Mouravi, George (2014), "Functional Clusters and Diverging Paths in Post-Soviet South: The Georgian Case" in Sophie Hohmann, Claire Mouradian, Silvia Serrano, Julien Thorez (eds.), *Development in Central Asia and the Caucasus: Migration, Democratisation and Inequality in the Post-Soviet Era*. Paris: I.B. Tauris, pp. 98–121.

Thorez, Julien (2014), "The Post-Soviet Space Between North and South: Discontinuities, Disparaties and Migrations", in Sophie Hohmann, Claire Mouradian, Silvia Serrano, Julien Thorez (eds.), *Development in Central Asia and the Caucasus: Migration, Democratisation and Inequality in the Post-Soviet Era*. Paris: I.B. Tauris, pp. 215–241.

United Nations (2010), *Multilateral Agreement on Establishing an International Think Tank on Landlocked Developing Countries*. https://treaties.un.org/doc/source/signature/2010/X-19.pdf

United Nations Conference on Trade and Development (2008), *Generalized System of Preferences: Handbook on the Scheme of the European Community*, United Nations: New York and Geneva. http://unctad.org/en/Docs/itcdtsbmisc25rev3_en.pdf

United Nations General Assembly (2015), 69th Session, Agenda Item 14, Culture of Peace, 25 June. http://www.unaoc.org/wp-content/uploads/UNAOC-Resolution-2015.pdf

Vatanabadi, Shouleh (1996). "Past, Present, Future, and Postcolonial Discourse in Modern Azerbaijani Literature" in *World Literature Today*, Vol. 70, No. 3, Literatures of Central Asia, pp. 493–497.

# 11

# Scripting the Change

## Bandung+60 Engaging with the Gender Question and Gendered Spaces

*Seema Mehra Parihar*


## Abstract

Emancipation of women even today after 60 years of evolution of 'Bandung spirit' as a concern is 'livid' and have coerced 'Gender question' immediate and urgent. Gendered spaces are largely fragmented and fractured in the contemporary world. The empirical evidence across the emerging and third world countries indicates that the neoliberal policies have not been successful in including those excluded in the mainstream development process. Even today in 100 countries around the world women are not allowed solely to do certain works because they are women (Indrawati, 2015). Noting the considerable criticism of research and studies into the status of women which were undertaken on a sectorial basis, entirely divorced from all circumstances of a given society, the paper contextualises gendered spaces, integrating gender expansiveness in existing social, economic and political space. This study engages the question of gender mainstreaming and presence of gendered spaces in Asia. The methodology adopted appraises gender, wearing largely an Indian lens through secondary data analysis from different government reports of India (2000–2014). Literature review from different parts combined with UN and World Bank Reports helped further in understanding the significance of the context. This paper aims to contribute and participate in scripting the change, raising and revisiting the gender related developments, tackling multiple intersecting inequalities to mainstream gender identities and concerns across policies, plans and programmes, without negotiating their presence and visibility.

*Key words:* Collocation of Equity and Inequity, Gender Expansiveness, Wave Narratives, Gender Mainstreaming, Gendered Spaces

"To young women in the global North, eating disorders are a major problem, but to women in the global South, eating disorder means not having enough rice in your bowl"
(Robin Morgan[1])

## Introduction

Gendered spaces are largely fragmented and even fractured in the contemporary world with existing post-feminist, post-patriarchal and gender equal spaces on one hand and to several spaces divided on gender lines physically and mentally with little or no role of women agency on the other. It seems that commitment to gender equality and empowerment is still in emergent stage in many parts of the Global South, especially in Asia and Africa. Noting the considerable criticism of research and studies into the status of women which were undertaken on a sectorial basis, entirely divorced from all circumstances of a given society, the paper contextualises these questions at Bandung+60 in a holistic way, integrating gender expansiveness in existing social, economic and political spaces. This study engages the question of gender mainstreaming and presence of gendered spaces in Asia based on following assumptions: (i) Gender equality is achievable; (ii) Gender identity is expansive, yet misunderstood; (iii) Gender wave narratives are misplaced in Asia; (iv) Social, political and economic development cannot ignore women work force; and (v) Mainstreaming gender cannot avoid the question of gender conflict. The adopted methodology appraises gender, wearing largely an Indian lens through secondary data analysis from different government reports of India (2000–2014). Literature review from different parts combined with UN and World Bank Reports helped further in understanding the significance of the context. The introduction of '*Gender Group*' for the first time at Bandung+60, as suggested in Paris meeting (Khudori, 2014[2]), aims at gender mainstreaming at all stages of policy process, be it local, state, national and international level through a formulation of new development framework (under negotiation) in 2015. This paper aims to contribute to this dialogue and participate in scripting the change raising and revisiting the gender related developments, tackling multiple intersecting inequalities to mainstream gender identities and concerns across policies, plans and programmes, without negotiating their presence and visibility.

## Background

The last century is remembered not just for the wars that devastated the world, but also for the rise of nationalism in the "Third World" (formerly colonised countries of Africa, Asia and Latin America, called also developing countries, now the South) and the process of widespread decolonisation. Non-Aligned Movement (NAM) contributed to the historic development and became a forum for the Third World to find one voice and to lay its claim to the world's wealth, power, politics, history and culture. It became not just a significant force because it had numbers, but it was also a progressive force. It militated against ideas of oppression, colonialism, discrimination, racism, imperialism, and neo-colonialism. The 1955 Bandung Asian-African Conference gave voice to one and many living in Asia and Africa through an idiom: *Bandung Spirit*, with one of the messages for building solidarity towards the poor, the colonised, the exploited, the weak and those being subjugated by the world order of the day and for their emancipation (Khudori, 2014[3]). However, today, 60 years after the Bandung Conference, domination by the powerful in the world order still persists. The empirical evidence across the emerging and Third World countries indicates that the neo-liberal policies have not been successful in including those excluded in the mainstream development process. Even today in 100 countries around the world women are not allowed solely to do certain works because they are women (Indrawati, 2015[4]). World Bank Report[5] (2015) validates the inequality and disparity: *"More than 150 countries have at least one law discriminating against women; 59 countries have no law against sexual harassment at work; 46 countries have no legal protection against domestic violence; 32 countries have different ways for applying for passport by men and women and in 18 countries women cannot get jobs if their husbands feel it is not in the family's interest. Only 18 countries are free of any law disadvantaged women and further only 9 countries have laws where at least one woman has to be board member of a publicly listed company"*. This only represents the need and support that so many women still need if the agenda is genuinely of inclusion and removal of poverty.

## Bandung+60 engaging with the Gender Question and Gendering spaces

Emergence and growth of women's movement since last century is engaged with liberation of women from centuries of oppression in different places and spaces across regions everywhere in the world. Emancipation of women even today after 60 years of evolution of 'Bandung spirit' as a concern is 'livid' and have coerced 'Gender question' immediate and urgent, as it was many decades before. Multiple theoretical analyses emerging from different women's movements and solutions have raised the urgency to missing gaps and newer oppressions. The women's movement has challenged the present patriarchal, exploitative society, both through its activities and through its theories. It is not that women were earlier unaware of their oppression. In fact, they articulated this oppression in various ways—through folk songs, pithy idioms and poems, paintings, and other forms of art to which they had access to. The present section helps us in understanding and raising new gender labelled questions amidst different spaces kindled by new agencies articulated through local women.

## 1. Insular Gender Spectrum and Gender Expansiveness: Nomenclature concerns

'Gender' and 'Sex' is all around us with different implication in different spaces and sections across social, economic and cultural hierarchy. Understanding of the Sex/Gender Distinction is very hazy and inadequate, and therefore delimits the choices assigned for their usage and usefulness. Sometimes, they are used interchangeably. The first clarification therefore emanates from the basic query related to its meaning and like any new discipline demands a need for discourse addressing itself to new hypothesis, questions and complications, thereby evolving and developing its own language and conceptual apparatus. Therefore, the most indispensable fundamental starting point should be the recognition of the nature and the basis of this division. Feminism did not however create the terminology of sex and gender. It was in English language that it was used while differentiating between sex and gender. The term 'Sex' whereas, was used to distinguish between male and female, the gender too though was given the same meaning and the examples can be found many centuries back. The more general usage of gender has reflection of grammatical usage—masculine, feminine or neuter (Edwards, 2010)[6]. Feminist writings were not the first to use the terms sex and gender differently, but a psychologist, Robert Stoller is usually credited with having introduced the distinction between 'sex', as the biological component and 'gender' as the cultural aspects of differences between men and women. In his own research on trans-sexualism, he argued for the primacy of gender over sex in the formation of individual identity as masculine or feminine. The distinction itself and the idea that 'man and women' are social creations than biological creatures, therefore, reflect the impact of surrounding spaces—social, cultural, political, economic and environmental.

It is very important for us to draw a distinction between sex and gender, because all actions of agency reflect around that. On one side, it offered a way of segregating between the predetermined, physiologically based, innate genetic character which are possessed either by men or by women, not by both, and the other learned or acquired environmental derived social differences (personality traits, attitudes, skills, type of activity). On the other, it definitely reflects the particular evaluation as the more important determinant of women's special treatment and unequal position.

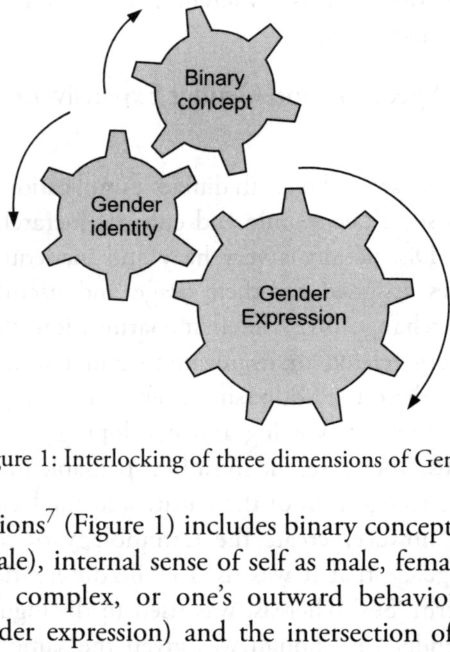


Figure 1: Interlocking of three dimensions of Gender

Three dimensions[7] (Figure 1) includes binary concept of gender (gender biology-male/female), internal sense of self as male, female, both or neither (gender identity) complex, or one's outward behaviour and respective presentation (gender expression) and the intersection of these reflects the individuals perception of gender as well as it reflects on how others perceive it. Gender expectations bombard us constantly and the social construct limits our choices of colour, dress, behaviour, attitudes, etc. The gender expansiveness loads understanding of the terms biological/anatomical sex[1]; Gender identity[2]; Gender expression[3]; Gender Role[4]; Transgender[5]; Sexual Orientation[6]; Gender normative/Cis gender[7]; and Gender Fluidity[8]. All enlarges the understanding of the gender discourse.

Self-expression of gender expansive individual may fall outside the commonly accepted and understood gender norm of their culture with their internal gender identity not synchronising perfectly with the sex assigned at birth like *calabai* and *calalai of* Indonesia; or *Hijra* of India, etc., demonstrating the presence of non-binary gender identity.

University of California (2015)[8], recognising the gender expansiveness and offer three gender related question to potential students, which is absent in almost all the universities across the globe, with one question framed as in other universities 'What Sex were you assigned at birth? With two choices: male or female'; a question on sexual orientation with three responses, including heterosexual or straight, gay or lesbian or a blank space and a question on gender identity, with six choices, including female, male, trans male/trans man, trans female/trans women, gender queer/gender non-confirming and different identity, such diversity raises the questions of clarification. However, changes are taking place but not as substantive as it should be. In 2014, one of the largest universities of India, the Delhi University, introduced in their admission forms too, recognising gender identity into three categories as male, female and other.

Largely, however, the policy makers even today in most parts of the world recognise binary gender. As for instance, Government of India, uses the term 'gender' based on the term as applied in different data sources across different Government departments such as 'Female' and 'Male' as per the data set of Census of India (2011), Department of Justice, Ministry of Law and Justice, Company Affairs (2005) and Ministry of Labour & Employment (2010); 'Girls' and 'Boys' from the District Information System for Education, Flash Statistics (2010–2011) or 'Women' and 'Men' for the data sets from the National Crime Records Bureau (2009–12), Ministry of Home Affairs (2012); National Family Health Survey (2009) and Ministry of Panchayati Raj (2008)[9]. Similar is the case in other parts of South Asia, Sub-Sahara Africa, Middle East, North Africa and other parts of the world, thereby indicative of the need for widening the lens for data collection for gender component.

Nepal however, has been the first country where in 2011 the entry of third gender is included in the Census and later in 2012 in their passports. But, largely the 'cis genders', with neatly aligned biological sex and gender identity, are embraced securely in every part of the world. Even the cues of being different are also a continuous reminder of being "other". What is to be however remembered that the new bridges between gender-expansive and gender normative are created, slow at present, but gaining visibility with changing times. This question needs thorough discussion today and affirmation to the context will lead to greater inclusion for individuals who challenge the norms of gender.

## 2. Redefining Wave Narrative: A Spatio-Temporal Generational Divide in Most Regions of Global South demanding new Gender Therapists

The wave narrative in feminist literature distinguishes three waves clearly and fourth in a fluid way. Gender spectrum across different parts of the world, especially in the Global South, are finding it difficult to match original wave narrative of first, second and third wave emanating from the United States and the United Kingdom on their different geographies. Today it seemed to have shifted to multiple transnational spaces as correctly illustrated

TABLE 1: Wave Narratives in Feminist Writings, merging yet missing concerns

| *Wave* | *Period* | *Focus As Delineated in writings on feminism* | *Merging yet missing concerns in Asia and Africa during the presence of particular narrative* |
|---|---|---|---|
| First Wave | $19^{th}$ and early $20^{th}$ century | Focus on absolute rights like suffrage<br>U.K.: Gaining the right of Women's suffrage, granted to some in 1918 and to all in 1928)<br>USA: Granting the women the right to vote with the passage of the Nineteenth Amendment to the United States Constitution (1919). | After 1948 UN Declaration on Political Rights the Women's suffrage, granted between 1949–1960 in 56 locations; 1960–1970 in 40 locations; 1970–1980 in 20 locations; 1980–1990 in 5 locations; 1990–2000 in 2 locations and 2000–2015 in 4 locations |
| Second Wave | Early 1960s & lasting through the late 1980s | Cultural equality issues, ending discrimination (through a lens of middle class: "essentialist" definition of feminity)<br>The second wave feminism saw cultural inequalities; political inequalities personal lives as deeply politicised, and reflective of a sexist structure of power. | Highly Visible even today in Asia, Africa and many other parts of the world, the presence of cultural & political inequalities; sexist structure of power; need for gender micropolitics; confusions in gender identities and expansiveness reactive activism; maximising the use of online technology for gender networking |
| Third Wave | 1990s-2008 | Post structural interpretation of gender micropolitics/intersection between race & gender/ sexual politics/young feminist | |
| Fourth wave | 2008 onwards | Activating the third wave movements through technology-online, reactive activism | |

by Nancy Fraser (2005)[10] in her presentation on *Mapping the Feminist Imagination: From redistribution to recognition to representation.* Original Wave narrative if on one hand helps in understanding the chorological and ideological development of feminism in the US and UK, it cannot fit in all the geographies pointing the gaps emulating generational divide and sluggish period of inactivity in many parts of Asia, Africa and Latin America (Table 1).

Relevance in the context, however, for building feminist theory and ideology, it is important to understand them. Different disciplines including feminist English writings, feminist geography, feminist history and others, based on different feminist movements have patterned the context. But, what is important today is that with cultural and political inequalities persisting in many parts of the world the need for insurgence of grassroots movements, including the young feminist self-expressions[11] is suggested. However, the need is for including 'self-obsessed' expression of young feminists, but with a caution to include the matters of public purpose, well understood by the experiences, yet so embryonic found in their spaces, cause of presence of multiple inequalities and conflicts in personal gender expressions and their gender orientation. Proto feminism is inclusive. The need is for creation of gender therapists (Figure 2) undertaking intergenerational conversations, continuous dialogue and exchanges of thought engaging the coordinates of the emerging fourth wave and preceding third and second wave feminism to bring sustainability in gender.

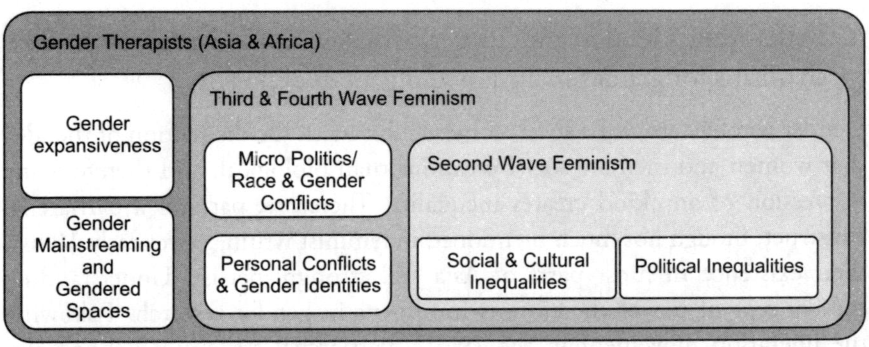


Figure 2. Creation of Gender Therapists (for Gender Integration) engaging the Conceptual coordinates of Second Wave, Third Wave & Fourth Wave feminism and Gender Expansiveness

## 3. Proto-feminism and contextualising the expression "Women's liberation" movements

Proto feminism, besides four wave feminism as discussed above, expresses the pre-feminist activities. One such phrase that occupied the large attention from 1964 to early 1980's was "Women's Liberation". From the time of the use of word 'Liberation' by Simone de Beauvoir in 1953 or mapping matchless aspirations of many women since 1895, the expression 'Women's Liberation' retained a presence among educated, middle class feminine movements from 1964 to early 1970's, occupying all women discussion forums, disillusioned by the new Left led by academia and/or activist of the United States with an introduction of the term 'libber'. However, the term 'Women's Liberation', could not be carried forward, because of the inability of the related feminists in balancing the vision and placing the voice of the cultural, social and political inequalities of the oppressed in forefront and subsequently getting divided. The earlier term women's movement replaced the expression of "Women's Liberation" because of exclusivity by the latter. Today, one is in the similar situation where new gender identities are attempting for liberation and expanding gender articulations. In many countries in South Asia where it took some time to recognise trans-gender communities like Swastika Lama, they are being documented by policy makers since 2011[12]. In India (2013) too laws are getting widened and trans-gender or third gender is expressed in policy forums. This expression had to be understood and redefined in the present times. When the women are still fighting for "liberation" in many parts, the new push is required to be inclusive and equality driven, re-contextualising gender concerns amidst economic and social development.

## 4. Redefining Gender and Power as a Social Construct with new mechanisms for gender inclusion and gender exclusion

Gender revolves around a social construction, with the distinction of the idea that women and men are social creations than biological, and therefore any oppression of any kind creates inequality. Therefore, parts of a patriarchal construct, though not much mentioned in feminist writings after early 1980's, their existence in most parts of Asia still strongly persist. Understanding the concept of power therefore is imminent in gender research. Following the liberation movement in the 1970's, patriarchal structures defined and delimited power. Women were consequently provoked "to Break out" (Bryld M. & N. Lykke, 1988). The inner and outer power structures were invoked. Inner structures tried to push the position of women as gendered subjects without social and cultural subjectivity. In 1980's and 1990's though the concept of patriarchy and feminism disappeared from gender research and women's studies in NORDIC countries, over 22 million women in the United States have been raped in their lifetime (National Intimate Partner and Sexual Violence Survey 2010). The presence of patriarchal mind-set just cannot be in any way ignored even today, including in most parts of Asia. According to a 2013 global review of available data, 35 per cent of women worldwide have experienced either physical and/or sexual intimate partner violence or non-partner sexual violence. However, some national studies show that up to 70 per cent of women have experienced physical and/or sexual violence in their lifetime from an intimate partner (UN Women, 2014). On average, 30% of women who have been in a relationship report that they have experienced some form of physical or sexual violence by their partner (World Health Organisation, 2014). One such example is a case study of India where around 40% of ever-married women age (15–49 years) who have experienced the emotional, physical or sexual violence from their husbands and 35.1% of women have experienced physical violence (NCRB, 2009). In 2014, there have been 1,19,538 reported cases of cruelty by husbands and relatives in India (NCRB, 2014)[13]. A women's crises Center in Jakarta, Mitra Perempuan (Friend of the Women), during the period of 1997–2002 received 879 reports of violence cases occurring in the surrounding cities and towns (ref.?).

Therefore, the relationships among gender, despite legal relationships (husband and wife) are tarnished, weakening physical, social and emotional power. Along with consciousness of the inferior status of women has come the concept of gender as an all-embracing socio-cultural variable, perceived in relation to other factors, such as class, race, ethnicity and age. Therefore, what becomes relevant today is the counter offensive of patriarchal structure, as already embraced by many (Knudsen, 2004)[14]. What emerged from this is the acceptance and usage of diffusion theory, inspired from the works of Michael Foucault. So, what is relevant today are generating new mechanisms for gender inclusion and gender exclusion, deeply understanding the mechanisms causing constant changes of power relations. In addition to this are the emerging concerns of women when she joins hand to work for economic development.

## 5. Re-Contextualising Gender Concerns amidst Economic Development

The growth of capitalism resulted change in social conditions and thought. The concept of democracy meant that people became important. Liberalism, as a social and political philosophy, led the charge in early phase. Women from the progressive social classes came forward as a collective. This movement has, as other social movements in history had, its flows and ebbs. The impact of capitalism however constricted and distorted in colonies like India, Indonesia, etc. did inspire progressive men and women. These movements had an international ferment but were rooted in contradictions of traditional society. The women's movement now looked for the roots of oppression in the very system of society itself. They analysed the system of patriarchy and sought its origins in history. They grappled with the social sciences and showed up the male bias inherent in them. They exposed how a patriarchal way of thinking coloured all analysis regarding women's role in history and in contemporary society.

In the recent decades, the global economic system increasingly featured the ideology of neo-liberalism, which harks back to the 19$^{th}$ century type old-fashioned laissez-faire liberalism with no labour protection. Its dominant institutional form has been Multinational Corporation, which expanded from the West/North and moved their operations to wherever the labour was cheapest. These masculine ideology and institution have been accepted by the equally masculine patriarchal governments of the global South, who promised to provide cheap, hardworking and docile female labour forces who would not complain about their conditions. As repeated in history, the financial crises has illustrated how women's rights and gender equality have been seriously undermined by economic, trade and fiscal policies that have increased militarisation, violence, poverty and inequality. While much of the relationship between development and gender inequality can be explained by the process of development, society-specific factors need to be studied. Poor countries by no means have a monopoly on gender inequality. However, disparities in health, education, and bargaining power within marriage tend to be larger in countries with low GDP per capita. Men earn more than women in essentially all societies and even labour force participate rate is significantly lower for females than for males. During 2011–12 NSSO Survey[15] conducted in India it was noted that only about 25 per cent of rural females were in labour force as compared to 55% of rural males. In urban areas, too, the gender gap was large with only 16 % of urban females in labour force to 56% of urban males. UN reported, *"Women perform 66 per cent of the world's work, produce 50 per cent of the food, but earn 10 per cent of the income and own 1 per cent of the property"*.(ref.?)

Even there is an anomaly in the presence of women on the board seats in the Corporate World. The percentage of board seats held by women are 17.1% for South Africa, 8.1% for China, 7.7% for Brazil, 4.8% for Russia and 4.1% for India (Catalyst Report: 2013). Contradictorily, what is to be noted is that women on the leadership roles are with higher qualifications than men.

Although the participation and empowerment of women endorse the thriving economies' efficiency, growth and development, their wages, working conditions and simple presence clamour and outcry for support. Existing related policy frameworks are not sufficient to meet the varied dimensions impacting women in both urban and rural working environment. The process of development need to be contextualised around the surrounding environment and the generic culture they represent. The urgent need is for creating gender sensitive policies and framework in work environment to meet the concerns including equality and non-discrimination in the work space. Essential is incorporating of the generic society demands, that exist where the women contributes towards economic development.

## 6. Gender Mainstreaming and evolving new gender spaces

Gender mainstreaming is an act of consciousness. "*Gender mainstreaming is a public policy concept of assessing different implications for women and men of any planned policy action, including legislations and programmes in all areas and levels*"(Stiegler, B., 2004)[16]. It aims at broadening women's involvement at all levels of decision making and therefore targets accountability. The issues across all areas of activity need to be defined so clearly to be able to enable gender differences. Presence of this is there in some degrees in every part of the world, but the moot question is the expansion of new gendered spaces. Let us elaborate this citing the case of India

Gender mainstreaming is evident in India through the popularity and recognition of various legislative measures intended to ensure equal rights, to counter social discrimination and various forms of violence and atrocities and to provide support services especially to working women. Participation in following activities illustrated the relevance and positive existence of few of the many gendered spaces in India. Some of them that showed positive gender mainstreaming include that of *Recognising Domestic Violence as a Public Health Concern* in Dilaasa, Maharashtra; The *Saurashtra Kachchh group on Violence against Women (SK-VAW),* Gujarat; *Mahalir Association for Literacy Awareness and Rights (MALAR),* Tamil Nadu; *Empowering Single Women - Ekal Nari Shakti Sangathan (ENSS)*, Rajasthan; *Engendering Livelihood Area Networking and Development Initiatives (ANANDI*). The women who participated in these activities not only got empowered in different spheres of life, with increased social, economic and political equity, and broader access to fundamental human rights, improvements in nutrition, basic health and education. In the same stride they created new gendered spaces.

Women agency is present everywhere contributing towards the resource management and development of mountain area of the Himalayas (India), though invisibly in most cases. Gendered spaces are visible at home; en route path when collecting water or fuel wood; or when happily working in their small agricultural field. Primary survey in Garhwal Himalayas denoted the fact that women bear substantially more of the domestic and farm responsibilities than their men folk or their counterparts in the plains and their dependence on money order economy. Women, both as participants and decision makers, share the responsibility of planting, transplanting, weeding, harvesting, and even collecting wood, water and fodder. Fodder collection, grazing and milking of cattle are generally performed by both women and men, whereas activities like feed preparation, feeding, cleaning sheds and preparing milk products are women's domain. The loss of nearby forest and water resources due to environmental degradation has an impact on women responsible for the collection and management of such resources, often forcing them to travel longer distances to meet their household's daily needs[17]. When compared to the already heavy work schedule, this added pressure comes as an unwelcome burden. Women are also extensively involved in informal trade: selling food, vegetables and snacks in roadside stalls and local market.

Women agency too is visibly present in India with the existence of women in the highest positions of decision-making. There is a presence of Pinki Anand as singular Law Officer (2014) and Smt R Banumathi as a Women Supreme Court Judge (2015). The representation of 82 women in the Lok Sabha, the lower House of Indian Parliament (2014); 29 Women Rajya Sabha, the Upper House of Indian Parliament (2014); 975057 Panchayat Representatives in Gram sabhas; 58191 in Intermediate Panchayats too speaks of presence of women in the top-most position of decision making in India thereby expanding the role of women agencies. For widening the gendered spaces in higher education, a University Grants Commission (UGC) Project on "Capacity Building for Higher Education" touched almost all parts of India. Two series of Gender Atlas Project of India (Series 1[18] and Series 2[19]) of Ministry of Women and Child Development (2012–present), Government of India and Kirori Mal College, University of Delhi, India also aimed towards this direction. The data has been categorised into seven themes preceded by context; demography; marital status, education; health, family welfare & nutrition; economy; public order & safety and representation of women in selected fields. It is pertinent to mention that the Gender Atlas Project has a wider vision and this atlas is one step towards translating this vision. The geospatial and thematic perspective of the atlas project incorporates 160+ gender disaggregated data (Parihar, S.M, 2015[20]). This aims to help social analysts, policy makers, research scholars and others in analysis of many relevant issues related to gender differentials in a holistic and integrated manner.

Gender mainstreaming definitely leads to gender equality and empowerment, but the strategy avoids the question of gender conflict, and articulates this as a new way of doing gender equality work. Feminism too is rejected because it is being seen as an opposition to professionalism and legitimate political issues. Simultaneously though, it is a well-intended response to feminism. What is therefore accepted in all discourses of gender mainstreaming is a notion that this type of gender equality work is to be performed without harming or threatening gender conflicts (Anderson, R., 2015)[21].

## Conclusion

Gender has a future with visible gendered spaces. The thought emanates from the inclusiveness of the term 'Gender', drawing clear distinction from gender identity and gender expansiveness. Gender expressions driven through gender therapists in the new world of mainstreaming gender would produce inclusiveness even among those as otherwise stated by Gerda Lerner[22], *"Women have a history; Women are in history they said"*. For attaining and sustaining this, insular gender spectrum and gender expansiveness have to be understood and accepted by one and all; wave narratives have to be redefined bridging the existing generational divide across spaces through the access of women agency and new gender therapists; contextualising Proto-feminism and upholding new mechanisms for gender inclusion and gender exclusion in social, cultural, political and economic expressions through gender mainstreaming using factual gender disaggregated data and performing balanced gender budgeting for gender integration.

## Endnotes

1. Biological/Anatomical Sex be understood as consisting of range of possibilities including the presence of a binary set of two options determined by chromosomes (XX for females; XY for males); hormones (estrogen/progesterone for females, testosterone for males); and internal and external genitalia (vulva, clitoris, vagina for assigned females, penis and testicles for assigned males).
2. Gender Identity. One's innermost concept of self as male or female or both or neither how individuals perceive themselves and what they call themselves.
3. Gender expression is not an indication of sexual orientation, it refers to the ways in which people externally communicate their gender identity to others through behaviour, clothing, haircut, voice, and other forms of presentation.
4. Gender Role includes the set of roles, activities, expectations and behaviors assigned to females and males by society.
5. Transgender includes all those whose identity or behaviour falls outside of stereotypical

gender norms and may additionally identify with a variety of other sexual identities as well.

6. Sexual Orientation refers to being romantically or sexually attracted to people of a specific gender. Our sexual orientation and our gender identity are separate, distinct parts of our overall identity.
7. Gender Normative/Cisgender refers to people whose sex assignment at birth corresponds to their gender identity and expression.
8. Gender fluidity conveys a wider, more flexible range of gender expression, with interests and behaviours that may even change from day to day. Gender fluid children do not feel confined by restrictive boundaries of stereotypical expectations of girls or boys. In other words, a child may feel they are a girl some days and a boy on others, or possibly feel that neither term describes them accurately.

## Foonotes

1. Robin Morgon is a co founder of Women's Media Center and refers to the mentioned statement while referring to feminisms–plural..."So feminism doesn't have a narrow definition; it's when anyone fights for women's rights".
2. Darwis Khudori, 2014, A Summary Report of BANDUNG 60 YEARS ON: WHAT ASSESSMENT? A one-day seminar at the University Paris 1 Panthéon-Sorbonne on June 27, 2014.
3. Ibid.
4. Sri Mulyani Indrawati (2015), Discriminating Against Women Keeps Countries Poorer, http://www.worldbank.org/en/news/opinion/2015/09/10/discriminating-against-women-keeps-countries-poorer
5. World Bank, Report on Women, Business and Law (2015). http://wbl.worldbank.org/
6. Edwards, Anne (2010), The Sex Gender Distinction: Has it outlined its Usefulness, *Australian Feminist Studies*, Vol. 4, Issue 10, pp. 1–12.
7. https://www.genderspectrum.org/quick-links/understanding-gender/
8. http://www.foxnews.com/us/2015/07/28/university-california-offers-six-choices-for-gender-identity/
9. Parihar, S.M. (2015), 'Gender Atlas of India, A Geospatial Perspective', India, p. 6.
10. Fraser, N., Mapping the Feminist Imagination: From Redistribution to Recognition to Representation. Constellation 12, 3/2005, pp. 295–327. (Original essay is from her presentation at Cambridge University, 'Gender Equality and Social Change', 2004 and later at a conference on 'Gender in Motion', at University of Basel, 2005).
11. Rubin, L., & C. Nemeroff (2001), Feminists Third Wave, *Women & Therapy*, Vol. 23, Issue 2, pp. 91–104.
12. See more at: http://www.dhakatribune.com/juris/2015/jan/08/ensure-rights-third-gender#sthash.J9pD96p0.dpuf
13. National Crime Records Bureau (2014), India.
14. Knudsen, S.V. (2004), Introduction: Gender & Power, *NORA*, No. 2, Vol. 12.
15. National Sample Survey Office (2014), NSS 68th Round (July 2011–June 2012), Employment and Unemployment Situation in India, NSS Report No. 554 (68/10/1), Ministry of Statistics and Programme Implementation, Government of India, pp. 123–124.
16. Stiegler, B., *Gender powers policy: ten questions and answers on the concept of gender mainstreaming*, Bonn: Friedrich Ebert-Stiftung, 2004. See http://www.un.org/womenwatch/daw/followup/main.htm
17. Parihar, S.M, et. al. (2013) 'Conceptualising Space and Indigenous Knowledge: Articulations

and Considerations for Natural Resource Management in Himalayas' in G.N. Devi, et. al., (Ed.) *Knowing Differently: the Cognitive Challenge of the Indigenous*, New Delhi: Routledge, pp. 198–224.

18. Parihar, S.M., Principal Investigator (2014) Gender Atlas of India, A Geospatial Perspective (Series 1) & Parihar, S.M., Principal Investigator (2015) Gender Atlas of India, A Thematic Perspective (Series 2), Convergent projects between Ministry of Women & Child Development, Government of India & Kirori Mal College, University of Delhi, India.
19. Ibid.
20. Ibid.
21. Anderson, R. (2015), 'The Question of Feminism in Mainstreaming Gender, A case of non-conflict in local Politics' in *Nordic Journal of Feminist & Gender Research*, Vol. 23, Issue 3, pp. 203–219.
22. Gerda Lerner (1920–2013) was the single most influential figure in the development of women's and gender history since the 1960s. "There was disappointment in her later years: indeed, Gerda's disappointments were as global as her ambition: growing inequality, religious fundamentalism, the rise of xenophobia and racism throughout the world, American military and security policy".

## References


Anderson, R. (2015), "The Question of Feminism in Mainstreaming Gender, A case of non-conflict in local Politics", *Nordic Journal of Feminist & Gender Research*, Vol. 23, Issue 3, pp. 203–219.

Catalyst Report 2008, *Census of Women Board Directors of the Fortune 500*, Appendix 3.

Catalyst Report, 2013, *Women on Board.*

Darwis Khudori, 2014, *A Summary Report of Bandung 60 Years On: What Assessment?* A one-day seminar at the University of Paris 1 Pantheon-Sorbonne (June 27, 2014).

Fraser, N., 2005, *Mapping the Feminist Imagination: From Redistribution to Recognition to Representation.* Constellation 12, 3/2005, pp. 295–327. (Original essay is from her presentation at Cambridge University, 'Gender Equality and Social Change', 2004 and later at a conference on 'Gender in Motion', at University of Basel, 2005)

Jamieson, K. H., *Beyond the Double Bind: Women and Leadership*, New York: Oxford University Press, 1995.

Knudsen, S.V. (2004), *Introduction: Gender & Power, NORA*, No. 2, Vol. 12.

NCRB (2009), *Crime in India: 2009*, National Crime Records Bureau, India.

NCRB (2014), *Crime in India: 2014*, National Crime Records Bureau, India.

National Sample Survey Office (2014), NSS 68$^{th}$ Round (July 2011–June 2012), Employment and Unemployment Situation in India, NSS Report No. 554 (68/10/1), Ministry of Statistics and Programme Implementation, Government of India, pp. 123–124.

Parihar, S.M., et. al. (2013), 'Conceptualising Space and Indigenous Knowledge: Articulations and Considerations for Natural Resource Management in Himalayas' in G.N. Devi, et. al., (Ed.) *Knowing Differently: the Cognitive Challenge of the Indigenous*, New Delhi: Routledge, pp. 198–224.

Parihar, S.M., Principal Investigator (2014) *Gender Atlas of India, A Geospatial Perspective* (Series 1). Convergent project between Ministry of Women & Child Development,

Government of India & Kirori Mal College, University of Delhi, India.

Parihar, S.M., Principal Investigator (2015) *Gender Atlas of India, A Thematic Perspective* (Series 2), Convergent project between Ministry of Women & Child Development, Government of India & Kirori Mal College, University of Delhi, India.

Rubin, L., and C. Nemeroff (2001), Feminists Third Wave, *Women & Therapy*, Vol. 23, Issue 2, pp. 91–104.

Stiegler, B., *Gender powers policy: ten questions and answers on the concept of gender mainstreaming*, Bonn: Friedrich Ebert-Stiftung, 2004.

World Bank, 2016, *Report on Women, Business and Law,* http://wbl.worldbank.org/

# 12

# More than Food Alone

## Food Security in the South and Global Environmental Change

*Trikurnianti Kusumanto*

## Abstract

Meeting global food and nutrition needs is a major challenge. In 2014, about 795 million people were undernourished globally, including 780 million in the South. Despite impressive increases in food production over the last five decades, eliminating global hunger and malnutrition will remain a main concern as well as dominate scientific and policy debates. While meeting food and nutrition needs is highly urgent, evidence is growing that common strategies of food production fall largely short to respond adequately. There is scope for increasing food production, yet efforts to that end are complicated by global environmental change, including climate change and declining ecosystem services. Dilemmatic is, however, that global environmental change is caused partly by food production practices themselves (e.g., excessive use of agrochemicals and deforestation leading to biodiversity loss).

Global environmental change is likely to compromise food security for every country on the planet, but securing populations of food and nutrition in the Global South is further jeopardised by multiple-level and multiple-scale complexities characteristic for southern regions with socioeconomic, policy, and institutional dimensions. This writing establishes the attributes of the food security challenge in the South in a context of global environmental change and explores a food system approach as a response to this challenge. For some obvious reasons, the food security issue is mostly relevant to Bandung Spirit led efforts. The writing also discusses the relevance of the food security challenge to the Bandung Conference. A food system approach provides a framework to identify which food system activities are vulnerable to what stress(es), thereby showing where given adaptation and mitigation interventions would be effective and what action points need to be prioritised. Furthermore, it underlines the importance of creating food systems that are resilient and equitable; allowing and supporting intensification of food production that is sustainable; making biodiversity and ecosystem services visible to informing decision and policymaking; viewing food and nutrition security as complex landscape covering different sectors, disciplines, institutions, and jurisdictions; governing interconnections between the diverse elements of food security.

Keywords: food security, food systems, South, ecosystem, nutrition, global environmental change

Meeting global food and nutrition needs is one of the major challenges of our time. In 2014, about 795 million people were undernourished globally, including 780 million in the South, which means that just over one in nine do not have enough to eat for leading a healthy and active life (FAO, IFAD, and WPF, 2015). The United Nations Food and Agricultur Organization (FAO) stated recently that with a global population estimated for 2050 to reach over 9 billion, global food production must increase by 70%, while food production in the South will need to double (Population Institute Website, 2015). Moreover, changing consumption patterns of a wealthier population is likely to raise global food demand even higher. Despite impressive increases in food production over the last five decades, eliminating global hunger and malnutrition will remain a main concern in the foreseeable future as well as dominate scientific and policy debates.

While meeting food and nutrition needs is highly urgent, evidence is growing that current strategies of food production fall largely short to respond adequately. There is scope for increasing food production, yet efforts to that end are complicated by global environmental change, including in relation to climate, land use, biodiversity, water availability, sea level, and stratospheric ozone. Dilemmatic is, nonetheless, that global environmental change is caused partly by practices of the food production itself, such as an excessive use of agrochemicals leading to hypertrophication of aquatic systems and deforestation to making place for agricultural land leading to biodiversity loss and declining ecosystem services.

Global environmental change is likely to compromise food security for every country on the planet, but securing populations of food and nutrition in the Global South is further jeopardised by multiple-level and multiple-scale complexities characteristic for southern regions with socioeconomic, policy, and institutional dimensions. This writing establishes the attributes of the food security challenge in the Global South in a context of global environmental change as well as explores a food system approach as a response to this challenge. Before doing this, however, it pins down the relevance of the food security issue to the Bandung Conference.

## Relevance to the Bandung Conference

For some obvious reasons, discussing and analysing the food security challenge and exploring possible solutions are mostly relevant for Bandung Spirit led efforts. From the outset, Bandung has called for building solidarity towards the poor and those marginalised by the world order of the day. A further relevance to Bandung relates to the idea of "emerging" country, a term designated to emerging national economies widely known as BRICS (acronym for Brazil, Russia, India, China, and South-Africa; whereas other than these five countries are potentially "emerging" too). A recently evolving Bandung Spirit discourse views this concept problematic in that economic growth of most presently "emerging" countries is largely based on an unsustainable exploitation of natural resources and one that results in a growing wealthy middle class yet at the same time widens the wealth gap between the rich and the poor (Khudori, 2014). One of the key features of an "emerging" country that often is considered, is its economic and food production capacity to feed its people in a sovereign way. Food sovereignty, as viewed in this writing, is the social-political way to attain food security, while the latter is more associated to the technical, institutional, and organisational aspects of food production and distribution. Furthermore, food security is relevant to Bandung Spirit endeavours where it relates to the theme of southern partnership. With China as frontrunner, South-South Cooperation has gained importance in recent years in attempts to reduce hunger and poverty by way of financial support and the exchange of food production experts and technologies. For instance, in June of the present year, China and FAO signed a US$50 million Memorandum of Understanding to build sustainable food systems in low-income food-deficit areas of Central-Asia, the Pacific Islands, Africa, and Latin America over a period of five years. China has done its very best to build southern partnerships by starting forums of cooperation and development initiatives, yet given its economic interests, enormous population to feed, and infatuated needs for energy and natural resources, there clearly are concerns for the local welfare and environment of partner countries (Kaplan, 2011). Lastly, food security is a key issue of the Bandung Conference as it closely interconnects to social and political conflicts, a major theme of Bandung. Food insecurity can directly result from political instability and violent conflict as well as intensify such situations. In the Arab Spring of 2011, for example, decrease of government subsidies for bread in the Near East, led to price rises that in turn evoked social turmoil and political violence. Besides, in conflict-ridden regions where infrastructures and service facilities for food production and distribution have been destroyed or fallen into the hands of opposing parties, populations face food insecurity due to a lack of physical access to foodstuffs.

## Taking Stock of Food Insecurity in the Global South

Developing further knowledge to adequately respond to food insecurity in the Global South is not only important and urgent, it is also timely. The year 2015 closes off the monitoring period of the Millennium Development Goals (MDGs), established in 2000 by UN member states with one of its goals (Goal 1c) set at "cutting by half the proportion of people who suffer from hunger by 2015". In addition, this year is also the point of time to reflect on what should be done to eliminate hunger on a planet under pressure while it moves into the post-2015 Sustainable Development Goals (SDGs) era. The most recent MDG monitoring exercise reported that the decrease of undernourished people had been fastest in east and south-eastern Asia, Central Asia, the Caucasus, northern and western Africa, and Latin America, all having reached above Goal 1c (FAO, IFAD and WPF, 2015). Southern Asia, Oceania, the Caribbean, and southern and eastern Africa had shown progress, but at such low a pace that they did not attain this target. In terms of number of countries, more than half of the countries monitored—72 of the 129 countries—had reached the MDG target. Hence, ceasing hunger in the South has shown an uneven progress.

## Food Security and Global Environmental Change Entangled

Natural ecosystems and biodiversity are the ecological foundation of the production of food for humans, whether in relation to agricultural land, forests, fisheries, or other natural resource systems. Agricultural production, in particular, is interwoven with ecosystems and biodiversity as it relies on the delivery of such ecosystem services as fresh water, pollination, and natural pest control. The value of these ecosystem services, however, is not always "visible" or remains "invisible until it is no longer available" (UNEP, 2014). Examples of such situations are those in which ecosystems can no longer provide pollination or natural predators to agricultural practices, necessitating these to call in human labour respectively the use of pesticides. If the value of natural capital is not sufficiently "visible", food production is likely to omit or undervalue nature's contribution to the production process—in either monetary or non-monetary terms. This, in turn, might lead to flawed production decisions and policies, such as those connected to investment needs for the maintenance, restoration, and creation of ecosystem stocks, flows, and service delievery.

Nonetheless, food system activities themselves—i.e. food production practices, distribution, and consumption—impose negative externalities on the health of ecosystems through, for example, soil erosion, nutrient run-off, biodiversity loss, and green house gas (GHG) emissions. The production of GHG, however, is largely inherent to common agricultural practices and involves, inter alia, processes of biological activities in agricultural soils and livestock's digestive systems, manure management, rice cultivation, synthetic fertilisers, crop residues decay, and field burning. The FAO (2014) stated that in 2011, 44 per cent of agriculture-related GHG emission occurred in Asia, followed by the Americas (25%), Africa (15%), Europe (12%), and Oceania (4%). Additionally, a relatively large environmental footprint can be related to food production increases through agricultural intensification and expansion —i.e., particularly expansion that involves deforestation. Global environmental change related to climate affects food production and hence food security —through, among other factors, extreme weather, changing patterns of rainfall and temperature, and biodiversity and soil losses, leading to water shortage, crop failures, plant diseases and pests, and shrinking availability of cooking fuelwood and livestock fodder. Those whose livelihoods are closely connected to food production as well as food production system has limited coping capacity, are therefore mostly vulnerable to the effects of climate change. Because in many southern localities women play vital roles as producers, resource managers, income earners, and family care takers and givers, women are the more susceptible to the consequences of global environmental change. Moreover, their low income and asset base, little access to resources—such as information, training, technology, and public services—as well as their limited engagement in decision-making, are likely to hamper women's adaptability to global environmental change. In indirect terms, global environmental change compromises food and nutrition security through an increase in food price volatility. This is more likely to occur in the near absence of adaptive food systems that could respond adequately and timely to increased food demands, disease outbreaks, and climate induced disasters and other crises. For vulnerable groups whose income is too low to cope with increasing food prices, food needs will never be met simply by meeting food demands as determined by markets. Indeed, food security is more than a mere matter of producing enough for meeting food demands. Current food production can in fact feed all, yet food distribution according to wealth as governed by markets, undermines a socially and economically equal access to food. What is more, food and nutrition security is at risk for those already prone to hunger and malnutrition, because global environmental change is likely to affect all aspects of food security—i.e. the stability of food availability, access, and use.

For above reasons, global environmental change tends to hit the poor, marginalised, and women the most. A nutrition predicament thereby is that in crises with skyrocketing food prices, these vulnerable groups tend to rely more on starchy diets as nutritious food—rich in fibres, essential vitamins, minerals, and proteins—are more expensive and hence less affordable. In crises, their diets are likely to become monotonous and carbohydrates-rich, while micronutrients-poor, in the end likely to lead to "hidden hunger". For tackling this, micronutrient requirements through food intake should be met over the longer-term (Jomo, 2014).

## Food Production in Southern Regions

A substantial portion of the food consumed in the South—in Asia and Sub-Saharan Africa even 80%—comes from smallholders with low-external inputs and low yields (IFAD, 2011). Most of these smallholders operate in remote areas with fragile ecosystems where interactions between natural systems and agricultural systems profoundly influence food production processes. Besides, these smallholders are confronted with high transportation and transactions costs and a limited access, if any, to such inputs as fertilisers, pesticides, as well as such services as extension and credit facilities. Albeit their central role in food production, small producers tend to receive little policy and institutional support, while most of them are nowadays experiencing declining agricultural yields and increasing market competition due to global trade and modern agribusiness. In addition, growing local, national, regional, and global demands for fibres, energy, and other goods derived from the land have led to market pressures they hardly can cope with. Global environmental change with likely negative consequences for yields and income, puts the small producers at even larger risks. For the women amongst them, the situation is still worse since female producers and workers bear often the largest risks.

Rather than by agricultural land alone, securing food and nutrition in southern urban, rural, and coastal areas is associated with food produced by a composite of interconnected and overlapping elements associated with farming land, forests, tree-based systems, aquaculture, and fisheries. Forests and tree-based systems, for instance, importantly complement diets with nutrition-rich food items (including fruits, edible tree leaves and flowers, mushrooms, honey, insects, and bush meet), provide cooking fuelwood, and deliver ecosystem services important for crop and livestock production

(Vincenti et al. 2013; Van Noordwijk et al. 2014). For especially the poor, marginalised, and women, forests and tree-based land use are a vital source of food, nutrition, cooking fuelwood, and income.

## A Food System Approach to Food Security in the Global South

Although the concept of food systems already emerged in the early 1990s, only since relatively recently it has been argued and promoted more widely, largely as a response to calls for attaining food security for all (UN, 2012). This section explores this approach in meeting food and nutrition needs in the Global South by discussing its conceptual foundations, why it emerged in the 90s, as well as the ways in which it responds to this challenge.

### Conceptual Foundations and Emergence

Recommended by the scientific community, the United Nations Conference on Sustainable Development in 2012 (Rio+20) adopted this approach to improve "*understanding of the interactions between food security and environmental or other stresses, thereby clarifying decision making regarding appropriate policy options*". The approach lays down in a systematic way the connections between a set of activities related to producing, processing, distributing, marketing, preparing, and consuming food on the one hand, and the outcomes of these activities on the other that could contribute to food security (stability for availability, access, and utilisation of food), social welfare (income, employment, wealth, human, social, and political capital), and environmental welfare (ecosystem stocks, flows, and services; access to natural capital).

As a concept, food systems emerged in the early 1990s as one of the outcomes of the search for alternatives to unsustainable industrial agriculture in the1920s-80s period—in the Third World taking the shape of the Green Revolution in the 1970s-80s. Influenced by critiques on the cultural foundations of industrial societies in the post-oil-embargo era of the 1970s, two notable works appeared that dealt specifically with agriculture. One was from a Western cultural perspective—Wendell Berry's work of 1977: *The unsettling of America: culture and agriculture*—and one from an Asian cultural angle—Masanobu Fukuoka's book of 1978: *One straw revolution.* Both works criticised industrial agriculture and offered alternatives that are more grounded on the local environment and cultural tradition (Dahlberg, 1993). The food system approach can be traced back to this earlier idea. Moreover, it has been broadened up to become a concept that among other theories refers to the hierarchy theory as used in ecology to include natural, social, and technological systems.

## Creating Resilient and Equitable Food Systems

It is obvious that possible solutions to food insecurity should be sought in the creation of resilient and equitable food systems. In socially and environmentally sustainable ways, such food systems match changing patterns of food supply and demands as well as have built-in mechanisms for meeting food needs of those vulnerable to price increases. Two central features of resilient food systems are that they endure environmental and economic shocks and can meet changing food patterns in times of crises (e.g., by having effective storage systems). Equitable food systems have built-in mechanisms that ensure food access for all (e.g., social protection of vulnerable groups in facing crises), are inclusive for all food producers (e.g., market access) and are supported by innovation systems that can respond to changing consumption patterns of all wealth groups.

### Allowing and supporting intensification of food production that is sustainable

Food systems should allow and support intensification of food production in ways that are sustainable. There are many different routes to intensify food production sustainably including through alternative agriculture such as agroecological approaches. Agroecology has ecology as its basis in the assumption that if farming systems harmoniously interact with their ecosystems, production will be sustainable. It focuses on the interactions between faming, social, and bioregional systems, institutions (e.g., land tenure, markets, trade regimes, and (global) policy frameworks. Intensifying food production can take place while simultaneously greening its process—thereby contributing to the transition to a greener economy—by increasing efficiency, reducing resource and energy waste along the food chain, improving health and nutrition, alleviating poverty, and creating rural employment. There is a common tendency to perceive sustainable development as competing to social development and poverty reduction. However, on the contrary, sustainable food systems can complement poverty alleviation and social development as they protect the natural and social assets on which the poor depend for their livelihoods. Ecological intensification is another example that can sustainably secure local communities of food and nutrition, i.e., by utilising trees in agricultural landscapes (Van Noordwijk *et al.* 2014). Approaches such as described here with a range of technological and food production levels should be better understood and promoted. Besides, analyses should also be made of the ways in which land and resources tenure, market, changing consumption patterns, and trade interconnect with these alternative approaches.

## Making Biodiversity and Ecosystem Services Visible

For food systems to be sustainable—i.e., embracing a long-term perspective socially and environmentally—it is key that the benefits delivered by biodiversity and ecosystem services be made visible, as well as the negative impacts that food systems have on biodiversity and ecosystem services (UNEP, 2014). The positive and negative values of biodiversity and ecosystem services respectively food systems should be recognised, understood, and captured in production decision-making and policymaking. Nonetheless, food production systems are not only featured by negative externalities impacting on the social and natural environment, but also by positive ones benefiting societies at large such as aesthetic and cultural amenities of rural, farming landscapes.

## Viewing Food Security as Complex Landscape

Applying a food system approach implies that food and nutrition security is viewed as a complex landscape with multiple interconnections at various levels of spatial, temporal and other scales, whilst covering different sectors (e.g., agriculture, forestry, fisheries, health, and education) and disciplines (e.g., resource and water management, energy, marketing, transportation, and consumption). Food systems are highly dependent on and influence socioeconomic processes, as well as natural ones (e.g., biophysiological and biogeochemical processes). For all these reasons, any food security strategy should have built-in coordination between policy, practice, and research.

## Governing Interconnections

In many countries, the management and governance of the diverse elements of food security are fragmented across different government departments and jurisdictions. Furthermore, research efforts that look in a more integrated way into this diversity of interconnected and overlapping components have only recently begun to attract attention from research institutions, governments, and the international community alike. For a strong and effective coordination between policy, practice, and research associated with food security, an integrated approach to governance is required while incorporating aspects of population, food, socioeconomic systems, environment, and climate. This necessitates laws and regulations to create legal and administrative space for institutional diversities with multiple actors responsible for different institutional frameworks and jurisdictions. The food system approach is a useful tool for governing food security as it provides a framework to identifying which food system activities are vulnerable to what stress(es), thereby showing where given adaptation and mitigation interventions would be effective and efficient, and what action points should be prioritised. Importantly, the approach necessitates recognition of the increasingly important roles that non-state actors play in seeking novel ways for tackling food insecurity.

## Concluding Remarks

For feeding the South on an increasingly interconnected globe that also faces environmental change, it is nothing less than sensible to search for interconnected solutions. The food system approach, as explored in this writing, offers a framework to better understand the multiple-level, multiple-scale, and boundary-crossing complexities that characterise food insecurity in many southern regions and localities. In seeking solutions, however, food insecurity analyses should put central aspects of equity, resiiience, and sustainability. In addition, as food security and the future of the planet concern us all, knowledge development should not be confined to scholarly debates and research, but also reaches out to policymakers, corporate actors, civil society, and not in the last instance, the food producers themselves. In this regard, the Bandung Conference might offer a platform for knowledge development and learning, as well as for laying down a basis for concrete action.

## References

Dahlberg, K.A. 1993. Regenerative food systems: Broadening the scope and agenda of sustainability. In: Allen, P. (ed.). *Food for the future: Conditions and contradictions of sustainability*. Pp. 75-102. John Wiley and Sons, New York.

FAO. 2014. *Agriculture, forestry and other land use emissions by sources and removals by sinks. 1990-2011 Analysis*. Working Paper Series ESS/14-02. FAO, Rome: http://www.fao.org/docrep/019/i3671e/i3671e.pdf.

FAO, IFAD and WPF. 2015. *The state of food insecurity in the world 2015. Meeting the 2015 international hunger targets: taking stock of uneven progress*. FAO, Rome: http://www.fao.org/3/a-i4646e.pdf.

IFAD. 2011. *Smallholders can feed the world*. Viewpoint. IFAD, Rome: http://www.ifad.org/pub/viewpoint/smallholder.pdf

Jomo, K. S. 2014. Tackling the nutrition challenge: A food systems approach. In: *Development, 2014, 57(2)*, pp.141-146. Society for International Development.

Kaplan, S. 2011. Fixing fragile states: Challenges and opportunities for multipolar cooperation. In: Berendsen, B. (ed.). *Common goods in a divided world*. KIT Publishers, Amsterdam.

Khudori, D. 2014. *Bandung 60 years on: What assessment? A one-day seminar at University Paris 1 Pathéon-Sorbonne on June 27, 2014*. Université Paris and Université Le Havre: http://www.bandungspirit.org/IMG/pdf/BANDUNG_60_YEARS-Seminar_Report-

Complete-281114.pdf.
Population Institute Website. 2015. https://www.populationinstitute.org/
UNEP. 2014. *The economics of ecosystems and biodiversity (TEEB) for agriculture & food. Concept note.* United Nations Environment Programme (UNEP), Geneva: http://www.teebweb.org/wp-content/uploads/2014/03/TEEB-for-Agriculture-and-Food_Concept-note1.pdf.
United Nations. 2012. *Food security for a planet under pressure. Transition to sustainability: interconnected challenges and solutions.* Rio+20 Policy Brief #2. United Nations Conference on Sustainable Development (Rio+20). Planet under Pressure. March 26-29, London: https://sustainabledevelopment.un.org/content/documents/880planetpressure.pdf.
Van Noordwijk, M., V. Bizard, P. Wangpakapattanawong, H.L. Tata, G.B. Villamore, and B. Leimona. 2014. Tree cover transitions and food security in Southeast Asia. In: *Global Food Security Vol. 3, Issues 3-4, Nov. 2014,* pp. 200-208, Elsevier: http://www.sciencedirect.com/science/article/pii/S2211912414000455.
Vincenti, B., C. Termote, A. Ickowitz, B. Powell, K. Kehlenbeck, and D. Hunter. 2013. The contribution of forests and trees to sustainable diets. In: *Sustainability 2013, 5,* pp. 4797-4824: http://www.mdpi.com/2071-1050/5/11/4797/pdf.

**Trikurnianti (Yanti) Kusumanto** is a social science researcher and activist in natural resource governance focusing on social and environmental sustainability in rural, agricultural and forest contexts. For over 25 years she has been engaged in international development and research agencies, such as the CGIAR and her own Netherlands-based consulting organisation. Her publications (e.g., with Resources for the Future, Washington D.C.) target at practitioners and policy makers, rather than scientists and underline the importance of adaptive management and collaborative natural resource governance that engage diverse actors.

# 13

# Bandung-Non Alignment-BRICS

## A Journey of the Bandung Spirit

*Beatriz Bissio*

## Abstract

The sixtieth anniversary of the Bandung Conference (April 18 to 24, 1955), the event that created the basis for the foundation of the Non-Aligned Movement, was celebrated in 2015. By consecrating the concept of the Third World, the Bandung meeting represented, symbolically, the moment in which a significant sector of humanity assumed consciousness of its role and made their voice heard. In the 1970s, when their level of intervention was rising, the Non Aligned countries adopted two new areas of struggle: the implementation of New International Economic Order (NIEO) and New World Information and Communications Order (NWICO). They failed in fulfilling most of their goals and sixty years later many of the problems that were analysed and debated in that pioneer conference continued to challenge a huge part of humanity. Therefore, the occasion inspired this paper's reflection on the legacy of this conglomerate of countries which reached its peak in the last decades of the 20$^{th}$ century. It also challenged us to seek points of convergence with the diplomacy currently developed by countries that used to be part of the Third World and today are identified as the leaders in their respective regions. Global players with prominent positions, called "emerging countries", they are outlining common goals and creating a formal political institutionality, giving rise to BRICS.

*Keywords:* BRICS, diplomacy, Bandung, Non-Aligned Movement, South-South relations, emerging countries

The Conference that took place in Bandung, Indonesia, from April 18 to 24, 1955, brought together leaders from some thirty Asian and African nations, responsible for the destiny of 1.350 million human beings. Sixty years later, in 2015, many of the problems that were analysed and debated in that pioneer conference continue to challenge a huge part of humanity. This observation justifies a reflection on the meaning and the projections of Bandung and invites us to think about the relevance today of some of the assessments and proposals made at the event, that constituted the landmark in the history of twentieth-century international relations.

By consecrating the emergence of the Non-Aligned Movement and the concept of the Third World, the Bandung meeting represented, symbolically, the moment in which a significant sector of humanity assumed consciousness of their role and made their voice heard. Richard Wright, a well-known journalist after his novel *Native Son (1940)*, which became the first book by an African-American writer to be selected by the Book-of-the-Month Club, attended the conference and wrote *The Color Curtain. A report on the Bandung Conference*[1]. In this book, he wrote:

> *The despised, the insulted, the hurt, the dispossessed—in short, the underdogs of the human race were meeting. Here were class and racial and religious consciousness on a global scale. Who had thought of organising such a meeting? And what had these nations in common? Nothing, it seemed to me, but what their past relationship to the Western world had made them feel. This meeting of the rejected was in itself a kind of judgment upon the Western world!*

It was true that there were differences among the participants. However, guided by the ideal of creating space of their own—an imagined community?—in the bipolar world of the period, this group of nations defined ten principles that directed their action in favour of the promotion of peaceful co-existence. And through these principles the "spirit of Bandung" marked the process of liberation of the colonial world and defined the path for the international insertion of the countries that formed the Non-Aligned Movement, with an explicit condemnation of racism, colonialism and imperialism. In the explosive scenario of the Cold War the ten principles of Bandung laid out the rejection of participation in any kind of military pact and the defence of non-intervention and non-interference in the internal affairs of other countries based on respect for the sovereignty and the territorial integrity of all nations and with respect for fundamental human rights at the top of the list. They recognised equality of all races, the right of any nation to defend itself individually or collectively, in the framework of the definitions of the United Nations Charter; they rejected arrangements for collective defence destined "to serve any particular interests of the big powers"[2], and they defended the solution of all conflicts through pacific means with respect for justice and international obligations.

In the 1970s, when their level of intervention was rising, the Non Aligned countries adopted two new areas of struggle: the implementation of New International Economic Order (NIEO) and New World Information and Communications Order (NWICO). This latter claim was incorporated by UNESCO, which in 1977 set up an international commission to study the problems of information flow. Three years later, this commission released a document known as the MacBride Report (Sean MacBride was the president of the Commission) with concrete proposals seeking balance in the production and access to information between the developed countries and the Third World, together with condemnation of the huge international information monopolies. The reaction of the United States and the UK was drastic: both countries abandoned UNESCO and cut off their funding for this UN agency which faced years of crisis and was finally forced to put aside any discussion of the issue.

Directly related to the proposal for a profound change in the rules of the game in the economy and in the production and distribution of information at a world level, the Non Aligned group questioned the division of the world according to the Cold War logic, based on ideological options, and they identified the real division as that based on the unequal capacity of nations to dispose of their own natural resources. That is to say, the real division was not between East and West, but between North and South. Therefore, for the Non Aligned countries, the economy and communications were strategic areas for achieving the most central goal of their action: the full development of every country. Ambitious goals of development were seen as the only way to eliminate every kind of exploitation and domination.

Although the diagnosis of the Non Aligned Movement was correct, the power balance at that historical moment did not allow for the implementation of this alternative, either in economics or in communications. The movement itself lost momentum in the face of economic and political impasses and took on a lower profile on the international scene. Nevertheless, in the first decades of the twenty-first century, in a world marked by globalisation and therefore very different from the scenario of the decades from 1950 to 1990 of the last century, new reality emerged. Some countries of what were known as the Third World—a designation that has been gradually replaced by that of Global South—have now become leaders in their respective regions, due to relative advances acquired in recent years that have transformed them into powers of medium importance. They began to be designated in the media as "emerging" countries, and they have come to identify common interests in their international action. The process that emerged from this situation was well known: in September 2006, the foreign ministers of

Brazil, Russia, India and China met during the sixty-first General Assembly of the United Nations and defined their own agenda, which aspired to be amplified and consolidated in ensuing years. In 2011, South Africa was formally incorporated into this dialogue mechanism, which came to be known as BRICS.

The BRICS have brought together the five largest emerging economies—with great disparities among them, of course, considering the Chinese economy represents the second GDP in the world (rapidly approaching that of the US), with India the third and Brazil and South Africa well behind. These countries represent 40% of the world population, approximately three billion people. Having for some time remained informal, the mechanism, originally established to promote cooperation in specific sectors, is consolidating through its successive meetings and has established important steps towards its institutionalisation.

The fourth meeting at the presidential level took place in the city of Fortaleza, Brazil in July 2014. There, an important economic agreement was ratified, the principal result of which was the founding of a new Development Bank, with its head office in Shanghai and India occupying the presidency. The initial capital authorised for the bank is 100 billion dollars. There will also be a Fund of Mutual Guarantees, with another 100 billion dollars. The objective of the new bank is to provide a source of funding for emerging and developing economies. Among its goals is the creation of conditions that will allow for overcoming the present dependence on the dollar as the principal global reserve currency (the agreement foresees a system of convertibility between the Brazilian real, the Russian ruble, the Indian rupee, the Chinese renminbi and the South African rand).

These projects of the BRICS group tally with the (frustrated) goals of the Non Aligned Movement. The proposal of the 1970s for a New International Economic Order depended, to great extent, on agreements that could have been made with some powers of the developed world, since the Third World countries did not have the political force to impose changes in the world economy by themselves. The only exception was perhaps the Organisation of Petroleum Exporting Countries, OPEC, that in 1973, a few days after the conference of the Non Aligned Movement in Algiers and the 1973 Arab–Israeli War war, determined an increase of up to 300% in the price of crude oil and the imposition of embargos on sales for western countries allied with Israel, resulting in the so-called "oil shock".

By 2014 the BRICS were beginning to modify the rules of the world macroeconomic game simply by using their own resources and acting with a clear political will. Not having an appropriate space for dialogue or negotiation under the structures of Bretton Woods, in particular in the IMF and the World Bank, the emerging powers had opted to use to use their weight to create alternatives that do not involve an open dispute with the hegemonic powers and that will allow them to create more inclusive conditions for global growth.

The presence of China and Russia in BRICS, in alliance with India, Brazil and South Africa explains, in part, the difference in the specific clout in the world scene between the BRICS group and the Non Aligned Movement. The proximity of China and Russia with the Non Aligned was already present at the time of the Cold War but the logic of that movement made coordinated action difficult. It is easy to understand that non-alignment did not imply, on the part of its members, an equidistant relation to one or another block. With the exception of one or another country that for historical reasons openly or implicitly defended a priority alliance with the West, the greater part of the Non Aligned Countries were fully aware that their potential allies were in the socialist camp and that they could not expect anything similar from the capitalist block, which included the old colonial powers. But in the bipolar context, they could not advance much more.

For this reason it is important to situate the BRICS alliance in the context of a historical process that calls into question the rules of the game that emerged from the Second World War. The BRICS today, even with diminished Brazilian involvement, can move forward with a project of gradual substitution of the architecture of Bretton Woods due to their own weight in the world economy. This was the essence of the project of the Non Aligned in looking for a new international economic order. The difference is in the concrete possibilities of these parties to achieve the goals of yesterday and today. As for communications, the BRICS block does not seek to challenge the large media conglomerates. This is not the terrain for their struggle.

What they propose is to change the rules of the game in cyberspace — the BRICS have outlined a project to guarantee access to Internet, in confrontation with US hegemony in the network. At present, the Internet system is connected through centres situated in Europe and the United States. The project defined by BRICS—called BRICS Cable—foresees the creation of an alternative infrastructure: an interoceanic system of 34 thousand kilometres of fiber-optic cables, with a capacity of 12.8 terabits per second, beginning in the Russian city of Vladivostok, passing through Shantou, Singapore, Cape Town and Fortaleza, connecting Russia, China, India, South Africa and Brazil before reaching the United States. The main objective of the project—in addition to reducing costs—is to ensure the autonomy of Internet communications of the BRICS in relation to the United States.

Non Aligned / BRICS: their diagnoses coincide. Their actions and, above all, the results do not. The international balance of power from the Bandung Conference to the golden years of the Non Aligned Movement did not allow either for achieving the goal of the New Economic Order, nor for changing the rules in the terrain of communications. The BRICS have not raised any major banners; they began with modest movements, but they are advancing towards the adoption of strategic measures that bring them closer to the definitions of the Non Aligned Movement. We are talking of two moments, two styles and the same objective: a less unequal world, with opportunities for development, prosperity and social justice for the great majorities, in a climate of cooperation and peace.

## Endnotes

1. WRIGHT, Richard, *The Color Curtain: A report on the Bandung Conference*. Cleveland and New York: The World Publishing Company, 1956.
2. The principle of collective defence is at the heart of NATO's founding treaty.

# 14

# Two Big Economic Crises
## The Indonesian Experience and Lessons Learned for Other Asian-African Developing Countries

*Tulus T.H. Tambunan and Ida Busnetty*

## Abstract

This paper aims to examine the Indonesian experience with two big economic crises in the past 12 years, namely the 1997/98 Asian financial crisis and the 2008/09 global economic crisis. The paper is based on secondary data analysis and a review of key literature. It has two main parts. The first part gives a theoretical explanation of the main transmission channels through which the two crises have affected the Indonesian economy. The second part is the empirical part of the paper about the impacts of the crises on such as economic growth, employment, remittances and poverty in Indonesia. One important finding from this study is that the Indonesian economy was much more resilience to the last crisis as compared to the 1997/98 crisis. During this first crisis, Indonesian economic growth was – 13 per cent and poverty increased significantly; whereas during the second one, Indonesia managed to keep a positive economic growth rate (though declined), and poverty kept declining.

*Keywords:* 2008/09 crisis, 1997/98 crisis, economic growth, remittance, poverty, unemployment

## I. Introduction

Indonesia now is much more vulnerable to any economic shocks than, say, 30 years ago, for the following reasons. First, since economic reforms started in the 1980s toward trade, banking, investment, and capital account liberalisations, the Indonesian economy has become more integrated with the world economy. Second, though at a decreasing rate, Indonesia is still dependent on exports of many primary commodities, i.e. mining and agriculture. This means that its economy is still sensitive to any world-price/demand instability for those commodities. Third, Indonesia has become increasingly dependent on imports of a number of food items such as rice, food grains, cereals, wheat, corn, meat, dairy, vegetables and fruits, or even oil. Any increases or instabilities of world prices or the world production failures of these commodities will have big effects on domestic consumption and food security in Indonesia. Fourth, more Indonesian working population, including women, went abroad as migrant workers, and hence livelihoods in many villages in Indonesia have become increasingly dependent on remittances from abroad. Any economic crisis hit the host countries (such as happened in Dubai during its financial crisis in 2009) will hit the Indonesian economy too. Finally, as a huge populated country with increasing income per capita, domestic food consumption is not only high but also keeps increasing. Accelerating output growth in agriculture is therefore a must for Indonesia, and this depends on various factors, including climate, which is an exogenous factor. As Indonesia is located between the Pacific Ocean and the Indian Ocean in the line of equator, the country is always vulnerable to El Nino/La Nina phenomenon, which may cause failures in rice (and other commodities) harvest and therefore will generate a hyperinflation.

Indeed, in the past 12 years, Indonesia has experienced two big economic crises, namely the Asian financial crisis started by mid 1997 and reached its peak in 1998, and the global economic crisis in 2008 and 2009. This paper aims to examine the Indonesian experiences with these two crises. It addresses two key questions. First, what were the main transmission channels through which the two crises affected the Indonesian economy? Second, was the impact on the Indonesian economy different between the two crises, and if yes, what made the difference?

The paper has three main parts. The first part (Chapter II) gives a theoretical explanation on the main transmission channels through which the two crises have affected the Indonesian economy. The second part (Chapter III) discusses the impacts of the two crises on the Indonesian economy focusing on economic growth, export, employment, remittances and poverty. The third part (Chapter IV) gives the most likely reasons that made the impact of the 1997/98 crisis different than that of the 2008/09 crisis.

## II. Transmission Channels

### II.1 The 1997/98 Crisis

In Indonesia, the 1997/98 Asian financial crisis was triggered by a sudden capital flight from the country which led its national currency, rupiah, to depreciate significantly against the US dollar. The depreciation was soon followed by a national banking crisis and ended up as a national economic crisis. Through the rupiah depreciation and higher interest rate (as the monetary authority's direct response in that time in order to stop capital flight), the crisis hit first middle and high income groups such as current employees in the financial/banking sector and large scale industries which strongly dependent on credits from bank or other financial institutions and imports. After several months, domestic inflation started to increase, and this accompanied with the increase in unemployment due to many laid off employees in crisis-affected firms than resulted in a significant increase in the poverty rate in 1998.

Thus, for Indonesia, the 1997/98 crisis was initially a currency crisis. Theoretically, the direct impact of currency depreciation will be mainly on export and import of the particular country (Figure 1). By assuming other factors constant, export, and hence, production and employment or income in the exporting firms/sectors and in their backward as well as forward linked firms/sectors will increase. This is the export effect of currency depreciation. On the import side, domestic prices of imported consumption and non-consumption goods will also increase. In the case of non-consumption goods, i.e. raw materials, capital and intermediate goods, components/spare parts, as a response to higher prices (in national currency) of these imported goods, two scenarios are possible: (1) imports decline and, consequently, total domestic production and employment also drop, or (2) imports may stay constant, but it means thus domestic production cost will increase and finally it will result in higher domestic inflation. This is the import effect of currency depreciation.

Besides the above effects, national currency depreciation also makes the value in national currency of foreign debts (in foreign currency against which the national currency has depreciated) owned by domestic firms to rise. Many highly foreign indebted domestic firms will face a serious financial crisis. If many of them have to reduce their production or even collapse, domestic total production and employment will then further decline. This can be called as the foreign debt cost effect of national currency depreciation[1].

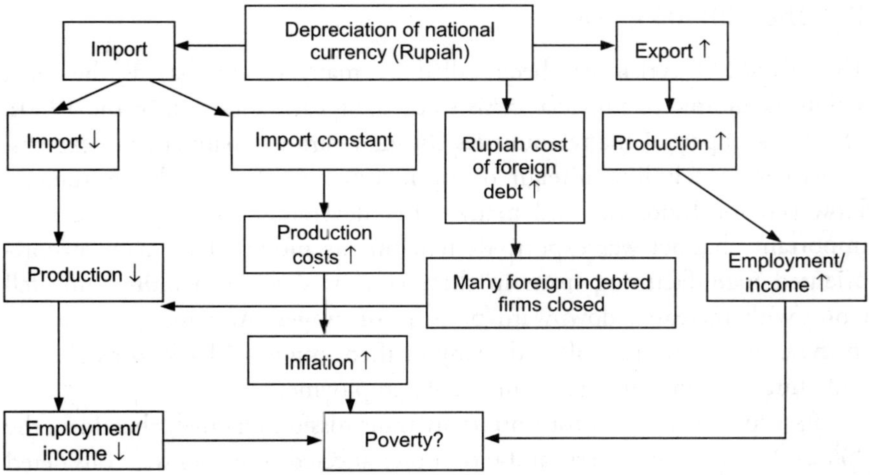


Figure 1: Transmission Channels of the Effects of the 1997/98 Crisis on the Indonesian Economy

The net result of all effects discussed above on poverty, however, can be positive, or negative, or no effect at all, depending on whether the export (positive) effects are larger, equal to or smaller than the import and foreign debts cost (negative) effects of the rupiah depreciation. The key issue here is whether export will increase when national currency is weakening. It depends at least on two main factors. First, the proportion of imported inputs in the export products, because it will determine to what extent the price competitiveness of the products will increase when national currency depreciates. Second, domestic production capacity of the export goods, which determines to what extent the production will increase when their price competitiveness increases.

So, in this 1997/98 crisis case, the key transmission channels through which the crisis affected the Indonesian economy were changes in export and import volumes and cost (in national currency) of foreign debts. With respect to the impact on poverty, the next transmission channels were changes in employment/income, and inflation. As export is usually increase (or at least not decline) when national currency depreciates, the most vulnerable group to the crisis is thus on the import side, especially imports of inputs. However, depends on what sectors are most severely affected by higher import costs (in national currency) and their response to the increased import costs: whether they keep the import volume the same as before depreciation and without any labour adjustment (e.g. lay off or less working hour) or reduce the amount of imports and hence production and employment.

## II.2 The 2008/09 Crisis

The 2008/2009 crisis has been called by many economists as the most serious economic or financial crisis since the great depression in the 1930s. The crisis impacted many countries through various channels, i.e. exports, investment (including foreign direct investment/FDI), and remittances. However, for Indonesia and many other developing countries, the most important channel was export. Retrenchments mounted in many export-oriented manufacturing firms in these countries, while working time fell along with increased downward pressure on wages. Also many employees in these firms were laid off and many of them migrated back to rural areas and shifted to informal and vulnerable employment.

As export was the most important transmission channel, therefore, the 2008/09 crisis for Indonesia and most other affected countries was considered primarily as a world demand/export market crisis. Theoretically, as illustrated in Figure 2, this kind of shock will affect the economy of these countries at the first stage through its effects on their domestic export-oriented firms.

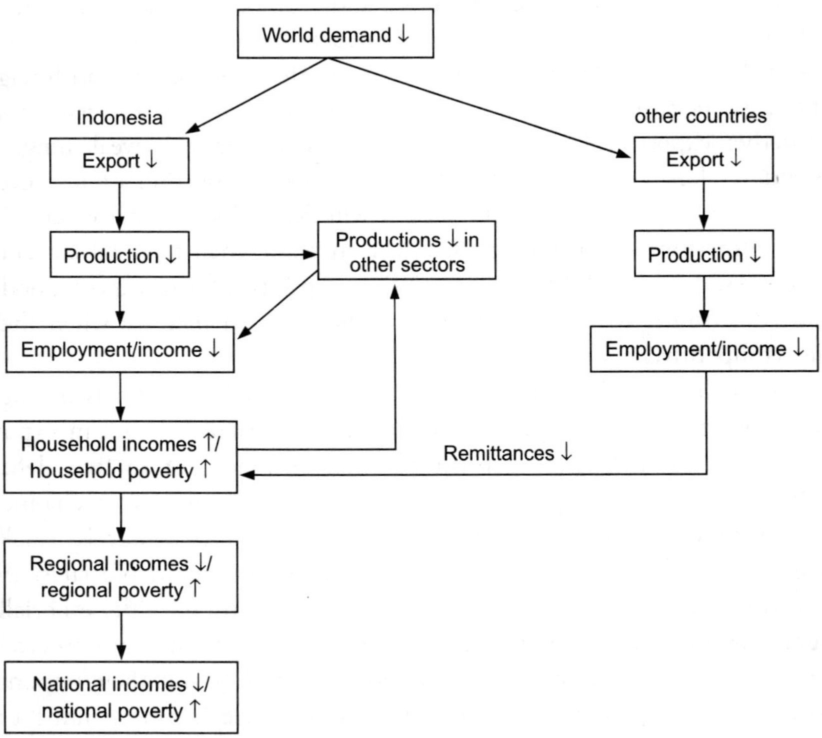


Figure 2: Transmission Channels of the Effects of the 2008/09 Crisis on the Indonesian Economy

It leads further to less production and employment in these firms and in other related firms. The employment reduction causes decline in incomes of many households, and it will result further in lower market demands for goods and services and hence production cuts in many industries/sectors. Finally, unemployment and poverty will increase.

In large countries like Indonesia, which consists of many islands or regions (i.e. provinces, districts and subdistricts), the impact may vary by region, or even the impact in some regions within the country may more severe than at the national level. For instance, if the decline in average household income in Java island (where most export-oriented manufacturing industries are located) is higher than in the rest of the country, and the proportion of the affected households in Java is significant large, then total income in Java will decline faster than that in the rest of the country.

If remittance inflows to Java also decline from foreign countries also affected by the crisis, then the income in Java will drop further. If remittances to other regions in Indonesia also decline, than the national income or the economic growth rate will decrease. In other words, if only one region in Indonesia was affected by the crisis, and the region's economy is not significant important for the national economy based on gross domestic products (GDP) distribution by region, the effect at the national level my insignificant, even if the impact for that particular region is significant. On the other hand, if Java is the highest Indonesia's GDP contributor, even a small impact of the crisis on Java will produce a serious shock for the national economy.

Thus, depending on: (1) the importance of the affected export commodities in Indonesia's total export; (2) the importance of the commodities and their related sectors (through backward and forward production linkages) in the economy of the regions of origin; (3) the importance of the regions' economy in the Indonesian economy; and (4) the crisis-coping measures taken by the affected firms to mitigate the effect of the crisis, the impact or outcome of the 2008/09 crisis on the Indonesian economy and hence poverty can be large or small. Therefore, in analysing the impact of the crisis on Indonesia's economy and poverty, the key are: (a) what export commodities have been hit by the crisis; (b) in what regions; (c) how are their linkages with the rest of the economy; and (d) what types of workers and their households are mostly affected?

## III. The Impacts

### III.1 The 1997/98 Crisis

The 1997/98 crisis hit many countries especially in East and Southeast Asia such as Indonesia, Thailand, Singapore, Malaysia Philippines and South Korea. However, the impact varied by country. Indonesia together with South Korea was among the most severely affected ones. The Indonesian economy had plunged into a deep recession in 1998 with overall growth at minus 13.7 per cent. The worst declines were in the construction sector, financial sector, trade, and hotel and restaurant. Other sectors, which had large contractions, were manufacturing and transport and communication. Mining and other services sectors also experienced a contraction. The agricultural and utility sectors still experienced positive growth (Feridhanusetyawan, et al., 2000). The crisis also led to a significant drop in income per capita, and a significant increase in poverty rate. All this evidence may suggest that the rupiah depreciation was more negative rather than positive for the Indonesian economy.

The increase in poverty and the decline in income per capita were consistent with output contractions in many sectors as explained before. There were three main reasons why the rupiah depreciation had caused a serious decline in Indonesia's aggregate output. First, despite the fact that Indonesia has adopted import substitution strategy during the New Order era (1966–1998), Indonesia, especially the manufacturing industry, has been increasingly dependent on imported capital and intermediate goods, components and spare parts, and some processed raw materials. So, the rupiah depreciation prevented many export-oriented firms from gaining better world price competitiveness, on one hand, while, on the other hand, many domestic market-oriented firms had to close down or to cut their production volume because they could not purchase any more very expensive imports. Second, many firms, especially conglomerates, during the New Order era had borrowed a lot money from foreign capital markets; mostly were short-term loans. They went bankrupt when rupiah depreciated and many other firms, which had business relations with them, were also in trouble. Third, the national banking sector was also collapsed. By the end of 1997 16 commercial banks were closed, and access to credit became very difficult and interest rate increased significantly. This has contributed significantly to output contractions in many sectors in Indonesia.

There is some evidence that the crisis not only increased poverty but also reduced the quality and supply of education and health services. Chhibber, at al. (2009) report that the crisis decreased enrolment rates among children aged 8–13 years and increased enrolment rates among children aged 14–19 years, although these changes were small, just one percentage point of enrolment. The impact on school enrolment, however, varied by region, suggesting that different regions in the country may have experienced differently with the crisis. Another important study is a 1999 report issued by the Australian Agency for International Development (AusAID). It shows that the crisis had numerous adverse health impacts in Indonesia, including: (1) declines in, respectively, personal and government expenditures on primary care. The use of health services for primary care also declined; (2) decline in purchases of medicines; (3) declines in DTP3 immunisation rates and polio rates. Vitamin A supplementation also fell. The declines most likely occurred among the poorer populations; (4) decline in the lowest wealth quintile in child visits to health facilities; (5) a halt in the 1990s downward trend in infant mortality; and (7) mortality increases (AusAid, 1999).

### III.2 The 2008/09 Crisis

Up to the end of 2008, countries like Thailand, Malaysia, Singapore, Philippines and Indonesia still shown some resilience towards the crisis. However in the first quarter 2009, they experienced deteriorating economic performance, except Indonesia. Singapore suffered the most and recorded –8.9 per cent in real GDP growth rate (year-on-year basis) in the first quarter 2009. This was not surprise at all, given the fact that as a tiny economy, Singapore is fully integrated with the global market for goods, services and finance. Consequently, its economy is fully sensitive to any external economic shocks. The country's economy then started to recover with positive growth again in the third quarter. Similarly with Singapore was Thailand, which has also been seriously hit by the crisis since the third quarter 2008, and the economy contracted by 7.11 per cent in the first quarter 2009. Thailand achieved again positive growth in the last quarter 2009. Malaysia, which experienced a slightly positive growth of around 0.1 per cent in the last quarter 2008, also suffered economic contraction by 6.20 per cent in the first quarter 2009. Meanwhile, Indonesia and the Philippines managed to keep positive growth although at declining rates during the crisis period. In the first quarter 2009, Indonesia achieved 6.2 per cent growth, but in the last quarter it was lower at 5.2 per cent.

While the economy of other countries in the group was deteriorated significantly especially during the first months in 2009, Indonesia has not only positive but also slightly higher GDP growth rates during the second and third quarters 2009. In overall, however, official data (National Agency of Statistics/BPS) show that the growth rate of Indonesian economy was at around 4.5 percent, much lower than the growth rate achieved in 2008. This may suggest that the Indonesian economy was also affected by the world economic recession in 2008/09, but nevertheless the country was able to keep positive economic growth rates during the crisis period.

Further as shown in Table 1, besides Indonesia, there were other few countries in the region, such as China, India, Pakistan and Bangladesh, which were also managed to mitigate the impact of the crisis on their domestic economy. Interestingly, the table shows that, within the developing world, countries in Asia and the Pacific region performed much better than those in other parts of the world during the crisis. Of course, many explanations can be thought, including that the variation in the impact of this kind of crisis on domestic economy is strongly related to the degree of integration of the particular country with the world economy. Rapidness and effectiveness of crisis-coping policy measures in the particular country may also played an important role.

TABLE 1: Economic Growth in the Developing World by Region, 2007–2010

| | *2007* | *2008* | *2009* | *2010** |
|---|---|---|---|---|
| East Asia and Pacific | 11.4 | 8.0 | 6.8 | 8.1 |
| – PRC | 13.0 | 9.0 | 8.4 | 9.0 |
| – Indonesia | 6.3 | 6.2 | 4.5 | 5.6 |
| – Thailand | 4.9 | 2.2 | –2.7 | 3.5 |
| Europe and Central Asia | 7.1 | 4.2 | –6.2 | 2.7 |
| South Asia | 8.5 | 5.7 | 5.7 | 6.9 |
| – India | 9.1 | 6.1 | 6.0 | 7.5 |
| – Pakistan | 5.7 | 2.0 | 3.7 | 3.0 |
| – Bangladesh | 6.4 | 6.2 | 5.9 | 5.5 |
| Latin America and Caribbean | 5.5 | 3.9 | -2.6 | 3.1 |
| Middle East and North Africa | 5.9 | 4.3 | 2.9 | 3.7 |
| Sub-Saharan Africa | 6.5 | 5.1 | 1.1 | 3.8 |

*Note:* * forecast by the World Bank.
*Source:* World Bank (2010a).

With respect to remittances, according to ILO (2009), the number of Indonesian workers abroad had been on an upward trend until the crisis deepened in mid 2009. Yugo et al. (2009) provide data which show that the number of Indonesian workers departed overseas increased with 258,000 workers by the end of December 2008 or around 54 per cent as compared to the end of September 2008 with 168,000 workers. However, total Indonesian workers went abroad in 2008 were less than in 2007.

However, according to Yugo, et als. (2009) estimation, total remittances inflows from overseas Indonesian workers declined slightly to approximately US$ 1.589 billion in the end of first quarter 2009 from US$ 1.61 billion in December 2008. It is not sure whether the less number of Indonesian overseas workers in 2008 compared to 2007 or the slightly decline in remittances inflows was caused by the crisis?

With respect to the impact of the crisis on employment, according to ADB (2009), unemployment in many Asian developing countries has risen during the 2008/09 crisis, particularly in the more export-dependent economies of Hong Kong, China; Singapore; and Taiwan. In Indonesia, the number of workers dismissal and homed in the formal sector has steadily increased during end December 2008 and early December 2009. While, according to ILO (2009) the crisis has prompted a steep fall in the growth of wage employment, which grew about 1.4 per cent during the period February 2008–February 2009, compared to 6.1 per cent during the same period in the previous year.

But, surprisingly, open unemployment has not increased significantly in that period. Even, it declined between February-August 2009. One explanation is that Indonesia has a large informal sector, which absorbed laid-off employees from crisis-affected firms in the formal sector. In other words, the impact of the crisis on Indonesia's labour market was not the significant increase in open employment but in disguised unemployment working in the informal sector.

TABLE 2: Poverty in Indonesia, 2000–2011

| *Year* | *Number of Poor (million)* | | | *Percentage of poverty (%)* | | |
|---|---|---|---|---|---|---|
| | *Urban* | *Rural* | *Total* | *Urban* | *Rural* | *Total* |
| 2000 | 12.30 | 26.40 | 38.70 | 14.60 | 22.38 | 19.14 |
| 2001 | 8.60 | 29.30 | 37.90 | 9.76 | 24.84 | 18.41 |
| 2002 | 13.30 | 25.10 | 38.40 | 14.46 | 21.10 | 18.20 |
| 2003 | 12.20 | 25.10 | 37.30 | 13.57 | 20.23 | 17.42 |
| 2004 | 11.40 | 24.80 | 36.10 | 12.13 | 20.11 | 16.66 |
| 2005 | 12.40 | 22.70 | 35.10 | 11.68 | 19.98 | 15.97 |
| 2006 | 14.49 | 24.81 | 39.30 | 13.47 | 21.81 | 17.75 |
| 2007 | 13.56 | 23.61 | 37.17 | 12.52 | 20.37 | 16.58 |
| 2008 | 12.77 | 22.19 | 34.96 | 11.65 | 18.93 | 15.42* |
| 2009 | .. | .. | .. | .. | .. | 14.20** |
| 2010 | .. | .. | .. | .. | .. | 13.51*** |
| 2011 | .. | .. | .. | .. | .. | 11.42*** |

Note: *= March; ** February' ***World Bank's estimates (World Bank, 2009a).
*Source:* BPS (www.bps.go.id).

Finally, the impact of the crisis on poverty in Indonesia was the most concern in that time. As shown before, in the aftermath of the 1997/98 crisis, poverty increased dramatically from around 17.47 per cent in 1996 to about 24.23 per cent in 1998, when the crisis reached its climax. However, in 1999 poverty started to decline gradually, though first very slightly, up to 2005. In 2006, due to the high increase in world fuel prices, and as Indonesia has become increasingly dependent on imports of oil, the poverty rate increased again, on average between 1.8 percentage point per year or about 4.2 million people fell into poverty between the period 2005–2006. Only after some policy adjustments and macroeconomic stabilisation, the poverty rate started to decline again in 2007. In relative terms, the poverty rate in 2007 was the same as that before the 1997/98 crisis. However, in absolute terms, the number of those living under the current poverty line was still higher than that in the pre-1997/98 crisis period. Although the difference varies by year, the poverty rate in urban areas is always lower than that in rural areas. According to World Bank's estimates, the poverty rate is likely to continue to fall, from 14.2 per February 2009 to around 13.5 per cent in early 2010 and 11.4 per cent in early 2011 (Table 2). This suggests that the 2008/09 crisis would not lead to an increase of the poverty rate in Indonesia (as compared to the 1997/98 crisis).

## IV. Main Factors That Made the Difference

By now it is well known that Indonesia was not only weathering the 2008/09 global economic crisis better than most other countries, but it was also much different than during the 1997/98 Asian financial crisis. The World Bank concludes the following: *One year after the global financial crisis and economic downturn, Indonesia's economy appears to be broadly back on track. Economic activity has been picking up, inflation has remained moderate, financial markets have risen, and the newly re-elected government, having established the strong fundamentals that supported Indonesia through the global crisis, appears to be now gearing up for new investments in Indonesia's physical infrastructure, human services and institutions of state. Indonesia seems well positioned to get back on its pre-crisis growth trajectory, with the possibility of further acceleration and more inclusive growth* (World Bank, 2009a, page iv).

Was the difference because the Indonesian government's response this time was quicker or was better prepared than during the 1997/98 crisis, or there were other factors? According to many discussions/studies[2], there are various reasons, and the most important ones are the followings:

1. from a regional perspective, the Indonesian economy performed well in the years before 2008 (with one of the best growth rates in Asia after

the 1997/98 Asian crisis up to 2008, particularly during the period 2005–2008);

2. the banking sector remains in good health (which was not the case in the years before the 1997/98 Asian economic crisis), although bank lending growth reduced in line with the slowing economy;
3. consumer prices kept stable, allowing Bank Indonesia (BI) to loosen monetary policy (which is important to keep consumption growth);
4. Indonesia's external position remained sound, the country's significant external financing obligations are being met, and foreign exchange reserves have risen slightly;
5. Indonesia's public finances are strong (which was not the case during the 1997/98 Asian crisis), allowing policy makers to quickly move to offset the global downturn's effects on Indonesia with a fiscal stimulus;
6. also based on the experience of the 1997/98 crisis, cautious policies by Indonesia's government, banks, and corporations, over the past decade have resulted in low debt levels and limited refinancing needs. This served the country especially well in late 2008 and early 2009, when liquidity tightened around the world;
7. compared with some Asian countries, Indonesia is a relatively "closed economy"[3];
8. consumers kept spending despite the fact that banks tightened credits in late 2008. Much of this spending might also relate to the election related activities; and
9. based on the experience of the 1997/98 Asian crisis, this time the Indonesian government was more quick and more active in response with appropriate measures to the crisis, e.g. by providing the stimulus through fiscal and monetary policies.

While, main reasons given by the Asian Development Bank that made Indonesia was more resilience than other countries during the 2008/09 crisis are the followings (ADB, 2010b):

1. the impact of a spike in risk aversion was muted by steady policy responses in Indonesia and the stabilising impact of co-ordinated global counter-measures on global financial markets;
2. the income impact of the fall in commodity prices was mitigated by the fact that the preceding years had seen record high prices for these same commodities, allowing rural households to build up a savings buffer to help them smoothen out consumption spending;
3. because the global recession was of relatively short duration, the lagged effects of the financial crisis were avoided;

4. the government's good housekeeping of previous years provided it with the space to take swifter and more effective policy responses than in previous episodes of external shocks; and
5. the balance sheets of the banking, corporate, and household sectors were much stronger.

## V. Lessons Learned for Other Asian-African Developing Countries

As shown in this paper, during the 1997/98 crisis the Indonesian economy performed significantly different compared to that during the 2008/09 crisis: after learning lessons from macroeconomic mismanagement and other related mistakes that led the country's economy to a big recession during the first crisis, Indonesia was much more resilience during the second crisis. Even, Indonesia weathered the 2008/09 crisis better than most other affected countries. The lessons that Indonesia learned from these two crises can also be learned by other Asian-African developing countries, and the key lessons are the followings:

1. maintain long-term high economic growth, supported by sound fiscal and monetary policies;
2. banking sector must remain in good health;
3. the balance sheets of the banking, corporate, and household sectors must keep strong;
4. prices must keep stable, allowing central bank to loosen monetary policy, which is important to keep consumption growth;
5. external position must remain sound (export must keep larger than import), external financing obligations must be met, and foreign exchange reserves must continue to increase;
6. rely on export of primary commodities in total export should be minimised by developing exports of especially manufactured goods based on the country's comparative and competitive advantages;
7. import dependency especially for consumers and industrial goods should be minimised by developing import-substitution industries based on the country's comparative and competitive advantages, not on protectionism;
8. public finances must remain strong allowing policy makers to quickly move to offset any regional or global downturn's effects on domestic economy with a fiscal stimulus;
9. both government and private sectors should always be careful in financing their activities with foreign debt, and their foreign funds should always be hedged.

10. government as well as private sector/consumers should keep spending, even if banks tight their credits;
11. government should always be ready for any types of crisis and it should quick and more active in response with appropriate measures to any crisis, e.g. by providing the stimulus through fiscal and monetary policies; and
12. above all: social and political stability is a pre-condition to implement all points mentioned above.

## Endnotes

1. Financial conditions of national governments which borrowed a lot of money from abroad will also deteriorate as national currency depreciates. However, in the case of Indonesia, the impact on domestic production and employment was not evident. Even, during the crisis the government could increase its expenditure on fuel, health and education to mitigate the impact of the crisis on the poor. A large part of the increased expenditure was from loans provided by the International Monetary Fund (IMF).
2. See for instance, World Bank (2009b, 2010b), Djaja (2009), Zavadjil (2009), and ADB (2009, 2010a).
3. In his study, Djaja (2009) shows that the share of Indonesia's exports to GDP was 29.4 per cent in 2007. The figure in the next three quarters of 2008 was 30.0 per cent on average. About 85 per cent of goods and services produced by Indonesian economy were used domestically in 2005, while only about 15 per cent went to foreign buyers. This indicates that Indonesia is not so strongly integrated with the rest of the world, at least from an export point of view. With such low exports, a sudden drop in world income and hence in world demand for Indonesian exports will not affect significantly domestic production.

## References


ADB (2009), *Asian Development Outlook 2009 Update*, Manila: Asian Development Bank.

ADB (2010a), *Asian Development Outlook 2010*, Manila: Asian Development Bank.

ADB (2010b), "Impact and Policy Responses: Indonesia, Philippines and Thailand", Report 6, ADB Regional Forum on the Impact of Global Economic and Financial Crisis, 14–15 January, Manila: Asian Development Bank.

ASEAN-World Bank (2009), "ASEAN Assessment on the Social Impacts of the Global Financial Crisis", A Snap-shot Report for notation at the 15th ASEAN Summit, 23 October, Cha-am Hua Hin, Thailand.

Berg, Andrew and Catherine Pattillo (1999a), "Predicting currency crises: the indicators approach and an alternative", *Journal of International Money and Finance*, August, 18(4): 561–586.

Berg, Andrew and Catherine Pattillo (1999b), "Are currency crises predictable? A test", IMF Staff Papers, June, 46(2): 107–138.

Berg, Andrew and Catherine Pattillo (1999c), "What caused the Asian crises: An early warning system approach", unpublished manuscript, Washington D.C., International Monetary Fund.

Edison, Hali J. (2000), "Do Indicators of Financial Crises Work? An Evaluation of An Early Warning System", International Finance Discussion Papers, No. 675, July, New York: Board of Governors of the Federal Reserve System.

Berg, Andrew, Eduardo Borensztein, and Catherine Pattillo (2004), "Assessing Early Warning Systems: How Have They Worked in Practice?", IMF Working Paper, March, Research Department, Washington, D.C.: International Monetary Fund.

Djaja, Komara (2009), "Impact of the Global Financial and Economic Crisis on Indonesia. A Rapid Assessment", paper prepared for the ILO, Secretary Coordinating Ministry for Economic Affairs, Indonesia.

Feridhanusetyawan, Tubagus, Haryo Aswicahyono and Titik Anas (2000), "The Economic Crisis and the Manufacturing Industry: The Role of Industrial Networks", CSIS Working Paper Series WPE 053, January, Jakarta: Center for Strategy and International Study (CSIS).

ILO (2009), *Labour and Social Trends in Indonesia 2009. Recovery and beyond through decent work*, Jakarta: International Labour Organisation Office for Indonesia.

Kaminsky, Graciela, and Carmen Reinhart (1999), "The twin crises: The causes of banking and balance of payments problems", *American Economic Review*, 89:3: 473–500.

Kaminsky, Graciela, Saul Lizondo and Carmen Reinhart (1998), "Leading indicators of currency crises", International Monetary Fund Staff Papers, 45: 1–48.

Masson, Paul, Eduardo Borensztein, Andrew Berg, Gian Maria Milesi-Ferretti and Catherine Pattillo (1999), "Anticipating balance of payments crises: The role of early warning systems", unpublished manuscript, Washington D.C., International Monetary Fund.

Tambunan, Tulus T.H. (2002), "Building 'An Early Warning System' For Indonesia With The Signal Approach", September, EADN Regional Project on Indicators and Analyses of Vulnerabilities to Economic Crises (EADNRP2–4), Bangkok: East Asian Development Network.

World Bank (2009a), "Migration and Development Brief 10", July 13, Washington, D.C.

World Bank (2009b), "Developing Indonesia's Crisis Monitoring and Response System", power point presentation, 6 June, World Bank Poverty Team, Jakarta.

World Bank (2009c), "Battling the forces of global recession", a World Bank economic update for the East Asia and Pacific Region", April 2009, Bangkok.

World Bank (2010a), *Global Economic Prospect. Crisis, Finance and Growth 2010*, Washington, D.C.

World Bank (2010b), "Indonesia's Crisis Monitoring and Response System (CMRS). Analysis and Presentation of CMRS Data". First Round Summary Report, 25 January, Jakarta.

Yudo, Teguh, Ira S. Titiheruw and Hadi Soesastro (2009), "The Impact of the Global Financial Crisis on Indonesia's Economy", Study Report submitted to The United Nations Development Programme (UNDP), September, Jakarta: Centre for Strategic and International Studies (CSIS).

Zavadjil, Milan (2009), "Indonesia's strong balance sheets—key to weathering the global financial crisis", 19, November, East Asia Forum.

# 15

# Dilemmas of Development and Challenges for Emerging Countries[1]

*Sit Tsui, Erebus Wong, Wen Tiejun and Lau Kin Chi*

## Abstract

Within the historical framework of the progress of global capitalism, we examine and compare the development experiences of developing countries over the past century particularly that of seven selected emerging countries (E7). Each country research team[2] has provided a report of historical review on their development experiences. Based on their studies, the E7 academic team completes an overall cross-country report entitled "E7: Comparative Study on the Objective Experiences of Seven Emerging Developing Countries". This paper outlines the categories, methodology and perspectives adopted by the report. Particularly, agrarian reforms and China's stock market crash of 2015 will be illustrated as two examples of encountering the development trap[3] of financial capitalism.

*Keywords:* financial capitalism, development trap, emerging countries, cost transfer, sovereignty externality

## 1. The Seven Emerging Countries, or E7

The seven countries that form the major subject of our study are (in alphabetical order): Brazil, China, India, Indonesia, South Africa, Turkey and Venezuela. This report adopts the term 'emerging countries,' which is generally accepted within international discourse to refer to relatively "successful" developing countries. By 'emerging' we mean—with the exception of Turkey—they were once subject to the yoke of colonial or semi-colonial rule, and gained national sovereignty through de-colonial struggle and later entered a period of development. We therefore emphasise that our use of the term "E7" invokes the notion of the above-named countries as emerging *economies*.

This concept is distinctly different from the notion of 'emerging market' deployed by the mainstream media and academy. 'Emerging market' implies a value judgment delineated by ideology; it implicitly connotes a cause-effect relation: the success of the countries said to fall under the rubric of 'emerging market' is attributed to 'marketisation'; hence, the concept is applied to the BRICS (Russia, Brazil, India, China, South Africa) countries for imposing an institutional transition towards free-market economy,' a change highly praised by the West. However, this framing as a historical category is unconvincing since it ignores the fact that Russia was one of the Western powers in the 19th century as well as one of the two super powers dominating the world in the 20th century. Accordingly, such a mismatching classification would fly in the face of anyone with a genuine appreciation of history.

This report seeks to examine the change of the global situation based on the perspective of and experiences of developing countries. Hence we understand the mainstream conceptual 'labelling' implies a sense of unease as the global power constellation is shifting and the existing historical categorisation becomes obsolete. Meanwhile, we willingly aspire to dialogue with "mainstream" discourses but on the other hand hope that the latter can understand that the basic position of E7 comparative research is not meant to be constrained by euro-centric ideological discourses.

## 2. The Rationale of Selection

We select these seven countries not only because they were once so-called 'successful' models of development or that their shares of the world economy are always significantly large. Most importantly, they have undergone many crises in modern history. Their development experiences can serve as a better revelation of the objective process of global capitalism, perhaps much more so than that of the developed countries.

Furthermore, the geo-political significance of every E7 country during the stage of industrial capitalism is obvious. Precisely because of their strategic importance in shaping geo-political constellation, the history of E7 is particularly instructive in helping us to understand the nature of global crises. The history of the E7 provides an account of how Latin America, Africa and Asia were and continue to be involved and imbricated in the progress of the world capitalist system. It is important to note that before their forced integration into the world economy, these countries and regions did enjoy a long period of prosperity, and their economies accounted for an overwhelming share of the world economy[4]. After Europe forced the historical "progress" of colonialism and capitalism, the West emerged from the margins of the world-system and became the core of the world. As a consequence the economic disparity between the West and the Non-West has been widening. No doubt industrial capitalism, which had completed primitive accumulation of capital through colonisation, is an economic system producing great material wealth. And it is always considered to be the proof of the superiority of Western culture and its social systems.

During the process of being forcibly integrated into the capitalist system through violent colonisation, the economic levels of these countries and regions not only stagnated, but also declined. Worse still, some experienced social disintegration (for example, the ancient civilisations of South America were totally destroyed by the Spanish). Except Turkey, all the other six countries were once colonised or being occupied.

Basically the E7 can be divided into two groups: the first, countries characterised by a *resources* economy (Brazil, Indonesia, South Africa, and Venezuela); the other, countries characterised by an *industrial* economy (China, India, Turkey and Brazil[5]).

## 3. Reflections on Methodology

Nowadays, there are many academic theories and public opinion too impregnated with strong ideological judgment that they cannot be useful for understanding reality (regardless of whether they are the intellectual products of leftists, rightists, conservatives, or liberalists). Moreover, these ideologies originally come from a Western milieu, their academies and polities, and are mainly derived from the historical experiences of Western countries. While they could be a useful reference for explaining certain social phenomena of these Western countries, their uncritical application into the study of Non-Western societies will not only fail in describing the realities of these societies, it is tantamount to falling prey to eurocentrism of the most fundamental kind. Relying on the ideologised criteria to judge the developing countries bespeaks a futile dependence on Western representations of realities to understand the former's experiences.

And even if such transportability of categories were epistemologically possible, the fact of the matter is that the developing countries are unable to compete with the developed countries at that same level. That is, we are here dealing with historically and ontologically distinct realities. In other words, there are irreducible differences in terms of the historical and politico-economic starting points between developing countries and developed countries. The former has not enjoyed the advantages of the latter which started to take off after occupying colonies (those European countries without the opportunity of large-scale colonisation usually had a history of militarism and authoritarianism). Therefore, it is difficult to transcendentally impose what is learnt from the experiences of the developed countries on to the developing countries.

In the first decade of the 21st century, the crisis of globalisation has finally exploded in the core nations of world capitalism. Under this pressure, the emerging countries have developed into non-neglectable economic entities (and widely recognised as an achievement). In regard of this, it is high time we should let go of eurocentric ideological judgments and ponder upon the following questions: what are the factors that allowed them to attain their present status? In comparison, many developing countries after years of endeavour cannot fulfil their original expectations, but worse still get trapped in a developmental pitfall, incapable of finding a way out. What are the factors that contributed to two such different trajectories?

In order to answer these questions, we not only have to study the contemporary, we also have to look into history. Not merely the developmental trajectories of the emerging countries, but also the macro background of the institutional transition of the advanced countries which continue to dominate the world. Then we make a judgment on the current status of these emerging countries. At the present, what is the current situation they confront in the global state of affairs? What will be their future scenario?

## 4. The 3S for Sustainability

When we emphasise the scientific methodology, we of course know that it is impossible to be totally value-free in the research of human and social sciences. In fact, mainstream discourse often claims to be value-free in order to cover its ideology. Hence, we prefer to advocate clearly that 'resources sovereignty, social solidarity and human security' should be the values embraced by developing countries, as alternatives to mainstream global capitalist ideologies.

Our initiatives are: 'from Resources Sovereignty, by Social Solidarity, for Human Security'. Only by upholding the three S principles do we have a chance to achieve eco-human sustainability. This is exactly the keynote of the Declaration of 3S for Sustainability during the First South-South Forum on Sustainability[6].

## 5. Alternative Perspectives

This report provides the following alternative perspectives:

> Industrial capital excess, be it in any kind of economic and political system, leads to outward industry transfer

The process of national industrialisation in the E7 is directly related to the overproduction (industrial capital excess) in developed and industrialised countries, which led to the outbreak of WWII as well as the subsequent outward industrial capital transfer. Moreover, during the Cold War overarched by the superpowers, and under the condition of vicious industrial competition, the ruling groups in the E7, in pursuit of modernisation, no matter what kind of ideology they advocate, invariably adopted a 'pro-foreign capital' policy owing to domestic capital scarcity. The pro-foreign capital dependency of the E7 meant that they had, in general, to acquiesce to foreign investors' demands for institutional changes as a *quid pro quo* for capital investment. This in turn calls up the question of sovereignty. Any country which subsequently attempts to defend and assert its national sovereignty encounters difficulties de-linking from the foreign capital that has been already introduced into the country. The typical result is an outbreak of complicated and intensive social conflicts.

> Capital formation is directly proportional to the socio-economic-ecological risks that beset a society, regardless of the social formation (capitalism, socialism etc.) under which it occurs.

The E7 is no exception. On the one hand, it is the risk caused by externality—when a country accepts the industry transfer, it also has to accept the intensification of social conflicts that originate from capital—labour confrontation; on the other hand, the over-exploitation of natural resources by capital and the subsequent environmental degradation often lead to ecological crisis. E-7 experiences show that once a country starts industrialisation, there will be a continuous accumulation of risks due to the endogenous 'capital intensification' of foreign capital and the primitive accumulation of domestic capital. This matches the regularity of cyclical economic crises as elaborated by political economy. The real experience of E7 is therefore how the ruling groups in the emerging countries deal with crises by making different macro policy adjustments which lead to endogenous institution transition or generally known as "reform".

> The nature of contemporary globalisation is the outward transfer of institutional costs by developed countries with an advanced economic structure.

The global economy at the stage of financialisation is dominated by developed countries' currency-political strategy, which is pivoted on the former's currency hegemony. In essence, it is the process through which developed economies transfer their debts crisis to the rest of the world through large-scale creation of financial credits. That is the reason why most of the E7 economies are unable to adopt effective domestic policy of macro-regulation to solve the crisis of imported inflation. Moreover, the lower position a developing country occupies in the international division of labour, the heavier the institutional cost transfer it has to bear—for example, those countries with manufacturing industries which are dependent on investments by transnational corporations, or those countries whose natural resources are under the control of transnational companies.

> Successful experiences of inclusive growth result from the formation of social capital based on localised economic sovereignty.

Because of their different economic structures and systems, countries within the E7 have responded differently to the challenges of globalisation—the countries without full economic sovereignty are prone to become "re-colonised"; although those countries with relatively full sovereignty adopt different ways to deal with the enormous cost transfer by the developed countries, they basically reinforce the government's (at central or local level) command over economic sovereignty. Those countries having intact resources sovereignty are thus capable of enjoying a portion of the gains from the capitalisation of resources through autonomic monetisation of resources. In this way these countries can have a better leeway to respond to the pressure of downward cost transfer implied in the currency-political strategy in a unipolar world.

## 6. Cost Transfer

In order to attract foreign capital, developing countries that receive industry transfer have to implement pro-capital policies regardless of the sort of political ideologies they endorse. They have to promote institutional transition according to the requirements of the investing countries during the process of industry and capital transfer. While the formation of industrial capital promotes economic growth, it also results in a double risk at the national level; namely, in the country's simultaneous exposure to an increasing probability of industrial and political (institutional) risks. A general rule is that the concentration of capital naturally leads to the intensification of risk.

Whether an emerging country can succeed in terms of avoiding the development trap when it accepts industry transfer very much depends on its ability to internalise the resulting externalities as an institutional cost at the national level[7].

The industrialisation of the developing countries after WWII was generally not endogenous as they were confronted with technological backwardness and the scarcity of capital and resources. Furthermore, colonisation was not a means they could take advantage of. As a result, developmental entrapment during industry transfer had become a general phenomenon. Only in a few exceptional cases could developing countries manage to escape the development trap.

It is a common experience among developing countries that when they accept capital and industry transfer to undertake industrialisation and urbanisation, they also have to bear the institutional costs endogenous to capital and industry. The same social problems once faced by the advanced countries have become even more serious as the developing countries cannot transfer such costs outward. In the meantime, the advanced countries enjoy larger capital returns transferring physical industry outward while upgrading their own economy to financial capitalism.

We believe that the course of development as led by advanced countries can be divided into three historical stages. The first stage is the primitive accumulation of capital through colonisation; the second is the development of industrial capital through industrialisation; the third is the globalisation of capital through financialisation[8]. Upon examining the three rounds of massive industry transfer out of the advanced countries after WWII, it is apparent that they have not simply been commercial decisions made by individual enterprises. Rather, these transfers are the natural consequence of the macroscopic contradictions in the world system.

Most of the problems in the comparative studies of E7 focus on the second stage. This emphasis can be explained by the fact that the stage of industrial capitalism involves the following general rule: in capital-intensive advanced countries the over-accumulation of capital leads to a decline in the average rates of profit of enterprises producing general commodities as well as the intensification of risks intrinsic to capital. It is due to the pressure of this tendency that enterprises have striven to reduce costs through industry transfer. This trend has intensified especially after the disintegration of the Bretton Woods System. An astronomical increase of money supply has led to an intensification of monetisation and financial leveraging. As a result, financial capital has alienated itself from the production of physical goods such as is involved in agriculture and manufacturing. Since the 1980s, under the influence of neoliberal ideology, advanced countries have become increasingly dependent on the profits derived from liquidity expansion; that is, through the creation of financial derivatives and other such financial products. They have thereby enjoyed the institutional gains of financialisation. Moreover, this trend has further raised the cost of manufacturing. As a result we have witnessed the second industry transfer.

## 7. Industrialisation led to Pro-capital Regime

Western economics is premised on the relative scarcity of production factors. However, the realistic condition developing countries generally have to face in pursuit of modernisation is the absolute scarcity of capital factor; there is hardly any capital available to substitute for labour. The difference between the conditions of relative scarcity and absolute scarcity is not quantitative but qualitative. Therefore Western economics based on the relative scarcity of factors is not totally applicable to developing countries encountering extreme scarcity in capital factor.

Developing countries in pursuit of industrialisation (modernisation) have to face the predicament of extreme scarcity of capital factor. Pro-capital policy is generally unavoidable. Most of the developing countries accepting industry transfer have to build a pro-capital government and educational system, irrespective of what they declare their political ideology to be.

For example, the newly established Chinese regime in the period of "New Democracy" during the early 1950s clearly objected to populism and established an economic institution of state capitalism. The situation was similar to Turkey's *étastisme* which in practice led to a de-politicisation of the population and weakened class consciousness. The similarity between Turkey and China resides in the fact that both nations were oriented toward national capitalism. After the anti-communist and anti-Chinese movements during the 1960s, Indonesia accumulated significant foreign debt stocks. The reason behind these manoeuvres was a reaction to the pervasive international leftwing movements in the 1960s, which were unfavourable to a pro-capital policy.

When transnational corporations march into developing countries, they not only push structural changes to its economic foundations but also promote a shift in ideology and values (the superstructure). In general, the introduction of foreign investment naturally leads to a more radical pro-capital institutional transition and corresponding ideology in the recipient countries.

Since the 1980s the free flow of capital—the centrepiece of the practice of neoliberalism—has been promoted by the developed nations of the world. This demand in economy, which is in fact an imperative of capital, has led to major institutional changes. Firstly the erstwhile general measure of physical production, gross national product (GNP), has been replaced by gross domestic product (GDP), which calculates the volume of commodities trade. In 1994 the General Agreement on Tariffs and Trade (GATT) was replaced by the World Trade Organisation (WTO). Accompanying the transition from GATT to the WTO was a significant change undertaken in two strategic sectors which are closely related to people's livelihood; namely, that finance and agriculture be incorporated into the institution of international free trade, which was an issue that was controversial and hotly contested in the Uruguay Round Negotiations.

## 8. Sovereignty Externality

By studying the history of developing countries, we discover a prevalent form of incomplete sovereignty. In many cases where nationalist liberation movements took the chance of the historical conjuncture of the WWII and the Cold War, the formal sovereignty thus achieved after independence was often the result of negotiations between the former colonial regime and political parties headed by the elites. In other instances, local social groups supported by foreign powers established political democracy through negotiations with the former rulers. Nevertheless whenever a government emerged from some sort of political deal, the country's sovereignty has often been compromised in the process of negotiations with the old powers (such as domestic capital bloc or foreign capitals). It is manifested in two aspects. On the one hand the new regime had to recognise the property right of the transnational capital and bureaucrat-capitalist class and forced to compromise on its economic sovereignty; on the other hand, it had to recognise the "soft power" of the former colonial suzerain by accepting the ideology indoctrinated by the latter. What it has achieved is merely *de jure* political sovereignty in the form of formal democracy.

In the contemporary history of national independent movements or civil resistance, China's experience is relatively exceptional. It is rare to find a country similar to it that has achieved a somewhat complete sovereignty through the mobilisation of the peasantry, which comprised the majority of the population, for a revolutionary war. A new government built by the people through revolution could be legitimised to smash the old regime and overthrow the institutions and laws in favour of the alliance of bureaucrat-capitalists and foreign capitals who have taken a major portion of the gains and transferred the costs to society. The new regime confiscated all properties and directly controlled all economic resources to take the gains. These institutional gains of compulsory institutional transition achieved by countless sacrifice by the peasants can be termed as "revolution bonus" without negative externality. This "bonus" is enjoyed by the majority of the people and the future generations without compensating the original owners.

However, a country enjoying the full revolution bonus (which implies complete economic and political sovereignty) will necessarily face hostility from the former colonial suzerain or the political bloc in exile as all the properties previously owned by the transnational corporations and bureaucrat-capitalist class are going to be confiscated without compensation. This hostility, be it manifested as conspiratorial manoeuvres or ideological influence through "soft power", has accounted for much Cold War and post-Cold War antagonisms.

## 9. Exogenous Crises

The emerging countries rise up in the world arena in a particular historical background. The development of capitalism has entered a new stage of financial globalisation. Like most of the developing countries, the emerging countries occupy a lower position in the international industry chain. They serve the advanced countries that have a highly developed financial sector and that occupy a higher position in the international industry hierarchy. At the same time, as a response to the tide of financial globalisation, the emerging economies have become increasingly financialised as their social assets become more monetised. Financial globalisation in its present conjuncture involves the advanced financialised country having international currency hegemony that injects huge quantities of liquidity into the global economic system in order to protect its own interest. Whether an emerging country keenly embraces the tide of financial globalisation or passively gets overwhelmed by it, it will inevitably have to encounter international economic fluctuations and increasingly frequent exogenous crisis. That is to say, it is forced to import crises from outside.

The emerging countries are confronted with these institutional hazards associated with industry transfer and globalisation. Many environmental groups suggest that as long as international trade agreements are endorsed with the power to override national laws of local ecosystem and resources protection, transnational capital will continue to have free rein to extract invaluable natural resources.

## 10. Case Study 1: "Revolution Bonus"—Agrarian Reform

Among the E7 countries, Brazil and South Africa are typically countries built along with the colonisation by the white people. Due to the historical and politico-economic context, the land and wealth are concentrated mostly in the hands of the descendants of the former colonists. For example, in Brazil, 1% of the population owns almost the 50% of the national wealth while 12 million peasants are labouring on lands that do not belong to them. Among the 1.24 billion hectares of arable lands, up to two thirds belong to 5% of the population, whereas only 15% of the land belongs to the tillers themselves. The concentration of land ownership is remarkably inequitable.

As the means of production is highly concentrated, the distribution of the benefits of the economic growth is naturally highly uneven: The situation is similar in South Africa, where most of the farms and mining fields are still owned by the white people, who accounts for the 14.1% of the total population but owns 87% of the land; while the black people who accounts for the 74.8% of the population but owns less than 13% of the land. In 2009, black people's share of the ownership of the mining field is merely 8.9%. In 1990, the average area of farms owned by white people is 1462.15 hectares, while those of the coloured, only 116.62 hectares. There exists huge difference of population density in the settlements for the white and for the black:

> In 1985, the population in the black homelands was 14,017,000. The total land size was 16,318,000 hectares; the per capita area was only 1.16 hectares. In the 1990s, the total population of the six homelands that had not claimed independence was 7.01 million, while the total land size was 8.83 million hectares; the population density was 86 inhabitants per square km. Even if all of the towns, roads, rivers and deserts are taken into account, the per capita land size was merely 1.26 hectares, only 0.34% of that of the white people. And the so called "black homelands" were composed of the remaining disjointed plots left by the early white colonists, most of which were located in the undeveloped remote regions, or even barren land... The limited land was not able to feed the huge black rural population, as there was no industry in the homelands... therefore the black homelands became an inexhaustible reservoir of cheap labour force for the white. Numerous black young workers left home early to the white area for work, and returned home late at night... They became commuter workers; more of them left their family and worked as migrant workers in mine and factories owned by the white. According to the statistics, in 1986 in the white regions, there were 556,000 commuter workers and 1.7 million migrant workers[9].

The government aims to transfer 30% of the 82 million hectares presumed to be in the hands of white farmers, Minister of Rural Development and Land Reform, amounting to 24.5 million hectares, to black farmers by 2014. 6.7 million hectares had been transferred by early 2012 via redistribution and restitution.

In 2009 the Gini Index of South Africa is 63.1, the second highest in the world. The situation in India is slightly better. 80% of the farmers own 40% of the country's arable land. Per capita arable land is less than 2 hectares. 11% of the rural households don't own land. 75% of India's labour force is in the rural areas.

In comparison, after the success of revolution in 1949, China launched the agrarian reform from which 85% of the country's peasants were benefited. Every household received a small patch of arable land although the per capita cultivated land was less than 1 mu. In reality, a majority of the population own a small amount of property. That is why when in 1970 Mao Zedong was interviewed by the American journalist Snow, he remarked: "China is an ocean of small bourgeois". The small plot of arable land has become the last safety net for the peasants. Under such condition, the villages are able to render great amount of labour which is of low reproduction cost and low opposability. For the moment, in China there are 240 million rural households and 220 million migrant workers. The institutional foundation for the remarkable achievement that China has made in the last two decades since merging into the globalisation, is the revolution bonus of 1949 China is still enjoying.

Through comparative studies of the developing countries we come to an understanding that if a newly independent nation does not have full economic sovereignty over its domestic resources, industry, currency and finance, the sovereignty is not a complete one even if it has taken over the superstructure and ideology from its former colonisers.

Similarly, a developing country may have a democratically elected regime. However if it does not have control over its natural resources, industry, currency and finance, etc., it cannot fulfil industrialisation on its own and promote pro-people policies beneficial that benefits the majority of the people. What is left is merely an empty institutional shell by the name of democracy.

## 11. Case Study 2: China's Stock Market Crash in 2015[10]

The stock market crash in China in the summer of 2015 was one episode in an on-going, developing battle between 'long' and 'short' positions that reflects the unique characteristic of the phase of financial capitalism. On the surface it was a showdown between the long-position of Chinese state capital and the short-position of private capital. It was the integration mutually of USA foreign capital and Chinese domestic capital. Given that the two are essentially the same, they would be able to collaborate with each other seamlessly.

After launching derivatives trade that could absorb great amounts of excessive supply of money, the foreign and domestic collaboration finally took place in line with the ways of financial capital markets and the mechanism of virtue capital. It only needed the trigger to be pulled to kick start the shorting.

Before this, Western financial capital had already had the intention of short-selling China's capital market. It has been going on for at least five years. However, they could not do the shorting because China's financial capital markets were not open to the outside. China had only given a token policy of QFII (Qualified Foreign Institutional Investors) to foreign capital. Given the small approval limit, it was not sufficient to cause havoc.

However, now the shorting was finally accomplished, a dream for years. In the recent two years, close to US$ 1 trillion of hot money had already flowed into China quietly. Ever since the initiation of the "Shanghai-Hong Kong Stock Connect", the "Shenzhen-Hong Kong Stock Connect" [under preparation], the so-called "Shanghai free trade zone" and so on which was the start to opening up to foreign financial capital, then followed by other coastal and even inland cities to follow suit, the opportunity for the long-short battle arose from the opening up of these capital accounts. In fact, all these so-called opening up has to do with giving approvals to coastal region's strong requests to directly deal with foreign capital! Thereupon, this "new deal" of deepening reform, in which China turns towards Western financial capital on all fronts, and of promoting "internet + finance", has indeed given the opportunity to foreign and domestic financial capital to mount a Trojan horse to go short on China. Therefore, no matter what measures the Central government is to adopt in this long-short battle in the stock market, it will be entirely different from the previous times.

Before the 2007 financial tsunami in Wall Street as a result of the sub-prime crisis in the USA, there had been a market crash in China that evaporated more than RMB 700 billion. In 2008, Wen Jiabao's market rescue tactic of using RMB 4 trillion to 'long' was successful in producing results because in his time domestic financial controls had not yet opened up. A decade before that, in 1998 Zhu Rongji had launched national debt investments to strengthen centralised adjustments, which was in effect a 'long', and it was also effective because at that time the Central government had strict control over financial capital. Internationally, this kind of system is referred to as capital controls, while the entire external financial capital system is known as capital flow. That was why after the 1997 Asian financial storm and the 2008 Wall Street financial tsunami, there were discussions around capital control or free capital flow. The conclusion was that China's strict control of capital market had effectively prevented the East Asian financial crisis from worsening and later buffered the impact of the 2008 financial tsunami. In this decade the Chinese government has effectively prevented the publicly pronounced attempts by international financial capital to short selling on China.

In 2013, Western financial capital had deployed various speculative schemes to cause emerging countries like Brazil, India, Russia and so on to fall into market crashes and large scale currency depreciation. China in 2013 still had not undertaken the project to deepen the reform on capital account, and hence fortunate enough to be spared.

Nevertheless, after the third plenary meeting of the eighteenth session of the CCP held at the end of 2013, China started to turn towards the Western model of financial capital economy on a large scale. During this phase, the authorities strongly pushed forward various trading tools such as margin trading, financial futures, over-the-counter financing and so on that would facilitate the development of derivatives. Because of that, it had actively created the historical opportunity for overseas financial capital to finally have the conditions for going short on China. This time, before the eruption of the global financial crisis which we are predicting, China preceded it with a stock market crash, evaporating over RMB 7 trillion.

Whether it is domestic or foreign capital, as long as you are working with financial capital, you would embody the 'statelessness' of finance. To be in the game of financial capital, there has to be a pursuit of liquidity. Profiting from liquidity is a major characteristic of financial capital. Of the so-called 'three new natures': liquidity, short-termness and concentration, the first is liquidity. Because of liquidity, there would be short-term, concentrated entries and withdrawals. In the previous phase of industrial capitalism, imperialism had the 'three old natures': because it was parasitic, so it was corrupt and dying. In the past, Marxism talked about the three old natures. What do the three new natures of financial capital of today refer to? Because it has to pursue liquidity to profit from capital, so it has no national boundary, no home nation.

Old Marxists say that "the proletariat has no home country". Yet as soon as imperialist countries were at war, the proletariat class immediately had home countries, all wanting to revert from internationalism to nationalism. This is a historical lesson. The reason that the proletariat class could not be 'countryless' is because industrial capital is "localised". The major basis for the proletariat class to have home countries is the re-distribution of the profits by industrial capital in the societies of the different home countries. Redistribution confers a fatherland to the proletariat. The 'countrylessness' of financial capital, this other form of internationalism, has finally been realised. Financial capital robs the whole world. Therefore financial capital can be registered in Cayman Island or Bahamas, any small country with a low tax rate. As long as profit is optimised and the speculative capital return is optimised, it can almost entirely ignore where the mother nation is. So although the Marxist internationalisation of the proletariat could not be realised in the phase of industrial capitalism, the financial capitalist class has finally become internationalist during the financial capitalism phase today. As long as they can rely on 'long-short' battles to arbitrage and make profit, they would wreak havoc anywhere in the world.

The market crash in China today as a case where the country-less international financial groups have finally gained the historical opportunity to short-sell on China is a result of a whole series of neoliberal policies since 2013. If the Central government as represented by various departments such as securities and financial supervision do not adopt emergency measures, then it would mean when the stock market crash erupts, international and domestic financial capital groups would be given the opportunity for shorting and bottom-fishing, and that would be even worse. The wealth of the physical economy that has been accumulated over the years would first be depressed to next-to-nothing, and then bought up at rock-bottom prices. It would be similar to the outcome of the 500–day reform in Russia in 1991. That had also been a robbery.

The Chinese government has dispatched "ten imperial decrees" during the time of stock market crash. There are certain "Chinese characteristics" that could have the capacity to do this. Since all big investment organisations like Central Huijin are owned by the state. If there is not the capacity of the state in controlling financial capital, the ten imperial decrees could not have been dispatched, and would be useless even if dispatched. It was not that the USA did not want to dispatch "imperial decrees" to stop the 2008 financial tsunami, but that even if they were dispatched there would be no stopping it. For China, given the system where most financial organisations are state-owned capital, they could do it.

## 12. Social Instability

As long as we put aside our ideological blinkers and look into history as it is, we come to understand how the costs of social institutions have been dealt with through cost transfer. For example, the so-called "democratic" city-states in ancient Greece were based on enslavement of the majority of the population. In modern Europe, only after amassing an enormous amount of wealth through colonial expansion and invasion, the emerging bourgeois class which reaped the gains could push democratic reform at home. As for the relatively progressive "welfare capitalism" of post-war Europe, it was made possible by the substantial increase in the capital earnings of the industry transfer abroad. The USA, a nation born of large-scale colonial expansion in the so-called "new" continent where the white colonisers alone could enjoy freedom and democracy, abolished slavery only when a transition from colonial agricultural trade to industrial capitalism occurred in the mid-19$^{th}$ century. Furthermore, it was not until the 1960s when industry transfer had almost been completed and domestic economic reconstruction and industrial upgrading began that the African-Americans gradually enjoyed a complete citizenship and civil rights[11].

Consequently, the late industrialising countries, including the E7, unlike the advanced countries, cannot enjoy the privilege of transferring abroad the costs of domestic social institutions. Any economic crisis will risk directly destabilising society as a whole. Generally, the traditional social self-protection mechanisms of developing countries disintegrate during rapid political modernisation. However, the government revenues of developing countries are typically not sufficient to afford a social security system covering the majority of the population.

The social problems are manifested as conflicts in the urban and rural sectors.

(A) Urban: Rapid urbanisation is common in developing countries that are committed to modernisation. However, accelerated urbanisation is usually not in a normalised manner. The cities attract a large number of labourers seeking employment opportunities but do not guarantee them of basic social security. As a result, large slums emerge in Brazil, India, South Africa and Indonesia. Crime is common in these slums. The urban sector is capital-intensive and therefore also risk-intensive. Economic crises usually strike the urban sector firstly in form of large-scale unemployment and increasing crimes.

(B) Rural: As a general rule, the rural sector has to shoulder a greater part of the institutional cost of urbanisation and industrialisation in the early stages of primitive accumulation and then in the development of the market. Typically the three major factors of production in the rural areas, namely land, labour force, and finance, will be "capitalised" and the capital gains then flow into the urban sector. The cities absorb a large portion of the financial resources and labour capital from the rural areas, which not only strangles the latter's development but also transfers the costs of urbanisation and of crises to it.

As for agriculture, pro-capital developing countries in the post-colonial stage often continue the institution by which transnational corporations control domestic agricultural resources. Furthermore, when a nation is seriously indebted, it will encourage mono-cultivation of cash crops in order to earn hard currency. There is usually the simultaneous promotion of industrial agriculture. These actions bring considerable impacts to bear on traditional rural society and its ecology. Many rural households become deeply indebted. Many peasants find it hard to make a living in the rural and are forced to leave the rural areas and end up in city slums. It is also a general tendency that labour-management conflicts escalate in developing countries accepting industry transfer.

## 13. Concluding remarks

The emerging seven countries embrace developmentalism, learning from and trying to catch up with the advanced countries. They strive after development at all costs. In essence, these endeavours originate from the eurocentricism that is embraced by the majority of developing-country peoples. It can be traced to the historical experiences of colonialism. Development seems to be the only way to escape the fate of invasion and enslavement. Maybe history has not afforded them another option. Nevertheless when all less developed countries strive after development, they should be aware of its limits. They should also undertake a profound reflection: playing the game only by the rules set by the advanced countries, even if they play it better than the latter, does not mean that they succeeded in surpassing the latter. On the contrary, they trap themselves by becoming the prisoners of eurocentric culture. We must understand that the game of globalisation set up by the West has reached a blind alley. The rules of the game have led to various ills. Only by a critical awareness of what is defective and what is truly valuable in the modern institutions established by the West can humanity look forward to a new era of ecological civilisation with genuine cultural diversity.

## Endnotes

1. This paper is the output of the Sub-project on "International Comparative Studies on National Security in the Process of Globalisation", led by Dr SIT Tsui, Southwest University, which is under the Major Project on "The Structure and Mechanism Innovation for Improving Rural Governance As Base of National Comprehensive Security" led by Professor WEN Tiejun, Renmin University of China. The Major Project is funded by the National Social Science Foundation of China (No. 14ZDA064).
2. Seven research team members are as follows: Brazil: Paulo Nakatani, Rogerio Naques Faleiros, Neide César Vargas Federal University of Espírito Santo; China: Zhou Li, Dong Xiaodan,

Renmin University of China; India: Vinod Raina (Center for Study of Development Studies), T. Gangadharan (All India Peoples Science Network), Arindam Banerjee (Ambedkar University); Indonesia: Indra Sakti Gunawan Lubis and Yulian Junaidi Jasuan (Indonesia Peasant Union/La Via Campesina); South Africa: Patrick Bond, Khadija Sharife (University of KwaZulu-Natal); Turkey: Galip Yalman, Aylin Topal Yilmaz (Middle East Technical University); Venezuela: José Felix Rivas (Central Bank of Venezuela), Ernesto Revello (PDVSA, Petróleos de Venezuela, S.A.).

3. By development trap we mean the more a developing country strives after development, the more it is entangled in structural underdevelopment or social contradiction. The syndrome includes exploding foreign debts, long-term balance and payments deficit, income polarisation, social and political instability, external dependency and even incomplete sovereignty. In a word, it is the vicious circle of underdevelopment.
4. Angus Madison estimates that in 1820, China's GDP is 32.9% of the world. But some scholars cast doubt on it. Liu Di thinks that actually China's GDP is only two-thirds of what Madison estimates (History of Economics, 2010, No. 5).
5. Brazil is a special case. Brazil has affluent natural resources, but it once implemented the import-substitution development model and so has developed a relatively complete industrial structure. However, recently there is a tendency of economic re-primitivisation. For details, please see Brazil Report: Historical Review, www.emergingcountries.org.
6. Please see the South-South Declaration, www.southsouthforum.org. The First South-South Forum on Sustainability, held on 12–14 December 2011 at Lingnan University, Hong Kong, was co-organised by Lingnan University, Renmin University of China, Peking University, Tsinghua University and the United Nations Development Programme (UNDP). All video recordings can be accessed at Global University for Sustainability website: http://our-global-u.org/oguorg/en/?page_id=175. A Second South-South Forum on Sustainability was held in Chongqing, China, at the Southwest University of China, on 8–10 December 2012. Please visit http://our-global-u.org/oguorg/en/?page_id=198.
7. Through a comparative study on the seven emerging countries, this report proposes the concept of "double risk at national level" which is different from the risk analysis in general micro-economics. We emphasise that developing countries when receiving external capital have to facilitate institutional provision according to the demand of institutional transition. In general, external capital and domestic interest blocs partake most of the gains whereas the state and the society have to shoulder the cost. As a result, most of the developing countries got ensnarled in the "national development trap" in which external and domestic interest blocs combine together in alliance.
8. Wen Tiejun, "Global Capitalization and Institutional Impoverishment," *Journal of China Agricultural University (Social Science)*, 2012(1).
9. Sun Hongqi, *Land and the Political Economy of South Africa*. Beijing: Central Compilation and Translation Press, 2011, pp. 12–13.
10. This case study is based on the seminar among several Chinese Founding Members of the Global University for Sustainability, conducted on July 6 and July 14, 2015, and then revised by the speakers. The translation is done by Alice Chow, and vetted by Kho Tungyi. First published in Our-Global-U website: http://our-global-u.org/oguorg/en/?page_id=799
11. The USA at the stage of industrial capitalism was once under the influence of fascism and witnessed the most intensified labor-management conflicts among the industrial nations. In 1934 alone there were 1856 cases of worker strikes. Over 2500 enterprises had employed hatchet men to sabotage the strikes (according to a report by The US Commission on Civil Rights). In a case of automobile workers strike, 27 were killed by the National Guard. See Wang Wen, "The US almost on the road to fascism, in *Global Times*, dated 8 April 2009.

# 16

# Toward a New Moral Economy

## Rethinking Land Reform in China and India[1]

*Lin Chun*

## Abstract

India and China were among the founding members of Bandung 1955. Since then both countries have undergone various transformations. This article focuses on their contrasting trajectories of land reform, which largely explains major differences in their socioeconomic developments. Yet, since the 1990s there have been trends of convergence between them and across the Global South. The upsurge of a neoliberal, increasingly financialised system of global capitalism intensified the question of land, threatening the livelihood of the world's massive remaining agrarian direct producers and the globe's environmental commons. In one way or another supported by state policies, big capital is further driving the "last peasantry" away from the land—land as a means of both production and subsistence. In the Bandung spirit of people's sovereignty and solidarity, I argue that building a new moral economy through rural (re)organisation would be the only alternative to this relentless process of commodifying land and labour. Many forms of such an economy can be created in China and India as elsewhere, which hold the promise for a future of flourishing eco-agriculture, cooperative farming, and self-governing participatory politics.

*Keywords:* Bandung, China, India, Peasant, Land Reform

India and China were among the founding members of Bandung 1955. Sixty years have since passed and much happened within each country as well as between the two. I will in this short paper focus on their different experiences with land reform, which may comparatively and collectively offer us some important lessons in terms of the Bandung spirit of sovereign social development.

One of Amartya Sen's long-standing observations is that there is a great gap between India and China in providing "essential public services". "Inequality is high in both countries," he wrote, but "China has done far more than India to raise life expectancy, expand general education and secure health care for its people" (Sen 2013). He considered China's efforts to improve the quality of life of its citizens, male and female, an "excellent achievement" (Sen 2000, 17; 2001). India, by contrast, has suffered "chronic undernourishment, a disorganised medical system [and] dysfunctional school systems" (ibid; see also Dreze and Sen 2002). According to recent World Bank data, 43% of Indian children are underweight, compared to 7% of Chinese children (and 28% of sub-Saharan African children) (Burke 2013). Approximately one-fifth of all Indian men and one-third of all Indian women over the age of seven are illiterate. China's literacy rate, meanwhile, is nearly 95% for both sexes (UNDP 2013). Sen thus argued that "for India to match China in its range of manufacturing capacity—its ability to produce gadgets of almost every kind, with increasing use of technology and better quality control—it needs a better-educated and healthier labour force at all levels of society" (2013). It is particularly notable that what China has achieved is not primarily due to market forces. In fact, compared with today's problems of social polarisation, collusion of bureaucratic power and private capital, and eco-environmental destruction, new China's track record of clean government and basic equality was built up before market reforms. In the Mao era, Chinese development had already advanced significantly and was laying the foundation for subsequent growth.

Comparing China to India is a common practice given the two countries' comparable sizes and starting points of development. In fact, China in 1949, ruined by decades of war (and soon to be mired in another in Korea), was thought to be even more backward than newly independent India, at least in terms of industry (e.g. electricity, steel, iron, and cement), infrastructure (e.g. railway mileage), and agricultural production. At the time of independence in 1947, India was the world's seventh largest industrial country by volume of output (Desai 2003). Over time, however, India's relative advantages have reversed in China's favour, a change reflected in a number of social indicators. Between 1950 and 1999, the overall HDI value in China increased from 0.225 to 0.718 while in India increased from 0.247 to 0.571 (Crafts 2002). In 2013, life expectancy in China was approximately 73.7 years, while in India it was 65.8 years (UNDP 2013). To be sure, uneven development features prominently in both countries. The Indian state of Kerala, for example, not only has higher human development scores than the Indian average, but also does better than China in several respects. At the national level, however, the general disparity between the two countries is striking: China is not a democracy, but the Chinese "have been strongly committed to eliminating hunger, illiteracy and medical neglect", as Sen notes (2013). But Sen is yet to answer his own question: why does India trail China?

While many works have sought to compare the diverse political-economic paths to modernisation in these two old agrarian civilisations, insufficient attention has been paid to the land relations as an answer. Concerning the complexities of the Chinese Communist Revolution centred in the peasant struggle for land, the late historian Maurice Meisner once remarked that "with an acute and painful awareness of all the horrors and crimes that accompanied the revolution," it is still true that "few events in world history have done more to better the lives of more people" (1999, 1, 12). The significance and fundamental justice of this truly great historical event lie in its transformative and emancipatory effects on the social conditions of the hitherto deprived and oppressed classes. Concerning land reform specifically, "While the landowning class had lost out in the socialist revolution in China, it effectively remained powerful in India as an integral part of the winning coalition of classes that gained independence, protected by and well ensconced in the ruling political party, and able to thwart any further redistributive or collectivist agrarian reforms" (Saith 2008: 727).

## The Land Revolution in China

Contrary to the typical 19th century European thinking about the East, private land-owning and a landed aristocracy are confirmed to have existed in both India and China early and widely. Where for millennia, a partially commercialised agriculture and cottage industry developed in addition to subsistence farming, sustaining booming markets for short-and long-distance trade. Such internal and external market activities arguably amounted to a peculiar form of commercial (as opposed to industrial) capitalism. Together with certain splendid achievements in science and technology, the oriental economies were once the most advanced in the pre-modern world. In China, despite an ancient moral ideal of equal land sharing and repeated top-down reforms to halt land annexation, powerful officials and landlords kept imposing heavy rents and levies, and encroaching on petty holdings. Almost every major Chinese dynasty was thus overturned by landless peasant uprisings, which aspired to see *junping*, or the equalisation of land, under an enlightened emperor. Yet over time, land concentration persisted, which took periodic social upheavals to break.

The Chinese economy began to lose its advantageous position in the late seventeenth century, undergoing monetisation while suffering from depleted silver inflows. The latter led to serious inflation, which was compounded by climate disasters and disease epidemics. By the mid-nineteenth century, the situation took a decisive turn for the worse in the wake of Britain's dirty drug war, which was then followed by encroachments from other Western powers and Japan. If the Opium War signified an unprecedented "national" crisis, the devastation of the Chinese countryside marked a profound social crisis as well. Entrenched nexuses of clan patriarchy and landlordism (involving both resident and absentee landlords) widened alongside exploitative gentry-official coalitions, aggressive foreign financial capital, monopolised trading, usury, and warlordism via profit-seeking brokers who marginalised the traditional gate-keeping rural elite. This trend of "state involution" was fostered by corrupt central, local, and village autocracies themselves (Duara 2010). Although very large landholding was not common in most parts of China, and peasant hardships not solely caused by unequal land ownership, the conjoined national and social crises deepened both tendencies. They were causally rooted in the re-institutionalised local land regimes. Revolution became inevitable.

The "awakening of Asia" was first marked by China's Republican Revolution of 1911, when the reactionary impulses of "cultured Europe" clashed with the progressive democratic platform of the "barbaric Asians" (Lenin 1913, 65–66, 99–100). The "three people's principles" of nationalism, democracy, and people's livelihood (proposed by the revolutionary leader Sun Yat Sen) entailed an agrarian policy of land to the tiller within a larger nation-building program of public land management in line with the industrial principle of "constraining capital" (Sun 1986). The idea of equalising land rights echoed an ancient yearning in China, which for Sun was directly translatable into "socialism or communism as *datong*-ism [great harmony]" (ibid., 355). However, the actual revolution was narrowly political: it overthrew the monarchy but did not change society. Nor did it consolidate national independence for the country. What the republican revolutionaries were unable to achieve, then, had to be taken up by the Communist Revolution, whose aim was liberating the Chinese nation and its toiling masses. The twentieth century communist transformation of China in general—and the transformation of rural China, in particular—can be viewed through three interconnected phases: 1) a land revolution in China's rural peripheries (1927–37) following the communist party's utter defeat in its infantile urban adventures; 2) nationwide yet unevenly proceeded land reforms (1947–51) during and after the civil war under communist local and, after 1949, national power against the Guomingdang regime that represented the interests of big landlordism and bureaucratic-comprador capital; and 3) the cooperative movements and communal organisation (1951–80) before decollectivisation in the early 1980s.

At its core, the Communist Revolution was a "land revolution." It was meant to overturn China's "semi-colonial and semi-feudal" conditions (as elaborated in party theory) and seize state power through a people's war of encircling the cities from the countryside. This original strategy counted on peasant mobilisation away from the powerful centres of counterrevolution, which required a firmly pro-poor land policy. But the policy also had to be flexible in its implementation to accommodate specific political considerations and constraints. Certain compromises were necessitated by the "united front" of a "new democratic revolution" to be distinguished from both classical bourgeois revolutions and a typically socialist one. The degree of rent reduction or land redistribution, for instance, was reined in at times by the need to win over an "enlightened gentry" or rich peasants. The policy of middle peasant inclusion was especially important and regionally occurred "ultra-left" measures which injured rural medium strata were quickly corrected. In the end, it was the communist success in tackling the land question that had facilitated the coordination between land reform, mass agitation, and military campaigns during the revolution. This novel process of state building and regime construction from below also fostered new subjective formations and innovative institutions in the new China.

During the Jiangxi Soviet period (from the guerrilla struggles in the Jinggang Mountain area beginning in 1927 to the Long March in 1934), land reform was central to the work of the party, with popular support garnered from a cross-section of grassroots organisations comprised of peasants, women, and youth. In 1928, the party passed two resolutions, calling for the expropriation of the landlord class. It subsequently tasked itself with enlarging Soviet territory, deepening the land revolution, and recruiting for the Red Army. As the brutal wars with Nanjing's military suppression left little possibility for consolidating land redistribution, the red base was lost to counterrevolution. In the wake of this defeat, the land revolution had to be suspended or mitigated until after the victorious national resistance against the Japanese invasion, resuming only when civil war broke out again in the 1940s. The monumental Outline of Land Law was promulgated in 1947[2], marking the beginning of a nationwide transformation in land ownership and rural relations. Ultimately, this helped determine the outcome of the war, as the peasant-soldiers chose to fight for their land. The GMD, losing the war to the communists largely because they failed the peasantry, learned the lesson and later conducted a highly effective land reform in Taiwan.

The principle of equality drove the project of land reform, in which all farming families and individuals were granted equal land rights. Technically, achieving this meant categorising all farmland by size, quality, and distance for the purposes of fair distribution and compensation, with the goal of equalising both possession and tax burdens. Although the male-dominated household was not challenged, women did enjoy the same rights to land, which they could own in their own names. This factor should not be taken as a mere byproduct but rather a central and deliberate component of the revolution and reform of land relations. It has had certain significantly positive social consequences for the conditions of female existence in China, as compared with India and large parts of South Asia more generally.

The pursuit of regime consolidation and economic recovery after 1949 under the guideline of "new democracy" (as opposed to the long-term goal of socialism) led to more moderate policy stipulated in the 1950 new Agrarian Reform Law and the Report on the Question of Land Reform. Industrial and commercial enterprises owned by landlords were excluded from confiscation, and the rich peasant economy was preserved. By the end of 1952, apart from certain minority regions, more than three hundred million poor peasants throughout the country had obtained their fair share of farmland along with farming tools, animals, and other means of production. Parts of pastoral and forest regions underwent similar reforms. Nationally, the lower- and middle-class peasants who accounted for 90% of the rural population owned their corresponding proportion of land[3]. Compared with the heavy rents and levies of the past (which were typically over 50% of peasant income), the gross tax rate was more than halved. Having first enjoyed an egalitarian land system, followed by the advent of cooperatives, the peasantry saw their economy grow apace. It was estimated that in 1952, about 35% of national gross investment was financed by the agricultural sector (Lippit 1974). Between 1950 and 1957, grain production achieved a 5.2% annual increase. The reforms also resulted in an equalisation of rural incomes (Khan 1977; Griffin et al. 2002).

Depending on expectations and local variations, any direct and immediate productive benefit of land redistribution is subject to specific analyses, although its purpose was indeed to "liberate productive forces" as stated by the Chinese Marxists. Indisputable however is its socio-political impact, from improving the lives and prospects of life chances for the vast majority in an agrarian society to winning the trust, support, and participation of the peasantry in creating a new social order. In the process, new rural subjectivity could be nurtured and created. Beyond land rights as an issue of redistributive justice, land reform was not just an economic matter. It was also a political one about state control over land and other natural resources and the organisation of production. As such it was a vital step in dismantling the rural infrastructure of economic, political, and cultural power of an *ancien regime* for modernisation. The land revolution as a whole thus endowed the communist rule its initial legitimacy, moral confidence, and practical authority indispensable for the country's subsequent construction. Although land issues were not the sole causes of the communist revolution, their redistributive resolve was a decisive contribution to both revolutionary triumph and post-revolutionary development.

## Land Reforms in India

Both India and China are huge, unevenly developed entities with a diverse eco-agricultural makeup of regions and cultures. But unlike China, whose territorial frontiers were historically plastic yet in one way or another definable, the territories of India of sub-continental scale were unsettled for many centuries. The Raj once controlled only about two-thirds of British India, leaving the remaining third of the so-called princely states and tribal areas ungoverned from the centre. It was not until the partition of 1947 that the borders of the Indian union were eventually clarified. Under the overlordship of ancient kings who ruled much of today's northern India, there was a complex set of land relations involving private owning, royal possession (land granted to the Brahmins for administration), custody claims by religious bodies, and customary communal holdings, along with various forms of bonded labour. Social stratification was centred on the hereditary and occupational castes. Land distribution and transfers, however, were mostly flexible in response to demographic changes and migration patterned by interregional, not caste, mobility (Bandyopadhyay 1993, 52). While the village evolved as a more or less self-sufficient unit, commercial ties developed in ports and towns to make the country a great global trader. Culturally, Pauranic Hinduism, which was established in the late classical period, was tolerated or even incorporated by the Islamic rulers from the early 12$^{th}$ century to 1750, whose power culminated in an expanded empire beginning in the mid-sixteenth century.

The British took over agrarian organisations from the Mughals while also superimposing those of their own. As they conquered more provinces, they systematically measured and recorded cultivated lands, making detailed field notes, even though they never completed the job. New land revenue systems were tried out, mixing Indian and European inputs. The East India Company Act of 1784 instructed the company "to inquire into the alleged grievances of the landholders, and if founded in truth, to afford them redress, and to establish permanent rules for the settlement and collection of the revenue" (Desai 2011, 81–3). A few years later, with the introduction of renewed land taxes under the Permanent Settlement Act of 1793, the Raj popularised a Zamindari system (along with Ryotwari and Mahalwari in different regions) at the cost of the *jajmani* relationship that the landless used to share with the landed to ensure minimal subsistence in a form of traditional moral economy (Sethi 2006). Generally speaking, under the British crown, land-use and landownership in India were managed in a way that eased the acquisition of land at low prices by colonial traders, settlers, and entrepreneurs for the establishment of mines, plantations, and other businesses in the empire's network of colonial extraction (Baden-Powell 1892, III, book iv, ch.1)[4].

Colonisation implies the institutionalisation of modern private property, which delegitimised the communal ownership of tribal societies in India as elsewhere. As such the capitalist transformation was "a scheme of destruction" that threatened "annihilating the human and natural substance of society" (Polanyi 1957, 163, 45ff). Global capitalism expanded "by destroying the two main sources of its own wealth: the land and the labourer" at home and abroad (Harvey 2006, 14). Empirical evidence in modern India shows that differences in historical institutions of property rights led to differences in productive organisation and policy choice, with repercussions for economic outcomes. Geographical areas in which land rights had previously been granted almost exclusively to landlords saw significantly lower levels of agricultural investments, productivity, and public goods provision than areas in which such rights were also customarily held by the cultivators (Banerjee and Iyer 2005).

The independence movement rightly blamed colonialism for the economic devastation and immense rural poverty caused in part by diverting agriculture away from food production and towards commercial crops (Bagchi 2009, 101–103)[5]. Independent India found itself in an inherited semi-feudal agrarian system, in which the ownership and control of land were concentrated in the hands of landlords and their intermediaries as rent collectors. Small landholders, tenants, and landless workers were mostly trapped in their fixed class-caste positions with little bargaining power. The land question was thus high on the agenda of the new government, which faced the daunting task of nation-building. Imbuing land reform with a sense of urgency, India then "was subject to the largest body of land reform legislation ever to have been passed in so short of period in any country" (Besley and Burgess 2000, 390). The legislation consisted of four main categories: 1) abolishing *zamindari* and tax farming[6], 2) tenancy contract regulation, 3) placing a ceiling on landholding, and 4) rationalising disparate tenure systems. The first two five-year plans allocated substantial budgetary support for these reforms, and local administrations made various strides to comply. Decades on, however, only the abolition of intermediaries had some tangible effect on increasing the security of smallholders and protecting tenants' rights (ibid., 395). The record of other areas of reform fluctuated across states and over time, with many of the central problems still not yet resolved (Ghatak 2007).

This seems not to be (as is often assumed) merely an issue of bureaucratic tardiness in policy implementation or such practical obstacles as lacking clear land records and titles in Bihar, for example. The design of land reform was itself weak in considering questions of redistribution of only "limited importance." The reform efforts were rather confined to the third category: the legislative abolition of landlordism by imposing ceilings (Besley and Burgess 2000, 390, 420). Yet, the landlords were permitted compensational retention, and the set ceilings were often compromised through dodging and even disguised forms of land expansion. Although legal measures were adopted with a view to redistributing surplus land to landless farmers, the latter was a secondary concern and was thus marginalised in practice. The opposition of large landholders amounted to a political hijacking of the reform agenda as they mobilised local and private interests to impede real change. In those states that attempted more serious efforts at reform, the process was also halted midway by beneficiaries other than the rural poor who succeeded in obstructing more radical policies. Essentially a matter of political power and class struggle, it was not surprising that throughout the post-independence decades, regardless of whichever party controlled the central government, "with many state legislatures controlled by the landlord class, reforms that harmed this class tended to be blocked" (Besley and Burgess 2000, 394). Land reform in India was also initially resisted by ideologically driven Western aid and lending agencies which put forward alternative programs to land reform. In effect, land reform in India, compounded by fragile state backing, ultimately permitted the landlords to resist any meaningful overhaul of the status quo.

As shown in the states of Kerala and West Bengal, successful land reform depended on the political power and determination of governments. In Kerala, the first communists elected to office in 1957 committed themselves to transforming agrarian relations. They introduced a radical ordinance followed by several reform bills and a landmark Land Reforms (Amendment) Act in 1969. With the goal of supporting self-cultivation, the reform set a non-negotiable ceiling on landholding to help farming families claim the excess land they had worked for generations. The new laws also secured tenure against eviction (Parayil 2000, chs. 2, 3, 4). However, these local measures alarmed big land owners nationally. Nehru, fearing political backlash and instability, invoked the President's rule to remove E.M.S. Namboodiripad, Kerala's chief minister, in 1959. In West Bengal, the communist-led government managed to survive more than three decades in power, beginning in 1977, over which time it rigorously implemented a series of land reforms. Operation Barga, launched in 1978, was among the first policies designed to implement the long-dormant tenancy laws of 1955, which were meant to regulate rents and ensure the security of tenure for sharecroppers (Sengupta 1981). The reforms reached deep and wide in the 1980s to empower the peasants by enforcing their legally protected contracts, along with providing additional support through multiple anti-poverty programs. Regrettably, it was state-sponsored land acquisition through the creation of so-called developmental zones in the wake of the neoliberal turn of economic policy in the late1990s that led to peasant unrest. Losing their rural constituents amid a perceive betrayal, the Left Front was defeated in the 2011 election.

Apparently, land reform in India was a subnational matter more than a national project. Unlike the Chinese pattern of using a central authority and a uniform policy and revenue system albeit with certain local autonomy and variation, India, with its manifold legal provisions and rival policy frameworks in different places, struggled to reform its agrarian sector amid locally different priorities, paces, and effects. The processes were uneven and torturous also in the face of complicated caste, language, ethnic, and religious diversities. In the end, "no land reform worthy of mention was attempted. ... As a party, Congress was controlled by a coalition of rich farmers, traders and urban professionals, in which the weight of the agrarian bosses was greatest, and its policies reflected the interests of these groups" (Anderson 2012)[7]. The land problem has remained unsolved in the post-Nehru era, despite Indira Gandhi's "war against poverty" or anti-corruption campaigns under other leaders, and despite changes in government coalitions after the Congress decline.

Today, land-related problems in India—from insecure tenancy rights to blocked or lost access to land for subsistence farming—continue to pose grave challenges. By 2005, although the agriculture's share of GDP had shrunk, about 58% of the national population still depended on farming for their livelihoods. 63% of these farmers owned less than one hectare of land, while large parcels of ten hectares or more were in the hands of less than 2% of the rural population. Agricultural labour classified as landless or land poor (those who had less than 0.2 hectares) accounted for 43% of all peasant households, which was actually an increase from 1950, while the wealthiest 10% of Indians monopolised more land (Sethi 2006, 74–75)[8]. Estimates based on a land and livestock survey in 2003 showed that if a uniform ceiling of 20 acres was assumed, there would be 15 million acres of above-ceiling redistributable land, which was "more than three times the total amount of land that has ever been redistributed under land reform programs in all states" (Rawal 2008, 47)[9]. By 2013, there were about 57.6 million landless households (Lerche 2013, 398–99). While petty cultivators, agricultural workers, and "footloose labour" fall prey to poverty and debt due to capital deprivation, remittance arrears, or usury, the landed class—traditional and capitalist alike—retain its control over wealth and power. In addition to land, members of this class also possess myriad resources in industry, commerce, and finance, as well as powerful positions in the educational and medical sectors, law, legislature, and government (Ramachandran 2011).

Worse still, agricultural growth has been slow, and surpluses are generally used to alleviate bureaucratic and military demands more than aiding the poorest segments of society. Over time, the absence of meaningful large-scale land reform has only highlighted its benefits in those places where it has been implemented. Fairer resource sharing and labour rewards in turn are bound to lead to positive social results—even just precarious reforms have reduced poverty through increased access to land by the poor in certain areas, initially nurturing a class of small-and medium-scale farmers and raising wages for hired agricultural labourers, thereby enhancing human development (Parayil 2000)[10].

Scholars continue to debate the relationship between land reform and agrarian productivity, but broadly agree on land reform's moral basis and social benefits. In India, there is an especially "robust link between land reform and poverty reduction" due to needed changes in the terms of land contracts and thereby productive relations (Besley and Burgess 2000, 391). As noted, beyond economic performance, at issue are social justice and welfare. Politically, land reform is also straightforwardly a matter of unshackling the hitherto oppressed people who otherwise cannot win the fight to secure their constitutional entitlements and rights. Even if, in the 21st century, two-thirds of all farming Indians appear to be small land holders, and even if they vote or rally around political parties, they are marginal or neglected in the policy decisions that directly affect their lives. Given the stubborn durability of feudal arrangements and bounded labour regime of dependent and subordinate relations—which have become increasingly infused with modern-day financial and corporate interests of both domestic and foreign capital—land reform remains instrumental for rural and national development.

## Collective Farming and Green Revolution

While land revolution in China overturned landlordism and its structural networks, India's crippled land reform omitted such a revolutionary break. Throughout the postcolonial world, as typified in the modern Chinese and Indian trajectories as two contrasting responses to the challenge of modernity, land reform explains important developmental differentiations. However, redistributing land alone would not definitively change economic structures and social relations for industrialisation. Such a change requires rural reorganisation so as to overcome the vulnerabilities of scattered and secluded petty farming and its political-psychological ramifications. That is, land reform is a pivotal precondition for independent domestic capital accumulation and thereby socioeconomic development (as also demonstrated by the experiences of East Asian "developmental states"). And any fundamental gains from such a reform need to be consolidated and widened through forms of cooperative agriculture. The latter is where the two national paths went further apart.

In China, alarmed by mounting signs of rural polarisation and pressed both to safeguard peasant livelihood and finance industrial growth during mobilisation for the war in Korea, the party adopted a draft resolution in late 1951 on agricultural socialisation. Mutual aid groups were quickly replaced by cooperatives by 1955, which then merged into much larger and more centralised communes in 1958 where all the factors of production were collectively managed. Notably, the movement proceeded by and large on a voluntary basis "with neither the violence nor the massive sabotage characteristic of Soviet collectivisation" (Selden 1982, 85; Nolan 1976). The unified government-communal system of management for the people's communes was an important institutional innovation. It had enabled not only labour accumulation and organisation for large scale infrastructural works and rural industries but also political participation and grassroots self-governance. The "mass mobilisation mode of transformation" demonstrated the superiority of the Chinese method (Saith 2008: 736–9). Distribution was based on a gradually refined system of work points calculated through regular, public, and practically democratic appraisals at the lowest gathering points of members on the grassroots. This was supplemented by communal rules and funds of social relief for the needy in the manner of a government-backed moral economy. The "five-guarantees", for example, ensured basic provisions for the security of handicapped and labour-deprived households. The day-to-day management was initially at the level of the productive brigade (a cluster of natural villages), and later readjusted in the wake of the failed Great Leap to that of the smaller productive team.

The advantages of collectively organised agriculture were evident. It saved land; larger fields encouraged a higher degree of mechanisation, which improved both land and labour productivity; collective cultivation facilitated the rapid diffusion of new seed varieties (especially of China's own revolutionary high-yielding hybrid rice), which enabled China to not only feed itself but also become a net grain exporter; communal management allowed the spread of locally produced chemical fertilisers, along with other green technologies in land use and crop planning; and local coordination facilitated labour and resource mobilisation for large-scale infrastructural construction and rural industries. Between 1952 and 1978, irrigated land in China tripled. This also entailed unprecedented land rearrangements and soil consolidation for efficiency in both grain and sideline production. Meanwhile, communal factories spread to absorb rural labour while boosting peasant income. Wherever non-farm enterprises could thrive, "the collectives became powerful internal agents of rural accumulation so obviously lacking in other parts of the developing world, including rural India" (ibid: 740). All these factors worked together to augment agrarian productivity and output that ensured national grain self-sufficiency, increased farming household purchasing power, while shoring up industrialisation.

Socially, the collectives mitigated inequality among members by depressing polarising forces and protecting basic security. They also promoted gender equality by bringing women from the confines of housework into united and gainful labour through such provisions as community nurseries and dining facilities. Communal clinics, schools, and mass campaigns for eradicating illiteracy and epidemics and for "cultured life" extended to remote villages. The phenomenal contribution of China's "barefoot doctors" to rural public health and preventive medicine was widely praised, such as by the World Health Organisation (Wang 2010). The process of collective agriculture was also one of elevating the lower classes and commoners to a politically esteemed stratum through a massive transformative politics of participation and recognition. The total absence of anything similar in India explains much of its social conservatism and developmental lag.

Acknowledging Chinese achievements, however, doesn't allow us to evade difficult questions concerning the moral dilemmas and many contradictions the socialist experiment had inflicted, including the failures of the Great Leap and the catastrophe of famine around 1960. Despite policies designed to balance economic growth and popular welfare, the kind of sectorial trades that would benefit peasants a great deal more were eventually unachievable. Rural development was curtailed to prioritise urban food supplies and price stability, hurting peasant incentives while sustaining urban-rural segregation. So-called internal accumulation—without what the first industrialisers enjoyed through the colonial extraction and "ecological relief" from exploiting overseas resources—took a heavy toll. Did the Indians do better? While having avoided a similar path of capital accumulation, India had to rely on foreign aid and international financing, which was a lasting drag on the national economy.

In India, betrayed by circumstances, weak and patchy land reforms resulted in "reverse tenancy" or "reverse rent", whereby small farmers had to lease their land to larger holders due to their own inability of accessing to credits, seeds, techniques, or water channels. The poorer the peasants, the more costly their cultivation could be (Ramachandran 2011). Unlike in China, cooperation was not an earnest policy response. In 1949, the Agrarian Reforms Committee of Congress did propose to promote rural coops, and in 1959 it put forward a resolution on agricultural organisational patterns. However, each move was eventually abandoned under the pressure of opposition from the landed elites. India's decision to first separate political democracy and social justice and then prioritise the former over the latter had a dire social consequence. As "most land reform interventions have languished in courts", there remains "endemic (near) landlessness, a dominance of uneconomic marginal, fragmented holdings, with the vast majority being below a scale which can guarantee a reasonable level of living" (Saith 2008: 734).

Nevertheless, in terms of mechanisation and technological upgrading, India managed to undertake a fairly successful "green revolution" after a prolonged period of stagnation in land pooling, techno-adaptation and labour productivity. First in Punjab in the 1960s, the World Bank in collaboration with the U.S. Agency for International Development advocated and subsidised the importation of chemical fertilisers, high-yielding and fertiliser-responsive seeds, pesticides, and farm machinery. "A combination of foreign knowledge, domestic subsidies, and rural private initiative brought a capitalist revolution to the Indian countryside" (Desai 2003, 9). This development into the 1970s and 1980s eased the situation of persistent hunger in some areas, as wheat production doubled over a period of twenty years while rice increased by 50%. Yet, since the foreign aid agencies sponsored monocultures from imported seed varieties, the revolution was costly. Emphasising commercial crops such as sugarcane and cotton at the expense of crops like chickpeas and millet, which were traditionally produced by the poor to feed themselves, the new direction had "steadily eroded the self-sufficiency of the small farmer in food grains". Seed commercialisation in general undermined not only natural biodiversity but also the autonomy and security of petty farmers. Moreover, rich farmers as the "principal beneficiaries" of the revolution were able to politicise subsidies and reinforce the concentration of land and dependency on capital intensive inputs (Harriss 2013, 355). Also lost were nearly 8.5 million hectares, or 6% of the crop base, to redundant water logging and excess alkalinity (World Resources Institute 1995, 79–81, chs. 5, 6).

A striking contrast between India and China in the cold war era was that while the latter had to be self-reliant after the Sino-Soviet split, the former was a recipient of substantial funds and aid, alternately or concurrently, from both camps of the East and West. The downside was that the World Bank, for instance, had compelled the Indian government to grant favourable conditions to foreign investment in local fertiliser and related industries, to remove several protective trade barriers, and to liberalise domestic price controls over basic food stuffs, from grains to milk (Kumar 2011; Sethi 2006, 78). The similar has increasingly happened to China since its accession to WTO in 2001. The approach of the WB, Ford Foundation and other multinational agencies in India took technology as the solution to underdevelopment. However, technological determinism did not fare well in reality. Despite India's many comparative advantages in geopolitics and natural endowments, including a more relaxed ratio of arable land to people, China's per capita output in terms of many essential agricultural products has been times larger than India's by 1980 and after. That is, at least before the "triple crises" peaked in rural China in the late 1990s, the country used its available land "far more productively than any other large-scale agricultural producer on the planet" (Bramall 2009, 245, 231) during the collective era and a "bonus" decade after. More specifically, green revolutionary technologies have proven to work better in collective agriculture.

A missing transformation in social attitudes and relations seems to have continuously held India back, even beyond the "impassable trenches" of caste. Legally denounced yet socially alive, "caste is about the worst form of inequality you can think of"[11]. In this context, throughout India, pervasively visible is electoral dependency on the landed elites who subordinate the poor and low-caste peasants and control their votes (Ramachandran 2011). These elites are politically powerful as they run the panchayats and local credit unions, making democracy a mockery at the village level. The regionalisation of Indian democracy and the emergence of caste-based party politics since the 1990s might be a blessing as much as a curse for political democracy without substantive social progress. Only against this backdrop, including the deprived *adivasis* or indigenous people who were left out by the green revolution and then exploited and increasingly dispossessed by the neoliberal wave of globalisation, can the Maoist insurgency be properly explained. To be sure, India's Westminster-style parliamentary rule was not a gift, but achieved through a daring freedom struggle. Democracy has also succeeded in many ways to make the Indians proud, given especially the country's extraordinary ethnic, religious and linguistic diversities. Yet even procedurally the system is stained by the incompetence, corruption, and criminality of its political class. Being not complacent, to defend democracy is to demand, with the Indian people, to have their democratic system socially substantiated.

## Agrarian Crises and Land to the Tiller: In Search of a New Moral Economy

The rise of an authoritarian market regime in China, meanwhile, only sharpened rather than solved the country's many contradictions. To be sure, market reforms saw a generally ascending standard of living, but this would not have been possible without the fundamental pre-reform transformations of socioeconomic structure and relations, especially an egalitarian land system. This system, a last defence of peasant security and prerequisite for rural reorganisation, is formally retained, though also seriously eroded. If India has never freed itself from global capitalist chains, China, by radically loosening its regulatory protections and capital controls, is chaining itself. The substitution effect, accompanied by improved access to inputs and markets, did boost agriculture in the first part of 1980s, but the gains were soon offset by looming problems from rural disorganisation. A manifold crisis in the countryside was duly identified to depict unprofitable farming, land loss and peasant displacement, enlarged urban-rural income disparities, and rundown public maintenance and grassroots governance (Wen 2005; Day 2013, 116–29). The crisis amounted to a testimony of the damages of decollectivisation, which paved the way for land and people to be eventually and thoroughly commodified, along the way producing classes of rich and poor. After a policy adjustment in 2006 in response to rural unrest, gone with state taxes were also the popular common funds from collective accumulation earlier established and historically indispensable for the communal moral economy. As the national strategy became centred on urbanisation with policies encouraging big capital agribusinesses, and as the debt ridden local governments promoted private land acquisition for cash returns, rural polarisation and landlessness have re-appeared decades after the greatest land revolution in world history. This in turn undermines the regime's initial power base.

In India, although not similarly pressed by land and water shortage and certain other ecological stresses, agriculture does have the same problems of soil degradation from accumulated overuse of chemicals and fertilisers, alongside fossil fuel dependence and, above all, unsustainable petty farming. The costs of cultivation in India, for marginal farmers in particular, have followed a relentlessly upward curve in the past two decades. Since inputs came to be progressively ineffective in a tired or resistant soil, the amount farmers needed keep piling up, while retreating water tables also reduced the aptitude of existing groundwater irrigation (Lerche 2013, 390; Harriss 2013, 357). Turning its agriculture into a global commercial hub through a neoliberal model has had a decidedly negative impact on the Indian agrarian sector. Rural conditions remain so calamitous that in some areas, village after village people are still starving. In large-scale contract farming (at times, of genetically modified crops), many cash farmers who "fail" in a fiercely competitive world market—unprotected from either cheap agricultural imports or expansive seeds and pesticides—have resorted to suicide (Deshpande and Arora 2010, chs. 6, 12). The subalterns may have crystallised themselves into regional and Dalit parties while toiling to boost a growing Indian economy, but little fundamental improvement of their lives is in sight.

The capitalist upsurge in rural Asia (as in the global South at large) since the 1990s has renewed and intensified the question of land. India has seen bold enclosures of farmland, pasture meadows, and forests done in the name of modernisation. Given that grain crops are the least profitable, and as farmers and pastoralists are ever more separated from their means of production and subsistence, the shrinking of arable land and agricultural degrainisation continue to impair common livelihoods. Endorsed by state policies, many large mining and water projects have gone ahead without sound, negotiated plans for either human resettlement or environmental rehabilitation, while ignoring desperate protests. Similarly, in China, dilapidated villages bear parcellised holdings, wasted farmland, hurdles in managing water and other common resources, and waning infrastructure. Between 1997 and 2008, at least 6.2% of the country's farmland had been engulfed by factories, construction sites, and sprawl, in addition to desertification, deforestation and worsening land, water, and air pollution. Meanwhile, foreign food and seed corporations led by Monsanto, DuPont, and other powerful multinationals found China a receptive place with brilliant investment opportunities. As transnational agro-capital invaded both productive streams and supply channels, its share in Chinese corn, wheat, rice, soybean and vegetables markets steadily rose. The heyday of self-reliance has become a distant memory under today's threat to the hard won "people's food sovereignty" (Yan and Chen 2013). In both countries, the encroachment of tribal or collective land and the deprivation of variously land-dependent communities is the work of capital—developers, investors, agro-businessmen, financiers, and the like—as much as the state.

The world's remaining communal land of all types—and its cultivators as the "last peasantry"—are targeted by attempts at "capitalising" agriculture so as to maintain a supply of cheap industrial labour for the global productive chain. Without organised efforts in the direction of desirable agricultural intensification and diversification, an artificial rural "surplus labour" is being constantly squeezed off the land. In the world's two greatest long-lasting agrarian economies, an unprecedented outflow of rural migration has created a "precariat" of footloose labourers. The official figure for such labourers in China in 2013 was 260 million. An unofficial estimate for India in the same year was "as many as 100 million" (including seasonal workers) (Harriss 2013, 358). In the evermore crowded and bifurcated cities across China and India, newcomers struggle with unemployment, job insecurity, low wages or wage arrears, and sweatshops in the poorly regulated and often informalised and casualised labour markets without strong government or union protection.

Yet, a global project that destroys the fertility of land and depletes the environmental commons through accelerating globalisation and financialisation would also be hopeless in countries like China and India where a vast number of people continue to live on the land. On a finite earth, the remaining hundreds of millions of farming households simply cannot resettle themselves elsewhere without ruining the basis of their livelihoods. An organic agriculture for need rather than profit is simply necessary for sustainable human existence. That is, it will be impossible at least in the foreseeable future for the majority of rural Indians and Chinese to become stable urban workers; less viable still for them all to depend on the market supply for food as urban dwellers. The size of their combined population alone predetermines the essential necessity of minimal national food sovereignty, as no global market could ever meet a demand of that scale. Moreover, the risks of international financial capital controlling and gambling on grain prices could precipitate political conflicts in addition to economic crises.

In both countries, focusing on "clarification" of property rights and expansion of a land market in close connection with the financial market, reforms are more geared toward rental and sales gains and local state revenue than agricultural growth. There is however a single most important difference between China and India that China's "family responsibility system" is not a simple resumption of post-land reform "private" petty farming. The dissolution of communes threatened to but not yet really altered either collective land ownership or equality of land rights, at least not formally or legally. Resumed on an equal per capita basis is only the use right to land along with household management. Class differentiation has now recurred, more polarising in some places than others; and the aftermath of decollectivisation was typically a case of the "tragedy of the uncommons." But so far, collective farmland remains functioning as a secure means of subsistence for most migrant workers who could return to farming in times of need (while many from the younger generation no longer possess any land as land redistribution in the early 1980s was largely consolidated without keeping pace with demographic changes). This distinction between displacement and dispossession is unique; it is indeed the secret of China's "cheap labour" as a "competitive advantage" in the global market. The two-tiered structure has allowed migrant workers to be paid below the cost of family reproduction, hence the country to evade the tribulations of landlessness or a visible urban underclass and massive slums (Wen 2005, ch. 3; He 2007; Lv 2011). By using the countryside as a social safety valve, the state can manage collaborating with capital, ironically by tapping into a socialist reserve (Day 2013, 192–93). That is, the essential benefit of equal land right has been permitted to share the cost of profits. The duality of China's postsocialist political economy of exploitation and security as a hidden contribution to capitalist global expansion has yet to be conceptualised. If, globally speaking, industrialisation is no longer dependent on rural sourcing, the classical agrarian question of capital may have indeed been bypassed (Bernstein 2009). China is nevertheless exceptional. Even in India, the on-going capitalist transformation from above and below endures, not independent of land and rural labour (Byres 1996).

As global and peripheral capitalism continue to trap nearly half of humanity in prolonged food insecurity and abject poverty, the question of moral economy hunts within the context of rampant private seizures of public and collective lands on the one hand and the aspiration of sovereignty and development of the Bandung nations on the other. The only alternative that holds promise for the future is "land to the tiller" and peasant (re)organisation into forms of a moral economy. In such moral economic communities eco-agrarian cooperation and a participatory socio-political life can flourish, provided support from central and local governments, urban workers, and society at large (Zhang 2012; Lin 2013, ch.7).

The concept of land as a commodity contradicts traditional and socialist notions of common property as a natural or social right. Given that the peasant population in the developing world still shoulders the largest proportion of global staple crops and food production, these peasants cannot be made "modernity's victims" in any responsible policy consideration (Watts 2009, 267). Their agency should be found in a great counter-transformation toward "the rational cultivation of the soil as eternal communal property" (Marx in Bensaid 2002, 313–24). Meeting "two of the greatest challenges facing humanity" in our times—environmental stresses and persistent poverty—requires land preservation for farming communities and redistribution of large private holdings (Pogge 2011, 335). A crucial clarification here, once again, is that for land reform to retain its normative appeal in the 21st century it must reject "the pursuit of individual solutions to the contradictions of social existence, through securing and setting in motion private property in means of production" (Bernstein 2009, 253). Neither land privatisation nor marginal petty farming in closed communities offers an answer.

Returning to Amartya Sen who raised the question of "why India trails China" (2013), has not a land revolution given China a decisive advantage? Will not losing that advantage altogether bear even more dire consequences? While promoting equal land rights needs to become a real political priority, and hence a matter of determined political intervention in India, policy reorientation away from the irresponsible and disastrous neoliberal utopia is pressing in both countries if they are ever to overcome the developmentalist impasse.

## Endnotes

1. This paper is an abbreviated version of "Rethinking land reform: comparative lessons from China and India", in Mahmood Mamdani, eds. *The Land Question: Socialism, Capitlaism, and the Market,* MISR book series, No. 5, 2015. I would like to thank Mahmood as well as Henry Bernstein, Giuliano Martiniello and other participants in the land relations workshop at the Makerere University, Kampala, Uganda, August 2012, along with Elizabeth Allen, for their valuable comments and editorial help. I am also grateful to Dr. Darwis Khudori for his support and kind inclusion of my contribution.
2. William Hinton sees the law as playing a role similar to that of the Emancipation Proclamation during the U.S. Civil War (1972, 7). If this is an adequate comparison in terms of historical significance, the enormous size of the population affected in China dwarfs the U.S. case.
3. Poor or landless peasants, who at the time made up 52.37% of the rural population, had increased their share of farmland from between 14.28% to 47.1%, while middle-class peasants, themselves enlarged from 33.13% to 39.9% of the rural population, also gained more land share, from 30.94% to 44.3% (*State Bureau of Statistics Yearbook 1980*).
4. In addition to land tax as a major source of revenue, the Raj also set up a debt repayment process that included not only the interest and dividends on the construction and operation of colonial management in India, but also the expenditure for reconquering northern India after the 1857 Mutiny. In other words, "the British imperial state made those who had been conquered responsible for paying for being conquered" (Bagchi 2009, 102).
5. The retreating British were also responsible for deindustrialisation and the drain of local treasure, rolling back the nineteenth-century gains made by India in terms of modern

infrastructure and industry (Desai 2003).

6. The system began to weaken before independence, but the 1950 Zamindari Abolition Act provided firm ownership rights only to "a class of superior tenants who formed the first land-operating layer under the Zamindars and taluqdars". And "these beneficiaries were strongly represented in the Congress Party, and this has much to do with the subsequent loss of all momentum" for further reforms (Saith 2008: 734).
7. Nehru, a "liberal individualist with socialist ideas," personally preferred more radical socioeconomic changes. But his fellow Congressmen were mostly "social conservatives" influenced by Gandhi's vision of consensual reform to reduce poverty by harnessing a cross-class alliance "with the landowners and industrialists firmly in the saddle" (Desai 2011, 319).
8. For a slightly different set of statistics from the *National Sample Survey for 2003–4*, see Harris (2013, 359). See also certain relevant regional data in Lerche (2013, 395–97).
9. "Inequality in ownership of land was the highest in Tamil Nadu, Punjab, Haryana and Andhra Pradesh", the states that had the highest levels of landlessness. "The Gini coefficient was higher than 0.8 in each of these states" (Rawal 2008, 47).
10. In *India's Human Development Report 2011*, Kerala tops the index in literacy rates, quality health services, and consumption expenditure. For example, the education index for Kerala is 0.92 as compared to 0.41 for Bihar, while the health index is 0.82 in Kerala, while in Assam it is 0.41. http://www.pratirodh.com/pdf/human_development_report2011.pdf.
11. Amartya Sen interview (Derbyshire 2013).

## References

Anderson, P. 2012. "After Nehru". *London Review of Books* 34 (15): 21–36.

Baden-Powell, B.H. 1892. *Land Systems of British India*. http://archive.org/stream/landsystemsofbri034947mbp/landsystemsofbri034947mbp_djvu.txt

Bagchi, A.K. 2009. "Nineteenth century imperialism and structural transformation in colonised countries", in Akram-Lodhi and Kay, eds. *Peasants and Globalization: Political Economy, Rural Transformation and the Agrarian Question*. New York: Routledge.

Bandyopadhyay, R. 1993. "Land System in India: A Historical Review". *Economic and Political Weekly* 28 (52): A-149.

Banerjee, A., and L. Lyer. 2005. "History, Institutions and Economic Performance: The Legacy of Colonial Land Tenure Systems in India". *The American Economic Review* 95 (4).

Bensaid, D. 2002. *Marx for Our Times: Adventures and Misadventures of a Critique*. London: Verso.

Bernstein, H. 2009. "Agrarian Questions from Transition to Globalization". In *Peasants and Globalization: Political Economy, Rural Transformation and the Agrarian Question*, eds. Akram-Lodhi and Kay. New York: Routledge.

Besley, T., and R. Burgess. 2006. "Land Reform, Poverty Reduction, and Growth: Evidence from India". *The Quarterly Journal of Economics* 115 (2): 389–430.

Bramall, C. 2009. *Chinese Economic Development*. London: Routledge.

Burke, J. "Indian school lunch poisoning: doctors race to save children". *The Guardian*, 17 July, 2013.

Byres, T.J. 1996. *Capitalism From Above and Capitalism From Below: An Essay in Comparative Political Economy*. London: Palgrave.

Crafts, N. 2002. "The Human Development Index, 1870–1999: Some Revised Estimates". *European Review of Economic History* 6: 395–405.

Day, A. 2013. *The Peasant in Postsocialist China: History, Politics, and Capitalism.* Cambridge: Cambridge University Press.

Desai, M. 2003. "India and China: An Essay in Comparative Political Economy". Presented at the IMF Conference on India/China, New Delhi. http://www.imf.org/external/np/apd/seminars/2003/newdelhi/desai.pdf

Desai, M. 2011. *The Rediscovery of India.* London: Bloomsbury Academic.

Deshpande, R.S., and S. Arora, eds. 2010. *Agrarian Crisis and Farmer Suicides*. London: Sage.

Dreze, J., and A. Sen. 2002. *India: Development and Participation.* Oxford: Oxford University Press.

Duara, P. 2010. *Culture, Power, and the State: Rural North China, 1900–1942.* Stanford: Stanford University Press.

Ghatak, M. 2007. "Land Reform". In *The Oxford Companion to Economics in India,* ed. K. Basu. New Delhi: Oxford University Press.

Griffin, K., A.R. Khan, and A. Ickowitz. 2002. "Poverty and Distribution of Land". *Journal of Agrarian Change* 2 (3): 279–330.

Harriss, J. 2013. "Does 'Landlordism' Still Matter? Reflections on Agrarian Change in India". *Journal of Agrarian Change* 13 (3): 351–364.

Harvey, D. 2006. *Spaces of Global Capitalism: Towards a Theory of Uneven Geographical Development.* London: Verso.

He, X. 2007. "New Rural Construction and the Chinese Path". *Chinese Sociology and Anthropology* 39 (4): 26–38.

Hinton, W. 1990. *The Great Reversal: The Privatization of China.* New York: Monthly Review.

Khan, A.R. 1977. "The Distribution of Income in Rural China". In *Poverty and Landlessness in Rural Asia*: 253–280.

Kumar, S.A. 2011. "Land Reform Policies for Growth and Poverty Reduction: Key Issues and Challenges Ahead". *International Journal of Business Economics and Management Research* 2 (11).

Lenin, V.I. 1913. "Backward Europe and Advanced China". Vol. 19 of *Pravda: Collected Works.* Moscow: Progress Publisher.

Lenin, V.I. 1913. "The Awakening of Asia". Vol. 19 of *Pravda: Collected Works*. Moscow: Progress Publisher.

Lerche, J. 2013. "The Agrarian Question in Neoliberal India: Agrarian Transition Bypassed?" *Journal of Agrarian Change* 13 (3): 382–404.

Lin, C. 2013. *China and Global Capitalism: Reflections on Marxism, History, and Contemporary Politics.* New York: Palgrave.

Lippit, V. 1974. *Land Reform and Economic Development in China: A Study of Institutional Change and Development Finance.* White Plains: International Arts and Sciences Press.

Lipton, M. 2009. *Land Reform in Developing Countries: Property Rights and Property Wrongs.* London: Routledge.

Lu, X. 2011. "New Ruralism or Urban Slums?", *Open Times* 4: 115–135.

Meisner, M. 1999. "The Significance of the Chinese Revolution in World History".

Working Paper. London: LSE Asia Research Centre.

Nolan, P. 1976. "Collectivization in China: Some Comparisons with the USSR". *Journal of Peasant Studies* 3 (2): 192–220.

Parayil, G., ed. 2000. *Kerala, The Development Experience: Reflections on Sustainability and Replicability*. London: Zed.

Pogge, T. 2011. "Allowing the Poor to Share the Earth". *Journal of Moral Philosophy* 8: 335–352.

Polanyi, K. 1957. *The Great Transformation: The Political and Economic Origins of Our Time*. Boston: Beacon.

Ramachandran, V.K. 2011. "Classes and Class Differentiation in India's Countryside". *World Review of Political Economy* 2 (4): 646–670.

Rawal, V. 2008. "Ownership Holdings of Land in Rural India: Putting the Record Straight". *Economics and Political Weekly* 43 (10): 43–48.

Saith, A. "China and India: the institutional roots of differential performance", *Development and Change,* 39, 5: 723–57.

Selden, M. 1982. "Cooperation and Conflict: Cooperative and Collective Formation in China's Countryside". In *The Transition to Socialism in China*, eds. M. Selden and V. Lippit. Armonk: ME Sharpe.

Sen, A. 2000. *Development as Freedom*. New York: Knopf.

Sen, A. 2001. "Quality of Life: India vs. China". *New York Review of Books,* 44–47.

Sen, A. 2013. "Why India Trails China?" In *New York Times.*

Sengupta, S. 1981. "West Bengal Land Reforms and the Agrarian Scene". *Economic and Political Weekly* 16 (25/26): A26–A75.

Sethi, M. 2006. "Land Reform in India: Issues and Challenges". In *Promised Land: Competing Visions of Agrarian Reform*, eds. P.M. Rosset, R. Patel, and M. Courville. New York: Food First Books, 73–92.

Sun, Z. [1924] 1986. "The Three People's Principles and Democracy". Vol. 9 of *Collections of Sun*. Beijing: Zhonghua Press.

United Nations Development Programme. 2013. "The Human Development Report". https://data.undp.org/dataset/Adult-literacy-rate-both-sexes-aged-15–and-above-/x22y-8m6h

Wang, S. 2010. "China's Double Movement in Healthcare". Vol. 46 of *Socialist Register*.

Watts, M. 2009. "The Southern Question: Agrarian Questions of Labour and Capital". In *Peasants and Globalization: Political Economy, Rural Transformation and the Agrarian Question*, eds. H. Akram-Lodhi and C. Kay. New York: Routledge.

Wen, T. 2005. *The Sannong Problem and a Fin de Siecle Reflection*. Beijing: Sanlian Publisher.

World Resources Institute Report. 1995. *World Resources 1994–5: A Guide to the Global Environment*. Oxford: Oxford University Press.

Yan, H., and Y. Chen. 2013. "Calling for the People's Food Sovereignty: Beginning with Discussing the Soybeans". *Humanities and Society.*

Zhang, L. 2012. *Land to the Tiller: The Reality and Logic of China's Land System.* Beijing: China University of Political Science and Law Press.

# 17

# Taking Subaltern and Ecological Perspectives on Sustainability in China

*Lau Kin Chi*

## Abstract

This paper examines the sustainability of China's economic development since the 1979 Reform by interrogating questions of socio-economic justice and ecological justice. It attempts to understand how the craze for Modernisation entraps China in socio-economic injustices and aggravating environmental crises. It argues for taking subaltern and ecological perspectives in challenging statist, elitist and anthropocentric discourses and practices in relation to the question of sustainability in China.

*Keywords:* China, sustainability, ecological justice, socio-economic justice, subaltern perspective, common

The year 2015 started with two interesting cultural events in China which may offer a glimpse into the perception of different sectors of the Chinese population on the question of sustainability in China after over 35 years of Reform. In the first days of January, a rock and roll song *My Tomatoes are Clean*, written and sung by the Peasant Brothers, topped the popularity list. On Feb 28, the tenth day of the Chinese New Year of the Ram, Chai Jing's documentary *Under the Dome* was screened on seven websites in China; within two days, it was viewed over 200 million times, at the same time provoking heated online debates and diverse political reactions[1]. What is worth analysis, apart from what the song or the documentary is about, is the way they are received by the public and what this tells about the "structure of feeling" of the time (Williams 1977: 128–135). The former concerns disparity between the nouveau riche and the ordinary folk, and between the urban and the rural. The latter concerns smog pollution in the context of intertwined political and institutional power and interests in China.

## This world is too much hustle and bustle

The first part of the lyrics of the song *My Tomatoes are Clean* goes like this[2]:

> This world is too much hustle and bustle
> I have a small piece of veggie plot
> This is far from Highway 107
> Free from auto exhaust and smog
> My home is not in that big big city
> No need to squeeze a smile to everyone
> No need to scramble for fame and money
> So long as my tomatoes are clean ....

The rural setting with tomatoes grown on a small plot is contrasted with the luxury lifestyle of the nouveau riche. It is intriguing is that this song should become popular by privileging a simple rustic life as against the hustle and bustle of the "modern" city. It is difficult to imagine massive numbers of peasants sharing this sentiment a decade back, but it seems the tide is somehow changing. Since the early 1980s, millions of peasant migrant workers have swarmed to the cities and the coastal regions for jobs, providing cheap labour and displacing the unionised urban working class that enjoyed high social status and social security until the Reform. The latter has been forced into unemployment through the imposition of bankruptcy of large numbers of state-owned enterprises in the late 1980s and throughout the 1990s. With the exodus to the cities, China's rural population changed from 89.36% in 1949, to under 80% in 1980, and under 50% in 2011; it was 46.3% in 2013[3]. At the end of 2014, peasant migrant workers numbered 274 million[4]. Thus, when the song expresses a wish to leave the cities, it articulates frustration and disenchantment with an upward-mobility dream once shared by tens of millions of peasant families. Indeed, life in the cities has remained untenable for peasant migrant workers. Not only is there the problem of low/withheld wages, meagre social security and harsh/hazardous working conditions, children of migrant workers cannot get regular education in the cities. Hence a slowdown in the exodus to the cities, and occasional complaints from factories in the south of difficulty in recruiting workers. If there is a lack of material improvement and sense of well-being on the part of the main sector of the population that has contributed to China's physical economy for over three decades, the sustainability of this mode of economic development is questionable.

The growth under the Reform has been largely propelled by the ideology of money, greed and individualism, and the iron law of the jungle seems to have been supreme: the winner is the one who amasses money, regardless of whatever means is taken; the loser is the one without money. Yet, is there no connection between the winner and the loser? In 1978, the Reform was launched with the promise that China was not going to practise exploitative capitalism for it was still embarking on a preliminary phase of socialism; the helmsman, Deng Xiaoping, pledged that a small minority should be allowed to get rich sooner so that they would take along those that would get rich later. It would only be a matter of time, sooner or later, for everyone to get rich and get a share of the cake.

The outcome of the Reform is obvious: the cake has indeed become bigger. There are undeniable achievements, for example, extreme poverty has been reduced. China prides itself as one of the very few countries meeting the Millennium Development Goal (MDG) in fighting poverty. Statistically, the 2015 MDG target of reducing the extreme poor of 1990 by half was already met in 2009—from 85 million to 35.97 million. Yet the fact is that 3.6% of China's population was still in extreme poverty in 2009; in 2010, China's extreme poor constituted 12.8% of the world's extreme poor[5]. Could, and should, China have performed better? Its economic growth has been applauded: continual annual per capita GDP growth at above 7.6% since 1991[6], China counts as the second largest economy in the world since 2010; in 2014, its total GDP was USD 10 trillion, foreign reserve USD 3.843 trillion, and total import and export value USD 4.3 trillion[7]. These are the statistics supporting the claim that China is now a global economy of consequence, a good developing-country student following the capitalist paradigm, and a model for the less and least developed countries.

But, the term "economic sustainability" can mean very different things to different interests. For the Chinese state or the global mainstream media, the primary reference is China's GDP growth. The term "sustainability" is used to refer to sustained growth, that is, continual expansion of the economy by the capitalist logic—more production, more jobs, more consumption, more material turnover, and more monetisation of all means of life. Such a position does not really care who benefits and who suffers in this paradigm of sustained growth, and for how long such growth can be sustained.

After 1949, the nation's wealth has been accumulated through coerced contribution by the whole population, channelled to the industries in the form of collective or state property. A study suggests that the contribution of peasants to nation building in the first 60 years of the People's Republic of China (PRC) was around 17.3 trillion yuan (equivalent to USD 2.8

trillion), made possible by policies such as the price-scissors system of agricultural and non-agricultural products, the mobilisation of cheap labour, and land acquisition (Kong and He, 2009). This is behind the "miracle" of China's industrialisation within three decades. With the Reform, since the late 1980s, institutional restructuring has legitimised massive privatisations of state-owned and collectively-owned enterprises and assets, and common/public wealth has been channelled to an elite minority through monopolised power and corruption[8].

From the position of the majority of the labouring population—peasants, migrant workers, and material and immaterial labourers —, economic sustainability means much more than selling waged labour in the immediate period; at least it means a decent livelihood with sustained income and social security, and a habitat with access to the basics of life—clean water, clean air, safe food. Yet, Chinese labour is in a precarious position, as the world factory mode of economic development is export-oriented and susceptible to the global economy externally, and internally dependent on exploitation and expropriation rather than social progress and social justice.

Furthermore, the fact that China has progressed into an era with finance capitalism dominating the economy is unsettling. Like the opportunities and crises that global finance capitalism engenders, China's economy is similarly susceptible to the vulnerabilities of casino capitalism, albeit in different ways due to state policies which are in general pro-capital, but specifically differentiated due to contentions of different vested interests[9]. According to the 2015 Report of the McKinsey Global Institute, China's total debt quadrupled from USD 7 trillion in 2007 to USD 28 trillion in mid 2014; China's debt as a share of GDP was at an alarming 282 %: half of loans were linked directly or indirectly to China's real estate market, unregulated shadow banking accounted for nearly half of new lending, and the debt of many local governments was likely unsustainable[10].

With the manufacturing sector going into demise, and profits from extraction of physical labour value being minimal, finance capital, speculative by nature, has flourished in the last decade in urban estate development and is targeting at the last bastion of the gains of the people from the 1949 revolution—rural land. Rural land, with some differentiation between residence lots and farmland, is gradually open to "circulation" (an euphemism for "transaction"). In 2008, a policy document formally legitimised the circulation of right of contract and operation of rural land[11]. In 2014, a policy document opened up mortgaging of rural residence lots[12]. Such major policy changes will have serious impacts on land entitlement and land access for Chinese peasants when, up to now, the right of use of land has been under the sovereignty of the village community. The peasant migrant workers, exploited by legitimised privatisation and capitalism, fed up with false promises about the nouveau riche extending a helping hand to those down below, may want to return to the mode of subsistence livelihood of their parents and grandparents. However, would they still be entitled to a small plot to grow clean tomatoes?

## I have a small piece of veggie plot

The mode of development of China's economy in the last three decades cannot sustain itself once the environmental factors are taken into consideration. China is dumping ground for electronic waste (rhetorically presented as a "recycling" industry) from the North, and the largest emitter of carbon dioxide in terms of volume (the blame lands with the producers rather than the consumers); the cost of cheap manufactured goods flooding the world (and subsidising low-income world population with low-priced daily necessities) is so low because of cheap labour as well as rampant environmental pollution... When "modernisation" at all costs is justified by Deng Xiaoping's famous motto "Development is the Hard Truth", the dire costs of such a development paradigm were not unforeseen. It is most important to understand how policy makers or the general public are not unaware of the consequences of environmental hazards that come with such a development paradigm, and yet, there are no radical efforts to reverse or abandon such a paradigm. We cannot simply dismiss this mind-set as idiocy or insanity, though there is no other word to describe such a collective ill. Thus the question need to be asked seriously: how is it that the ecological problems present themselves again and again, every time with more severity, and any one of them could turn into a major catastrophe, yet, no radical reversal is effected.

I think we need to examine the severity of the ecological problems, understand their connectivity to each other, and make sense of the way the problems are perceived and the logic of reasoning, of policy makers as well as the general public, that relegates them to secondary significance. For example, the following "reasoning" has been in currency in China: we need to be utilitarian and pragmatic, we must make a choice between starving today (economic needs) and being poisoned next week (ecological concerns), and obviously the former takes precedence; get rich first, become strong first, and then the problems can be resolved with money and national power; the problems are "tuition fees" that China must pay for its development modelled after the advanced countries, as the economic powers of UK or USA also encountered these problems in their industrialisation phase; science and technology somehow can solve the problems and we have faith that even if science and technology cannot redress the problems today, a solution will be found tomorrow... As for the elite minority, or even for the upper middle class: if China becomes uninhabitable, we have an alternative—migrate abroad.

The middle-class perspective is predominant in discourses about China's ecological problems. The middle classes, mostly professionals and entrepreneurs, are estimated to be about 20% of the population. Some may have taken advantage of the property boom to secure a few apartments, most have benefited from economic growth and good income, own a house and a car, and enjoy a lifestyle of travelling abroad and eating out. They are the ones subscribing to notions of slow living, organic food and healthy lifestyle, and are concerned particularly with issues immediately affecting their health. They are the ones most receptive of the articulations in Chai Jing's documentary *Under the Dome.* This documentary has become a major cultural and political event. Receiving over 200 million online hits means that one in three of the 637 million netizens in China watched the documentary in the first 48 hours. The interesting question for me is how this Chinese version of "Inconvenient Truth"[13] illuminates the mindset of the middle classes, and the constraints of their perspective and formulation of alternatives.

While raising the smog issue which certainly need to be urgently addressed[14], Chai Jing's reading of the cause of the problem and her recommendations for solution are typically middle class oriented: she proposes that the polluting steel factories be closed down, and that the monopoly of China National Petroleum Corporation and China Petroleum Chemical Corporation be broken by introducing market competition which she thinks will rationalise control over contamination. The challenger of corporate monopoly does not challenge the logic of the market, modernisation and capitalism.

This liberal, humanistic approach is typical of mainstream civil society discourse in China. There has been an upsurge of environmental NGOs in China in the last two decades, partly because they were not regarded as too politically threatening in the eyes of the authorities, and partly because they echoed the mainstream middle class, liberal agenda[15]. Examining their limitations helps us explore radical and effective alternatives from the perspective of subaltern classes.

In my view, it is not adequate to explain away the environmental problems in China today largely as an outcome of its industrialisation or its export-oriented economic paradigm. Surely the environmental degradation has to do with such a development path. I think the probe has to go further to understand this craze for Modernisation that not only dominates the pursuit of state authorities, but also pervades common sense in general, so much so that it is not as if the problems do not present themselves, yet they are not genuinely recognised. Like the subalterns that cannot speak, that is, they speak but cannot be heard, (Spivak 1988; Lau and Hui 2005) nature cannot scream, that is, it screams, but cannot be heard.

## So long as my tomatoes are clean

I will take one example, water.

Water is the source of life. China's per capita access to fresh water is only 25% of the world average. Since the early 1980s, the decentralisation of industries and mining to be run by township and village enterprises (TVEs) was for some time seen as an impetus to developing China's manufacturing sector and giving the rural an opportunity for "development". This was the reason per capita income in many rural regions increased from the mid 1980s onwards. However, rural industries exploit not just local labour, but also water resources, as a consequence of which soil is also contaminated. Apart from industrial contamination which is the first major source of contamination, untreated urban sewage disposal, and excessive use of pesticides and chemical fertilisers, are the second and third major sources of water contamination.

The quality of water resources has deteriorated rapidly since the early 1980s, and by the mid 1990s, the situation was so grave that the state was forced to intervene. Water quality reached an alarming low level in 2001–02, when 40% of water from the seven major rivers in China was worse than Grade V. Even with state efforts to clean up, and the situation improved gradually, in 2010, still 20% of the water quality was worse than Grade V.

According to the Inclusive Wealth Report 2014, between 1990–2010, China's growth in terms of GDP was 523%, but only 47% in terms of Inclusive Wealth. The IWI adjusted average growth rate for China was –6.2% in 1991–1995, -2.0% in 1996–2000, -1.7% in 2001–2005, and –5.2% in 2006–2010[16]. Thus, if the environmental cost of China's growth is taken into account, its spectacular GDP growth is demystified. China's Environmental Ministry estimates that redressing and preventing water contamination will cost RMB 2,000 billion (USD 320 billion) and at least 40 years, and experts estimate that the three most severe contaminations—water, air and soil—will take RMB 6,000 billion (USD 960 billion) for remedy[17].

The unchecked contamination of water by industries, mining and agricultural production is a manifestation of anarchy rather than autocracy.

The logic of "Development as the Hard Truth" permeates all levels. While clean water resources remain scarce, China continues its export-oriented economy: shoes, electronics, vegetables, fruits... China's population is 19% of the world population, but it produces 67% of the world's vegetables, 50% pork, 30% rice, 50% apples, and 40% oranges; 80% greenhouses in the world are in China, heavily consuming water. This means with its agricultural exports, China is at the same time cheaply exporting its rare water resources (Wen Tiejun 2014).

Hence, the term "world factory" is ironic. Some Chinese scholars critical of such a development paradigm call China a "factory owned by the world". One third of China's carbon emission comes from its net export; 7–14% of its carbon emission comes from China's manufactured goods supplying the USA market[18]. The mainstream rhetoric in China's negotiations on climate change policies takes a position of a "developing country": developing countries have a right to develop, the burden should fall primarily on the developed countries; China's per capita carbon emission is only 10% of that of the USA; why are we not entitled to enjoy a lifestyle of the North, now that some of us can afford it; it is a conspiracy of the Western powers to contain China's economic growth... All these have some truth in them, but they emanate from the position of the state or the middle class, rather than from the subaltern, and more from industrial than agricultural concerns. China is most vulnerable to the effects of climate change, and draughts in the north and floods in the south have been the pattern since the 1990s, which directly affect food production and the conditions of livelihood of hundreds of millions of peasants. A research from the Chinese Academy of Sciences estimates that with global warming, water shortage and reduction in arable land, China's food supply by 2050 would be reduced by 14–23%[19].

What underpins the Modernisation fantasy is science and technology, which is nothing but progressive. Emanating from a mindless exploitation of nature is an arrogance and vanity coming from an anthropocentric urge to control. There is the exhilaration about human control over Nature.

Thus, many mega projects have been undertaken in China, not only for practical reasons, but also represented with a gesture of defiance of Nature's constraints. In relation to water, two mega, and potentially catastrophic, projects have been implemented since the 1990s: the Three Gorges Dam project, and the South-to-North Water Diversion Project. Both are unprecedented in their scale.

Building a dam at the Three Gorges of the Yangtze River had been in the mind of leaders since Sun Yat Sen in the early 20th century. One deterrent was a strategic concern of national defence, fearing a mega dam would be an obvious military or terrorist target. The consequence would be devastating: the population along the Yangtze River is around 400 million, one third of China's total population. Average population density is 220 persons/sq.km., reaches 600–900 persons/sq.km. in downstream regions, and 4,600 persons/sq.km. in Shanghai[20]. There have been a lot of controversies among scientists and engineers on the pros and cons of the project. When the project was finally put to a vote at the National People's Congress (NPC) in April 1992, the approval rate was the lowest ever approval rate in NPC history: of the 2,633 deputies, 67% voted in favour, and 33% against, in abstention or no vote. The Three Gorges Dam was built to be the largest in the world: the dam is 185 metres high and 2.15 km long, water level reaching 175 metres, with the dam reservoir extending 600 km in length and on average 1.12 km in width. It contains 39.3 cu.km. of water and has a total surface area of 1,045 sq. km (Hui, Lau et al., 1997). There was conjecture as to whether the Wenchuan Earthquake of 2008 was a consequence of the Three Gorges Dam, though "scientifically" it is difficult to prove or disprove the cause and effect relation.

The other mega project is the South-to-North Water Diversion Project. It is planned to supply water from the south to regions in the north. The water to be diverted for all three Eastern, Central and Western routes is planned to amount to almost 45 billion cubic metres per year. The Central Route is 1,264 km long, and takes one third of water from the Han River to the north; Beijing and Tianjin will each get over 1 billion cubic metres per year while Hebei and Henan provinces will also have a share of 3 billion cubic metres each. This is a classic example of metropolitan cities being unsustainable in terms of water and energy resources, and instead of reducing metropolitan population and de-urbanisation, the supreme human will is asserted. The resources are mobilised to the power centres to cater for their needs. In Beijing, the seven rivers it relied on half a century ago are now almost dried up or so polluted that they can no longer provide the 3.6 billion cubic metres per year consumed by Beijing. Excessive drawing of underground water has caused underground water level of Beijing to drop from around 12 metres in 1999 to around 24 metres in 2010[21]. Yet, the question is not just about spending almost 200 billion yuan (over USD 30 billion) on the Central Route, the question is the contempt for Nature that will definitely invite Nature's revenge. The south-to-north diversion crosses over 7,000 rivers, tributaries and streams which flow largely from west to east. It is not difficult to imagine the huge disruptions and the immense difficulties in engineering the water to flow above, below or across west-east flowing rivers. The water will flow in a tunnel under the Yellow River, while water pipes will hang in the air in some regions, and if they should break at some point, an avalanche of water will flood the area. Some scientists also warn that such diversion causes mixing of river waters and contaminations that can be disastrous.

This is yet another example of maintaining sustained provisions to Beijing and cosmopolitan cities, regardless of the huge disruptions in the habitat sustaining the livelihood of rural and provincial populations. So long as Beijing continues to get water, "sustainability" seems to be assured, however irrational the project may be in terms of costs, technological flaws, or transfer of the burden on to other sectors. The "sustainability" of Beijing is what goes into the vision of the state leadership and urban middle class, of the upper echelons of the social and political hierarchy; such partial "sustainability" of the power centre is presented as universal "sustainability". The rural, the marginalised, and those who cannot afford to live in cities and to pay for highly priced water do not come into the horizon. Hurrah! Beijing finds its sustainability in the supply of water, energy... And if clean air for Beijing is a problem, industries in the vicinity should be removed to more remote places, which does not require lifestyle changes from the capital's middle class with their automobiles.

## Modernisation and Growth at All Costs

The reality of the ecological crisis is too real for the ruling elite to ignore. In response, again and again, they resort to measures of management at the hands of experts serving the status quo. The experts managing the crises set out to do so with a very different agenda than that of the affected people who resist. Where can the experts lead us with their effort to maintain growth so that the development of "affluence" will not be disrupted? According to Andre Gorz, the exit from capitalism will happen one way or another. "De-growth is... imperative for our survival. But it presupposes a different economy, a different lifestyle, a different civilisation and different social relations. In the absence of these, collapse could be avoided only through restrictions, rationing and the kind of authoritarian resource-allocation typical of a *war economy*" (Gorz 2010: 27).

In the modernisation discourse in China, "de-growth" is almost unthinkable, even if it is an undeniable fact that China's so-called "growth" in the last 35 years has fostered gross economic and social injustice and has incurred environmental devastation which renders large sections of the population vulnerable, and undermines the conditions for the quality of life for the majority population. Man-made ecological catastrophes could in one moment wipe out the "gains" of decades of so-called "progress".

Yet, the Modernisation paradigm has gone unchallenged in the discourse of the ruling elite and the mainstream intellectuals. Some all too familiar assertions are, for instance: China must rise above its humiliation and violation by the imperialist powers; its only salvation lies with self-strengthening movements starting in the late 19$^{th}$ century, unequivocally articulated during the May 4 Movement of 1919 with the banner "For Science and Democracy", and practically pursued after 1949 with a modernisation path modelled after the West. After a century, the 2007 launch of lunar orbiter Chang'E1 and the 2008 Olympics were applauded as a triumphal return of China's power: the slumbering dragon has awakened. The Asia Infrastructure Investment Bank, launched in October 2014, rivals the World Bank, International Monetary Fund and Asia Development Bank. "To be a strong power", or "to resume being a strong power", unfortunately takes the development paradigm of the western powers almost as the only point of reference, and the only way for China's nation-building.

For those identified with the subject position of the ruling elite, China is forced to modernise itself in order to protect its pride and sovereignty; however, the "forced" modernisation of China is not simply a cure with extremely destructive side effects. It is destructive in such a way that people who are made to embrace it are also made oblivious to its force of destruction by being deprived of any other vantage point except those made proper by the dominant forces of modernisation and capitalism.

The ruling elite in China succumb to the developmentalist ideology for the pursuit of "growth" and "development"; the pursuit of modernisation after the fashion of "the west" provides them with powerful machines to establish hierarchical structures in the maintaining and producing of disparity, privilege, and system of inclusion and exclusion. The forces of the state and the capital that gain from and defend such a development paradigm by all means are substantial vested interest power blocs: the party-state regime retaining its legitimacy of rule through continual economic development; the nouveau riche exercising their political, monopolistic power in appropriating public and state property; the state and private capital in China and global finance capital partnering and contesting between and among themselves.... The ways in which finance capital has permeated China's economy and created havoc have demonstrated their force with the stock market crash in China in June 2015[22].

## Articulating Socio-Economic Justice with Ecological Justice

In this paper, I argue for taking seriously the cultural dimension which, rather than being relegated to the level of "superstructure" or of secondary/complementary importance, is part and parcel of the development paradigm. A radical change in the perceptions, values and preferences of the majority of the population must be pursued for a meaningful reversal of the current developmentalist trajectory. Most people would subscribe to the "idea" of "sustainability" because this buzzword is so much in vogue in the mass media, in school education, or in state and UN discourse. The questions we have to probe are: How is this term so much accepted but so little heeded? How do we enable the majority to see how partial, minority interests displace majority interests in the hegemonic interpretation of what "sustainability" means in our political and social life, thus rendering "sustainability" void of "justice"? How can people be convinced to struggle for a paradigm of sustainability *with* justice, seeing the two as interdependent? How can the relations between humans, and relations with nature, be de-monetised?

In debates among progressive intellectuals in China, in my opinion, the major conceptual issue on Modernisation is still inadequately pursued. The evils of Modernisation may be reckoned: it is a logic of an elite minority plundering the majority within and among nations; it is savagery clothed in civilised suit and tie; it is taking the human species along with the earth to imminent destruction... yet, Modernisation is still largely accepted as a necessary evil. Perhaps, it is a political formulation of "revolution by stages", that only after going through capitalism can the basis be laid for socialism and communism; or a nationalist formulation that only going through Modernisation can China become powerful enough as a nation-state to rival the imperialist powers; or a Darwinist formulation that the more one lags behind, the more exploited one is, therefore the faster China is modernised, the higher it goes up the chain. And a utopian formulation can come "afterwards"—when China is modernised to a certain extent, it can progress to alter-modernity or even anti-modernity.

However, this paper has shown how China is deeply mired in the dangerous mud of ecological and socio-economic injustices in its modernisation path. Confronting China is not the question of more progress or more growth, but multiple tasks of reversing dire damages already done to its ecology, society and culture. Alternative ways of reading history and conceptualising sustainability are most urgent, and there are theoretical formulations and empirical experiences on the common and the community that are useful for rethinking China's trajectory.

On the question of articulating ecological justice with socio-economic justice, C.A. Bowers (2001) criticises the progressive left for uncritically embracing the legacy of Enlightenment, allowing themselves to be trapped in the anthropocentrism, Eurocentrism, rationalism and racism of modernity, the driving force behind imperialism, colonisation and modernisation. Michel de Certeau (1986) points out in "The Politics of Silence" that the destructive onslaught of modern development has deep cultural roots in the divide between subject and object which enables both nature and human beings to be regarded as resources and open to optimal exploitation with the declining regulating hold of ethics and religion on scientific reason. "Development" and "progress" cannot be taken for granted as unquestionable direction of humanity. The ensuing ecological crisis is certainly directly linked to the intense techno-scientific transformation the Earth is made to undergo in order that capitalism can "flourish" throughout all corners of the world.

The ecological destruction of modernisation is not simply a mistreatment of nature. It is certainly a political question of placing the social cost of development on those lacking the muscle to protect themselves, of the destruction of cultures and communities through modern development and education in the name of empowering them for and integrating them into the modern world while in fact eradicating any defence against rampant commodification. Hence, ecological justice demands that the question of social justice should take the ecological destruction of nature, habitat and livelihoods into consideration. It is not simply a question of future sustainability of mankind, but more importantly the question of destroying the basis, the knowledge and the skills for communities to organise their interdependence into productive and creative cooperation and self-management in the production of autonomy and the commons.

The anti-modernity impetus emerges from below, from the initiatives and resistance of the subaltern, defending the common for survival, livelihood and community bonding. In two significant practices for sustainability based on the traditions and wisdoms of indigenous communities—the Aymarans in Peru, and the Zapatistas in Mexico (Dai and Lau 2006), neither contends for statehood. They demand and practice local community governance. They demonstrate self-organisation and cooperation evolving in the process of living together as part of the habitat in and through which they obtain their means of subsistence, and together with which they maintain the ecological balance of the habitat. Their idea of the commons covers all means of living together defying reduction to the claims of property, whether private or public. The means of living together refer not only to the so-called "natural resources" such as water, land, and air; knowledges, languages, social relations, affects, cultures, beliefs, customs, etc., that evolve in the processes of self-organisation and cooperation are also necessary means of living together. They are all of the nature of the common, not meant to be owned privately or publicly, but to be shared. They come into being and change in the course of things in and through sharing wherein lies their creative power in responding to the call and demand of the changing environment in which people cohabit.

In China, the movements and struggles for socio-economic and ecological justice require active participation of the people, not as individuals but as communities. In the last two decades, there are people's initiatives to counter the adverse effects of developmentalism and marketisation, and there are self-organised peasant cooperatives, local trading of organic food products, community-supported agriculture, food safety campaigns, rural-urban interactions, and environmental protection efforts (Wong and Sit 2015). The rural reconstruction movements that started some 15 years ago have involved thousands of people, especially the younger generation (Wen and Lau 2012)[23]. These efforts are, however, inadequate if they cannot be articulated into the agenda for ecological justice *with* socio-economic justice. The initiatives in China can learn much from interacting with groups such as the Commons Strategies Group for a paradigm shift towards the commons (Bollier and Helfrich 2012), or the movements for food sovereignty across the world (Herrera and Lau, 2015).

## Endnotes

1. *Under the Dome* 穹顶之下 with English subtitles: https://www.youtube.com/watch?v=T6X2uwlQGQM
2. *My Tomatoes are Clean* (我的番茄是干净的), http://mp3.9ku.com/mp3/654/653116.mp3
3. National Bureau of Statistics of PRC, 7 July 2014.
4. *Guangming Daily*, 1 March 2015.
5. *The Millennium Development Goals Report 2014*, p. 9. Relative to most other countries which have failed to attain the MDG goals, China is a success story. However, this should be seen not so much as China's "success", but as the dismal failures of global capitalism in most developing countries today.
6. According to the World Bank Report, China's GDP growth rate registered two digits growth in 16 out of 34 years during 1980–2013. The rate did not go under 7.6% except for the years 1981 and 1989–90. http://data.worldbank.org/indicator/NY.GDP.MKTP.KD.ZG
7. National Bureau of Statistics of PRC, 20 Jan 2015.
8. According to a report by the Chinese Academy of Social Sciences, between 1990 and 2011, 18,000 corrupt officials fled from China, taking up to 800 billion yuan (USD 235 billion) with them. *China Daily*, 31 Dec 2014.
9. I am Co-director of a research project comparing China with six other emerging countries, and after the first phase of the seven-country reports in 2011–12, the second phase with a critical analysis of the experience of the seven countries is conducted in 2013–15. Please see http://www.emergingcountries.org/pdf/China%20Historical%20Review.pdf for the historical review of China in the first phase. This is based on Wen Tiejun's Eight Crises (2013).

10. McKinsey Global Institute: *Debt and (not much) Deleveraging*, Third report, Feb. 2015, p. 8. http://www.mckinsey.com/insights/economic_studies/debt_and_not_much_deleveraging
11. "The CCP Central Party Committee Decision on Major Issues Concerning the Advancement of Rural Reform and Development", 2008.
12. "Opinions on Comprehensive Deepening of Reform to Accelerate Agricultural Modernization", No. 1 Document of 2014. The rural in China is now open to firstly, private transfer of rural land use, and secondly, to finance capital, which are the two main threats on the rural in this decade.
13. The documentary is a recorded 103–minute lecture delivered by Chai Jing during which she relates her personal experience as a mother concerned with the health of her baby to the issue of PM2.5 smog pollution, with clips of her journalistic interviews with experts and officials in China and the North, presentation of charts and cartoons to explain the severity of the issue, and recommendations for action.
14. The World Health Organization's World Cancer Report 2014 found that China, home to 19% of the global population, accounts for one-third of global deaths from lung cancer. The lung cancer mortality rate in China has risen by ten times from 5.46/100,000 persons of 40 years ago to 45.57/100,000 persons in 2013. ScienceNet.cn, 18 March 2013.
15. According to the China Federation of Environmental Protection 2013 Annual Report, till the end of 2012, there were 7,881 environmental organizations in China, an increase of 38.8% from 2007 to 2012. http://news.xinhuanet.com/local/2013–12/05/c_118433538.htm
16. Inclusive Wealth Report 2014: Measuring Progress toward Sustainability http://mgiep.unesco.org/wp-content/uploads/2014/12/IWR2014–WEB.pdf
17. Ou Changmei reporting on 4 March 2015 on www.thepaper.cn http://www.thepaper.cn/newsDetail_forward_1307689
18. Wen Jiajun: "Climate change and the absence of climate justice in China", BCR Magazine, 1 March 2015.
19. "Water shortage will endanger China's food security", Chinese Academy of Sciences, 5 March 2009. http://www.igsnrr.ac.cn/kxcb/dlyzykpyd/qybl/200903/t20090305_2114042.html.
20. Changjiang Water Resources Commission of the Ministry of Water Resources, http://www.ctgpc.com.cn/sxslsn/
21. "The South-to-North Water Diversion Project will bring huge catastrophes", Shanshui Xiaoyaoyou, 29 Dec 2014.
22. See essay discussing the stock market crash in China on the Global University for Sustainability website: http://our-global-u.org/oguorg/en/?page_id=561
23. This co-authored paper reviews a movement of urban youth voluntarily going to the countryside or taking up organic farming in the last decade in China.

## References

Bollier, David and Silke Helfrich. Eds. 2012. *The Wealth of the Commons: A World Beyond Market and State*. Amherst: Levellers.

Bowers, C.A., 2001. *Educating for Eco-Justice and Community*. Athens: University of Georgia Press.

Dai Jinhua and Lau Kin Chi. Eds. 2006. *The Knight in Mask: Collection of Writings of Sub-Commander Marcos*. Shanghai: Shanghai Peoples Press. (in Chinese)

De Certeau, Michel. 1986. "The politics of silence", *Heterologies: Discourse on the Other*. Manchester: University of Minnesota.

Gorz, Andre. 2010. *Ecologica*. London: Seagull.

Herrera, Remy and Lau Kin Chi. Eds. 2015. *The Struggle for Food Sovereignty: Alternative Development and the Renewal of Peasant Societies Today*. London: Pluto.

Hui Po Keung, Lau Kin Chi et al. 1997. "Three Gorges Dam: case study". *The Dispossessed: Victims of Development in Asia*. Eds. Raina, Chowdhury and Chowdhury. Hong Kong: ARENA, 37–44.

Kong Xiangzhi and A. He. 2009. "The contribution of peasants to nation building in the first 60 years of the People's Republic of China", *Teaching and Research*, No. 9. (in Chinese)

Lau Kin Chi and Hui Shiu Lun. 2005. Eds. *Subaltern Studies*. Beijing: CCTP. (in Chinese)

Spivak, Gayatri. 1988. "Can the subaltern speak?", *Marxism and the Interpretation of Culture*. Eds. Nelson C and L. Grossberg. Basingstoke: Macmillan Education.

Wen Tiejun. 2013. *Eight Crises: Lessons from China 1949–2009*. Beijing: Dongfang. (in Chinese)

Wen Tiejun. 2014. "Financialization of grain challenges China's food security", Dec 4, *Economic and Finance Web*, http://news.cenet.org.cn/show-16–65389–1.html (in Chinese)

Wen Tiejun, Lau Kin-chi, et al. (2012) "Ecological civilization, indigenous culture, and rural reconstruction in China", *Monthly Review*, Feb., 63:9, 4–8.

Williams, Raymond. 1977. *Marxism and Literature*. Oxford: Oxford University Press.

Wong, Erebus and Sit Tsui. 2015. "Rethinking 'Rural China', Unthinking Modernisation: Rural Regeneration and Post-Developmental Historical Agency", *The Struggle for Food Sovereignty: Alternative Development and the Renewal of Peasant Societies Today*. Eds. Herrera, Remy and Lau Kin Chi. London: Pluto.

# 18

# Towards a New Movement
## Aligned Trans-Internationalism

*Aziz Salmone Fall*

Reflecting on sixty years after the Non-Alignmed Movement presents us with an opportunity to start a new page instead of enduring the unipolar era and its fatal spiral downwards. Most of the Non-Aligned Movement's agenda and its demands are still relevant today notably: resisting the military control over the planet, advocating national and international policies for a more equitable management of resources for all people, safeguarding the rights of nations to choose their own independent development while ensuring peace and solidarity amongst nations. The demands and the measures that arose from the Non-Aligned Movement of Bandung constituted, in the Cold War era, a middle ground for nationalisms defending independent democracy. They were advancements of national "bourgeois or petty-bourgeois" interests and the essential elements are still important, though considerably without breath. Unfortunately, the scattering of the states of the South has exhausted the potential of the group of 77.

The era of the West-East polarisation of the world has ended. However, the North-South polarisation persists, like imperialism, but in more sophisticated forms. Having survived the Cold War, the Non-Aligned Movement has had a positive impact on international relations and development. Yet it has suffered, more than ever, from the geopolitical and economic uni-polarity of the global market order. National sovereign spaces, have been considerably destabilised by arbitrary, unjust practices of multi-national financial institutions, whether public or private.

However things have evolved. It is time for the new generation to take a stand; to align on the Southern front and update internationalism. The aligned, resolutely anti-imperialist movement, crystallising in the wake of the internationalism of the 20$^{th}$ century, articulates its strategy to defend the Commons and regain the sovereignty of nations towards a People's Fifth International Trans-internationalism. This new aligned movement offers a bolder formula to adapt internationalism to the economic and geopolitical order imposed by the globalised capitalist expansion. By adapting to a new internationalist transnational dimension, we advocate for a global reorganisation, a movement towards a universal ethical and socio-ecological transformation. This resistance, finding its energy mainly from the Global South, and gradually spreading to areas of the North, rediscovers in the global ecological emergency, issues of egalitarianism, feminisms, social justice, and the individual commitment of each human. This personal commitment must be multiplied by the collective strength of the human community.

The logic of the market order is destructive of social relations and the environment. Like a trojan horse, it is embedded in development. But development has gone astray. However, globalisation, a historical reality which is centuries old, has become an euphemism to describe the acceleration of capitalist accumulation and the redeployment of imperialism. This is done under the leadership of oligopolies, plutocracies, and remaining strong pockets of State power that are still geopolitically dominant. The puncture that this conjunction of oligopolies, plutocrats and dominant states still exerts on the exploitation of labour and surplus value works to accentuate global polarisation. The economic asymmetry is aggravated by a confusion between modernisation and westernisation that accentuates tendencies towards homogenisation and standardisation without being able to achieve it, despite capturing the attention of the hypnotised masses.

Submitted to structural adjustments policies and harsh conditions over the past three decades, the countries of the periphery seem paralysed and the ranks scatter under the brutal dispossession they undergo. The state has been sorely lacking in the development of public politics. The negative socio-political and ecological consequences of these measures will inevitably take decades to stamp out in our countries.

People and societies are not passive. But the 'depoliticisation', endemic of the neoliberal era, has undermined political organisation. However, resistance persists everywhere. With the "emergence" of the BRICS—who make up less than 15% of world's GDP—some countries have managed to control their accumulated wealth. This threatens the hegemony of the dominant blocs of the imperialist Troika—United-States-Europe-Japan. Having lost in the economic field, the Troika is reduced to co-opt the so called emerging countries to reinvigorate their own declining growth rate and to maintain all of the other countries in stagnation. This is no accident. It is done by strategic and geopolitical interference to reaffirm supremacy in the South. It is_accomplished through the dispossession of natural resources, by exploiting conflicts, and supporting various terrorist actions. Their strategy entails summoning all countries to align under their "safe crusade" or face an end to international cooperation and direct investment.

North-South solidarity remains a mirage maintained by the global elites. It has never reached 0.7% and the famous Millenium Development Goals and the crusade for poverty reduction were mainly diversions in the neoliberal agenda. But there are objective ways out through the active inclusion of the Southern countries in the world economy, despite the 'compradorisation' of most of their executives. However, the spirit of Bandung persists in many stratas of our societies. Here are some examples:

1. Objecting to capital flight
2. Attempts to regulate investments
3. Struggles to defend the agrarian question with land reforms against land grabbing
4. Efforts to ensure food security and the protection of production and the peasantry
5. Developing antibodies against the neoliberal virus

It is important to build on the historical struggles that have been fought and to work more boldly on others to affirm the genuine credentials of our people. The substantial gains of the Left in Latin America have occurred while the breaks have been placed on the popular uprisings in North Africa, and the Middle East or recently in the spring of Burkina Faso. Yet, despite the end of colonialism, imperialist and militarist domination through territorial occupation continues to take place in the Global South. Africa's very sovereignty depends on dismantling all foreign military bases, mainly AFRICOM. In the Middle East, the persistence of the brutal occupation of Palestine since the mid 20$^{th}$ century by the Israeli military forces, which constitute the fourth biggest army in the world and which is one of the biggest arms suppliers in the Southern hemisphere constitutes perhaps one of the biggest flaws in the capacity of the Non-Aligned Movement to put an end to all forms of colonial domination. All such factors which leave the Left in disarray should be opposed. There remains a great need for a democratic re-politicisation of the masses.

United against the oppression of nations, the potential to regain the path of self-reliance and strengthen the 'Tricontinental' front are the only solutions possible to the crisis in the Global South. But this radical reform of the Bandung front is eminently political and must pass through a rediscovery of internationalism and the defence of the common good of humanity. Democratic re-politicisation of our masses to resist the tide through the rebuilding of the 'Tricontinental' may counter the military momentum of collective imperialism.

Since the regulatory mechanisms, whether multialateral or transnational, that exist globally, to protect the commons, have become archaic or inoperable; the Non-Aligned Movement should address the issue of the commons, the last non-commodified public spaces and promote the adoption of a Universal Declaration for the common good of humanity. This strategy must reflect viewpoints from progressive forces in the South but also those in the North who are willing to offer their support.

To do this, we must now pass this phase of indignation, engage more deeply and show even more audacity. We must organise towards the development of a 'tricontinental' internationalist political platform of convergence. We must do so until we reach the trans-internationalist phase. That will be a second decisive step towards affirming democratic and popular sovereignty. Here, it will be important to firmly complete the gains of the preceding era and affirm an alignment with Nation-States, popular movements, social groups, associations, individuals, on the basis of internationalism in a transnational era. Beyond Bandung will provide a roadmap for a social project. This must be a global social project, in a polycentric world where popular forces of the South, fed up with the North-South monologue, reorient globalisation towards a development that is truly about balance, social justice, protecting Mother Earth and human well-being.

BANDUNG SPIRIT

BANDUNG+60

Rethinking Emerging Forces:

BUILDING SOVEREIGNTY, PREVENTING HEGEMONY

Challenges for Emerging Forces in the Globalised World

International and Multidisciplinary Conference in Commemoration of the 60th Anniversary of the 1955 Bandung Asian-African Conference, Jakarta-Bandung-Jakarta, October 27–31, 2015

# Bandung+60 Declaration

## I. General Statement

Coming from twenty-six countries (Brazil, Burkina Faso, Chile, China, Egypt, France, Gambia, Germany, Ghana, India, Indonesia, Japan, Malaysia, Morocco, Myanmar, Nepal, Netherlands, Nigeria, Palestine, Philippines, Russia, Senegal, Sudan, Switzerland, Thailand, Zimbabwe), representing the Global South and progressive elements of the Global North, we, scholars, intellectuals and activists assembled in the conference to commemorate the 60th Anniversary of the 1955 Bandung Asian-African Conference have issued this declaration with consensus.

The conference took place on October 27, 2015, at the LIPI (Indonesian Institute of Sciences) in Jakarta, on October 28 and 29, 2015, at the Gedung Merdeka (Independence Building) in Bandung,—the same venue where sixty years ago delegates from twenty-nine newly independent countries or nations which were about to gain their independence had assembled for the historic Asian-African Conference,—and on October 30 and 31, 2015, at Trisakti University, in Jakarta.

The 1955 Bandung Asian-African Conference gave birth to an idiom 'Bandung Spirit', which we summarised as a call: 1) for a peaceful coexistence between nations; 2) for the liberation of the world from the hegemony of any superpower, from colonialism, from imperialism and from any kind of domination of one country by another; 3) for the equality of races and nations; 4) for the solidarity with the poor, the colonised, the exploited, and the weak and those being weakened by the world order of the day; and 5) for a people-centred development.

Now, sixty years after the Bandung Conference, the colonial occupation has by and large disappeared, the "Cold War" has ended, and the Non-Aligned Movement has been marginalised. Yet, similar systems of domination by the imperialist powers in the world order persist, especially through the monopoly control at global level over the access to natural resources, the sciences and technology, the financial system, the weapons of mass destruction, and the media.

We have debated on other threats that continue to destroy our peoples in the Global South. They are: wars often orchestrated by the same imperialist powers who sell arms or through military interventions (such as in Afghanistan, Iraq, Libya, Syria, Yemen); social injustice; the plunder of the natural resources, particularly the mineral and land; propaganda and disinformation in the international media; impediments artificially created to limit the freedom of movement for human beings; neocolonial economic agreements; and the oppression of women. These unlawful activities still affect the majority of our peoples and communities. Likewise, injustice has surfaced in more sophisticated forms and larger dimensions.

We, therefore, salute all the initiatives aimed at reinvigorating the Bandung Spirit, including the Bandung+60 conferences, especially the Asian-African Conference of heads of state and of government held in Jakarta and Bandung in April 2015.

We must struggle against the ongoing domination of former imperialist and colonialist powers in the Global South. We must rely on our people everywhere for concepts like *kedaulatan rakyat* (popular sovereignty) and *TRISAKTI* (political sovereignty, economic self reliance, cultural self assertion) in Indonesia, or *N'an lara an sara* (we must not stay lying; we must stand up) in Burkina Faso.

We want the United Nations programmes, in its 70$^{th}$ anniversary, to contribute effectively to the genuine world-wide development based on the values of global *Swaraj*, Pan-Africanism and *Ubuntu*, the values of solidarity and mutual respect between humans in harmony with the nature.

We, intellectuals, activists, researchers have focused our discussion and deliberation on the following themes:

1. *Bandung Conference: Memory of the World and Emerging Forces* (LIPI, Jakarta, October 27)

2. *Enhancing the Role of Scholars in Promoting People-Driven Asian-African Partnership* (Gedung Merdeka, Bandung, October 28–29);
3. *In Search Of Sovereignty: Old and New Challenges for Emerging Forces 60 Years After the Bandung Asian-African Conference 1955* (Trisakti University, Jakarta, October 30).

After five days of vigorous and fruitful debates and deliberations, we uphold the following commitments:

1. We express our gratitude to the people and Government of Indonesia for their warm hospitality that was helpful to rekindle in our hearts and deeds the immortal spirit of Bandung. We would particularly like to thank the following institutions for their support to our conference: the Advisory Council of the President of the Republic of Indonesia; the Indonesian Ministry of Foreign Affairs; the Governor of Jakarta; the LIPI (Indonesian Institute of Sciences); the ANRI (National Archives of the Republic of Indonesia); Universitas Trisakti Jakarta; the MKAA (Museum Konperensi Asia Afrika) Bandung; the PKAA (the Centre for Asian-African Studies) Universitas Padjadjaran Bandung; and the CODESRIA (Council for the Development of Social Science Research in Africa). We extend our gratitude to the Prime Minister of Nepal for his message of support and to the Embassies of Brazil, China, Ecuador and Palestine for their presence in our conference.
2. We proclaim our commitment to convey through our writings and actions the spirit of Bandung, which is the same spirit that lives in the struggles for sovereignty and justice across the Global South as well as in other fora, such as the Tricontinental Conference, the World Social Forum, and conferences such as New Dehli (1947, 1954), Cairo (1957, 1958), Tashkent (1958), Conakry (1960), Belgrade (1961), Moshi (1963), Cairo (1964), Havana (1966), Lusaka (1970), Algiers (1973), Colombo (1976), Havana (1979), Jakarta and Bandung (2005, 2015). We will strive to build on the historic struggles that have been fought, and work more boldly to uphold the aspirations of our people. For this, we must go beyond the nostalgia and engage more deeply and show even greater determination in consolidating the sovereignty of our respective countries and peoples, by working towards the protection of the commons.
3. We assert our determination to contribute practically to the revival of the Bandung Spirit through the implementation of the *Declaration on Reinvigorating the New Asian-African Strategic Partnership* adopted by leaders of Asian-African countries in April 2015 for building an alternative intellectual agenda by providing tools for the progressive

political initiatives based on the spirit of Bandung. We will strive to work with our brothers and sisters from Latin America whose leaders and peoples have successfully challenged the empire.

4. We affirm our willingness to contribute in our respective countries to the creation of a genuine Bandung Academic Agenda, based on the Tricontinental (Asia-Africa-Latin America-ASAFLA) academic cooperation as a means of resistance against the hegemony of superpowers and the violation of the rights of our states and peoples. We need to achieve our intellectual sovereignty, and challenge the dominant paradigms that provide the intellectual foundation for the existing global order. These are the very paradigms the peoples of the world are seeking to transform.
5. We condemn the repressive and unjust policies and practices of the Israeli occupation in Palestine. We salute the resistance and steadfastness of the Palestinian people against the Israeli occupation and its impunity, and for achieving their national sovereignty and genuine democracy. We express our solidarity with their struggle for their liberation, right of return, and independence. We urge the academic institutions in Africa, Asia and Latin America to empower the Palestinian academic institutions, to collaborate with progressive Israeli scholars and to boycott the Israeli academic institutions.
6. We pay our tribute to the martyrs fallen during the heroic struggle of the people of the Global South for democracy and social justice. In the African Continent, as in Burkina Faso, the African youth must aim at reinvigorating the effective decolonisation and reassertion of sovereignty of the continent and at rekindling the spirit of Pan-Africanism.
7. We appeal for the protection of peoples and communities, such as the Rohingyas in Myanmar, who face the risk of genocide.

## II. Outcome of the Conference

The following principles and decisions were debated in seven working groups based on academic disciplines: two general thematic groups (HISTORY and GENDER EQUALITY AND WOMEN EMPOWERMENT) and five specialised thematic groups (CULTURE, ECOLOGY, ECONOMY, POLITICS, SPIRITUALITY & RELIGION). In addition, two special sessions were dedicated respectively to the questions of PALESTINE and of ROHINGYA. Other important topics like youth, civil society's role, diaspora will be included in the next meetings.

## History

1. We congratulate the ANRI (National Archives of the Republic of Indonesia) and the LIPI (Indonesian Institute of Sciences) for the adoption of the archives of the 1955 Bandung Asian-African Conference as a part of the UNESCO's Memory of the World. It can be considered as a progress of Africa and Asia in the writing of their own history as well as of world history.
2. For long, the history of the world was written within the framework of colonialist interest. Colonialism entailed accumulation of knowledge on all aspects of life of the colonised by the colonisers, and this knowledge has been stocked in the colonialist countries. Africa, Asia, Latin America and the Caribbean should stop this process of dispossession of knowledge and write their own history.

We call for the writing of a BANDUNG HISTORIOGRAPHY starting with the following themes:

(a) The Bandung Conference in Local and National History: The history of the Bandung Conference has been written in many ways. However, none has yet revealed how the Bandung Conference was perceived by the people (communities, associations, organisations) and the government at local and national levels in the countries of Africa, Asia and Latin America. It is high time now to look at national archives, especially of the countries that participated in the conference, and also at the archives of the national liberation movements, the media and the oral sources, particularly the testimonies of the remaining living witnesses in any country of the Global South. In this context, we support the initiative for a series of conferences on the archives of Pan-African Movements to be organised in Africa and in other countries with the people of African descent.

(b) The Bandung Era as a Historical Period in the World History: The Bandung Era, between 1955 and 1990, has been a turning point in Global History. It marks the rise of the peoples of the South against the domination of the North. During the Bandung Era, the North was forced to adjust itself to the demands and aspirations of the South. After this era, the North took back its control of the world through the neoliberal globalisation. We need to write in detail what exactly happened in every Asian and African country about the development experiences during the Bandung Era to draw lessons for the future.

(c) The Bandung Constellation: Origin, Development and Impacts: Like a big bang generating a constellation of stars, planets, comets, meteors, the Bandung Conference generated a Bandung Constellation of conferences, cultural festivals, social and solidarity movements, associations/organisations/institutions, business fora, research institutes, study centres, academic periodicals, news magazines and many other efforts. The contours and the content of the Bandung Constellation have not yet been known completely. It is the right time now to define them by tracing back their origin, development and impacts. We should write the history of every event from the perspective of every participating country. Compiled in a document, it will form at the same time a history and a directory of the Bandung Constellation. We, therefore, appeal to Asian, African, and Latin American historians to establish an Association of Asian African and Latin American Historians.

## Gender Equality and Women Empowerment

The constantly reinvigorated women's movement since the last century has been engaged with the liberation of women from centuries of oppression in different places across the regions everywhere in the world. Multiple theoretical and analytical studies have highlighted the newer oppressions of women even while there were expanding demands for gender justice. Women's rights and gender equality have been seriously undermined by the economic, trade and fiscal policies that have increased militarisation, violence, poverty, and inequality, especially under the regime of neoliberalism. It is necessary, therefore, to historicize the women's movement and to explore the complex trends in the relationship between the sexes.

We call for the following actions to be taken:

(a) To support gender equality and women empowerment as an integral pillar of the Bandung Spirit Community.
(b) To advocate for the expansion of the gender spectrum.
(c) To transform the existing patriarchal structure, heteronormative practices, social and cultural norms into a gender sensitive society.
(d) To revise the way women are presented in publicity and in mainstream mass media coverage.
(e) To implement in letter and spirit the elimination of all forms of violence against women in personal, public, and cyber spheres.
(f) To create multiple gender narrative models relevant to the South.
(g) To empower women to combat discriminations, inequality and injustice generated by globalisation.

(h) To work towards gender mainstreaming through universal gender budgeting, gender policies and programme, and gender sensitive monitoring and evaluation as a way to advance gender equality within the Bandung Spirit Community and beyond.

(i) To create inter- and intra-gender networks and gender support spaces, and to exchange knowledge, experiences and ideas about gender issues, about violence and crimes against women, and about the maternal health that cut across differences within the Bandung Spirit Community.

(k) To disseminate knowledge about gender equality, to raise gender awareness through manuals and books, training programmes, seminars and conferences.

(l) To urge governments to agree politically to promote 'Gender Justice' and address essential structural dimensions of gender inequality by taking the following measures: (i) to transform and deepen the normative framework for women's human rights and achieve them through effective implementation of laws and policies along the key dimensions; (ii) to ensure that the resources for and attention to access, affordability and availability of basic services are not curtailed, and that the women's entitlements, rights and health, and gender equality are protected and promoted; (iii) to expand women's capabilities, particularly through education, so that their ability to challenge gender inequality individually and collectively is strengthened; (iv) to increase women's participation in the political and other decision-making processes from the household to national and international levels so as to increase their voice and agency.

## Culture

1. We interpret culture as a core of knowledge based on the collective experiences of a people over time—including their ideas, belief systems, history, language, music, literature, and customs—in regards to their vision of their socio-political and socio-economic environment and how they behave with respect to it.
2. History shows that hegemony is often based not only on coercion but also on domination of hearts and minds through culture. It is, therefore, logical that if any group of people looks forward to "Building Sovereignty, Preventing Hegemony"—the main theme of our conference—culture has to be an important tool, a defence mechanism. We underline one of the points of the Final Communiqué of the 1955 Bandung Conference that Asia and Africa have been the

cradle of great religions and civilisations, which have enriched other cultures and civilisations while themselves being enriched in the process. Unfortunately, contacts among Asian and African countries were interrupted during the past centuries. The peoples of Asia and Africa are now animated by a keen and sincere desire to renew their old cultural contacts and develop new ones in the context of the modern world.

3. We have put emphasis on the theme of "Comparative African and Asian perspectives of culture as a resource for building sovereignty and preventing hegemony". We think we should not only adopt a celebratory approach to culture as a tool at the disposal of African and Asian societies to tackle external hegemony; we also need to take stock of ways in which certain aspects of culture might indeed be inimical to building sovereignty and preventing hegemony.

We call for the following actions to be taken:

(a) Countries of Asia and Africa, which are able to do so, should give more facilities for the admission of students and trainees from sister Asian and African countries to their institutions. These exchanges are a way to deepen intercultural dialogue between students, researchers, and communities.

(b) Countries of Africa and Asia should also encourage the organisation of periodical Bandung Spirit intercontinental cultural events involving local communities as main actors.

## Ecology

1. Humanity has prospered for millennia under the favourable conditions of the Earth System—a planetary entity encompassing Air (atmosphere), Water (hydrosphere), Land (geosphere), and Life (biosphere). However, this habitable environment has been destroyed over the years by the productivism that commodifies natural resources. This drive reflects the Western anthropocentric visions (subsequently reproduced everywhere), that seek human hegemony over the nature. It conceptualises Earth as 'resources' to be exploited for profits, causing an adverse change in the interactive patterns of the various spheres on and above the Earth.
2. Global Warming and associated Climate Change, resulting from the intensification of carbon dioxide and other greenhouse gases in the atmosphere, are the most visible and threatening aspect of change today. The massive burning of the fossil fuels, deforestation, and

other human activities are causing the harmful impacts in the form of unprecedented heat-waves, droughts, storms, floods, and the rise of the sea levels.

We call for the following actions to be taken:

(a) Politically, governments must urgently agree on moral-legal questions of 'Inter-National/Human Justice' like who is responsible for the transformation of Earth, and on what grounds. Earth System transformation is also an issue of 'Inter-Generational Justice', requiring urgent deliberations and action because each succeeding generation faces more adverse environment than the previous ones.

(b) Economically, we must transcend the capitalist regime as it commodifies and mutilates the Earth System. The neoliberal mode of production cannot confront the metabolic system of Nature, evidently exemplified by the capitalism's failure. Regarding the degradation of tropical forests, the Global South should establish a specific mechanism to secure them. Moreover, as mine exploitation also destroys ecosystems, we must minimise such practice to sustain ecosystem for the coming generations.

(c) Studies have convincingly shown that today's eco-catastrophes are principally traceable to the paradigms embraced by the modern West. We must, therefore, transcend: 1) the image of human domination over nature; and 2) the segmentation of the "Search for Truth" and thereby a dangerous division of knowledge into the physical, chemical, and biological sciences on the one hand, and the social sciences and humanities on the other. To secure human well-being, social scientists can no longer exclude climate and other Earth System transformations from their paradigms, just as bio-geo-chemical-physical scientists on the Earth can no longer exclude humanity from their subjects.

(d) We observe how the "haves" have promoted today's eco-catastrophe from which the "have-nots" are suffering disproportionally. Thus, scholars are urged to engage the communities affected by the ecological crises as agents for human progress and survival. Ecological justice cannot be dissociated from economic and social justice. A universal declaration of the Ecological Commons should, therefore, be advocated.

(e) We realise that Food Security requires healthy ecosystems. Since food insecurity occurs with ecological (as well as social) degradation, the world can be fed only by upholding the ecological principles. We observe that food insecurity emerges not so much from the tension between population growth and food production, but from the tension between the latter and its commercialisation along with ecological destruction that has accompanied it.

(f) Governments should promote Food Sovereignty because it secures local control and ecological sustainability. To maintain the essential ecosystem services, governments should conceptualise agriculture as part of the ecosystem, and empower small farmers, agricultural workers and the landless.

(g) Research should explore strategies to attain food systems that are ecologically sustainable and socially equitable. Academia should support the development of knowledge of policymakers and societies related to the complex interconnections between the diverse elements of the food system.

## Economy

1. We have noted that since centuries many Asian countries had significant trade links with some parts of the African continent, especially East Africa. However, in the recent decades, trade between the majority of Asian developing economies and African countries have not been so significant compared to their trade with other regions.
2. We recognise that governments in Africa and Asia have been giving their efforts to reinvigorate the Bandung Spirit and enhance cooperation between African and Asian nations. This was started with the first Asian-African Sub-Regional Organisations Conference (AASROC) in 2003 in Bandung (Indonesia) and followed by the second conference hosted by Durban, South Africa in 2004. These conferences were important as they outlined the concept of New Asian-African Strategic Partnership (NAASP). In 2005, Jakarta and Bandung co-hosted the commemorative golden jubilee Africa-Asia summit, resulting in the adoption of NAASP. It marked the beginning of new cooperative agreements focused on attaining mutual prosperity and development by countering the threats of globalisation. And, most recently, in 2015 Indonesia again hosted the 60$^{th}$ Anniversary of the Asia-Africa Conference, and they again discussed strategies to strengthen cooperation between them. However, the majority of private economic players in many countries in both Asia and Africa never took note of all these agreements or efforts.
3. In our view, there is too much focus on the neoliberal framework in the economic fora and other gatherings in Asia, Africa and Latin America. There is a conspicuous lack of contribution of scholars and

intellectuals to include issues related to the grassroots communities in the policy deliberations in the regional meetings in the South.

4. We notice that the North-South free trade agreements are detrimental to the South due to the asymmetric economic powers between the two sides. There is a need to strengthen South-South cooperation for the benefit of our peoples. We note the recent establishment of the TPP (Trans-Pacific Cooperation) and hope that it will not be used to further accentuate North-South disparity in world trade. We also hope that the trade and investment policies of India and China and their financial assistance to other Asian and African countries in support of their economic development will not undermine the sovereignty of these countries. In this context, we denounce the lack of will of certain African governments to implement the sovereign currency policies vis-à-vis the North.
5. We have found considerable evidence to suggest that SME (Small and Medium Enterprises) are vital to increase the people's prosperity in Africa and Asia. Good examples for this are numerous as are noticed in the work of the ATC (Asia-Africa Trade Center) in Jakarta,—which is the initiative of Asian and African SME in trade between the two continents,—the annual Trade Expo Indonesia and the biennale *Salon International de l'Artisanat de Ouagadougou* (International Arts and Handicrafts Trade Show of Ouagadougou) in Burkina Faso, both of which provide opportunity to SME of the respective countries to expose their products.

We call for the following actions to be taken:

(a) To recommend Asian and African governments to encourage trade and investment links among domestic private sectors in the two continents. Either the governments in the two continents can initiate such links with state-own companies as the leading players, or facilitate trade and investment links by private sector with measures such as tax incentives, export financing and subsidised credit schemes. Asian embassies in Africa and vice versa should be the front runners in this effort by providing up-to-date information on trade and investment potentials/opportunities and macroeconomic as well as social and political conditions in the host countries.

(b) To call governments of Asian and African countries for an active information campaign and publicisation about all the agreements they have adopted to promote trade and investment links between the two continents. In establishing regional economic blocks or in creating free trade areas, African and Asian countries should harmonise, standardise and simplify trade procedures, customs, official documentation, health and safety procedures, regulatory bodies, trade financing schemes, and other measures required to do international trade.

c) To urge the governments of the Global South not to conclude the Doha Development Round without a meaningful development package and no other round should be launched without addressing the core development issues that the Doha Development round was mandated to address at the 10th WTO Ministerial Conference held in Nairobi in December 2015, or at other relevant fora.

(d) To support the project introduced by Ecuador at the UN Council of Human Rights for a legally binding international instrument regarding Transnational Corporations (TNCs) and other business corporations.

(e) To encourage the initiatives of African and Asian SME in their exchanges between the two continents and to appeal to African and Asian scholars to contribute to their development through their research and publications in diverse scientific disciplines such as economics, management, history, anthropology, linguistics, political science and sociology.

(f) To suggest to the governments of African and Asian countries to organise periodic exhibitions of African-Asian Arts and Handicrafts involving African and Asian SME.

## Politics

1. As formulated in our own languages and visions, *kedaulatan rakyat* (popular sovereignty), *permusyawaratan* (collective deliberation), *N'an lara an sara* (we must not stay lying; we must stand up) must be the principles and values as the corner-stones of true democracy in our countries.
2. Bearing this in mind, the conference considers that the conflicts in Syria, Libya, Iraq and Afghanistan, and the destabilisation of Nigeria, Mali, Niger, Cameroon and other countries in the Global South by armed groups, and the so called crisis added by the migrants are mainly the consequences of the deeds of the imperialist forces. Only through state and popular sovereign agency can the root causes of these wars and destruction be eradicated.
3. We express our total solidarity with the legitimate struggle of the people of Palestine and will stand together with the Palestinian scholars and activists for this cause.

4. We advocate for peace and peaceful coexistence. Countries should settle disputes based on the 'Bandung Spirit' and avoid the direct or indirect interference in sovereignty space.
5. We salute the affirmation of popular and national sovereignty and integration processes in Central and South America, and express our solidarity with their popular democratic resistance.
6. We believe that foreign military bases in the Global South must be dismantled in order to create conditions for the exercise of popular sovereignty.

We call for the following actions to be taken:

a) To increase the public funding for research in humanities, sciences and technology and to encourage more South-South cooperation.
b) To promote an alternative framework in place of the current regime of intellectual property rights for the sake of common good and build an open source in the sphere of information and communication technology.
c) To support and strengthen the tricontinental front of the Global South, through organisations such as the G-77, as well as networks of civil societies and social movements of the Global South with special attention to enhancing academic cooperation.

## Spirituality and Religion

1. We found that human rights, religious diversity and peaceful co-existence among religions are threatened by four historical and systemic types of religious domination: (i) Abrahamic monotheism over other belief systems; (ii) Majority over Minority and in many cases Minority over Majority; (iii) Communitarism over individuality; and (iv) Men over Women.
2. We have learnt from the iconic leaders of the Bandung Era, which included Mao Zedong, the Atheist and Soekarno, the Muslim that the concepts of good and evil, morality and integrity are primarily intimate and personal undertakings of every citizen. From that standpoint they are constructively reflected in the civic codes of a community or social policies. This legacy of the Bandung Era should be reiterated today.
3. We recall that the rise of the Liberation Theology in Latin America during the Bandung Era duly challenged the governments to acknowledge the intangible ideals of the poor endangered by unrestrained market-driven policies.

4. We observed the trend of escalation of violence at global level, including wars, terrorism in the name of religion and counter-terrorism. We noted that international terrorism is a complex reality, concerning not only religious issues but also a challenge to the present international order. We realised that mass unemployment among the youth and brutal political repression increase the risk of religious fanaticism and the use of terrorism for political aims.
5. We decry the persistent loss of lives, in some cases the number being tens of thousands, motivated by ethno-religious rivalry and/repression in Africa and Asia (e.g. Central African Republic, China, India, Indonesia, Iraq, Mali, Burkina Faso, Myanmar, Nigeria, Palestine, the Philippines, Thailand, just to quote a few glaring examples).
6. We underline that not all political and social movements based on religion are "communitarian" in the sense of acting for the interest of their own community. Some of them are "pluralist" (acting for the interest of religious diversity and of common well-beings). We witnessed the rise of inter-faith and inter-religious movements for the common concerns: peace, human-rights, democracy, ecology and social justice.

We call for the following actions to be taken:

a) We call for a conscientisation among our communities about the danger of the aforementioned four historical and systemic types of religious domination, and for the empowerment of the dominated religious communities, as a means to preserve religious diversity and peaceful co-existence among religions.
b) We condemn all forms of terrorism, including state terrorism, mourn the dead and sympathise with those in pain. While being in solidarity with the victims of terrorism, we call for the eradication of its causes at local, national as well as global level.
c) We encourage actions that promote "pluralist" social policies in spiritual and religious domain and prevent the development of "exclusivist" religious movements.
d) We call for an inter- and intra-religious dialogue in our countries, schools, community organisations, national and international organisations.
e) We support the civil authorities in creating an appropriate public sphere for all citizens to practice freely the spiritual or religious traditions of their choice. We warn that proselytism by any religious group may generate conflict.

f) We appreciate actions such as *"The African Initiative on Education for Peace and Development through Inter-religious and Inter-cultural Dialogue"* held in Benin (West Africa) in May 2015, as it offers pertinent ideas to advance responsible citizenship, and we call for the emulation of such initiatives in other parts of the world.

## III. Roadmap

We need to take the following measures:

### 1. Institutional Strengthening

a) Formalisation of the BANDUNG SPIRIT NETWORK as a legal-formal organisation registered in one or more countries. The international coordinator and the eight working groups coordinators (History, Gender, Culture, Ecology, Economy, Politics, Spirituality & Religion, Final Declaration) are in charge of the implementation of this plan in consultation with the Bandung+60 conference participants and working group members.
b) Setting-up of an ASAFLA (Asia-Africa-Latin America) Secretariat.
c) Collaboration of the BANDUNG SPIRIT NETWORK with the PKAA (Pusat Studi Asia-Afrika / Centre for Asian-African Studies) at the Padjadjaran University, Bandung.

### 2. Academic Cooperation

As a step towards implementation of the Declaration, a draft proposal for academic cooperation is presented as an appendix of this document.

In addition, a special programme will be dedicated to building up academic cooperation with Palestinian scientific institutions and Israeli scholars who oppose Israeli violation of human rights and international law.

### 3. Opportunities

2016 will be the year of the 55th anniversary of the Belgrade Conference of Non-Alignment, the 50th anniversary of the Havana Conference of Tricontinental Movement, and the 20th anniversary of the UN Declaration on the Right to Development.

It will be an opportunity to organise a series of Bandung Spirit-based events in African, Asian and Latin American countries. They may be organised in conjunction with the International Decade of People of African Descent (2015–2024). It is the right time for the Bandung Spirit Network to join hands with the Asian, African and Latin American Diaspora networks to move towards the concretisation of the Bandung Spirit message.

# BANDUNG CONFERENCE 1955 AND BANDUNG COMMEMORATIVE CONFERENCES 2005 AND 2015

## EXCERPTS FROM THE DECLARATIONS OF HEADS OF STATE AND GOVERNMENTS

*Presented by* Darwis Khudori

Under the auspices of Indonesian government, States of Africa and Asia have been involved in the 1955 Bandung Asian-African conference and its commemorative conferences in 2005 and 2015. At every conference, they produced an official statement, communiqué or declaration.

This article is aimed at presenting briefly the content of those documents. It is not intended to review the whole documents in exhaustive way, but to quote the passages considered to be significant in relation to the evolution of socio-cultural and politico-economical situation in Africa and Asia during the last 60 years.

## The 1955 Bandung Asian-African Conference Final Communique

The 1955 Bandung Conference was held during the Cold War following the WW II. The world order was dominated by two blocks of superpowers: West (capitalist) and East (communist). The African and Asian countries who just took back their independence from Western colonial occupation were struggling for securing their independence, living in peace in order to improve their living condition and helping other colonised countries to get out from colonial occupation. The Final Communiqué of the 1955 Bandung Asian-African Conference is marked by these preoccupations. It gave birth to an idiom "Bandung Spirit". This idiom has however never been defined in any official document. It was identified sometimes as "anti-colonialism", "non-alignment", "solidarity", etc. I personally found that "Bandung Spirit" represents a common wish for: 1) a peaceful coexistence between nations; 2) the liberation of the world from the hegemony of any superpower, from colonialism, from imperialism and from any kind of domination of one country by another; 3) the equality of races and nations; 4) the solidarity with the poor, the colonised, the exploited, and the weak and those being weakened by the world order of the day; and 5) a people-centred development. It seems to me that these are the core or the permanent elements that characterise the following "Bandung Spirit-based" conference declarations. The last part of the Final Communiqué of the 1955 Bandung Asian-African Conference represents those points.

> The Asian-African Conference gave anxious thought to the question of world peace and cooperation. It viewed with deep concern the present state of international tension with its danger of an atomic world war. The problem of peace is correlative with the problem of international security. In this connection, all States should cooperate, especially through the United Nations, in bringing about the reduction of armaments and the elimination of nuclear weapons under effective international control. In this way, international peace can be promoted and nuclear energy may be used exclusively for peaceful purposes. This would help answer the needs particularly of Asia and Africa, for what they urgently require are social progress and better standards of life in large freedom. Freedom and peace are interdependent.
>
> The right of self-determination must be enjoyed by all peoples, and freedom and independence must be granted, with the least possible delay, to those who are still dependent peoples. Indeed, all nations should have the right freely to choose their own political and economic systems and their own way of life, in conformity with the purposes and principles of the Charter of the United Nations.
>
> Free from mistrust and fear, and with confidence and goodwill towards each other, nations should practice tolerance and live together in peace with one another as good neighbors and develop friendly cooperation on the basis of the following principles:

1. Respect for fundamental human rights and for the purposes and principles of the Charter of the United Nations.
2. Respect for the sovereignty and territorial integrity of all nations.
3. Recognition of the equality of all races and of the equality of all nations large and small
4. Abstention from intervention or interference in the internal affairs of another country.

5. Respect for the right of each nation to defend itself singly or collectively, in conformity with the Charter of the United Nations.
6. (a) Abstention from the use of arrangements of collective defence to serve any particular interests of the big powers.
   (b) Abstention by any country from exerting pressures on other countries.
7. Refraining from acts or threats of aggression or the use of force against the territorial integrity or political independence of any country.
8. Settlement of all international disputes by peaceful means, such as negotiation, conciliation, arbitration or judicial settlement as well as other peaceful means of the parties own choice, in conformity with the Charter of the United Nations.
9. Promotion of mutual interests and cooperation.
10. Respect for justice and international obligations.

## The 2005 Declaration on the New Asian-African Strategic Partnership

While keeping the ten principles of the 1955 Bandung Asian-Conference as reference, there is something new in the 2005 Asian-African Conference declaration: *"people-to-people interaction, particularly business, academia, and civil society."* This corresponds to the evolution of socio-political structure in African and Asian countries. The Bandung Era (approximately 1955-1970) was marked by the struggle for independence and for nation building during which people and government formed a sole socio-political entity. The following period, in which the countries had re-conquered their independence and the government stressed its policy on economic growth, the socio-political entity started to split, the government policy and the parliament behaviour did not always represent people's aspiration, people's organisations started to appear and develop into N.G.Os, trade unions, neighbourhood associations, social and solidarity movements, gender mainstreaming… This new reality has been integrated into the 2005 declaration. Yet, the stress of African and Asian government policy remains economic development without putting into question the world economic order. In their agenda, African and Asian States planned to organise *"A Business Summit in conjunction with the Summit of Heads of State/Government will be held every four years"*. On the other hand, nothing was planned for academia and civil society. There is no statement either in what way African and Asian States deal with academia and civil society. The following passages represent this reality.

> We underscore the urgency of promoting economic development in the Asian and African regions, as stipulated in the 1955 Bandung Conference. We stress that poverty and under-development, gender mainstreaming,

communicable diseases, environmental degradation, natural disasters, drought and desertification, digital divide, inequitable market access, and foreign debt, remain as issues of common concern which call for our closer cooperation and collective action.

To this end, we hereby declare, as an expression of our new political will, the establishment of a New Asian-African Strategic Partnership (NAASP) as a framework to build a bridge between Asia and Africa covering three broad areas of partnership, namely political solidarity, economic cooperation, and socio-cultural relations. The strategic partnership provides a momentum in achieving peace, prosperity and progress, and will be based on the following principles and ideals:

1. The Ten Principles of Bandung of the 1955 Asian-African Conference;
2. Recognition of diversity between and within the regions, including different social and economic systems and levels of development;
3. Commitment to open dialogue, based on mutual respect and benefit;
4. Promotion of non-exclusive cooperation by involving all stakeholders;
5. Attainment of practical and sustainable cooperation based on comparative advantage, equal partnership, common ownership and vision, as well as a firm and shared conviction to address common challenges;
6. Promotion of sustainable partnership by complementing and building upon existing regional/sub-regional initiatives in Asia and Africa;
7. Promotion of a just, democratic, transparent, accountable and harmonious society;
8. Promotion and protection of human rights and fundamental freedoms, including the right to development;
9. Promotion of collective and unified efforts in multilateral fora.

We resolve that the sustainability of the NAASP shall be conducted through three tiers of interaction: an intergovernmental forum; sub-regional organizations; and people-to-people interaction, particularly business, academia, and civil society.

We are determined to develop an institutionalized process of the NAASP through convening: a Summit of Heads of State/Government every four years; a Ministerial Meeting of Foreign Ministers every two years; and Sectoral Ministerial and other Technical Meetings when deemed necessary. A Business Summit in conjunction with the Summit of Heads of State/Government will be held every four years.

## The 2015 Asian-African Conference Documents

Unlike the previous conferences, the 2015 Asian-African Conference produced three documents successively: 1) The Declaration on Reinvigorating the New Asian-African Strategic Partnership; 2) The Bandung Message; 3) The Declaration on Palestine. These documents seem to be in line with the orientation of the Indonesian government under the leadership of President Joko Widodo. Inspired by Soekarno's teachings, Joko Widodo's political line is oriented towards national (cultural, economical and political) sovereignties, social justice, people-centred development, solidarity toward the sufferings. He is also surrounded by advisors from progressive scholars, intellectuals and activists of social movements. His opening statement to the conference clearly expressed his political orientation (see Joko Widodo's opening statement in the Introduction of this book). The three documents of the 2015 Asian-African Conference show clearly their affinity with this political orientation. We find in the documents many terms familiar to the discourses of social movement and alter-globalisation like "South-South", "North-South", "Stakeholders", "Food Security", "Energy Security", "Gender Equality", "Women Empowerment"...

## 1) Declaration on Reinvigorating the New Asian-African Strategic Partnership

This is the outcome of the 2015 Asian-African Conference held in Jakarta on April 22-23, 2015. Let us quote some passages:

> 10. While reaffirming that South-South Cooperation and its agenda have to be set by countries of the South, we call for the active involvement of development partners and other related stakeholders in various mechanisms within South-South Cooperation and triangular cooperation to inter alia, mobilize their supports, share and exchange best practices, as well as promote transfer and development of technology, to further enhance South-South cooperation initiatives based on the principle of mutual benefit, non-conditionality, equality, national ownership, respect for national sovereignty, as well as non-interference in domestic affairs. We also recognize that South-South Cooperation continues to serve as a complement to, and not a substitute for, North-South development cooperation.
>
> 11. We are committed to carrying forward the NAASP by implementing ambitious goals and practical initiatives, with the aim at enabling Asia and Africa to play a more active, coordinated and leading role on various issues of common concern. We, therefore, call on our Ministers and officials to galvanize necessary actions to arrive at a successful conclusion on the 8 Focus Areas of Cooperation as recommended by the NAASP Senior Official Meeting in Jakarta, October 2009, namely Counter Terrorism; Combating Transnational Organized Crimes; Food Security; Energy Security; Small and Medium Enterprises; Tourism; Asian-African Development University Network; Gender Equality and Women Empowerment. We instruct our officials to conduct future review and evaluation of the NAASP's activities periodically.

29. We will revitalize the New Asian-African Strategic Partnership by improving its operational framework by:

- Organizing a Commemorative Asian-African Summit every ten years;
- Consolidating the institutionalized process of the NAASP by rotating the co-chairmanship of NAASP every four years as stipulated in the NAASP Declaration 2005;
- Organizing biennial ministerial consultations at the sidelines of the UN General Assembly in New York to provide strategic direction for Asian-African partnership;
- Organizing annual meetings between Co-chairs;
- Strengthening people-to-people interactions, particularly in business, academia, media, youth and sports as well as civil society. In this regard, we encourage inter-regional University to University (U to U) cooperation, including the establishment of an Asian-African Academic Forum to strengthen closer collaboration among higher education institutions and academicians in the two regions. We also see the benefits of establishing a network of Asian-African think-tanks to enhance research and assist policy development.

## 2) The Bandung Message 2015: Strengthening South-South Cooperation to Promote World Peace and Prosperity

This document was declared during the commemoration of the 60$^{th}$ anniversary of the 1955 Bandung Asian-African Conference in Bandung on April 24, 2015. Here are some essential passages.

> 8. We reaffirm the importance of building harmony among cultures, religions, faiths and civilizations. We commit to collectively combating violent extremism, racism, racial discrimination, xenophobia and related intolerance, while recognizing moderation as an important value in countering all forms of extremism, and to promoting dialogue, mutual respects, understanding and acceptance.
>
> 15. We express our strong opposition and condemnation to all unilateral coercive measures including sanctions which violate the Charter of the United Nations and undermine international law as well as the norms and principles governing peaceful relations among states.
>
> 25. We also recognize that each country faces specific challenges to achieve sustainable development, and we underscore the special challenges faced by the most vulnerable countries, which include least developed countries, landlocked developing countries and Small Island Developing States, as well as the specific challenges faced by the middle-income countries and the countries in situation of conflict or emerging from conflict.

34. We reaffirm the importance of promoting democratic values. While acknowledging there is no single model of democracy, we are committed to forging cooperation in strengthening democratic institutions built on people's aspiration. We, therefore, underline the importance of strengthening democracy through dialogue and cooperation.

35. We stress the importance of strengthening people to people contacts by facilitating and encouraging interaction and exchange among youth, women, business, intellectuals, scholars, experts, athletes, artists, and media of the two regions.

36. We are determined to promote cooperation on gender equality and women empowerment, and vulnerable groups, particularly on the issues of better access to education, healthcare and employment opportunities, in order to increase their participation in all spheres of life.

## 3) The Declaration on Palestine

The Final Communiqué of the 1955 Bandung Conference took care of five concrete questions: 1) the independence of North Africa; 2) the integration of West Irian into Indonesia; 3) the reunification of Vietnam; 4) the end of apartheid in South Africa; 5) the independence of Palestine. The first four questions have been settled before the 2005 Asian-African Conference, leaving Palestinian question unsettled until up to the present. Faithful to the Bandung Spirit, the 2005 and 2015 Asian-African Conferences maintained the Palestinian question in their declaration. The last conference considers the question urgent and present it in a special declaration. Let us read some passages.

> 1. We, the leaders of the Asian and African countries remain committed to the principle of self-determination as set forth in the Final Communiqué of the Bandung Conference in 1955, and in accordance with the Charter of the United Nations. We deplore the fact that sixty years since the Bandung Conference, the Palestinian people remain deprived of their rights, freedom and independence, and that millions of Palestinians are still living under occupation and as refugees, and that this historic injustice continues.
>
> 2. We, in the spirit of Asian African solidarity, pay tribute to the resilience and steadfastness of the Palestinian people in the face of the illegal Israeli occupation, and reaffirm our full support of the just struggle of the Palestinian people to regain their inalienable right to self-determination, including the realization of the sovereignty and independence of their State of Palestine with East Jerusalem as its capital, based on the 4 June 1967 borders and relevant United Nations resolutions, as set out in the two-State solution.

3. We stress that the only viable solution to the Israeli-Palestinian conflict is an agreement, which ends the illegal Israeli occupation that began in 1967, resolves all permanent status issues—Palestine refugees, Jerusalem, settlements, borders, security and water—and justly fulfils the inalienable rights and legitimate national aspirations of the Palestinian people. We further reaffirm that a just, lasting and comprehensive settlement of the Israeli-Palestinian conflict is imperative for achieving peace and security in the region.

# Notes on Contributors

Writer, architect and historian specialised in the Contemporary Arab and Muslim World, **Darwis Khudori** is Associate Professor of Oriental Studies at the University of Le Havre, France, member of GRIC (Group of Research on Identity and Culture) and director of Master's Degree in International Management specialised in Exchanges with Asia, at the same university. He is the initiator and coordinator of the Bandung Spirit Network, an academic and civil society movement based on the spirit of the 1955 Bandung Conference, and Bandung Spirit Book Series as a way to develop sciences in developing countries through book publication in cooperative way in order to make academic books affordable to readers in developing world. The last book published in this framework is *Religious Diversity in a Globalised Society: Challenges and Responses in Africa and Asia,* a co-publication of Indonesian, Philippine, French, Lebanese and Dutch academic institutions, 2013.

**Naoko Shimazu** is Professor of History, Birkbeck University of London. Her major publications include *Imagining Japan in Post-war East Asia* (co-editor, Routledge, 2013), *Japanese Society at War: Death, Memory and the Russo-Japanese War* (Cambridge University Press, 2009), *Nationalisms in Japan* (editor, Routledge, 2006), *Japan, Race and Equality: Racial Equality Proposal of 1919* (Routledge, 1998). She serves on the advisory boards of *The Historical Journal, Modern Asian Studies, Reviews in History, Theory, Culture and Society,* and *Japan Forum*. She is a Fellow of the Royal Historical Society, and Professorial Associate of Japan Research Centre at SOAS. She is currently completing *Diplomacy as Theatre: The Bandung Conference and the Making of the Third World.*

**Manoranjan Mohanty**, formerly Professor of Political Science and Director, Developing Countries Research Centre at the University of Delhi, is Honorary

Fellow, Institute of Chinese Studies, Delhi and Distinguished Professor and Editor, *Social Change* at the Council for Social Development, New Delhi. His recent publications include *Ideology Matters: China from Mao Zedong to Xi Jinping, Red and Green: Five Decades of the Maoist Movement in India and Building a Just World* (Co-ed.)

**Noha Khalaf** is Palestinian researcher specialised in International Affairs: BA (AUC Cairo), MA (AUB, Beirut), PhD (INALCO, Paris). She published several studies on International Politics and the question of Palestine in *Shu'un Falastiniyeh* and *Al Fikr al Stratigi el Arabi (1978–1982)*, Beirut, articles in various Arabic newspapers such as al Quds al Arabi, Rai al Youm, Al Arabi al Jadeed, as well as in the Algerian periodical Naqd (in French), and the Jerusalem Quarterly (in English), a book in French entitled the *Memoirs of 'Issa al 'Issa: Palestinian Intellectual and Journalist (1878–1950)*, Karthala, 2009. She coordinated recently two major conferences: the first as a Visiting Fellow at the Columbia University Middle East Research Center (CUMERC), Amman, entitled "A Hundred Years of Journalism In Palestine" in Commemoration of the Founding of Falastin Newspaper in Jaffa, 1911, and the second conference at the Institut du Monde Arabe, Paris, in June 2013, entitled "A Hundred Years of Arab Nationalism, in Commemoration of the Centenary of the Holding of the First Arab Congress in Paris", in 1913.

**Adams Bodomo** is currently Professor of African Studies at the University of Vienna, with key research areas in African linguistics, African language literatures, and global African diaspora studies. He has published widely on Africa-Asia comparative studies in many journals, such as *African Studies, African Diaspora, China Quarterly, China Review, West Asia and Africa, African and Asian Studies, African and East sian Affairs,* and *Journal of African American Studies*. His pioneering book on the African diaspora in Chin is titled: *Africans in China: A socio-cultural study and its implications on Africa-China relations* (Cambria Press, NY, 2012).

**Lazare Ki-Zerbo** has studied philosophy at the Husserl Archives of the Ecole normale supérieure in Paris and earned a Ph.D at Poitiers University in 1994, on *a Contribution to a phenomenological approach to the social ontology departing from Edmund Husserl.* He then taught at Ouagadougou University in Burkina Faso where he contributed to the founding of the Movement of the intellectuals for freedom. His research fields concern history of Pan-Africanism, particularly W.E.B du Bois, Richard Wright; the right to development. Dr. Ki-Zerbo has edited African studies in geography from below (CODESRIA, Dakar, 2008); The Pan-African Movement in the 20$^{th}$ century (OIF, Paris, 2013), The Pan-African Ideal (forthcoming, CODESRIA, 2016), The African diaspora (translation into French of a book by Patrick Manning). Dr. Ki-Zerbo is also member of the African network for global history, and is deputy chairman of the International Joseph Ki-Zerbo committee for Africa and the diaspora.

**István Tarrósy** is currently Associate Professor of Political Science and African Studies and Director of the African Research Center at the University of Pécs, with key research areas in African state development, African regionalism, Afro-Asian linkages and global African diaspora studies. He has published widely on the international relations of Sub-Saharan African states, Africa-Asia comparative studies and African migrations in many journals, such as *African Studies Quarterly, International Journal of Area Studies, Society and Economy, Portuguese Journal of International Affairs, Croatian International Relations Review, Ibadan Journal of the Social Sciences* and the *Hungarian Journal of African Studies*. His latest book is titled: *The African State in a Changing Global Context: Breakdowns and Transformations* (LIT Verlag, Münster-Wien-London, 2011).

**Mérick Freedy Alagbe** holds a PhD in Political Science and International Relations with research activities focused on the new dimensions of the Chinese presence in Africa. He conducted field researches throughout African countries engaged in a strong partnership with China. After completing his PhD, he embarked on an international career with some of the biggest humanitarian organizations (Caritas; Oxfam; International Committee of the Red Cross...). He is member of the Edition Committee of the Humanitarian Think Tank at the Institute of International Relations and Strategic Affairs in Paris (IRIS). He published several articles in journals such as Affaires Stratégiques; Diploweb; Grotius International etc.

**Jason E. Strakes** is an associate research fellow of the Politics and Security Programme at the OSCE Academy in Bishkek, Kyrgyz Republic. His current research interests include the participation of former Soviet states in Asian-African regionalism and Global South institutions. He will publish "Incapacity, Endowment and Ambivalence: Deciphering Azerbaijan's Regional Leadership Strategy" in Jacqueline Ann Braveboy-Wagner ed., *Diplomatic Strategies of Leading Nations in the Global South: Asia, Africa, Latin America, and the Middle East* (London: Palgrave-Macmillan, 2016). Strakes has served as a member-at-large on the executive committee of the International Studies Association Global South Caucus (GSCIS) since 2011, and chairs the Developing Eurasia Initiative (DEI) academic working group.

**Seema Mehra Parihar**, Ph.D. in Geography (Delhi School of Economics, University of Delhi, India) and PDF at Department of Geoinformatics, Cartography and Geovisualisation (ITC, Enschede, The Netherlands), is an Associate Professor at Department of Geography, Kirori Mal College, University of Delhi for more than 28 years. During the last three decades she has worked on Gender & Space; Natural Resource Management, and Geospatial tools and technologies. She has also transacted manual 'Women & Research' as a Trainer of the Trainer at many universities, as well as conducted 29 workshops for college faculty, school teachers, and researchers and for government-based projects. She has published more than 34 articles and presented more than 60 papers in national and international conferences and has undertaken 9 research-based projects. She is currently working on Climate Change and inter-sectoral convergence projects, including Gender Atlas of India: Geospatial Perspective (Series 1) & Thematic Perspective (Series 2) & has collated more than 160 Gender Disaggregated Data. A trained behavioural assessor and an avid trekker, she has also been actively associated for more than thirty years in spreading the movement of National Integration.

**Trikurnianti (Yanti) Kusumanto** is researcher in the area of collaborative governance of natural resources and social and environmental sustainability. After almost ten years engagement in CGIAR, she established a Netherlands-based consulting organisation that views the need to link research to action. Her writings show the importance of knowledge development which not only involves scientists, but also communities, policy makers, and other stakeholders. Her publications (e.g. with Resources for the Future) target at practitioners and policy makers, rather than scientists. She is the first author of a gender mainstreaming training manual in forestry focused on Asia and the Pacific for publication by RECOFTC and FAO.

**Beatriz Bissio**, PhD in History (Universidade Federal Fluminense, UFF, Brazil), is Associate Professor and Director of the Department of Political Science IFCS/Universidade Federal do Rio de Janeiro (UFRJ). Uruguayan naturalized Brazilian, Beatriz Bissio has worked for more than two decades as a journalist in the international arena, as a correspondent for various media in Latin America and as founder, director and editor of the magazines Third World (1974–2006), Ecology and Development (1991–2006) and

Revista do Mercosur (1992–2006). She has interviewed personalities such as Sean MacBride, Nelson Mandela, Agostinho Neto, Fidel Castro, Yasser Arafat, Samora Machel, Muammar Gaddafi, Saddam Hussein, Xanana Gusmao, Julius Nyerere, General Omar Torrijos, General Velasco Alvarado. Former Coordinator of the International Relations Committee of the Government of the Brazilian State of Maranhão (Dr. Jackson Lago's administration—2007–2009). Chair of the NGO "Dialogues of the South". Vladimir Herzog Prize and Golden Dolphin 2000 of Journalism. She received on May 8, 2013 the Victory Medal, awarded by the Brazilian Minister of Defense, Celso Amorim.

**Tulus T.H. Tambunan**, graduated and holds PhD in economics in the Erasmus University in Rotterdam, the Netherlands, is a lecturer in the faculty of economics, Trisakti University (Indonesia). He is also the director of the Center for Industry, Small and Medium Enterprises, and Business Competition Studies, and the chief editor of the International Journal of Small and Medium Enterprises and Business Sustainability. Some of his publications are *The Readiness of MSMEs in Facing ASEAN Economic Community 2015* (2014); *Economic Crisis and Vulnerability: The Story from Southeast Asia* (2011), *Global Economic Crisis and ASEAN Economy. Theory and Empirical Findings* (2010); and *SME in Asian Developing Countries* (2009).

**Ida Busnetty** was born in Bukittinggi, West Sumatra, Indonesia, on November 16, 1967. She graduated in Economics from the Faculty of Economics, Andalas University, Padang, West Sumatra, Indonesia. She obtained a Master of Management and Doctorate Degree from the Faculty of Economics, Trisakti University, Jakarta, Indonesia, of which she has been lecturer since 1992. Since 2010, she is Secretary of the Centre for Industry, SME and Business Competition Studies, at the same university. She is also advisor of the Chamber of Commerce and Industry of West Jakarta since January 2015.

**Sit Tsui**, Margaret Jade is associate professor of the Institute of Rural Reconstruction of China, Southwest University, Chongqing, China. She is involved in Global University for Sustainability, Asian Regional Exchange for New Alternatives, and South South Forum on Sustainability. Her research areas include globalisation, rural reconstruction, cultural studies, and feminism.

**Erebus Wong** is senior researcher of Kwan Fong Cultural Research and Development Programme, Lingnan University, Hong Kong. He is involved in Global University for Sustainability, Asian Regional Exchange for New Alternatives, and South South Forum on Sustainability. His research areas include philosophy, ecology, economy, and critical policy studies.

**Wen Tiejun** is Executive Dean of the Institute of Advanced Studies for Sustainability of Renmin University of China, Beijing; the Institute of Rural Reconstruction of China, Southwest University, Chongqing; and the Institute of Rural Reconstruction of the Straits, Fujian Agriculture and Forestry University, Fuzhou. He is a renowned expert on sustainability, agrarian issues, policy studies, macro-economics, south-south cooperation, and inclusive growth.

**Lau Kin Chi** is associate professor teaching Cultural Studies at Lingnan University, Hong Kong. She is involved in several global projects such as Global University for Sustainability, World Forum for Alternatives, Peace Women Across the Globe, Asian Regional Exchange for New Alternatives, and South-South Forum on Sustainability. She has published on issues of agriculture, rural reconstruction, food sovereignty, ecology, resistance, pedagogy, and feminism.

**Lin Chun** teaches at the London School of Economics. She is the author of *The British New Left* (1993), *The Transformation of Chinese Socialism* (2006), and *China and Global Capitalism* (2013). She is also the editor of *China I, II and III* (2000) and co-editor of *Is Mao Really a Monster?* (2009). Her articles appear in various journals and languages. She publishes books, chapters and articles in Chinese as well, including *Reflections on China's Reform Trajectory* (2008) and (coedited) *Women: The Longest Revolution* (1997). She co-edits Palgrave's *China in Transformation* book Series.

Political scientist from Senegal and Egypt, **Aziz Salmone Fall** teaches political sciences, anthropology, international relations and development at McGill University and at the Université du Québec à Montréal (UQAM). A dedicated internationalist, he is the former coordinator of the Quebec anti-apartheid network and a founding member of GRILA (Groupe de recherche et d'initiative pour la libération de l'Afrique), where he is coordinating CIJS a collective of 21 attorneys against impunity in the murder of president Thomas Sankara. President of the Internationalist Centre (CIRFA), he is in charge of the follow-up of the *AFRICOM go home Declaration*, a campaign against military bases and the plundering of Africa's resources. He advocates for the revival of the tricontinental.